CRY into the WIND

CRY into the WIND

(a true story)

Othello Bach

Othello Bach

SEVEN LOCKS PRESS

Santa Ana, California

Seven Locks Press
P.O. Box 25689
Santa Ana, CA 92799
(800) 354-5348

Individual Sales. This book is available through most bookstores or can be ordered directly from Seven Locks Press at the address above.

Quantity Sales. Special discounts are available on quantity purchases by corporations, associations, and others. For details, contact the "Special Sales Department" at the publisher's address above.

Printed in the United States of America

Library of Congress Cataloging-in-Publication Data
is available from the publisher
ISBN 1-931643-61-X

Cover and interior design by Heather Buchman

To our mother
Anna Bernice Birdwell James

Russell and Bernice James' wedding picture, 1929.

Table of Contents

Chapter 11

Chapter 12

Chapter 13

Chapter 14

Prologue

I first wrote about my childhood in 1963, four years after leaving the orphanage. At twenty-two, I had little else to write about. I mailed the piece to a magazine whose editor rejected it with a standard rejection slip, and a note scribbled on the bottom: *Who are you trying to kid? Things like this haven't happened since Dickens wrote about them. And, by the way, you need to choose a less pretentious pseudonym.*

Having been a non-reader until I was fourteen, my vocabulary still didn't include the words *pretentious* or *pseudonym*, so I picked up my dictionary and learned that he didn't care for my name. I stared at the note, knowing I could change my name, but I wasn't sure what to do about a life that wasn't believable. The next day, I decided to write something believable: *fiction.* I sold a couple of short stories then wrote a novel that was bought by Avon Books. They, too, thought my name "wasn't quite right" and gave the credit to someone named *Heather Peters.*

Forty years and twenty-two books later, I've decided to use my pretentious name and tell my "unbelievable" story about growing up in two different orphanages in the '50s, and the deplorable circumstances that led to my placement there.

Both homes still exist but today they're known as "children's homes." It is not my intent to defame or even suggest that what I experienced forty years ago is "standard practice" today. I don't know. This book merely tells the way it was for me and my family.

While I realize my life would have been far more traumatic had I not been taken to the orphanage, it is my hope that revealing "how it was" will positively influence the way homes are managed in the future. I also hope that what I learned along the way will help others move beyond the effects of abuse, and to happier, more rewarding lives.

Memories . . .

are like initials carved deeply into the tender bark of a young tree; as the trunk grows and expands, so do the carvings. Those who labor passionately, or thoughtlessly, leave their mark, and although they may never again return to that site, the tree forever bears witness to that encounter.

Other events never quite become memories, but like an unidentified fragrance carried on a breeze, they prompt ripples of joy or sadness in unexpected moments. These not-quite-memories sometimes act as rudders, steering us in one direction when we want to go in another, or nudging us into action when nothing else could.

Bitter or sweet, they are ours to do with as we choose.

Othello Bach

Chapter 1

The Great Escape

My brother, Don, says the first four years of my life were lived in the back of a flat bed truck. For sure, I remember climbing in and out of a truck but Don is ten years older than I, so I was spared some of his early and sordid experiences.

The oldest girl and the middle sibling of seven, I recall excitement, love, joy, and sometimes gut-wrenching terror as we moved from the truck to live in a ditch, from the ditch to a shack that burned down, and then to an orphanage where we were torn from each other's arms and never allowed to be together again.

The earliest of these memories formed between 1945 and '46, when I wasn't quite five.

"Let's go!" Momma's face glistened with a fine layer of perspiration as she hurried around, balancing our baby brother, Gordon, on her hip and grabbing the last of our things with her free hand. "Come on, girls! Your daddy's ready to leave!"

We had been in a panic ever since Daddy rushed home, shouting, "Ol' man Dunlap's coming for the rent at ten o'clock!"

Momma made a little crying sound in the back of her throat, but all she said was, "Oh, Lord, Russell!"

After that, there wasn't a quiet mouth or still foot in the house for the next hour. Daddy honked the horn and revved the truck's engine, adding to the confusion as we searched to make sure we didn't leave something precious behind.

"Bernice! Get the kids out here!"

Momma shooed Jenny and Amy away from the pile of junk left laying in the corner. Amy clutched a small pink sandal with chubby three-year-old hands as Jenny tried to explain the situation to Momma. "We was huntin' for her other shoe."

Momma herded us out the door and down the porch where Amy dropped the sandal and squatted to pick it up. Momma sighed, shifted the bundle of assorted clothing tucked under her right arm, and grabbed Amy's hand.

"Did you find the other shoe?" Momma asked, half-dragging Amy toward the truck while Gordon bounced on her hip, partially hidden by the bundle of clothing.

"Nope. Jes' found one." Jenny and I hurried to keep up. Although Jenny was eighteen months younger than I, she was already a little taller and faster.

"They're too small, anyway," Momma said, "She might as well go barefoot." She hoisted Amy up to the back of the truck where Don waited to take her. Once Amy was safely behind him, he grabbed Jenny's hands, then mine, and lifted us up.

"Get in! Get in!" Daddy yelled. "Dunlap's comin' round the corner!"

Momma quickly counted heads to make sure we were all there. I had settled next to my brother, Thurmond, who huddled in the corner near the cab, crying.

"Where's Mason?" Momma's eyes frantically darted from face to face.

"Right here!" Mason sprinted up behind her and hopped into the truck. He hugged a brown paper bag protectively. "Had to get my books."

"Bernice!"

Momma gave Mason a quick smile and approving nod, handed him the wadded clothes, then turned and ran for the cab. I watched through the sideboards as Gordon laughed in her arms. His eyes wide and bright, his head bobbing with every step, it was obvious he liked all the rushing, running, and yelling.

The engine revved and the truck started to move just seconds after she opened the door. I held my breath, afraid Momma might fall out. A second later, the door slammed and I relaxed. I hated it when Daddy started driving before the door was closed.

"Here he comes!" Daddy yelled out the window.

I looked between the slatted sideboards. An old gray car, moving in the opposite direction, sped by, throwing up a cloud of red dust that made me squint. Ol' man Dunlap shouted and waved his arms like a crazy man.

"Damn thieves!" was all I heard before he disappeared behind the rust-colored dirt roiling in the air.

I leaned around to peek through the back window of the cab and saw Daddy laughing. Momma bounced along on the seat, hugging Gordon to her shoulder and staring straight ahead, her long hair a dark cloud whipping around her face as air rushed in the window. Daddy leaned forward, hands and forearms on the steering wheel, his eyes wide, his face reddened by the excitement. He laughed and spat out words so fast, I couldn't guess what he was saying.

Momma, the tallest one in the family, sat a good six inches higher on the seat than Daddy. I probably wouldn't have noticed that, except I had just heard Daddy tell ol' man Dunlap, four weeks ago, when we moved into the house, that Momma was shorter than him when they married.

"Course, she was only fifteen, then." Daddy chuckled, glanced away, then added, "I guess you might say she sort of grew on me."

For a moment, looking through the window at them, I thought about the way Daddy's eyes always "slinked" about, darting up quickly then away again, never quite looking anyone in the eye. He did it with all of us.

"Shee-it!" The anger in Mason's voice made me turn. I settled down next to Thurmond again and watched the others. Don and Mason had taken positions on opposite sides of the truck, near the rear, their backs against the sideboards.

"Shee-it, what?" Don asked.

Mason looked scared enough to cry. "I forgot the tarp."

Don chuckled. "You're gonna get your butt kicked. You know it."

"Well, I had to get my books," Mason said. "The last time we moved I ran off and forgot 'em. It was months before I could get any more!"

Don sighed. "You're still gonna get your butt kicked."

Neither of them spoke for a long time after that conversation. They stared back at the cloud of dust erasing the road from our sight, while the six of us bounced and jiggled in silence.

We had never run from the landlord before because we had never rented a house before. Generally, we ran from angry farmers who found us living in the truck, parked on the back of their property. Sometimes it took them a month to stumble upon us, but more often we were caught within a couple of weeks. The shouting and running always created a lot of excitement, until we got away, but after a while a sadness would set in and no one would speak. We just bounced along, listening to the motor and the tires rumbling down the road. During those times I was more aware of the vibrations coming through the floorboards. They jiggled my legs and insides and made my cheeks quiver, and later, I liked the tingling that stayed with me for several minutes after the truck stopped.

I stared at Don and Mason. To me, they seemed grown, and were the handsomest men on earth. Don, about fourteen, had red hair and intense brown eyes. Before he said anything, I could tell if he was happy or sad just by looking at his eyes. Either they sparkled and danced or made me want to cry. On days like today, when the sadness set in, his brows drew close and his eyes seemed to focus on something I couldn't see. But I could tell it was a big, important problem.

With Don around, I never got scared. I knew that whatever might go wrong, he could fix it. Strong and stocky, there was nothing he couldn't lift or move. He didn't go to school anymore because he had a job. "Gotta help feed the young'uns," is the way he put it. I knew Momma depended on him a lot because Daddy was usually gone. I wasn't sure why Daddy was gone so much, and I probably never asked because I didn't miss him and there was always something interesting going on with one of us.

Mason, twelve, was as different from Don as a deer is from a bull. No one would have ever guessed they were brothers, except that they both had those wonderfully expressive eyes. Mason's leaner and finer-boned body seemed to move with less effort than Don's, and his thick dark hair seemed to irritate him when it fell over his forehead, so every few minutes he brushed it back with his fingers. The only time Mason's hair didn't seem to bother him was when he was reading. Then, the whole world disappeared for him because he wanted to know how everything worked or how come it didn't. Not just trucks, cars, and machines. He wanted to know about things on the other side of the stars, and things so small nobody could see them, so he read everything he could, and wondered about the rest.

Mason and Don sometimes talked about invisible things, like electricity or thoughts or germs, and I eavesdropped but never interrupted. I didn't understand but I wanted to, because they were like gods to me—very different gods, but equally important. Don's strength and good nature made me feel like everything was okay, and Mason's polite, quiet-spoken way made me want to listen carefully so I didn't miss anything.

But now, as I watched them and waited to learn where we were going and what was happening, they were silent.

"Stop wiggling and gimme that!" Jenny took the sandal away from Amy.

"It won't go on!" Amy whined, grabbing the sandal back and trying to stuff her foot into it. "It won't go on!"

Jenny scooted Amy around so that she could help. "It don't fit no more, that's why."

"But I want it on! I want it on!"

Jenny patiently unbuckled the toe strap so that Amy's toes could slide forward. Once the shoe was buckled in place, Amy sat back and smiled. Jenny, who was always combing or brushing someone's hair, began to run her fingers through Amy's. "Wearing one pink shoe is pretty stupid," she said under her breath.

Thurmond, the only blue-eyed blonde in the bunch, had fallen asleep and now slumped heavily against me. Just eighteen months older than I,

Thurmond wasn't just my brother, he was one of my best friends. Jenny was the other. But I loved Thurmond in a different way than I loved Don and Mason because I knew him better, and because I felt sorry for him because Daddy whipped him harder than he whipped the rest of us. Even on those rare occasions when daddy was home and would play with us, somehow, he would always hurt Thurmond, and it always made me so sad. I cried more for Thurmond than I ever cried for myself.

"What makes Momma so pretty?" Jenny asked wistfully. "I wanna look like her."

"She just is," I said. "Her face is . . . " I tried to find the right word.

"Delicate." Mason interrupted. "The word is delicate. Momma's got a kind of soft and delicate—"

"Shee-it!" Don laughed. "Momma's not soft! She's tough. She can handle more than—"

"I mean the way she looks!" Mason snapped.

Jenny sighed, her fingers still moving gently through Amy's hair. "I wanna look like Momma."

When we fell silent again, with only the grumbling of the engine to hold my attention, I became aware of Momma's dresser and headboard tied against the sideboards. Other than the few paper sacks and cardboard boxes haphazardly filled with assorted clothing and a box of crackers, the dresser and headboard were our only belongings.

"You know what?" Don spoke in a sober, quiet tone. "I hate the old man."

Mason stared intently at him but didn't respond.

"This ain't no way to do your family."

Mason still didn't reply but held steady eye contact while he thought about Don's words. Then lowering his eyes, Mason said, "I don't know how Momma stands it."

Don grunted and nodded. "Last time we were in Altus, I heard Aunt Lola Mae say those same words to Momma. They were in the kitchen and Aunt Lola Mae had Momma kind of backed up against the table and was saying things like, 'you oughtn't to put up with it!' and I saw Momma hold her hands up kind of like this," Don held his palms up to Mason, "and she said, 'Don't talk like that about Russell! He's your brother! And I love him!' or words something like that."

Mason shook his head. "She has a way of making things seem better than they are. That's for sure."

Don chuckled and nodded. "I don't know if she does that for her sake or ours." He seemed to consider his own words for a minute then added, "Probably ours. It don't seem to do her much good."

Mason nodded and glanced toward the cab window. "I think you're right. But when Daddy—"

"Daddy, shee-it!" Don's instant anger pulled his mouth down and narrowed his eyes. "Think about this . . . what's Mr. Berry gonna think when I don't show up for work tomorrow?" Don flung his arm outward in exasperation. "That I just up and quit? That makes me look like some sorry bastard, don't it?"

Mason nodded slowly. "Yeah."

"I mean a man's entitled to know if you're quittin'. He's expecting me to show up just like always!" Disgust darkened his voice.

Mason took one of his books from the paper bag and rubbed his palm over the cover. "I hate to think of going to another school. Stupid kids will all laugh at me again. Laugh at my clothes being too small. Laugh at that silly Roy Rogers' jacket. At my shoes, all wore out."

"I gotta dookey!" The urgency in Amy's voice left no doubt she had waited too long. She scrambled up and grabbed her behind with both hands. "I gotta dookey!"

"Oh, boy," Don groaned. "There's about to be a stinky accident, I think."

"Hurry!" Amy said. "Make Daddy stop!"

Don waved at me. "Bang on the window. See if you can get him to stop."

I turned and pounded the glass with my palm. Momma looked over her shoulder. "Amy's gotta dookey!" I yelled over the roar of the engine. "Tell Daddy to stop."

I saw her mouth the words. After a few seconds the truck slowed and pulled off the road. Daddy left the engine running and climbed out. "I'm not gonna stop every fifteen minutes! All of you get out and pee, whether you have to or not!"

We scrambled toward the rear and let Don and Mason help us down. Momma left Gordon in the cab and came back to help Amy. Then, like a pack of wild dogs, we scattered in different directions, into the weeds and brush alongside the road. I know the others hated it as much as I did because everyone griped and complained, but none of us dared to miss the opportunity.

I found my place out of sight of the rest, just as they did. Squatting behind a bush, with weeds scratching my bare bottom, was the only time I ever envied my brothers.

Climbing back into the truck, Don said to Mason, "I'll bet we've fertilized half of Oklahoma and Texas." Momma laughed with them and handed Amy to Don. I didn't get the joke and it aggravated me. For a long time I had wanted to make jokes because I knew it would feel good to make everyone laugh, but I couldn't think of one.

Underway again, I stood behind the cab, placed my hands and arms on the sun-warmed metal, and stared ahead. Miles and miles of flat farmland lay on either side of the road. Occasionally, a little cluster of trees would mark a farmhouse and eventually, we'd pass the cutoff path that ran out to the farm. The two-lane dirt road became a paved road at some point, but the pavement was riddled with holes and ruts, and almost as rough as the dirt road had been.

Stolen Bologna and Warm Rain

The sun was straight overhead when my stomach began to growl about being empty. I turned to complain when Thurmond handed me some soda crackers. Within minutes, between the six of us, the whole box of crackers was eaten, leaving no trace of crumbs, but my hunger remained.

"Momma!" I beat on the window. When she looked back, I yelled, "I'm hungry! I wanna eat!"

She nodded and said something to Daddy.

"I'm hungry, Momma! We all are! I want something to eat!" I pounded again. She closed her eyes and took a deep breath, and when she opened her eyes again, she motioned for me to move toward her door.

Scooting as close as I could, I put my face against the sideboards, leaving my ear exposed between the boards, to catch her words.

"Eat the crackers!" she yelled back.

"We did!"

There was a long pause. "Then you might as well cry into the wind."

I felt my shoulders sag. Turning around, I sat down with my back against the sideboards. Some words made me feel a slow sadness and others robbed me instantly. The words, *cry into the wind* were the quickest thief. They meant, *it's hopeless*, or in this case, *there's no more food.*

I stared at the empty cracker box that had become Amy's new toy.

We bumped and grumbled into a pretty little town sometime later and Daddy drove right into the center of town. He parked on a street that had stores from one end of the block to the next, and across the street stood the biggest building I had ever seen. It stood on a little hill, and thick, green grass ran from the building to the sidewalk. Thrilled at the beauty of it, I momentarily forgot my hunger.

"Ain't that the prettiest yard you ever seen?" I asked Thurmond.

He peered between the sideboards. "Be fun to roll down that hill, wouldn't it?"

"Think we could?"

"Let's ask."

Don and Mason jumped down from the truck. Daddy walked toward a grocery store and motioned for them to follow. Momma came back to talk to us, Gordon in her arms.

"Let's ask Momma," Thurmond urged. "Come on. Let's ask her."

We scrambled down from the truck. "Can we go over to the big green yard?" I asked. "Thurmond and me want to go over and run on it."

Momma turned and studied the situation. "Well, I don't know why not. It's the courthouse. I reckon it's all right."

"I wanna go!" Jenny said. "If you get to go, so do I!"

Momma nodded. "Wait for Jenny." She held her hand up quickly to stop Amy. "But you stay with me, Sugar. You're too little."

While we waited for a pickup truck to pass, Momma said, "And Othello, that big green yard is called a lawn."

Who cared what it was called? We'd never had anything but dirt to play on, and regardless of what it was called, it was just made for running up and rolling down.

We dashed across the street and up the little hill, laughing like fools and squealing like pigs. When we reached the top of the hill, all three of us fell to the ground and rolled down the carpet of *lawn*. It felt good, it smelled wonderful, and it didn't get us dirty. Breathlessly, we ran up the incline a second and third time, flung ourselves down and rolled to the bottom. I was thinking that this had to be the best place in the whole world when suddenly loud, angry voices made my heart leap into my throat. We all stopped in mid-roll and stared in horror at the three men storming in our direction. Suit jackets flapping behind them, they ran at us like snorting bulls, yelling words I couldn't understand until they were upon us. We scrambled to our feet, and at that moment, our confusion heightened.

Don yelled for us on the other side of the street, and the words of the angry men suddenly became clear.

"Get out of here! Go! Filthy white trash!"

"This is a courthouse! Not a playground!"

The words hit us in the back of the head as we dashed for the truck. Momma looked worried, waving us on. Amy cried and screamed from the shouting and anger, while Daddy yelled from the driver's seat, "Come on! Let's go!"

Gasping and frightened, we practically jumped into the truck without help. Momma rushed to the cab and as soon as she was inside, Daddy pulled out into the street and took off. The three men who had chased us, stood on the curb and yelled, shaking their fists and shouting words like "filthy," "no good," and "trash."

No one dared to speak until we were well beyond the town. It took me fifteen minutes just to catch my breath, so I couldn't have talked if I had wanted to. But if I had, I would have talked about how those words had hurt the back of my neck, my head, and created an awful ache inside me. I would have asked questions about those words, like, why was it filthy to roll on the lawn when it didn't even get you dirty? Why were we "no good" for wanting to do a fun thing like that, or "trash" for doing it?

While I was pouting, Thurmond nudged me and handed me some baloney with a piece of white bread folded around it. Suddenly I realized I was so hungry, I wanted ten more before I took the first bite.

Now distracted from my personal injury, I watched Don and Mason making the sandwiches for us. Don had a foot-long length of baloney and was cutting it with his pocketknife. He handed the cuts to Mason who took slices of white bread and folded them around the meat, then passed it along to whichever set of hands was closest.

"He better not stop till he's out of Oklahoma," Don grumbled. "Damnedest thing I ever saw! Could you believe that?" he asked Mason.

"Naw. It's a wonder the law's not behind us right now."

"They're looking, all right. You can count on it. Shee-it! I couldn't believe it when he told me to stick this goddamn thing in my shirt!"

Mason laughed. "In your pants, would've made more sense. No one's gonna look there. Besides, it's shaped like—" He glanced back to see who was listening and the two of them burst out laughing.

When the laugh was over, they ate their sandwiches. "He just walked right out with a whole bag of groceries! Customers standing right there!" Don spoke around the lump of baloney and bread in his cheek. "I had no idea he didn't mean to pay for the stuff."

Slowly, I began to understand the panic behind our sudden departure. Rolling on the lawn hadn't been the only reason for all the screaming and yelling. Daddy had stolen the food.

My initial reaction was to defend Daddy, to justify his behavior, because somewhere deep inside me, I loved him. What I couldn't understand was why Don and Mason weren't doing the same thing. But I loved them, too, so it was too difficult a problem to resolve immediately. Unwilling to compromise my love for any of them, I decided not to think about it at all.

Amy, suddenly preferring the company of her older brother, toddled toward the rear in one pink sandal, and Don let her cuddle up in his lap while he and Mason talked.

Thurmond, Jenny, and I, bored for lack of something to do, stood behind the cab, stretched our arms out over the cab, and let the wind rush over us. It whipped our pigtails straight out behind us and flattened Thurmond's blonde hair against his scalp. We squinted against the wind to watch the passing countryside.

As the day lengthened and our faces grew raw from the wind and the sun, we sank back to the bed of the truck.

"It's gonna rain." Mason's voice thickened with dread. "And we don't have the tarp."

Following Don's upward gaze, I saw the thick dark clouds piling up on the horizon. When I fixed my eyes in one spot, I could see how fast they were moving.

"I'm gonna catch hell," Mason said.

"Too late to worry about that." When Don spoke, Amy woke up, rubbed her eyes with both fists, and looked up, smiling. Sometimes she didn't look real. She looked like the big dolls in the store windows, and this was one of those times. I held my arms out and she ran to me, off-balance, the too-small sandal almost tripping her. She fell against me, laughing. An instant later, Jenny was running her fingers through Amy's hair again, trying to straighten the tangled mess.

The sky continued to darken over the next hour and Mason's frown deepened. When the truck began to slow, both he and Don stood to see what lay ahead. "It's a filling station," Don announced. "Let's get out and stretch our legs." They both jumped off the truck and walked toward the station as soon as Daddy stopped the truck.

Through the sideboards I saw two gas pumps and a small station not much bigger than the back of the truck. Traces of white paint still clung to the little building, but most of it had been eaten away by years of wind and rain. Now, only dull, raw wood remained to soak up the heat of the sun.

Behind the station, a dull-wood shack squatted close to the ground, looking lonely and small against the expanse of flat, open country. Empty oil drums lined the side of the shack, holes rusted through in several places. As we approached, a small brown dog darted from one of the rusted oil drums, and, with its tail wagging, ran out to be patted. Not a single tree could be seen anywhere in the distance, just scrappy brush, soon to be tumbleweeds, covered the fields as far as I could see.

We moved toward the back of the truck, eager to go to the bathroom. Momma left Gordon sleeping in the cab and came back to help us down. I winced as the sharp edges of gravel bit into my bare feet. "Walk easy," Momma said. "Don't run."

Stinging red dirt and sand, flung from the fields by the wind, bit at our arms, legs and faces, and whipped our hair about.

Hobbling over the gravel, we headed toward the back of the gas station while Daddy started pumping gas. Some of the gas stations had sinks and flush toilets. This wasn't one of them. Two outhouses, which couldn't be seen from where we parked, stood between the sad brown shack and the station. Don and Mason stepped out of one outhouse, zipping their pants and tucking in their shirts.

"Can't use that one," Mason instructed, pointing toward the other outhouse. "It's private. This one's for customers. But it's a two-seater."

Momma took Amy inside while Jenny, Thurmond, and I waited.

"Sure wish I had a soda pop," Jenny said. She turned to Thurmond. "You think that man in there has soda pop?" She pointed toward the station.

"What's it matter? You ain't got no money." He scratched an old mosquito bite on the back of his arm, then twisted his arm around to examine the welt.

Jenny looked away, trying not to cry. "It matters 'cause I want some. I'm so thirsty I can't hardly swallow."

Amy squealed and pushed Momma away as they came out of the outhouse. "Lemme do it! Lemme do it!" She tugged at her underpants, trying to pull them up. Thurmond darted inside the outhouse and shut the door. Regretfully, I stared at the half moon carved above the door, until Amy began to cry in frustration because she had her panties twisted into an unmanageable roll and she couldn't get them up.

Momma, her long dark curls blowing about her face, gently leaned down and said, "My, what a good job you did! Look at that. You're getting to be such a big girl!"

Amy's crying stopped immediately with the praise. She smiled, unaware that Mamma had quickly unsnarled the roll and had her panties straight again.

"Big girl!" Amy repeated proudly, running over to stand beside Jenny.

"Can we get a soda pop?" Jenny asked. "I'm thirsty."

Momma smoothed loose strands of hair away from Jenny's face. "I'll go see." Then, taking Amy's hand, she headed back toward the truck. "You girls come on as soon as you're through."

Squatting in weeds was miserable but there, at least, we didn't have to hold our breath.

Bursting from the outhouse, we ran as far as we could before gasping for fresh air. Once we had cleared our noses and our lungs, we saw how Jenny's thirst was going to be relieved. Don, Mason, Thurmond, Amy, and Momma stood at the side of the station, and Momma was holding a garden hose so Mason could wash his hands. When he finished, he took the hose and drank, then passed the hose to Don.

I had no doubt that Mason discovered the hose. He hated being dirty more than anyone I knew. Thanks to him, we would also be "watered" before we left.

"I wanted a soda pop," Jenny grumbled.

More baloney sandwiches filled our stomachs toward the end of the day, and dark clouds spread from horizon to horizon, except for a small margin in the west where a brilliant sun gently lowered itself. Daddy pulled the truck off the road in a stretch of loneliness where nothing was except a now-and-again tree and endless miles of shrubs and pastures. If cows filled those pastures during the day, they had been put up for evening.

When Daddy turned off the ignition, the surrounding silence rushed upon us, and perhaps because we were tired, no one moved for several seconds. We sat like statues, allowing our senses to absorb the sudden quiet. The only sound disturbing the silence was the gusting wind, torturing the weeds beside the road.

Then cab doors opened. Don and Mason sprang down from the rear of the truck. Don stretched and ran his hand through his mop of red curls and looked around, orienting himself. Mason glanced nervously toward Daddy, who was striding toward them.

"It'll be dark in half an hour," Daddy said. "We'll spend the night here."

Jenny and I lowered ourselves from the truck. Thurmond grabbed Amy and kept her from following us. She started to cry and Momma immediately appeared to take her. With Gordon balanced on one hip, Momma reached for Amy and let her straddle the other hip.

"Pee," Amy whined. "I gotta pee."

"Okay. Whoever has to go, come on."

Only Don, Mason, and Daddy were left standing by the truck.

Following Momma, I scanned the sparse accommodations. Thurmond, able to run faster, picked the thickest growth to hide behind, while Jenny and I studied the possibilities. Eventually, the problem was relieved, and as we bounded back toward the truck, I heard Daddy shouting. Mason grimaced and cowered as Daddy yelled. "How the hell could you forget it? It's the only thing you had to remember! One goddamn thing and you forget!"

I approached slowly.

"I know. I know," Mason admitted. "First, I couldn't find it, then I remembered my books and went to get them. After that, you were telling us to get in the truck, and well—"

'Well, hell! Now you've fixed it for all of us! Look at those clouds!"

Momma hurried back with Amy and Gordon. She slowed her steps as she approached the angry faces. "What? What happened?"

Mason ducked his head and averted his eyes.

"Stupid idiot forgot the tarp!" Daddy yelled, taking a cigarette from his pocket. "How can anybody be that stupid?"

Momma glanced toward Mason, then at Daddy. "Now, Russell. We all forget things. It's not like the end of the world."

"The hell it's not!" Daddy flipped the top on his lighter and lit the cigarette. "The sky's covered with rain clouds."

Mason looked pleadingly at Momma. "I remembered my books, but—"

Momma took a long, shaky breath and turned to Daddy. "Even so, that doesn't mean it's going to rain. And even if it does, we won't shrink. We won't dissolve." She smiled uneasily and kissed Gordon and then Amy. "Well, these two sweet things might dissolve like sugar, so I'll keep them dry."

Daddy threw her an angry, darting glance and strode back to the cab. A few seconds later we heard the door open and slam shut. Don rolled his eyes skyward, turned on his heel and walked several yards away, down the road. I didn't have to see his face to know how angry he was. His stiff movements and hard steps left no doubt.

Daylight diminished rapidly as we stood there, waiting for instructions. Momma put Amy down, and still holding Gordon, moved to Mason. She put her arm around him. "You're not stupid and you're not an idiot. You did the right thing, getting your books. Books are far more important than a silly ol' tarp. There's nothing going to happen to us because we don't have the tarp."

Mason blinked back tears. "We'll get rained on."

"Maybe, maybe not. You just remember what I said. You did the right thing." She patted his shoulder and turned to glance toward Don, who was now staring back in our direction. She waved for him to return. "We still have a lot to be thankful for, Mason. We're all healthy. We have each other and . . . and . . . you have your books."

"We're gonna be cold and wet," he said, "and it's all my fault."

She shushed him. "Come on, now, and help your brother spread out some blankets in the truck."

Don hoisted himself into the truck and Mason reluctantly followed. They fumbled through the cardboard boxes until they found two blankets, then pushed everything aside and spread them out. By the time the blankets were down, darkness had almost overtaken us, and my brothers were shadows moving within shadows.

"Okay," Don said. "Gimme a hand." He leaned down and helped us up, one at a time. Momma carried Gordon to the cab as we all wiggled to find our place between the blankets.

The cab door opened.

"Leave me the hell alone!" Daddy shouted. "I'm sleeping up here!"

The door closed. In the dark, we listened to Momma's footsteps move slowly back to the rear of the truck. Gordon fussed.

"Here, Momma. Take my hand." Don.

"Gimme Gordon." Mason.

"Scoot down. Make room for Momma." Don.

Everyone twisted and moved.

"I wanna sleep next to Momma." Thurmond.

Lots of shuffling, grunting, wiggling. Gordon cried.

"Here, Mason, let me feed him."

Once settled against Momma's breast, Gordon hushed and the world seemed to stop breathing. We lay in absolute darkness. Even the wind seemed to pause in respect for Momma.

"I seen him drinking," Don said. "He's been drinking all day, hasn't he?"

"It's okay," Momma said. "Don't worry yourself."

Even the crickets were quiet.

"I'm sorry I forgot the tarp."

"There's nothing to worry about, Mason. Let's be thankful that it's a warm night."

"But it's gonna rain."

"Maybe. Maybe not."

I spooned up against Jenny who had grown so still I knew that she was asleep already. I glanced upward, wishing I could see the millions of stars that were usually the last thing I saw each night, but tonight the clouds wouldn't allow it.

A large raindrop splattered against the side of my face. We all moved at the same time.

Mason groaned. "I told you it would rain!"

"It's just sprinkling," Mamma said. "We'll get under the truck."

"I'll get the flashlight." The truck bed shook as Don sprang down and ran up to the cab. We heard the door open, heard him fumble through the glove compartment, then slam the door.

"He's passed out cold," he said, shining the light over us.

The sprinkles grew heavier.

A few minutes later, Don and Mamma had us lined up like sausages under the truck. Rain pelted the cab and plunked against the floorboards but for the moment, we were dry.

"I told you it was gonna rain," Mason complained.

"Shhh."

We lay still and listened to the rain until it started to seep through the bed and drip on us.

"See?" Mason agonized. "Now we're all getting rained on!"

Momma's voice was soft. "But, it's a warm rain, Mason. It's a warm rain."

Chapter 2

The Ditch

The next morning we finished off the baloney and bread, watered and fertilized the bushes, and piled back into the truck. Daddy probably hadn't gone more than a couple of miles when he slowed and pulled off the road by a big tree. Other than the one big tree, only grass, bushes, and weeds grew.

We all strained to see why he had stopped. An old truck pulling a trailer with some kind of big machine on it, rumbled toward us from the opposite direction.

"Why'd he stop?" Mason asked. "He didn't have to stop to let a truck and backhoe pass."

"Damned if I know." They jumped down. Uncertainty kept the rest of us in the truck.

As the other truck approached, Daddy opened his door and stepped to the asphalt. He stood in the middle of the road and waved for the man to stop. The truck slowly ground to a halt.

"Got troubles?" the man yelled.

Daddy hurried over to talk to the man but the wind blew away their words before we could hear them.

The stranger took off his cap, scratched his head, frowned, and seemed to be asking questions. Finally, he shrugged, nodded, and got out of his truck. He walked back with Daddy.

"You kids get out of the way so this man can see the headboard and dresser."

We scrambled to the other side of the truck. The man hopped up, examined the headboard, then the dresser, and turned to Daddy. All he said was, "Okay."

A few minutes later the man pulled the backhoe out into the field about fifty feet off the road. Since Daddy had followed him on foot, we all made our way out of the truck and followed Daddy. Don and Mason stood with Momma, who was holding Gordon, and they all looked like someone had just hit them in the head with a board. With stunned, wide-eyed expressions, they watched in silence.

The fellow unloaded the backhoe, moved it into position, and lifted its shovel. "Here?" he yelled.

"Yeah!" Daddy yelled back. "Right there."

The shovel came down and for the next several minutes, the stranger dug a trench in the field. When he had finished, a gaping hole about six feet wide and twenty feet long lay before us. The pile of freshly scooped dirt called fiercely to Thurmond, who couldn't stay out of it. He tried to run up it, and only slipped and slid because it was so loose. The rest of us simply stared.

When the digging was finished, the man drove the backhoe onto his trailer, hopped into his truck, and pulled it up next to ours. He and Daddy unloaded our headboard and dresser, set them on the back blade of the backhoe, and tied them in place with rope. Without another word, the stranger climbed into his truck and slowly drove on down the road.

Momma didn't even try to blink away her tears. Eyes wide open, fixed on the trench, the tears flowed, uninterrupted. She didn't even look away when Daddy said, "I'll be back later with a tarp." Clinging to Gordon, her skirt whipping in the wind, her hair blowing curls around her head, she just stared.

Don and Mason glared at Daddy. I had no idea what was happening and didn't understand their menacing faces.

Daddy turned and left. As the truck's engine faded into the wind, I realized that I was looking at our next home, and I couldn't have been more pleased. This was a thousand times better than living in the truck. In fact, as far as I could see, this was about the greatest place anyone could live. Like rabbits! Sliding into our house and burrowing beneath the earth.

Thurmond, Jenny, and Amy obviously agreed with me because they were already busy having a good time.

At that moment, I thought of my first joke. Eager to share it, I slid down into the trench, stood in the middle of it, and shouted, "Momma! Would you say we're in a rut?"

At first, I thought no one got it, so I explained. "A rut! Like—a rut! Would you say we're in a rut?"

To my great delight, Momma wiped her tears and laughed. "I'd say you're right, Othello. I think we're in a rut."

"Shee-it!" Don and Mason scowled at me and turned away. They didn't get it.

Momma spread a blanket under the tree and nursed Gordon while most of us played in the rut or on the mound of dirt. Don and Mason left to look for a stream or creek.

Jenny, Thurmond, and I explored every rock and bush, unaware that our new home was less than ideal. We chased a jack rabbit but not for long. It lost us within seconds. All the while we played, a part of me felt sad for Momma and I tried hard to think of a new joke.

Sometime later, daddy returned and unloaded a big canvas tarp. He took all of the boxes out of the truck and set a little two-burner coal oil stove just outside the rut. He told Thurmond to go find the biggest rocks he could carry and bring them back. Thurmond groaned and complained as he left, but did as he was told.

Don and Mason came back about then, and Don said, "The creek's not far, but if you don't know where it is, you can walk forever. It's over—"

"Help me spread the tarp," Daddy interrupted.

Don took one end and together, they put a roof over our new home. Using the rocks Thurmond carried up, they weighted the edges down.

"I went by the body shop while I was in town." Daddy lit a cigarette as he spoke. "I can hire on in the morning." He blew a stream of blue gray smoke into the wind. "But I gotta be there early so I'm spending the night in town. Don can go with me and find something. I saw a couple of places that—"

"But . . . Russell," Momma said, "what about school? Mason's got another month of school to finish."

I glanced at Mason who suddenly looked half his age. Like a little kid, he chewed at his thumbnail and listened, wide-eyed, for Daddy's answer.

Daddy shook his head impatiently. "Then he can go into town with me tonight and find the school tomorrow." He took another drag on the cigarette. "Don can stay here tonight with you and the little 'uns, and walk in tomorrow to look for work."

Momma nodded and rushed around, looking through the boxes to find something clean for Mason to wear.

"Don't worry, Momma. I'll just find the school tomorrow. I won't need clean clothes till I find it. I want to see where it is, first."

She sighed and stood. "Okay." Closing her eyes, she reached back, bundled her hair in one hand, fumbled for something in one of the boxes and came up with a broken shoelace. She tied her hair back and said to Daddy, "Tell the boss that you have kids to feed. See if he won't pay you at the end of the day."

Daddy frowned and gave a short jerk of a nod, as if it irritated him for her to tell him what to do.

Daddy and Mason left well before dark. Momma went through the boxes quickly, found a pan, some canned peaches, and two forks. Don opened the peaches with a can opener on his pocketknife and we shared the forks to empty the can of peaches. When the last of the peach juice was gone, Momma pointed toward the road. "You girls go over there by the road and pick some wild greens for supper."

I groaned the loudest. We had eaten wild greens all of my life and I hated them almost as much as I hated chicken livers. We were eating weeds and I knew it. God never meant for them to be eaten. They grew wild because they were weeds, and they grew by the road because cars were supposed to run over them. Or maybe cows and horses were supposed to eat them, but pure and simple, they were weeds and that's exactly what they tasted like.

Later, after Momma boiled the weeds, I ate them like everyone else. I was too hungry to argue.

"Wish we had some vinegar," Thurmond grumbled. "They's a lots better with vinegar."

Nothing made them better, but I kept the thought to myself. At least, they made the hunger go away.

About sundown, Momma had us wash up in the creek but by the time we walked back to the trench, our feet were as dirty as they had been.

"But this is clean dirt," Jenny said. "It'll brush off."

Momma climbed down into the rut with us, and using the flashlight and a coal oil lamp, bedded us down on the blankets. She rummaged around in the boxes looking for something, and suddenly came up laughing. Shining the light around the sides of the trench, she found a root sticking out about an inch and moved over to it. She hung something on the root and stood back laughing.

"What is it?" I asked

Don chuckled and shook his head. "It's a little embroidery thing. It says 'Home, Sweet Home'."

I got the joke! For once, I got it! I laughed harder than anyone else.

I wasn't sure when Momma stopped laughing and started crying but I became aware that somehow the feeling changed. Everyone felt it and sat up to look at her. Don went to her, put his arm around her and together, they sat down against the dirt wall.

I had never heard her cry out loud before.

Wind ruffled the tarp all night, knocking dirt and little clods down on us.

Don was gone when I got up, and Momma was outside by the stove. She had found half a loaf of bread in the bottom of a sack and was happy enough to celebrate. One by one, we crawled up and ate the squashed slices of white bread with eager mouths and grateful hearts. Anything was better than weed greens in the morning.

After we had eaten, Momma handed Thurmond a bucket and a bar of lye soap and gave Jenny and me an armload of clothes to carry. She carried Gordon, held Amy's hand, and together we walked to the creek. The morning sun shone brightly and as far as I could see, it was going to be another beautiful day.

While Momma washed clothes, we took turns watching Amy and Gordon, and fought over a frog that Thurmond found until it finally leaped from our grasp and into the water. Then we carried the heavy, soggy, wet clothes back to the trench and draped them over the bushes to dry.

Mason came running up about noon, just in time to eat weed greens. He was breathless from running and excitement. "Did you wash my clothes?" He scanned the laundry strewn over the bushes.

"Yes, I did," Momma said. "You'll be clean tomorrow."

In his excitement over finding the school, he ate the weed greens without a trace of resentment, something I never managed.

"It looks like a good school, Momma. It's not too big." He couldn't help smiling.

"Did you go in and talk to anyone?" She asked. "Did you tell them you would be there tomorrow?"

"Naw." He shook his head shyly. "I couldn't do that. But I peeked in the window."

Momma smiled. "And what did you see?"

"I saw some kids at a long table and they were doing some kind of science experiment. They even had a microscope."

Momma looked up toward the sky. "Thank you, God," she said. Then smiling as big as I ever saw her smile, she said, "Oh, Mason! I'm so glad!"

"Yeah," he grinned. "Me, too."

What seemed to be the best stroke of luck Mason ever had soon turned into his worst nightmare. Determined to protect his books, he climbed down into the trench, and with a screwdriver and a stick he dug a rectangular hole in the wall of the trench to hold his books. Then, one by one, he brought each of us to look at it, and said, "This is *my* drawer for *my* books. Never touch them. Never! Okay?"

We all agreed, each so impressed with the perfect "drawer" that we were darn near speechless. The books fit in the "drawer" so perfectly there was no doubt that Mason was a genius!

Don came home about sundown, carrying a sack of groceries. We rushed out to meet him like a bunch of eager puppies and when he smiled, his face was so sunburned the skin around his eyes crinkled white.

"Helped lay pipe for a construction company," he said to Momma. "Shee-it! That's hot work." He set the bag of groceries on the blanket under the tree. "Gotta wear a long sleeve shirt tomorrow. My arms are all burnt up." He extended his arms and we cringed to look at them.

"Oh, Don!" Mamma gasped. "Go down to the creek and get in the water awhile. It'll help take the sting out."

"Yeah, I will in a minute." He dug into his pocket. "Anyway, here's a little change. Spent plumb near all of it so we could eat tonight."

Momma kissed him, careful not to touch his arms.

While Don and Mason went down to the creek, Momma put weenies into a big pot of beans and heated it up. She let us each have an apple while we waited for the banquet to be served.

Daddy didn't come back that night. I probably wouldn't even have noticed except Momma seemed to sit up a long time after the rest of us were asleep. Crowded together on blankets in the bottom of that trench, with hardly room to turn over, we listened to the crickets chirping above our heads and heard an occasional car pass on the road.

It wasn't the thunder that woke me—it was the mud. I tried to push myself up but my elbows sank into the ground and I couldn't move. Muddy water rushed down the sides of the trench and swirled around us. I scrambled to get up. Everyone suddenly thrashed about yelling and complaining.

"God almighty!" Don yelled. "We gotta get out of here!"

Momma flipped on the flashlight. "I've got Gordon!" she said. "Get Amy!"

Both Gordon and Amy screamed with indignation. The rest of us whined and grumbled, disoriented by the rude awakening. Before we could begin to get organized and out of the trench, a loud clap of thunder reverberated around us, instantly followed by a torrential downpour.

"My books!" Mason cried. "My books will be ruined!"

No one assured him they wouldn't be. We all knew they had to be covered with mud, but at that moment, there was no time to think of anything except getting out of the flooding hole.

Water and oozing mud hindered our escape. Don climbed out first then pulled the rest of us up one at a time. Covered in mud, with no shelter in sight, we huddled together like drowned rats, while the rain poured down on us. The storm didn't last long, but it was enough to help me understand why Momma had cried, and why Don and Mason were so angry when Daddy had the trench dug. My "rut" joke didn't seem funny at all after the rain.

Mason cried so hard and for such a long time, that I thought he might be sad forever. When the sun came up, he climbed back down in the trench and pulled his books from his mud-filled "drawer." For a while he lovingly tried to wipe each page clean but eventually gave up and with a loud, frustrated sob, flung them to the ground and walked toward the creek, crying.

Everything we owned dripped, including our clothes and the sagging boxes that held them. The blankets lay in the bottom of the trench, floating in six inches of muddy red water or stuck under globs of mud. Don and Mason's shoes lay in the trench, as soggy as the blankets. Momma's shoes, kicked off outside the trench, were also soaked. The rest of us didn't have to worry. We had no shoes to ruin.

Momma pulled the wilted, wet paper sack away from the remaining groceries and took stock of what she had. Don recruited Thurmond to climb down in the trench and hand him the end of the blankets. "Nothing to do but wash them," he said. "Might as well get started."

Thurmond's usually shiny blonde hair stuck to his head with a dull red paste. Always eager to be included by his older brothers, he wasted no time sliding down into the muddy trench.

"God! It's heavy!" Thurmond strained to lift the soggy blanket.

"It'll be lighter if you get off it, stupid!" Don yelled.

The rest of us laughed, waiting for Thurmond to discover his mistake. When he did, he tugged one end of the blanket up high enough that Don could reach it. Once within his grasp, Don yanked it up and out of the hole. Thurmond sloshed around, retrieved the second blanket, handed the corner to Don, then pitched the shoes out of the hole.

"Find mine!" Amy instructed from the edge of the trench. "Find my choo, too!"

Thurmond scowled up at her and flung mud from his arms. "Naw. It don't fit no way!"

Amy, already distracted by the mud oozing between her toes, forgot her request and squatted to play with her muddy toes.

The sun burned hot all that day. The washed blankets dried on the bushes by noon, along with the rest of our belongings. Mason gave up on the idea of going to school and left with Don as soon as the heavy work was finished.

Jenny, Thurmond, and I spent the afternoon making mud sculptures and drying them on sun-warmed rocks. Jenny and I labored over dolls and birds, while Thurmond's interest ran more toward cars, dogs, and other strange animals. Amy played close to Momma and Gordon, who were rarely more than a few feet from us.

The whole summer passed in that field but we never slept in the trench again. Rainstorms sometimes left a foot of water in the hole but we didn't care. Don, Mason, and Momma fashioned a tent out of the tarp and our meager belongings were kept dry, day and night. Don insisted that Momma, Gordon, and Amy sleep inside the tent, which they did. The rest of us shared the blankets—and the mosquitoes—in the open air, unless it rained. Then, as before, we huddled together under the tarp to keep dry. Daddy came by once in awhile, and when he did, he took the tent.

A Black Eye for Money

One hot night before we left the field and the trench, I eavesdropped on a conversation not meant for my ears. Don had taken a job in another town and only came back on the weekends, and Daddy had been "gone" longer than usual.

"Mason! Mason!" Momma's urgent whisper woke me. "Mason, get up. I need to talk to you." She held the flashlight so that it shown on the ground beside him.

Mason stirred and sat up. "Huh?"

"You said you know where your daddy works and where he stays—in town, I mean."

He blinked and rubbed his eyes. "Uh-huh."

"What's the name of the shop?"

He stopped rubbing his eyes and stared at her. "Why?"

"Because I'm going to walk into town. I need to talk to him."

Mason shook his head. "Don't do that, Momma. He told me not to tell you. He said he'd beat me within an inch of my life if I told."

"I've got to know!" she said desperately. "If I don't' get some money from him, my babies are going to starve!"

Mason lowered his eyes and looked away. "He'll blow up, Momma. Don't make me tell."

"I think it's Otis' Body Shop, isn't it?"

Mason's quick, apprehensive glance confirmed her suspicions.

"I thought so. I thought I heard you and Don talking about it one day."

Mason got to his knees in front of her. "Let me go, Momma. Let me find him and tell him. Even if he beats me, I—I don't want you to go. It's too far. And . . . "

"And what?"

"Well, you just shouldn't go. Let me."

Momma stared at him for a long time before she sighed and said, "You're smart. I'll trust you. But you've got to find him tomorrow and tell him I've got to have money for food."

"I will. I'll go tomorrow."

She patted his arm. "Thank you. I hate it that you to have to do it, but—"

"No. It's better that way," he assured her. "It's better if I go."

She kissed his forehead then stood and followed the circle of light back into the tent. I sensed the urgency in both Momma and Mason, but for the life of me, all I could think of, was the promise of real food instead of weed greens.

When Mason left the next day, and when he returned, later, both escaped my attention. But towards suppertime, I noticed that something wonderful was cooking in the pot on the two-burner stove. Lifting the lid, I discovered plump, yellow-white butter beans bubbling in a thick broth. The smooth, shiny joint of a ham bone danced among the beans.

Don wandered up just after we had eaten. "Where's Mason?" he asked.

Momma, helping Amy finish her beans, nodded toward the tent. "Sleeping."

Don laughed. "Sleeping? Well, I'll just get the lazy bum up!"

Momma held up a cautioning hand. "Well, he's not feeling too good right now."

Having not seen Mason come home, I was surprised to find out he was sick. I waited until Don was inside the tent and no one else was watching, then I sneaked around to the back to listen. They were already talking.

"Damn!" Don said. "He smacked you good! You got a shiner the size of Texas!"

"He 'bout broke my arm!" Mason said. "Look at this."

I assumed he was displaying bruises.

"Shee-it!" Don whistled through his teeth "So, where was he?"

"Beer joint. God, I hate going in, looking for him."

"Yeah. Me, too."

They were quiet for a while and then Don asked, "Was he with someone?"

Mason must have nodded because Don said, "I thought so. He usually is. What'd he say?"

"That was the thing!" Mason said. "He got so mad when he saw me, he told me to get out! But I didn't. I just stood there, remembering what Momma said to tell him." His voice cracked and I heard the disgust in his voice. "He had his arm around this lady in the booth with him, and he said, 'Go on, now! Get!' The woman laughed and I wanted to leave but . . . anyway, I finally stood right next to him and said, 'Momma's got to have some money for food. She said I can't leave till you give me money.'"

My heart drummed in my ears. Until that instant, I had forgotten all about him being sent to find Daddy. I thought someone else had beat him up.

"That's when he hit me," Mason continued. "Right there in front of everybody. I fell on my butt. Everyone was staring. And I said it again, 'cept I yelled it this time. I yelled, '*Momma needs money for groceries!*' He jumped up then, madder than a rabid dog, and I thought I was a goner. But he reached into his pocket and handed me money. He jammed it in my hand like I was wrong for taking it. Then he yelled, '*Now, get out of here and don't ever come back! When I'm busy, I'm busy*!' Mason hesitated for a moment then added, "Then I left as fast as I could."

Don cleared his throat. "Well, I see you got home with some groceries, so I'd say you did pretty good, little brother. You got nothing to be 'shamed of. Now, come on and eat something with me, before it's all gone."

I was shocked to see Mason's face. The left side of his face was black and blue and his eye was swollen shut.

Thurmond and Jenny called for me to play but I stayed near Gordon and Amy so that I could be close to Don, Mason, and Momma.

"This ain't right, Momma," Don said, as he ate his beans. "This just ain't right."

Chapter 3

A Shack but No Shoes

I don't think Daddy ever spent a night at the ditch, but in the late fall, when it became too cold to stay out in the open, we left the ditch and Daddy, Momma, and Don pitched a tent in some farmer's pasture, where another family had already claimed a place. Amid the cow plops and salt licks, we played with the neighbor's children. Nights in the tent became unbearable as the weather turned colder and we coughed until no one could sleep. Momma made a tonic of coal oil and sugar and it helped a little, but the coughing didn't stop until Daddy finally moved us into a shack, still outside the city limits, but a little closer to town.

Moving created a lot of excitement, especially for Mason, because he now had a place to keep his things out of the dirt. Even though there was no plumbing in the house, and only one bedroom, eventually we had three beds and we were separated a little. Jenny, Amy, and I slept on a bed in the living room; the three boys shared a bed on the back porch, which had been haphazardly enclosed to serve as a room; and Momma, Daddy, and Gordon slept in the real bedroom.

A wood-burning cook stove in the kitchen heated water and cooked food and a pot-bellied stove in the living room warmed the shack, when we had wood or coal to burn. Little by little we acquired a few pieces of furniture—a long wooden table and benches for the kitchen, a free-standing cupboard, and an overstuffed green chair in the living room. Outside, on the rear of the property was an outhouse, a faucet, a smelly little chicken coop, a thick stand of tall trees some fifty feet in back of the house, and a #2 washtub propped against the wall near the back door, for washing clothes and bathing on Saturdays.

Daddy was rarely home, and many evenings were passed with wishes for this or that, as we slowly browsed the Sears & Roebuck catalog. When wood or coal was available, we gathered around the stove in the living room. When it wasn't, we gathered at the kitchen table.

I swooned over the shiny shoes and ribbons, and Momma dog-eared the pages with ugly high-top boys shoes and said, "These would be warmer and last longer."

"But I want these!" I would turn back to the pretty shoes.

She would sigh, shake her head and say, "Well, Othello, if you want 'em bad enough, you can have 'em."

"Well, I do," I would insist with all the conviction I felt. "I want 'em really bad."

Deep gutters straddled the dirt road in front of the house and filled rapidly after a rain, washing the town's debris past our yard. On one occasion, the gutter delivered a five-dollar bill, which Jenny and I grabbed at once. Running our treasure inside to Momma, she gasped and hugged us. "Shoes!" She laughed. "You'll both get shoes!"

She placed our feet on paper, drew around them, and said she'd have Daddy take her to the store when he came home. Two days later, when he hadn't returned, Momma called us inside. She explained that the woman who lived across the road had just had a baby, but it died, and she said the woman had no money to bury the baby or buy flowers for its grave. She asked if she could use the $5 to help the woman with the funeral.

I thought about the shiny shoes and grudgingly remained silent while Jenny nodded quickly. Shamed into agreeing, I finally gave my consent. I did, however, intend to step up my campaign for shoes.

When school started, I still had no shoes, and walked barefoot on the dirt road into town. Momma had made me a second flour sack dress, and washed and ironed daily to keep me clean, and everything seemed okay for a couple of months until we awoke one morning to find three inches of snow on the ground. Not about to let me skip school, Momma wrapped my feet in burlap bags and tied them on with bailing wire. She said I should throw the sacks on the bushes when I got to school and hopefully the sun would come out and dry them before I started home.

Unaware that burlap shoes weren't common snow gear, I expected to see the bushes covered with burlap bags from other kids. Instead, I saw kids wearing red and black rubber boots, and quickly removed the bags and hid them under the bushes. When I entered the room barefoot, the teacher drew back and gasped. Embarrassed, I quickly took my seat, avoiding everyone's eyes. Throughout the morning, I sat on one foot, then the other, to keep them warm, dreading lunchtime when I had to walk home to eat. However, the trip home wasn't nearly as miserable as it had been in the morning. Although cold, the snow had melted enough that, while cold and muddy, I wasn't freezing. Momma washed my feet in warm water and was just saying I shouldn't go back after lunch, when a car pulled up in front of the house. It was my teacher, delivering a pair of shoes. Momma cried as she thanked her, and said I would eat quickly and not be late in the afternoon.

The shoes were ugly, brown, and scuffed, but warmer than gunnysacks, and I knew I would only have to wear them until spring. As much as I hated dirty feet, I preferred dirty feet to ugly boy's shoes.

Friday evenings dragged mercilessly as we waited for Daddy to come home so he and Momma could go to the store. One Friday, Mason came home from school and said he had stopped and talked with Daddy at the shop, and Daddy would be home for supper about six o'clock. Momma sang and joked with us as she peeled the last of the potatoes and fried them in the big cast-iron skillet. When the potatoes were ready, she covered the skillet and pulled a chair over to the kitchen window, where we clamored around and sang songs that she made up. "Won't you come home, dear Daddy, won't you come home? You're gone the whole week long," was sung to the tune of another song I'd heard her sing. While we sang, we took turns at the window, watching for the truck lights to appear on the road, while Momma made biscuits. When we had sung every song we knew, and Daddy hadn't arrived, we finally sat down in front of the pie tins that served as plates, and spooned out fried potatoes.

Jenny, who had been asleep, came to the table late. Rubbing her eyes, she yawned and said, "Pass the taters."

"Ain't no more taters," Thurmond said. "Just grease."

She nodded, took a biscuit, and said, "Pass the grease."

"If he don't come home tonight, Momma, these kids are gonna freeze to death." Don's fourteen-year-old face suddenly looked very grown up. "We're burning the last of the coal."

Momma's eyes were wide and frightened, but she kept rocking Gordon as if everything was okay. "He'll be here," she said. "He'll come. He told Mason."

An hour later, the stove in the living room was as cold as the air, the warmth from the kitchen stove faded fast, and the wind outside howled to get in. Jenny and Amy slept on the living room bed and I huddled against them while Momma and Don stared out at the snow blowing past the window. Mason and Thurmond sat in the kitchen to keep warm, reading old comic books in the wobbly light of the lantern.

Finally, the truck's engine grumbled into the yard. Don and Momma turned toward the door but didn't move until Daddy stumbled inside, along with a flurry of icy wind and snowflakes.

Daddy swore at the cold and rushed to the stove to warm himself. From the bed, I could see into the kitchen and all of the living room, too. Momma and Don exchanged frowns and Mason, at the kitchen table, turned away in disgust. "He drank the paycheck again," he said to Thurmond.

"Where have you been?" Momma asked. "You told Mason—"

"What the hell do you know about it?" Daddy yelled. "Don't start yappin' at me now! I gotta warm up to even think!"

"You won't do it, here," Don said.

Daddy glanced up angrily then touched the stove. "We'll ain't that great! I'm half freezing to death and there's no fire!"

"Did you spend it all?" Momma asked, her mouth tight, her face pinched. "Did you spend every last cent of it on whiskey?"

Daddy ignored her. "Well, Don can just go pick up some coal along the railroad tracks. There's always coal spilt along the—"

"You'll do it!" Momma snapped. "You're not sending him out on a night like this! If you'd have come home, like you said—"

"I ain't goin' by myself!" he yelled. "He can go with me!"

"No!" Momma yelled. "He's worked all day and gotta get up early tomorrow! If it weren't for him, we would all have starved by now!"

"He's going, too!" Daddy yelled. "One person can't get enough! Come on, Don! There's tow sacks in the truck."

Don nodded, zipped up his coat, pulled his cap over his ears, and followed Daddy out.

I was asleep when loud stomping on the porch woke me. The door opened and frigid air took my breath away as Don and Daddy came inside. Covered with snow, both were almost white. They dropped their sacks on the floor and stood like statues, too cold to move. Momma rushed to bring Don a pan of water to thaw his red and swollen hands. She ran a wet cloth over his face, removing ice from his eyebrows and from under his nose. "I'm so sorry," she said. "So sorry."

All the while, Daddy stood to one side, saying nothing.

"Daddy's cold, too," Jenny said, scooting out of the bed and going into the kitchen. "I'll get some warm water for him."

"No, Jenny," Momma said. "Warm water hurts too much. I'll take care of him."

Jenny dived back under the covers and Mason and Thurmond, still at the kitchen table, grabbed a sack of coal and dragged it over to the living room stove.

The next morning, I saw Daddy take a small gasoline can from his truck and walk across the road to the house where the baby had died. He peeked through their window, then moved to a large drum beside the house, turned the spigot, and filled the small can with kerosene. He stayed beside the house for a minute, then trotted back across the road. When he brought the small can inside, Momma said, "Did you pay for that?"

"'Course, I did!" he snapped.

Minutes later, the neighbor lady ran into our yard screaming that she had seen Daddy steal kerosene. He denied it and said that she was crazy and seeing things.

The Last Christmas

Two weeks before Christmas, I started a campaign for a rubber doll. Each time I asked, Momma said, "We'll see."

Then, two days before Christmas, Don and Mason dragged home a Christmas tree and set it up in the living room. Momma's mood instantly brightened and we were quickly caught up in the idea of decorating it. Momma whipped powered soap and water with a whisk until it looked like beaten egg whites. Then, using a large spoon, she laid every branch with "snow." Jenny and I watched in amazement as Momma drew angels with very wide skirts on brown paper sacks and painted them with white shoe polish. Next, she made a thick flour-and-water paste and glued the bottom of each angel's wide skirt together in the back, and stood it on the tree branches.

That night, as we ate biscuits and gravy, we talked about our beautiful tree, and after supper, we sang Christmas carols.

Around noon on Christmas Eve, Grandma and Grandpa Birdwell, Momma's parents, brought presents for everyone and placed them under the tree. Grandpa Birdwell, a huge man with wild white hair rearing out of his head like a mane, spoke firmly, making all of us hush. I wanted to like him and tried sitting on his lap once, but he quickly scooted me off and told me to go play. Grandma was not much bigger than Thurmond, but she had a sour face and I didn't even try to talk to her. But after they left, we erupted with noise and curiosity, and dropped to our hands and knees to crawl around the tree and try to imagine what hidden treasures awaited us on Christmas morning.

That evening, Momma bundled us up and we all walked into town to a Salvation Army Christmas program. She held Gordon close, a blanket over his head, as we trudged through the few inches of snow, finally arriving at a little church where people crowded together inside and spilled out the door. Elbowing her way inside past the adults, she kept saying, "I have children here. Please let us inside." The sea of bodies reluctantly opened enough that we could squeeze through. Once inside, the heat immediately felt good, but just as quickly, it became stifling as we found ourselves trapped between stinking wet wool coats, unable to move. Loud Christmas music blared around us and people yelled over our heads, as we held hands and followed Momma deeper into the crowd. She led us down an aisle and finally found a pew where we could squeeze in and sit.

We heard Santa's bells ringing and a loud "Ho-Ho-Ho!" from the front of the room, but we were too short to see beyond the heads of adults in front of us. Mason and Thurmond worked their way to the front.

After a while, someone announced that all children should hold up their hands so Santa could see them. Our hands shot into the air, where they remained until they ached, but Santa didn't come. Locking one arm behind my head to hold the other, I tried to keep my arm up. Eventually, I became too tired to care.

"Get your hands up!" Momma said, "Get your hands up!" I looked around and noticed that Jenny and Amy had given up, too. We tried again. The oppressive heat and stench of wet wool made me nauseous. Without knowing it, I let my arm slip down again.

"Over here!" Momma called to someone. "Please! Over here! I have some little girls. They've waited so long—" She glanced at us. "Get your hands up so you'll get something!"

I pushed my hand into the air, hoping I wouldn't throw up, frightened by the panic I heard in Momma's voice. "It don't matter, Momma! Let's go!"

"It does matter! You've got to have some Christmas!" She waved her arm at someone in the aisle. "Please! Over here!"

A woman in a Salvation Army uniform and a Santa hat struggled through the crowd to get to us. Leaning as far as she could, she reached into a bag and handed each of us a small wrapped gift.

"Thank you," Momma said then slumped heavily against the seat. "Oh, I had hoped you'd get a doll." Like her, I knew it couldn't be a doll. Still, I tore away the paper and looked at the rubber truck. I ran it along my leg but the wheels didn't turn. Jenny had been given a car and Amy, a sack of marbles.

"Can we go, now?" I looked up just in time to see her wiping tears from her cheeks.

We made our way back through the noisy, smelly, overheated crowd and stepped into the cold, clear night. On the way home, our mood brightened considerably as Mason walked on new stilts and Thurmond swung at the air with a new bat. He had also received a ball and we couldn't wait to help him put his gifts to use.

On Christmas morning, we awakened to the sound of Momma singing carols as she nursed Gordon. Daddy had come home sometime during the night, and sat in the kitchen drinking coffee and smoking. When we were allowed to open our gifts, I thought I would explode with happiness. Grandma and Grandpa had given Jenny, Amy, and me, each, a coloring book with eight pictures and a box of four crayons. Mason said they were "giveaway" samples, but I didn't care. I poured the crayons on the floor and became lost in the magical process of coloring.

Moving from picture to picture, I delighted with every mark I made, and when suddenly my book was finished, a terrible sense of disappointment engulfed me. Jenny and Amy were still working. I watched their every stroke, hoping they would ask me to finish their pictures, but they didn't.

When all of our pictures were colored, Momma praised our work and said, "I know how much you wanted rubber dolls, and well, I don't have rubber dolls, but I do have something I made for you."

"You do?" We followed on her heels as she went into her bedroom and took a box from the closet. "I'm sorry these aren't the dolls you wanted," she said before reaching into the box, "but maybe they'll do."

At first glance, I couldn't tell what it was, except that it wore a red and white checkered dress and matching bonnet and looked sort of like a doll. When she handed it to me, its orange face with button eyes and an ink-drawn mouth smiled up at me. Bundled in little blankets, cut from one of Gordon's blankets, the orange-faced baby stared at me. I opened the blanket, lifted its dress, and discovered that my homemade baby was once a sweet potato. For sure, it was a homely child but I could see how hard

Momma had worked to make it acceptable. I didn't really love it but I suddenly loved Momma so much I hugged it.

"What's it?" Amy pulled at my arm to see.

"You like it?" Jenny asked tentatively, her nose wrinkled and her mouth turned down.

I looked at Momma who watched closely, her hand still inside the box, her eyes wide as she watched me.

"I love it," I lied to Jenny.

Instantly, Jenny and Amy wanted one, too, and Momma smiled and handed each of them a sweet potato doll, their dresses a different fabric, so that we wouldn't get them mixed up.

"How'd you stick its eyes in its head?" Jenny asked. She pulled at one and lifted it off, discovering that a straight pin held it in place. "Oh." She pushed the eye back down.

Momma suddenly started to cry.

"Don't you like 'em?" Amy asked Momma.

She wiped her eyes on her apron. "I just wish they were real dolls."

That Christmas night, the three of us fell asleep hugging our sweet potato dolls.

White Trash Ways

Throughout the winter, I awoke each morning to see Momma sitting in the kitchen, writing by the light of the kerosene lantern. Both she and Don would stop by local businesses when they were in town and ask the secretaries to save unwanted correspondence for Momma, so that she could use the clean back side to write her stories and poems. Other times, when the paper was gone, she would cut up brown paper bags or use the backs of envelopes.

More than once that winter, she opened the mail and danced around the house waving an acceptance letter or a check from a magazine. "Three dollars and fifty cents! I can't wait to tell your grandpa!"

Grandpa was a teacher, a preacher, a sometimes inventor, and a poet. When he came over, he often brought food, and Momma always sat with him in the kitchen, waiting patiently for him to read her latest work. One evening, he slid her writing back and said, "Is that supposed to be funny?"

"It *is* funny!" she insisted. "I know it is!"

"It's not funny to me!" He frowned and folded his arms. "I told you to stop spending your time on stories. You have a fine ear for poetry. Concentrate on poetry."

She reached to the top of the cupboard and handed him a letter. "Read it for yourself," she smiled. "They thought my story was funny and paid me three dollars and fifty cents for it!" She showed him the check.

Grandpa read the letter, handed it back to her, and folded his arms again. "There's no such thing as good literature anymore."

Grandpa stayed for the beans-and-weenies he had brought for our supper, and after we were all seated and had our heads bowed, he began to pray. I hated Grandpa's prayers because they went on until my neck felt like it would break and never stop hurting. That night when he finally finished, I said, "Finally!"

Both Momma and Grandpa glared at me until I wanted to crawl under the table. And I might have, except for the weenies, which I loved.

"Pass the weenies, please," I repeated as the pan of weenies made its way around the table. Everyone talked until I couldn't be heard. "Pass the weenies, please!" Still I was ignored.

Momma and Grandpa were discussing someone called Mussolini, and I couldn't get eye contact or make my request heard. Finally, deciding a rhyme might make them pay attention, I said, "Pass the weenies, Mussolini!"

Momma's hand shot across the table and smacked my cheek, almost knocking me off the bench.

"Don't ever call anyone Mussolini!"

"I just wanted the weenies," I cried, "and no one would pass 'em."

She handed me the plate of weenies. "All you have to do is ask," she said. "But never call anyone Mussolini!"

I didn't know who Mussolini was, but if it hadn't been for him, I wouldn't have gotten the weenies.

When Don bought Momma a radio, we climbed all over her while she dialed through the stations to find music she liked. However, when she was working, mending, or ironing clothes, she listened to preaching. Lifting the heavy iron from the stove, she would sing along with the choirs and nod and laugh at the preachers as she ironed.

We generally played on the floor at her feet, cutting paper dolls from old newspapers while preachers shouted and screamed until we couldn't hear ourselves talk. I hated all the hollering but was afraid to say anything because I knew preachers were supposed to be people that God really liked; but one day I became so cranky from all the shouting, I yelled, "Is he mad at us?"

"Who?" Momma asked without looking up.

"The radio preacher. Why does he yell at us?"

She laughed. "He wants us to listen and understand."

"Well, I don't understand why he wants us to listen to shoutin'," I complained. "It hurts my ears and makes me mad!"

She laughed again, and changed the station to music. "Do you like that? That's Frank Sinatra."

"Leave it there!" Jenny yelled. "Don't ever go back to preachers!"

Stolen Supper

Late one afternoon, while it was still too cold to play outside or even open the windows, a loud knock sounded at the door. Don answered it, and two of Momma's brothers, Calvin and Stanley, stepped inside. Both carried bags of groceries, and everyone laughed and talked instantly. They had brought chicken, potatoes, canned peas, bread, flour, and shortening.

Momma thanked them for the food, shooed us out of the kitchen, and immediately started cooking. Calvin and Stanley sat at the table with Don and Mason while Momma hurried around, laughing and enjoying the visit.

I heard Calvin say that he and Stanley had just gotten out of prison that day. I had never seen Momma so happy as when she listened to their stories and cooked. The smell of chicken frying and potatoes cooking, mingled with the sound of their excited voices and laughter, created the most festive mood I had ever felt or seen.

With the table piled high with food, we scrambled to our places and waited for each dish to pass our way. As when Grandpa visited, there was so much noise and talking, it was hard to be heard over the crowd.

My eyes followed the mashed potatoes. "Pass the taters, please."

I said it half a dozen times. I had chicken and peas on my plate, but I didn't want to eat until I also had potatoes. "Pass the taters, please."

Just then a loud, booming knock rattled the front door. Before Don could get to it, the door burst open and two policemen stepped inside, one with his gun drawn.

"Okay, Calvin . . . Stanley . . . let's go."

Momma jumped up. "Roy Richardson! Don't wave that gun around my children! For God's sake, I'm your cousin! You don't wave a gun at your own family."

"There's no family here that I'd claim," Roy said. "You're just a bunch of white trash. Now get up, Calvin!"

Uncle Calvin leaned back against the wall and stared at the policemen. "Come on, Roy, let the kids eat. They're hungry."

Roy waved his gun at the table. "Stop eating! Stop eating right now! That food is stolen! These two assholes walked right out of prison and stole food at the first grocery store in town! Now, they're going back to prison, and that food is evidence!"

I watched helplessly as Roy and his partner bagged all the uncooked food, then dumped the cooked food into paper bags, and with guns drawn, marched Uncle Calvin and Uncle Stanley out into the night. Once all of the excitement died down, I wasn't nearly as upset about what happened to my uncles, as I was that I didn't get any mashed potatoes.

Broken Heads and Hearts

The first day that it was warm and dry enough to play outside, Thurmond grabbed his ball and bat, and Jenny and I ran out after him. Thurmond wanted to bat first and since it was his ball and bat, we let him. I pitched and Jenny played catcher. His first two swings missed and the third one caught Jenny on the head and knocked her to the ground. She screamed and cried while we tried to shush her, afraid that Momma would stop the game. Putting Jenny in a cardboard box, we dragged her around to the rain barrel beside the house and splashed cool water on her sore head. We promised her that she could bat next, if she would stop crying.

Finally, she hushed, and keeping our end of the deal, Thurmond pitched, Jenny got up to bat, and I played catcher. Before Thurmond pitched the first ball, I saw that Jenny's eye was already swollen shut. Still, she waited for the pitch.

She shouldn't have. Thurmond let it rip, hit her in the head, and knocked her down again. Once more she cried, screamed, and kicked, and once more we put her in the cardboard box and dragged her around to the rain barrel. This time, however, Momma heard her crying and ran out to check.

"Oh, my Lord!" she said. "What have you done?"

"We was just playing and she got hit!" Thurmond tried to explain, suddenly so scared he could hardly talk.

"It's true!" I said. "He didn't mean to!"

"My Lord! You've half killed her!"

Momma turned and ran across the road, where she banged on the neighbor's door and came back with a handful of bacon fat. She laid two slabs on Jenny's face, covering both her eyes, then carried her into the house and laid her on the bed. Later that afternoon it began to snow so all prospects for finishing the game were doomed.

That night, after supper, Daddy came home. He stomped into the house yelling about some man at work, and when he saw Jenny's swollen lumpy, black-and-blue face, he stopped and said, "What the hell happened to her?"

Momma said, "Now, Russell, calm down. It was an accident."

But Daddy wouldn't calm down. Little by little Momma told him what happened, and when Daddy had heard enough, he grabbed Thurmond's bat, smacked it against the floor, and broke it. Then, he threw the pieces into the fire in the living room stove. Thurmond cried and begged, "No, Daddy, no! Don't burn it up!" But Daddy closed the door and let it burn. Then he took the ball, opened the living room door, and threw the ball as far as he could into the snowy night. All the while, Momma pleaded, "Russell, stop! It's their only real toy! Russell, stop!" Thurmond buried his face in his hands and sobbed, but Daddy still wasn't through. He took off his belt, grabbed Thurmond by one arm and beat him again and again. Momma tried to stop him but Daddy kept flinging his arm back, hitting her, too.

I watched the whole thing from behind the green chair in the living room, the place I usually went to suck my thumb when things started happening too fast. When the whipping ended, Thurmond ran to the back porch room, crying, and Mason went in after him. Jenny and Amy huddled on the living room bed, while I hid behind the chair, staring at Daddy and hating him. It had all been an accident. He didn't need to do that.

The next morning, after Daddy left, and Momma was in her bedroom with Gordon, Don and Mason talked in the kitchen. From my place on the living room bed, I could hear everything said. Mason told Don about the beating and Don said, "You know why he hates Thurmond, don't you?"

Mason shook his head.

"Well, I guess you were too little to remember," Don began, "but when you were about five and I was seven, we went to California and lived for awhile in an Okie camp." He then told Mason about an evening when Daddy was sitting around drinking with the other men in the camp, and Momma put on her good dress, fixed her hair, put on lipstick and rouge, and walked past Daddy and out to the road. When Daddy asked her where she was going, she said, "My babies are hungry. Someone has to feed them." Then she flagged down a shiny, new yellow convertible and a tall, good-looking blonde man followed her into the tent.

Mason listened intently and said, "She didn't!"

"Didn't you ever wonder why Thurmond is the only blue-eyed blonde in the bunch?" Don asked.

Mason stared for a minute then shrugged. "Guess I don't have to ask now."

Their discussion ended when Momma carried Gordon into the kitchen and joined them. I thought about what Don said and wondered why a tall blonde man that Momma met years ago had anything to do with why Daddy hated Thurmond. Thurmond wasn't even born yet.

Chapter 4

Dead Sweet Potato Dolls

I loved my sweet potato Christmas doll until it sprouted.

"Momma!" I screamed the morning I woke up and found awful wart-like growths covering its face and body. Horrified, I flung it off the bed. It skidded across the floor and bumped the leg of the stove. "It's ugly!" I whined. "Momma! My doll got ugly last night!"

Jenny sat up beside me and rubbed her eyes. "What?"

I pointed to my sprouting doll. "It's got things on it! Worms is coming out of its face or something."

Jenny crawled to the edge of the bed and squinted at the doll. "Not as ugly as mine was yesterday," she said matter-of-factly. "Mine had white things too but it also had a rotten spot. And it stunk, too."

Momma hurried into the room, buttoning her sweater. "Shhh! You'll wake up Gordon."

"Looky, Momma!" I pointed to the doll. "There's things on it."

Momma picked up the doll and chuckled. "It sprouted." She brushed her thumb over a sprout and flicked it to the floor.

Jenny and I recoiled. "It's ugly, ain't it?"

Momma laughed. "Well, I guess you might as well take it out and bury it today, beside Jenny's and Amy's." She moved into the kitchen and put it on the table. "They didn't last as long as I thought they would." She shivered. "Right now, I've got to get a fire started."

Momma warmed up leftover biscuits, pushed her finger in them to make a hole, then poured them full of syrup. Holding them so the syrup wouldn't drip, she handed us our breakfast.

"Don't step on my baby's grave," Jenny said later, as we approached the sweet potato doll burial site. "I put a cross on it yesterday."

"She did mine, too," Amy said, struggling to keep up with us.

The icy February air reddened our cheeks and fingers as we squatted on the ground and scraped at the earth with tin cans and a bent spoon, only a foot or so from other freshly dug graves. Two twig crosses, tied with dirty string and standing lopsided in the crumbled earth, marked the spots.

"There," I said, wiping my nose on my coat sleeve, "that's deep enough."

"No, it's not!" Jenny argued. "Its belly will stick up."

With numbed fingers, I placed my ugly child in the hole. "I don't care. I'm freezing and it's just a dumb ol' sweet tater, anyway." I quickly scooted loose dirt over and around it.

"See," Jenny said solemnly, "its belly's sticking out."

I pushed on its belly.

"You gonna sing or pray?" Amy asked.

"No. It's too cold."

"We did," Jenny said. "We had a real nice funeral for ours."

Only mildly shamed, I stood and brushed dirt off my clothes.

"You gonna make a cross?" Amy asked.

"No." I turned and ran for the house. "I'm going inside where it's warm!"

Amy and Jenny scrambled up and ran after me. "I'm gonna tell Momma," Jenny said. "I'm gonna tell her you didn't sing or pray or make a cross or anything."

Knowing how Momma liked singing, praying, and such, I stopped dead in my tracks, turned, and stared at her. She halted in front of me and raised her arms as if she thought I was going to hit her.

"If you do, you'll go to hell," I told her.

"I won't neither!"

"Yes, you will! The Bible says so."

"No, it don't!"

I glared at her and growled menacingly. "It says . . . little sisters cain't tell on big sisters cause it's a sin!"

"I don't believe you!" Jenny wiped her nose on the back of her hand and sniffed. "I never heard that."

"It's in Jerusalem," I said authoritatively. "The book of Jerusalem. That's in the Bible. So you better not tell anything bad on me! Hell is hot and lots of little sisters are in it right now!"

Amy wrinkled her nose, scrunched up her face, and started to cry.

"Did you tell something bad on one of us?" Jenny asked her sternly.

Amy shook her head no, her eyes wide, her mouth puckered in silence.

"Good! Now, let's go inside where it's warm," I ordered. Obediently, they followed. If my transgressions against my sweet potato baby's corpse were ever reported to Momma, I never heard about it.

Barefoot Birthday

As March approached and my seventh birthday neared, I began to pester Momma again for a rubber baby doll.

"Can I have one, Momma? Huh? Can I have a rubber doll?"

"If I had the money, you could have lots of rubber dolls."

"I just want one," I begged. "Can you get just one?"

"I'll do the best I can, Othello. That's all I can promise."

Every night I imagined holding a real doll, changing its pretty dresses, and feeding it with a tiny bottle like the one in the Sears & Roebuck catalog; and regardless of how many times Momma said, "I'll do my best. That's all I can promise," I never gave up hope. Maybe she would have the money by my birthday.

By March, I had outgrown my ugly brown winter shoes, but it didn't matter. Although the air was crisp and the earth was cold, the first week of March was filled with sunshine and warmth. I walked barefoot to and from school and took my time doing so.

Spring touched all the trees and shrubs, and fresh green life poked its brilliant self from every plant. Birds sang and flitted from branch to branch, and dogs barked and darted up to fences as I approached. People working in their yards smiled and waved at me as I passed. It was a glorious week, with everyone glad to be out in the sunshine again, so I took advantage of it and made friends with anyone who would stop and talk with me.

Mr. and Mrs. Granger, who seemed to love rocking in their porch swing, always came to the fence to talk to me. She kept a cookie in her pocket, which she gave me just before I headed on home.

"It's my birthday this week!" I announced. "I'm gonna be seven."

"Oh, how nice!" Mrs. Granger said. "Will you be having a party?"

I wasn't sure what a party was but I didn't want her to know. "Momma said she's gonna bake me a cake!" I said proudly.

"That's nice," Mrs. Granger said, and Mr. Granger nodded and smiled. "But are you going to have a party?"

"Is that when lots of people come over?" I asked hesitantly.

"Yes!" She nodded eagerly. "And play games and eat ice cream and cake."

I had never eaten any ice cream except what Momma made from snow, so I looked around, puzzled. There wasn't a snowflake in sight.

"Well, we're lots of people," I said, "so I guess we'll have a party." Embarrassed, sure I was missing some important information, I decided to leave.

"Don't forget this!" Mrs. Granger said, reaching for the cookie in her pocket.

"Thank you."

The next afternoon, as I passed their house on the way home from school, Mrs. Granger hurried off the porch to meet me. Mr. Granger followed.

"Othello," she said with a playful smile, "will you ask your mother if we can have a birthday party for you next Saturday?"

The question excited me so, I could hardly breathe. "A party?"

Her head bobbed rapidly, making her curls dance on her head. "Would you like that? I can invite a bunch of little girls I know. We'll play games. I'll get a special cake with your name on it!"

I stared, enthralled and speechless. "Y-yes, ma'am! I'd like that a lot!"

"Good." She handed me a piece of paper. "Give this to your mother It has the time and date and everything on it."

"I will." I took the note. "I'll give it to her."

Propelled by excitement, I ran almost all the way home, feeling as though I would never be sad again, no matter what happened. This was the most exciting thought I had ever had. A party!

Sadness crossed Momma's face when I repeated the Grangers' conversation. She sat on the edge of the bed beside me and looked at me a long time before speaking. "I wished you hadn't said yes without talking to me first."

Confused, I frowned. "Why?"

She patted my leg then brushed my hair back with her hand. "Because all of the other girls will have on pretty dresses," she explained. "They'll be wearing shoes and socks and have ribbons in their hair. And you don't have those things."

"I don't care!" I insisted. "I want to go, anyway. It's *my* party!"

Sighing, she rubbed my neck a moment, then said, "Well, let's wash and roll your hair tonight so it'll be shiny and pretty."

After supper, she heated water, filled the tub, and bathed Jenny, Amy, and me, then rolled our hair on rags. Between my excitement and the lumpy curls, it took forever to fall asleep.

The next morning, I awoke to find Momma in the kitchen ironing a dress. Jenny and I were almost the same size and had flour sack dresses exactly alike, except that one had a small black spot on the front, where a fly had landed just as Momma set the iron down. I climbed out of bed to see which one she was ironing.

"I wanna wear the one without the fly spot."

She laughed. "Okay."

As I left that afternoon, Momma stood on the porch and called to me across the yard. "I'll bake you a cake while you're gone." I could tell from the sadness in her eyes that she still didn't want me to go.

I was the first to arrive, and Mr. and Mrs. Granger greeted me at the door and walked me into the kitchen where a beautiful sheet cake waited on the kitchen table. It said, "Happy Birthday, Othello," and had roses on the corners and on either side of my name. I stared at it, too excited to notice anything else, except that Mr. and Mrs. Granger were standing on either side of me, smiling.

When the other girls arrived, we were all ushered into the backyard to play a game called croquet. I'd never seen or heard of it, but it was fun whacking the balls toward the wickets. Caught up in the game, I didn't notice when Mr. and Mrs. Granger left the yard. When it was my turn, I kept my eyes down and concentrated on my shot, completely unaware of myself or what others might be thinking or doing.

"Why don't you have on shoes?" one of the girls asked.

Startled, I glanced up. A pretty girl with long, shiny blonde curls, stood next to me. "Huh?" She repeated. "Why don't you have on shoes?"

Suddenly, I became aware of her yellow, ruffled dress, tied with a glossy ribbon at her waist. Yellow socks and shiny black shoes with straps and buckles covered her feet. Self-consciously, I glanced at the other girls who now stood in a circle around me, staring at my dirty, bare feet. "I don't like shoes," I lied.

"I'll bet she doesn't have any," someone else said.

"I do, too!" I lied again. "I have lots of shoes."

"Your feet are nasty!"

"If you have shoes, why don't you wear them?"

"Because they make your feet stink!" I worked hard not to cry.

Just then, the Grangers rushed into the back yard. "Come on, girls! You can't play and talk at the same time! The game will take forever!"

Most of the girls moved back and away from me, and as they did, I noticed that each wore a pretty, brightly colored dress. I glanced down at my own faded blue flour-sack print that hung belt-less and shapeless from my shoulders to my knees. And, of course, beneath the hem of my dress I saw my dirty bare feet. They had been washed just last night, but now dirt settled between my toes and dust covered my feet to my ankles.

The Grangers worked with other girls, showing them how to hold their mallets but I had suddenly lost all interest in the game and the party. Dropping my mallet and unable to contain my humiliation and tears, I ran inside.

The Grangers followed.

"I wanna go," I said. "I don't like it here."

Mr. and Mrs. Granger walked me over to my cake. "Well, certainly you can leave, but wouldn't you like to take some cake with you? You can have any piece you want."

I nodded. I wanted the piece that had my name on it. "I want the middle, with my name and two roses."

"Well, you can sure have it," Mrs. Granger said. "We'll cut it right out of there for you."

I watched as they cut the center out of the cake, then placed it in a pie tin for me to carry home. I was beyond the gate when I remembered I hadn't said thank you. Glancing back, I saw them in the doorway watching me.

"Thank you for the pretty cake."

They smiled and waved.

All the way home, I thought about Momma asking me not to go, and wondered how she knew what would happen.

Momma met me at the door. "You didn't stay very long."

I shook my head. "They was mean," I said, trying to hold back the tears. "What difference does it make if you wear shoes or not." I handed Momma the pie tin with the cake.

"Must have been a beautiful cake." She smiled and patted my arm.

I nodded. "They had on pretty dresses and shoes, and I didn't care. I didn't even notice till they started making fun of me. I was just having fun."

Momma nodded, blinked back wetness, and smiled. "Come on, you can have the cake with your name on it, and some of what I made, too!"

Jenny, Amy, and Momma sang "Happy Birthday" to me, and then we ate cake together. The greatest fun was feeding Gordon some of the icing. Momma scooped some of the red icing from a rose onto the end of her finger and tucked it into his mouth. At first, he seemed startled. Then he smacked a couple of times, grinned, and leaned forward for more. When he had eaten the whole rose and we had laughed at how much he liked it, the disappointment of the party began to drift away.

Jell-O and Rich People

Later in the spring, I became friends with a girl in my class named Kathryn Severe. Her long blonde hair fell over her shoulders in soft, shiny curls and her clothes were prettier than anything I saw in Sears & Roebuck. The ribbons tied on top of her head blew with her hair, and when she bent over, I could see that her panties also had ruffles on them. I felt honored that Kathryn wanted to play with me.

One day, she asked if I would come to her house the following day for lunch. She said she lived near the school and we wouldn't have to hurry. That evening, Momma rolled my hair on rags and washed my dress so it would be perfectly clean. Unfortunately, the next morning I woke up with a fever blister on my lip and, to make matters worse, I realized that Momma had washed the dress with the fly spot on it.

"I can't wear it!" I cried. "She'll know it's a fly! She has beautiful clothes!"

"You don't have to go home with her today," she said. "I'm sure she'll invite you again."

"But I want to! I just don't want to look ugly!"

When I arrived at school that morning, it seemed to me that even the boys looked better than I did. This, however, didn't change my mind about going.

I liked the long, skinny houses where Kathryn lived, and gaped at all the tiny front yards with little white fences around them. Colorful flowers bloomed in pots just outside everyone's door and the houses seemed very narrow and close together.

"Why are the houses so skinny?" I asked Kathryn.

"They're trailers," she said. "You can't see the wheels because they're hidden." She was right, I saw no trace of wheels. Then, as we entered her yard, I noticed the beautiful green yard and marveled at how clean and inviting it seemed.

"What's this?" I pointed at the lawn.

She frowned as if I were stupid. "It's grass."

"Grass? Grass grows tall, like this." I held my hand about a foot off the ground.

"Well, my daddy cuts it!"

I squatted to examine the evenly cut blades and imagined her father on his hands and knees with a pair of scissors. "How long does it take?"

"Just a few minutes." She opened the door and waited for me to follow.

"Boy, it would take me a week!"

"Not if you use a mower," she said. "Come on."

I supposed a mower was a giant pair of scissors, and was amazed that grass could be cut so short and evenly. I would tell Momma about it and maybe we could get some grass and cut it short and even, too.

When Kathryn opened the door, her mother stood just inside. "Mother, this is Othello."

Mrs. Severe had a pretty smile on her face when I entered but it faded quickly. Self-consciously, I covered the fly spot with my hand and touched the fever blister with my tongue.

"Where are your shoes, Child?" Mrs. Severe had a panicky look on her face.

"I don't wear 'em much," I answered.

"It doesn't matter," Kathryn said, scooting into a booth with a shiny white table. "She's not cold."

Mrs. Severe recovered her manners and smiled at me again. "Of course not. Scoot right in beside Kathryn. I have your sandwiches ready."

Accustomed to eating from pie pans and drinking from tin cans, the beautiful dishes took my breath away. I stared, feasting my eyes on the whole room. White lace curtains covered the windows and white paper with little flowers covered the walls. A lamp with a ruffled shade lit the table at the end of the room.

Kathryn picked up her sandwich and began to eat while I stared at mine. The sandwich had been cut diagonally, and I could see meat, lettuce and tomatoes between the bread. Until this moment, a "sandwich" was a piece of baloney with a single slice of bread folded around it, and now my hands trembled as I carefully lifted it off the plate, afraid I would spill or break something.

The first bite, however, convinced me that *this* was a sandwich. I decided to remember everything about it so I could tell Momma how to make it. Then Mrs. Severe poured us a cup of hot chocolate and served it in cups that matched our plates. "I also made some Jell-O. Would you like some?"

I didn't know, so I looked at Kathryn.

"It's cherry," she said. "I love it."

"Yes, thank you."

Mrs. Severe smiled at me, sat down with us, and folded her hands on the table.

"You're rich, aren't you?" I looked at Mrs. Severe.

Her eyes widened and she laughed. "No, no. We're not rich. Why would you think that?"

"I'd say you're pretty rich because—look at your pretty things. Flowers on the walls and curtains and—look!" I pointed to the plates and cups. "Even your dishes match."

Mrs. Severe stopped smiling, cleared her throat, and stood quickly. "Well, maybe . . . maybe I just, ah . . . just didn't know. But . . . " She opened a white box and reached for something. "Maybe you're right, Othello. I guess maybe we're rich." She turned and set two little pedestal dishes on the table. They were filled with something red and shiny.

"What's that?" I wondered if I was supposed to eat it or drink it.

"Jell-O," Kathryn said. "Haven't you ever had Jell-O?" She poked hers with her finger and it jiggled. I laughed and looked at her finger, amazed that it wasn't wet. She poked it again and it tickled me so that I couldn't stop laughing.

Mrs. Severe laughed with me and handed me a spoon. I ate the first bite, delighted with the coldness and texture. I poked it with my finger, shook the dish to watch it wiggle, and the three of us laughed and played with the Jell-O until every last bite was scraped out of the pretty crystal dish.

Enthralled by the whole experience, I thanked Mrs. Severe and asked if Kathryn could come to my house tomorrow for lunch. Her smile faded a little but she finally nodded and said, "Yes, I suppose."

There was so much Momma didn't know! She didn't know about lettuce on sandwiches or Jell-O, and she didn't know about pretty paper for the walls and dishes that matched, or that grass could be cut no more than two inches high and be as even as a rug.

Momma, Jenny, and Thurmond sat on the front porch listening to all the marvelous things I had to tell. I talked for almost an hour and when I finished, I was startled to learn that Momma knew about these things.

"But you have to have a refrigerator to make Jell-O and keep lettuce crisp," she explained. "And when I get one, I'll make some Jell-O."

"What about the pretty flowers for the walls? They're better than newspapers."

She patted me again. "Come on. I need to start supper."

In the excitement of relating my experiences, I forgot to tell Momma that I had invited Kathryn home for lunch tomorrow. And when that hour arrived, I bounded up the box that served as a step to the porch and yelled at Kathryn to follow as I ran into the house. Hopping over the piles of laundry sorted on the living room floor, I ran into the kitchen where Momma stood holding Gordon and stirring something on the stove.

"Kathryn's eating with us today!" I announced. Momma's eyes widened, and her mouth moved but no words came out.

Kathryn carefully stepped around the clothes and moved toward the kitchen.

Mamma's breath caught before she said, "I—I wish you had told me, Othello. There's only some greens—" Her eyes frantically scanned the kitchen. "—and a couple of cold biscuits. Hello, Kathryn. Please come in."

Momma knew I hated wild greens and I knew that she wouldn't have cooked them if she'd had potatoes, so I didn't complain. "Come on, Kathryn." I sat down on the bench.

Momma smiled and talked with Kathryn, telling her how beautiful her hair was, and talking about school, as she placed a pie pan and forks in front of us and served the greens.

"We have some vinegar," I told Kathryn. "That makes 'em better."

Kathryn, who hadn't said a word since she entered the house, slowly looked around the kitchen and down at her greens, then jumped up and ran out of the house.

"Wait!" I yelled. "Come back!" I ran out after her, following her down the road we'd just walked together. She had a good head start and as I chased her, I watched her pretty pink dress bounce with every step, her hair flying back with a trail of ribbons. I begged her to stop but she wouldn't slow down, and when I realized I would never catch her, I stopped and stared after her as she disappeared down the road.

Confused and crying, I walked back home. Momma waited on the box step, holding Gordon, while Jenny and Amy ran out to meet me.

"Why'd she do that?" I asked Momma. "I was nice to her."

She pulled me close and let me cry against her for a moment. Jenny and Amy watched, as confused as I. When I stopped crying, Momma kept her arm around me, and said, "Poor folks sometimes scare people. It scares them and they don't know what to do but run."

"You think she'll ever come back?"

"I don't know."

"I liked her dress," Jenny said. "I would look pretty in it."

Amy nodded in agreement. "Me, too."

I didn't return to school that afternoon, and the next day I was too embarrassed to look at Kathryn. I longed to recapture our friendship but she never spoke to me again, and I never really understood how being poor could be so scary.

Chapter 5

Daddy and Mason; Othello holding Gordan.

Unhappy Truths

When Mason came home with thirty baby chickens squeaking and peeping from inside a big flat box, he couldn't stop smiling. We pushed and shoved each other out of the way, trying to peek through the holes as the little fuzzy yellow heads moved and bobbed inside the box. Mason set the box on the ground and pointed out that it was taped shut and had better remain shut until he could build a little fence around the chicken coop.

More or less content to squat on the ground and peek at them, the rest of us watched him work. When, at last, he had a small area secured to suit him, he opened the box and we squealed and laughed as the baby chicks climbed over each other to get out.

"How's he plan to feed 'em?" Daddy asked when he saw them.

"Well," Momma explained, "he got a job at Langer's Feed Store, and Mr. Langer said he could pay for them and buy their feed if he worked two hours a day after school, and half a day on Saturday."

Daddy nodded, lit a cigarette, and laughed as he watched them.

The chicks pleased Mason more than anything else ever had. He smiled as he tossed them feed and laughed as they tumbled over his feet and each other trying to get to it.

When Daddy said, "They won't be big enough to eat for a long time," Mason looked like he might faint. The color left his face and his mouth hung open.

"I'm not raisin' 'em to eat!" he said, "I just want to have 'em!"

Daddy laughed and went inside.

A few days later, Grandpa Birdwell brought us a wooden wagon with sideboards like the truck's, and he let us play with it while he went inside to talk to Momma. Thurmond, Jenny, Amy, and I almost wore out the wagon while Grandpa and Momma talked the afternoon away.

Our only toys were old truck tires. Two hung from trees in the backyard, and one was used for rolling each other down the hill at the end of the road. We took turns curling up inside and being pushed.

When Grandpa left, he left the wagon with us and gave Momma a stack of papers, which she put on her dresser and told us not to touch. The next Saturday, while Don and Mason were working, and Daddy was gone, Momma took us with her to hand out papers for Grandpa. Thurmond didn't want to go so she said he could stay home alone if he wanted. Then she loaded Jenny and Amy in the wagon, put Gordon in Jenny's lap, and told Amy to hold the stack of papers. Momma pulled the wagon and I walked beside her into town. Then we began a slow trek up and down every street, handing a sheet of paper to someone at every house.

"A tent revival meeting, all next week," Momma told them. "Be sure and come!" Most of the people smiled and nodded and read the paper as we walked away. Around noon, we began to complain about being hungry and she said, "We'll eat something at home, later. Don't ask anyone for food. Do you understand?"

We nodded, but not without grumbling.

"If someone should offer, that's different. But never, never ask. We're not beggars."

"Why can't we go home now?" Jenny whined. "I'm hungry."

"Because I promised your Grandpa I'd help him." She strode ahead, knocking on doors and handing sheets to everyone she met.

At one house, it surprised her to find someone she knew. The lady invited us inside, and while she and Momma talked in the living room, and Momma nursed Gordon, Jenny, Amy, and I were given a game of tidily-winks and told to play on the kitchen floor. At one point, a tidily-wink flipped under the drape that hung around the lady's sink, and without hesitating, we lifted it. To our surprise and delight, we discovered a bowl of hard Christmas candy on a shelf with some fancy dishes.

I glanced toward the living room, then at my sisters. "Just one piece?" They nodded. By the time we left, the bowl was empty and we scooted out the door without mentioning our crime.

"Thank you, Bernice," the woman said as we left. "Your father's a wonderful preacher. I'll be there."

On Saturday night, all of us except Daddy walked into town to the revival meeting and sat right on the front row, while Momma sat at the piano and played for the singing. Although I didn't know many of the songs, I sang them all, and as loud as I could so the Lord would hear me, too. After the singing ended, a man prayed, then Grandpa stood up in front of all those people and yelled and screamed just like the radio preachers, and by the time he finished, his yelling and screaming had made me feel just as angry as the radio preachers did.

During the last song, five or six people walked to the front, crying, and Grandpa shouted, "Hallelujah! Hallelujah!" Then he announced that tomorrow night, after the meeting, we would all go to the Baptist church for baptisms.

When most of the crowd had left the tent, Momma remained, still talking with Grandma and some friends. She motioned for Don to come to her. "Find your Grandpa," she said, "and invite him to supper before the meeting tomorrow."

I heard the instruction and went with him. We looked everywhere and were about to give up when Don walked around to the back of the tent. It was dark and I didn't see anything, but we both heard grunting sounds coming from the tall grass a few yards away. I stayed by the tent while Don walked out, listened, then turned and hurried back. Mason rounded the corner just then. "Did you find him?"

Don jerked his head, as if to say, "come on," and when we were back inside the tent, Don said, "He's out there rolling in the grass with Miss Templeton!"

Mason drew back and frowned. "That's a sin!"

"So he says." Don laughed. "Maybe once they're saved, there's nothing to worry about." They both burst out laughing.

A few minutes later, Don told me to stay put and he went outside again. When he came back a few minutes later, he told Momma that he'd delivered her message.

The saddest thing about Grandpa coming to that Sunday dinner was what happened to Mason's chickens. They weren't little yellow peepers anymore but they weren't much bigger than quail, either.

"No!" Mason screamed, trying to guard his flapping, squawking brood. "Don't kill 'em! I didn't raise 'em to eat!"

"Mason, be reasonable! We need some meat! You need some meat, and so do the others! And besides, Grandpa's coming. He wants meat, too!"

When it was clear he couldn't win, Mason ran off crying, swearing that he would starve to death before he ever ate another piece of chicken.

Once he was out of sight, Momma wrung a few necks then took an ax and loped off the heads of the others. We let them flop around the yard awhile, then dropped them into scalding water. Thurmond and I helped pull out the feathers. Other than it being such a stinky mess, I didn't hate it too much, except for the pain it caused Mason. He didn't talk to anyone for three days.

Several times during the summer, heavy rain turned the bar ditch in front of the house into a rushing river and the temptation to "ride the rapids" was more than Thurmond, Jenny, and I could resist. The minute Momma turned her back, the three of us stripped to our underwear, ran outside, and jumped in. It was no more than a foot and a half deep in front of the house, and a little deeper beside the pasture, but deep enough for us to be pushed along on a thrilling ride.

Momma called us from the porch, trying to get us home, but we would yell and splash, letting the current carry us farther away. Only when our energy was spent were we willing to take the punishment waiting for us at home.

"Polio! Polio! Polio!" was every other word out of her mouth. "Don't you understand it can cripple you and kill you?" First, she would spank us and then scrub us down with water so hot we could hardly stand it. Using a washcloth made from a burlap bag and a bar of homemade lye soap, she rubbed our skin raw, working her fingers into our ears, scrubbing our scrapes, and washing our hair. Then she'd say, "Bend over," and wash our private parts until we hardly had any skin left. Once we were out of the tub, she poured salt into every cut and scrape, trying to kill the polio germs.

The Dead Baby

A few days after such a rain, Jenny and I were digging in the mud for treasures, when something fluttered from the window of a passing car. A sheet of stamps floated down between us. We grabbed it and ran inside to see if it was valuable.

"Sugar stamps!" Momma picked us up and kissed us a dozen times. "Oh, yes! They're sugar ration stamps. You found something valuable!"

"Can you buy shoes or rubber dolls with them?" I asked hopefully.

"No, but I can buy sugar!"

"Shoes and a rubber doll!" Thurmond mocked. "That's all you think about!"

Then, one afternoon, not long after finding the stamps, as Jenny, Amy, and I played beside the house, a car pulled up near the porch and a doctor and nurse rushed to the door. Someone inside let them in. I left Jenny and Amy playing alone and slipped inside. Momma's bedroom door was closed, so I hid behind the green chair in the living room, sucking my thumb and waiting for the door to open.

When it did, I almost stopped breathing. Momma lay on her bed, her knees bent, her legs spread wide, and the doctor was scooping large clots of blood out of her. The nurse hurried out of the room carrying a bundle of newspapers. Over her shoulder, she said, "I'll get one of your sons to bury it."

Momma said to the doctor, "Just get it all. I can't afford to get sick. I have too many kids to take care of." The door closed again.

Momma's tone told me that she probably wasn't dying, so my heart slowed a little, and I hurried outside to see what the nurse was doing. She had walked to the far side of the backyard, beyond the outhouse, and Mason walked beside her, a shovel in his hand. When the nurse stopped and put down the bundle, Mason started to dig. The nurse turned and headed back toward the house, and I ran past her to Mason.

"What is it?" I asked.

"Nothing. Get out of here."

"It's something," I said. "I saw the doctor pulling guts and clots out of Momma."

He kept digging. "He wasn't pulling guts out of Momma. She had a dead baby inside her. The doctor got it out."

I stared at the bundle of paper now seeping blood. "There's a baby in there?"

"It's dead. Now, go away so the others won't come out here."

Later, Mason walked me back to the grave and showed me a special, large, smooth rock he had placed on it. "Don't ever step here," he said solemnly. "That's your dead brother or sister."

I never stepped there.

Thurmond's favorite place in the summertime was the tree house in the backyard, set far away from the house in the middle of a small forest. One afternoon he said, "If you still want a rubber doll, I can get you one."

"How can you get one if Momma can't?" I asked.

"I just can. But you have to come up to the tree house."

Usually, he wouldn't let me near the tree house, so that, in itself, was enough to make me listen. We climbed the rickety ladder and once on the solid floor of the tree house, I said, "Where's the rubber doll."

"It's not here," he said, "but I will bring it here if you'll let me do it."

"Do what?"

"It."

"What's it?"

"Take your pants off."

"Why?"

"I'll show you."

"No."

"Do you want the rubber doll?"

"Yes." I took my panties off.

"Now let me touch you there, with mine."

"With your pants off?"

"Yes."

"You swear you've got a rubber doll?"

"Yes, and I'll get it as soon as you let me do it."

I squinted at him, trying to see if he was lying. I couldn't tell. Finally, I nodded.

He quickly unzipped his pants and laid on top of me. He pushed and bumped and wiggled against me until the boards hurt my back and I told him to stop. Then he jumped up, zipped his pants, and climbed down the ladder.

"You going to get the rubber doll?"

"Yeah."

"You better or I'll tell!"

"You tell and you'll get in trouble, too!"

An awful sinking feeling passed through me. I had let him do a terrible thing and he probably didn't have a rubber doll, and would never come back! Furious, I sat in the tree house and waited. The sun made a slow pass over the trees and I knew I had been a sucker.

"Thurmond!" I yelled over and over. "Thurmond! You'd better come back!"

Too ashamed to come down, I waited until I heard Momma calling us for supper before I moved to leave. Just then, Thurmond's head appeared at the tree house door. "Here's your rubber doll!" He flung something over my head and quickly descended the ladder. I turned and picked up what he had thrown, and stared in disbelief. He had cut a rubber doll out of a pink inner tube. It looked like my paper dolls, except it was made of rubber. Initially, I felt cheated and angry. But the more I stared at it, the more impressed I was that he had kept his promise. Pure and simple, I had been outsmarted. It was the best trick I had ever heard of, and I had to admire him for that.

Cut Foot, Drunk Doctor

While Momma hung the laundry on the line, we played in the backyard. Gordon, who was just beginning to toddle around after us, laughed and squealed with his new freedom until his tender feet crossed a sticker patch. Then he would drop to the ground and cry until one of us rushed to remove the stickers and head him in another direction. On this particular day, however, as we marched around playing soldiers and swinging swords made from cardboard boxes, Gordon suddenly plopped down and screamed with a terrible urgency.

Momma dropped a piece of laundry and we all ran to him. The bloodied bottom of a broken jar lay inches away, and the back of his foot gaped from ankle to ankle.

Momma yanked him up and carried him inside. She tied a cord around his leg, just under the knee, and used a wooden spoon to make a tourniquet. "Don't leave the house!" she yelled back at us as she ran down the road to the nearest neighbors with a car.

I picked up the broken jar, carried it to the outhouse, and dropped it down the hole.

"Could he die?" Jenny asked.

No one knew, so we didn't answer.

With Momma and Daddy gone, and Don and Mason working, we stayed close to the house. When Don and Mason finally arrived, we ate cold biscuits and syrup, all of us too worried about Gordon to be very hungry.

Daddy brought Momma home after dark, and Momma looked tired and worried. Her hair frizzed about her frowning, pinched expression. "I know the doctor was drunk!" She cried. "He didn't sew that foot up right! Look how it turns!"

Momma held Gordon, now asleep, and let his legs dangle for all of us to see. The bandaged foot hung sideways, turning inward.

The next week Momma insisted that Daddy take her to another doctor, one she trusted in Altus, Oklahoma. Grouchy Grandma Birdwell stayed with us for the several days that Momma was gone, and when she returned, Gordon's foot was in a cast, hanging straight from his leg. She said the doctor in Altus had to undo what the drunk doctor did, and sew it on right.

The next morning, when Gordon smiled at us, our hearts all melted. He seemed oblivious to the cast, but what he lacked in awareness, we made up for in sympathy and kisses. We dragged him around like a rag doll, assuming that he couldn't walk with the cast.

"Put him down!" Momma shouted. "If you stop carrying him, he'll learn to walk on it just like he learned to walk in the first place!"

Doubtful that she was right, but knowing she meant it, we sat him on the floor then stood around him, waiting and watching. Confused at being suddenly abandoned, he looked at each of us and held up his arms. In turn, we looked at Momma.

"Leave him alone," she said. "Go play! He'll be all right. I'm right here, watching."

Reluctantly, we scattered. Gordon cried. We turned back.

"Go!" she yelled. "He's okay."

He didn't sound okay, but his howls only lasted a few minutes. Then he pulled himself up on Momma's chair and stood there patting her leg. She smiled at him and wiped his face with her apron. "You can go play, too," she told him.

We pretended not to watch as he turned himself, keeping his balance with one hand on the chair.

"Gordon!" Jenny called, slapping her thighs to get his attention. "Come to me!"

He grinned and just stood there.

"Come on! Come over here!" She inched forward.

He laughed and turned loose of Momma's chair, clapping as if to applaud his own efforts. Then, with the gleeful bright-eyed look of a jack-o-lantern, he took three steps before toppling over. The cast banged against the floor and Gordon sat up, startled, but not crying. We all rushed forward to help, but Momma held up her hand and we stopped.

Gordon patted the cast and looked up at Momma.

"Go play," she said to him. "I've got work to do."

He grinned and, again, crawled back to her chair and pulled himself up. This time, he turned loose and went clunking across the floor with uncertain, uneven steps. When he made it to Jenny, we all laughed and clapped. By the next morning, the sound of his cast clunking around the room became just another accepted noise that said everything was okay.

Thurmond's Skeleton

A week or so before Halloween, Thurmond came home with a paper skeleton. His blue eyes danced with excitement and his cheeks flushed pink from the chilly autumn air, as he held the skeleton by a string attached to its head.

The minute Momma saw it her hands went to her hips and her dark eyes narrowed suspiciously. "Where'd you get that?"

Thurmond didn't answer, but kept jerking the skeleton around to make its joints jump and swing in every direction.

"Thurmond!" Momma snapped. "Where did you get that?"

Without looking at her, he said, "From school."

She looked it over carefully, then with a deep frown pinching the skin between her eyes, she said, "Empty you pockets."

Thurmond paled, leaving his cheeks looking chapped from the wind. His wide blue eyes blinked nervously. "W-why?"

"Just do it." She stood over him, her hands still on her hips.

Slowly, Thurmond reached into his pocket and after fumbling around for a minute, he took out his pocketknife and laid it on the table.

"Everything."

Tears built on his lower lids as he reached back into his pocket. Slowly, he extracted two candy bars and six pieces of bubble gum.

"Aaah!" Sounds of happy expectations escaped our mouths.

Momma picked up the candy and gum. "Where did you get that?"

Thurmond's face now reddened and wrinkled as he began to cry.

"I know you stole it!" Momma said, "Now, where did you get it?"

Through agonizing sobs, he finally managed to say, "The drugstore."

"I thought so!" Momma turned to me. "Watch the little ones. We're going to return this." She grabbed Thurmond by the arm and half dragging him, marched him out the front door. "You're going to return it and apologize for taking it!" She swatted him hard on the butt, making him yelp and cry louder. "My kids are *not* growing up to be thieves!" She stuffed the candy back into his pockets.

We watched them disappear down the road, hearing her scold him every step of the way, and swat his bottom every few steps.

"I'm glad," Jenny said. "The skeleton was ugly."

"Was scary," said Amy. "It made me wanna cry."

The Piano

I stood at the far end of the pasture, sucking on a chunk of salt I'd just knocked off a cow's salt lick, when I heard piano music in the wind. Squinting toward the house, I listened carefully. It danced through the air, sounding a lot like the fast, happy music Momma played at church when Grandpa preached.

I knew it wasn't radio music, and I knew real piano music couldn't be coming from our house; but just the same, I ran across the pasture, dodging the cow plops, wanting to find out where the music was coming from. The closer I got to the house, the louder the music floated past my ears. Bursting through the door, I ran into Daddy and knocked myself down. The whole family crowded around Momma who sat at a big upright piano placed against the wall, just inside the front door.

Daddy had a big grin on his face.

"Is it ours?" I asked. "Can we keep it?"

"It's ours." He looked pleased with himself.

I had never seen a piano this close and as Momma ran her fingers up and down the keys, and I heard the high and low notes, I could see how it worked and knew I could play it. For over an hour, I stood at her elbow, listening and watching. When she stopped playing and went to make supper, everyone took their turn banging on the keys, except me. I waited. I wanted to sit down with her later, alone, and have her teach me a song.

My opportunity came the next day. "I can do that, Momma. I know I can."

"That wouldn't surprise me," she laughed. "Here, sit down."

"Show me a song. I can play it."

"Okay." She played only the low notes, a rhythm that I liked at once. "It's called *Heart and Soul.*"

I asked her to play it twice more, and then I tried. Nothing had ever felt more natural in my life. My hands seemed to know what to do, even when I didn't. Then she began to play the melody that went with the low notes, and my mind slipped into another zone, a place more comfortable than drawing and coloring, a place where nothing existed except what my ears wanted to hear and my fingers wanted to do.

Momma taught me the "top and bottom" parts of three duets that day and I went to bed with music dancing in my ears and the image of my hands moving over the piano keys.

Bad News About Shoes

For the next several days, I screamed and yelled at my sisters every time they banged on the piano while I was practicing. When Momma closed the lid and forced me outside, I resented it. Maybe some day I could be good enough to play at church, too, and maybe I could even do it by Sunday if everyone would leave me alone and let me practice.

I sullenly settled myself beside the house, on the ground beneath the kitchen window, refusing to play with the others. I smoothed a patch of ground and wrote my name with my finger. To play the piano at church, I would need shiny shoes and ribbons. The thought prompted me to go inside and get the Sears & Roebuck catalog.

Momma stood at the kitchen stove with Gordon riding her hip, using a stick to punch at laundry boiling in a tub of sudsy water. I hoisted the catalog onto the table and opened to the page with shiny patent leather shoes. "See them shoes?" I pointed to the pair I wanted.

Momma glanced back but kept pushing the clothes around. "I see them."

"I want them shoes, Momma."

"I know." The steaming tub moistened her face. "If you want them bad enough, Othello, you can have them."

My heart lightened, as it always did when she said that. "I want them really, really bad."

"Good. Then you can have them."

I moved around to look directly into her eyes. "I want them really, really bad," I repeated in my most serious, adult-like voice.

She turned away from the wash and fixed her eyes intently on mine. Then with a steady, no-nonsense tone, she said, "And I said . . . if you want them bad enough, you can have them."

I smiled and took a deep breath. Then it was done. She would get me the shoes. Filled with deep contentment, I closed the catalog, put it back on the cupboard, and went back outside. Settling myself beneath the window again, I erased my name with the palm of my hand, created a new fresh surface to write it again, and labored for several minutes to make every letter perfect.

Then, it hit me. She hadn't said she would buy me the shoes. Like Thurmond's rubber doll, which *was* a rubber doll but not the one I wanted, Momma had said, if I wanted them bad enough I could have them. What did that mean? That I would have to get them for myself?

Furious, realizing I had been tricked again I jumped up, ran inside, and threw the catalog on the table. "Momma!" I tried not to cry. "I said I want them shoes!"

She turned slowly from the stove and put a hand on my shoulder. "I heard you," she replied calmly, "and I said—"

"I know what you said! If I want 'em bad enough—!"

Her hand still on my shoulder, she looked directly into my eyes and nodded. "That's right."

A sickening feeling weakened my stomach. Feeling betrayed, I stormed out of the kitchen and ran back to the side of the house. I would have to get the shoes myself. That's what she meant. But how was I supposed to do that? If parents couldn't get shoes, how could kids?

Arms wrapped around my shins, I pulled myself into a ball and leaned against the house. Did Don, Mason, and Thurmond already know this? Did they know they weren't going to get help . . . that they had to do it themselves? They probably did, but wouldn't tell me. They had heard me begging for shoes and dolls, and still they wouldn't tell me. I felt cheated that they had let me build up my hopes for nothing.

What could *I* do to make money? What did I have that someone would buy? All I knew was how to cut out paper dolls.

Paper dolls . . .

Maybe I could cut paper dolls and sell them to people driving down the road. The thought appealed to me and I considered it further. If I cut out a string of girl dolls and a string of boy dolls, maybe I could sell two strings to each car. The money I made wouldn't be like money found in the ditch that I had to share, so I could save it all for shoes.

For the next several minutes, a strong sense of independence and excitement replaced my anger and allowed me to glimpse a freedom I hadn't seen or felt before. I smoothed the dirt once more and wrote my name. No sooner had I finished than a sow bug crawled across my careful lettering. Jenny and Amy came and squatted beside me.

"Whatcha doin'?" Jenny asked.

Feeling smug over my new revelation, I decided to be like my older brothers and keep it to myself. "Watching the bug," I said.

Jenny picked up a rock and whacked the bug.

"Why'd you do that?" I scolded her. "He wasn't hurtin' nothing!"

"He wasn't helping neither." She tossed the rock aside and ran off to play. Amy followed, her underpants coated with dirt and drooping beneath the hem of her dress.

Maybe it was a stupid idea, selling paper dolls. Everybody could cut paper dolls. But I would think of some way to get those shoes.

At supper, as we heaped gravy over biscuits, Thurmond talked endlessly about Halloween. I had learned about Halloween in school, but I didn't really understand what he meant by "tricker-treating." I knew he was good at tricks and thought maybe he had a pocket full of rubber doll tricks for other girls, but Momma said he couldn't go to town in the dark, so it didn't matter. He left the table crying.

Momma sat next to Don and discussed how the nights were getting colder, and how he was trying to get her a new stove. Both Don and Mason were bigger than Daddy now, so when they talked, I eavesdropped, knowing their words were important.

Mason scowled at Don. "Why buy another stove? There's no wood or coal for the stoves we've got!"

"I mean a gas stove," Don said. "They're gonna lay gas lines out here in a few weeks."

Mason glanced up skeptically and Momma ran her hand over Don's head. "I don't know what I'd do without you, Don. You're gonna have a lot of stars in your crown when you get to heaven." Then she glanced around the table and added, "I don't know what I'd do without every one of you."

Mason shrugged. "You'd probably get some rest once in awhile. And a little quiet now and then."

We laughed, extra loud, because Momma laughed, too.

Chapter 6

The Fire

Later that Halloween night, bitter cold fingers of frigid air sneaked through the cracks of the shack's flimsy walls, stealing the last of its warmth. Daddy had come home earlier and had enough of his paycheck left to go to the grocery store. Now, he, Momma, and Gordon were gone.

As night closed in around us, we waited, and our empty stomachs growled, making us more impatient and quarrelsome by the minute. The six of us listened for the familiar rumbling of Daddy's old truck, signaling that he and Momma were home.

Although I was seven, and considered myself almost grown, I still took all of my cues from Don and Mason. At the moment, they seemed to be working as hard as the rest of us to keep from fighting and squabbling.

Wind howled as it tore around the corners of the shack and pushed through the cracks, puffing out the newspaper covering the walls. Momma had laboriously pasted it from corner to corner, not only to hide the ugliness of unpainted boards but to try to keep the wind's icy breath away from us. Now, as Don and Mason huddled close to the stove, trying to start a fire, I thought I might starve to death before Momma and Daddy returned.

Daddy had arrived home late in the afternoon. We'd been expecting him "any minute" for a week. While my urge was always the same, to run up and hug him the minute I saw him, lately, I tended to hold back. Sometimes his mood was no better than a pestered snake's.

But today, he came in smiling and seemed happy to see us. Don, who had gotten off work early, was washing up in the tub outside the back door. Momma lifted the speckled granite coffeepot from the wood burning stove and poured Daddy a cup of coffee, while Jenny, Amy, and Gordon crawled all over him, vying for long-overdue attention.

The screen door banged shut behind Don as he entered the kitchen, drying his face and arms on a thin, tattered dish towel. "Got another cup of that?" He nodded toward the coffeepot.

"Sure." Momma lifted the pot again. "You kids go play in the living room." With her free arm, she shooed us out of the room. Reluctantly, we went.

The best part of living in that little three-room shack was that no matter where you were, you could hear everything said. The living room, like the other rooms, had a bed pushed against one wall. Other than that, it had the green chair with scratchy fabric, a pot-bellied stove, two straight-backed, cane-bottom chairs, and an unfinished cabinet that stood just outside the kitchen door.

The cabinet held our most precious possessions—canned food, when we sometimes had it, a little white vase, the Bible, and a varnished wooden box about ten inches wide, twelve inches long, and a foot tall. Other than the Bible, the box was the most precious thing in the cabinet. It protected the stories and articles that Momma wrote on the backs of envelopes, brown paper bags, and sometimes real tablet paper. It sat on the top shelf, well out of the reach of small hands and inquisitive fingers.

Our newly acquired piano stood against the wall, just to the right of the front door. Now, as Jenny, Amy, and I rolled half a yo-yo back and forth across the cold, wood floor, only a few feet from the kitchen, I watched and listened to the grown-ups.

Momma smiled at Daddy. "Don has some good news." Her eyes danced as she spoke and glanced at Don. "He bought a new gas stove today."

Daddy threw a suspicious scowl in Don's direction. "Why in the hell did you do that? We ain't got no gas lines to hook it up to."

Don nodded, cupping both his hands around his coffee. "It's butane. But it can be converted to gas, as soon as the lines get out here."

Daddy listened but the skepticism didn't leave his face.

"He went by the gas company," Momma said. "They told him that the lines would be out this far in a few weeks."

Don's head bobbed in agreement as she talked. "It's already paid for," he said. "I paid for it. But they can't deliver it till tomorrow."

Daddy grunted and took a noisy sip of coffee. When he set the cup back on the raw plank surface of the table, he smiled. "All right."

After taking a long breath, Don exhaled slowly, as if trying to steady himself, and said, "That goddamn wood burner is dangerous. One of these kids is gonna fall against it and get seriously burned or . . . or they're gonna freeze to death 'cause there's no wood or coal to burn."

"Now, Donald Earl," Momma reached over and patted his arm, "you worry too much." Then, smiling, her eyes sparkling again, she added, "It's sure gonna be easier cooking with a new stove."

Don's expression didn't change. He threw a sour look at Daddy. "You going to get some groceries today?"

Daddy nodded and slurped his coffee again. For the first time, I noticed how small he was compared to Don and Momma. With his black hair combed straight back, and his shoulders hunched, elbows on the table, he looked like a little boy. "Yeah," he answered Don. "We'll go soon as your Momma's ready."

"Supper!" Momma turned to us, laughing. "I'll make us a big supper tonight!" She stood, scooted the bench back under her side of the table, and turned to leave. Don pulled a kerosene lantern to the center of the table, lit it, and replaced the globe. Momma left the kitchen and headed toward the bedroom.

Just then, Mason opened the front door and stepped inside. He carried his .22 rifle to the cabinet in the living room and carefully laid it on top. "Didn't get one lousy rabbit," he groused before he realized that Daddy was sitting in the kitchen. "Oh, hi. When did you get here?"

Daddy lit a cigarette. "Few minutes ago."

Mason lifted the coffeepot, looked around for a cup, and seeing that both cups were being used, poured coffee into one of the tin cans that substituted for glasses. After filling the can, he wrapped a pot holder around it and sat down with Daddy and Don.

"Nary a rabbit, huh?" Don cast a sympathetic glance toward Mason.

Mason frowned, disgusted. "I seen a couple. Thought I hit one of 'em but couldn't find it." He looked at Daddy expectantly. "Getting some groceries tonight?"

Daddy nodded.

More interested in watching Momma get dressed than listening to Mason complain, Jenny, Amy, and I wandered into the bedroom. Momma had already slipped on her good dress and stood in front of the dresser, leaning close to the mirror. We watched in amazement as she carefully ran the lipstick tube over her lips and transformed herself into the most beautiful woman in the world.

"You's pretty." Amy, just tall enough to place her fingers along the edge of the dresser, looked up in glowing admiration.

"Not as pretty as you . . . or you . . . or you!" Momma touched each of our noses in turn. Then, with quick strokes, she ran the black-bristled brush down the length of her hair. Millions of tiny curls burst from the brush and fanned out around her face.

"Ooooo!" Jenny gasped. "Your hair goes out so pretty! I wish mine would."

Momma smiled, dabbed the lipstick on her cheeks, and rubbed vigorously to smear the color around. When her cheeks looked as though she had just come in from a cold, breezy day, she removed her hand and stepped back to appraise her reflection.

"Jenny," she said, "I'll never be as pretty as you!"

Jenny screwed her face into a mask of doubt and Momma laughed. Then turning to the baby bed in the corner where Gordon slept, she said, "You girls, go on, now. I've got to bundle up Gordon."

"Don't take him!" Jenny whined. "Leave him here, so you can hurry faster."

Momma quickly removed Gordon's soggy diaper and pinned a fresh one on him. "I could, but you'd be sorry in a few minutes. He's been asleep all afternoon. And when he wakes up, he's gonna be hungry and screaming at the top of his lungs."

She wrapped a thick blanket around him and whispered, "Isn't that so, Pun'kin?" She kissed Gordon, who jerked back and started to cry. "See what I mean?" She hustled us into the living room. "But I'll feed him on the way to the store and he'll be happy again. Now, scoot!"

Thurmond, who had been under the covers on the living room bed, looking at a well-worn comic book, sat up when Momma walked by. "Can we have taters and gravy tonight?"

Momma nodded and smiled. "Taters and gravy. Chicken and biscuits."

Suddenly, we couldn't wait for her to leave and return to cook our supper.

Minutes later, Don cranked the truck and we waved goodbye, urging them to "Hurry up!" As soon as they were out of sight, Don and Mason left with gunnysacks to scavenge along the railroad tracks for chunks of coal that had bounced free of the boxcars. Thurmond stayed near the fading warmth of the pot-bellied stove, continuing to study the old Superman comic book.

Jenny and I decided to cut out paper dolls—no easy task with the dull scissors we had, and the wiggly little sister who wouldn't leave us alone.

An hour later, odd scraps of newspaper littered our laps and the bed around us. Jenny sat cross-legged, facing me, straining to force the scissors to cut.

"Do yours have noses?" she asked, not taking her concentration off her careful cutting.

"Sure," I said, "but you can't see them."

"You can see mine!" she announced. "See?" She worked her fingers out of the scissors and sucked at the painful red impression left by the handles.

Amy, who had kept herself happy by licking her arms and sticking scraps of paper to herself, leaned over to see the noses on Jenny's paper dolls. "Lessee."

"Watch what you're doing!" Jenny grabbed her best dolls and turned away.

Just then, Don and Mason clamored onto the porch and into the house. A rush of cold, stinging air swept into the room and took our breaths away. Don booted the door shut behind him.

"Close the door!" Thurmond yelled after the fact, trying to protect his warm spot by the stove. Jenny, Amy, and I grabbed the blanket and pulled it up around us, scattering paper dolls everywhere.

Faces raw and red from the icy wind, and hands blackened by the coal, Don and Mason dropped their half-filled sacks beside the stove. Groaning and shivering, they rubbed their hands together and extended them toward the warmth.

"Shee-it! There ain't no fire in there!" Mason grumbled, placing both his hands against the cooling sides.

Thurmond quickly dragged one gunnysack toward the stove. "It's 'bout dead but we can start another'n." He opened the metal door and tossed heaping handfuls of coal inside, then poked them around with a broken broom handle already blackened with use. "There's live ones on the bottom."

"Sorry, girls," Don scooped up the pages of newspaper we had earmarked for future paper dolls. "You kids gotta clean up some of this mess. You've got paper scattered everywhere. This bed looks like the bottom of a damn bird cage."

He rumpled the paper, tossed it into the stove, and lit it.

Mason stared at Amy. "She's got some kind of disease or something. Half her face is black . . . and looky there . . . so's her arms!"

"Godalmighty!" Don yelled. "She's eatin' the goddamn paper!"

"She ain't eatin' it!" I corrected him. "She was just lickin' it."

Amy, frightened by all the loud attention, started to cry.

"I'm hungry!" Thurmond complained, scooting as close to the stove as he could.

"You ain't alone, cry-baby." Mason unbuttoned his coat and held it open toward the stove. "I ain't only hungry, I'm froze half to death!"

Don wiped coal dust off his hands and handed the dirty towel to Mason, who dry-scrubbed his own hands and forearms.

The rumble of the truck's engine sent us all scurrying. The boys raced toward the door, almost knocking Amy down. I grabbed her and pulled her out of the way. The bed was the safest and warmest place to be while they tramped in and out with the groceries.

Jenny quickly gathered the remains of her favorite paper dolls and stuffed them into a shoe box. Then she climbed under the blanket and huddled against Amy and me to watch the exciting flurry of activity.

Momma hurried in first, with Gordon bundled tightly to her bosom. She rounded the corner into the bedroom and cheerfully called over her shoulder, "A good supper tonight, girls! Anybody hungry?"

"Yes!" we chorused and she laughed. Daddy and the boys charged through the living room with sacks and boxes piled high with food, and between their long strides and anxious remarks, Jenny, Amy, and I darted into the bedroom with Momma.

Busy tying her apron behind her back, she smiled at us. "I'm hurryin'! I'm hurryin'!"

"Can I help fix supper?" I wanted to be in the middle of the action.

"Not tonight." She adjusted the apron. "I've got to hurry. But I'll tell you what . . . we bought some apples. I'll give you each an apple, right now. Okay?"

She checked on Gordon, who was sleeping soundly, tucked the blanket tightly around him, and hurried toward the kitchen. We followed closely behind. She handed each of us an apple, then prodded us toward the living room. "Don!" she called over our incessant chattering, "you and Mason take the others to the back room. Keep 'em out of my way so I can cook supper."

Don groaned and turned his face away.

She rummaged through a sack and brought out several new comic books. "Here. You can read these till supper's fixed."

Don looked insulated. "I don't wanna read a funny book!"

Momma leaned toward him and whispered, "I gotta talk to your daddy 'bout things."

"Oh." Don's face softened. "Come on, Mason. Help me get these little piggies into the back room."

"Sooey! Sooey!" Mason waved his arms, rooting us from our places and scattering us toward the door. We giggled and ran ahead of him.

The back room was actually a porch enclosed with odd boards, large pieces of tin, and almost anything else that was flat and could have a nail driven through it. An ironsted bed, shoved to one end, took up half the floor space. A ladder-back chair and a three-drawer chest stood on the opposite end. What had been a side door to the house now opened into this makeshift room and there was no other exit. A window with a single pane of glass had been installed for light and did not open. The head of the iron bedstead rose up the uneven wall, its rounded iron bar crossing in front of the window.

"Gimme a funny book!" Thurmond pestered Don as he struggled to get us all on the bed and covered with a blanket.

"Here!" Don shoved a magazine at his younger brother. "Now, shut up and be still!"

I scooted as far down under the covers as I could and leafed through the colorful pages of pictures. Thurmond, Jenny, and Amy snuggled next to me and one another. The constant chatter and crunching of apples contented me for a moment.

"You think she'll ask him about that woman?" Mason asked Don, his voice so low I could hardly hear him.

Don and Mason had flopped across the foot of the bed. I peeked from behind my book to watch them, knowing I wasn't supposed to be listening.

Don made a scoffing sound. "Which one?"

"The one I saw him with. The one in the beer joint."

Don shook his head. "Nope. Don't think so. Didn't she tell you to forget it?"

Mason took a deep breath, turned on his stomach, and put his head on his folded arms. "You think *she* can forget it?"

"Probably. She has a way of doin' that, you know. She just forgets things that make her sad and goes right on being happy, like nothing was wrong."

I knew from the tone of their voices and the squint of their eyes that, deep down, they were very angry about something. My stomach drew tight around the cold bits of hard apple I'd eaten. Bundling my sweater about me, I wiggled from the blanket and sneaked over by the door. I wanted to be in the kitchen with Momma.

"Where do you think you're goin', Squirt?" Don glanced at me but didn't bother to move.

"I just wanna sit by the door." I stood waiting for his permission. He nodded. "Don't go in there." He jerked his head toward the kitchen.

"I won't."

If it hadn't been so cold, I would never have been able to isolate myself. Usually, where I went, Jenny and Amy followed. But for the moment, they preferred the warmth of the blanket.

I eased down on the little braided rug by the door, careful to keep my legs and feet off the cold floor. For several minutes, I sat very still, knowing that everyone would forget about me and I could sneak the door open just a fraction of an inch. That's all I wanted. A peephole. I knew I had just the right angle to look into the kitchen, if I could get the door open a little.

I waited. The moment came. Using my thumb, I reached under the edge of the door and moved it so slightly that no one noticed. I moved it a little more.

"Would you guys cut it out!" Don snapped at the others. "You're so wiggly, we can't even talk!"

"I want another funny book," Thurmond complained. "I read this one twice already."

"I'll trade." Jenny exchanged books with him.

At last I had it! The tiny sliver of an opening that looked directly into the kitchen. Momma had the lifter in her hand and was about to remove one of the round iron plates from the top of the stove. Daddy stood at the far side of the kitchen, smoking a cigarette and staring out the window. He glanced back and said something to Momma. Without looking at him, she chuckled, and set the plate aside. She searched around the stove, looking for something. After a moment, I realized that she was trying to locate the little tin can she used to sprinkle a small amount of kerosene on the coals or wood to get the fire started. I'd seen her do it dozens of times before.

A twinge of guilt nipped at me. Jenny and I took the little can every chance we got. Its size, and the neat little spout Momma had pinched in it, made it irresistible.

Momma sighed, looking tired and upset now. I tried to remember where I'd seen the can last. But before I could think, she shook her head, squatted down, and lifted the big five-gallon can of kerosene from the floor. She unscrewed the lid and then hoisted the can up and directed the spout toward the open grate.

Daddy turned just at that instant. "Bernice! Don't—!"

I saw no threat. I felt no threat. It happened so fast, I didn't know what happened. With a deafening roar, the kitchen exploded into a ball of fire. Instantly, the door slammed shut, cutting off my view; but in that instant, I saw Momma lifted off the floor and being blown back against the wall.

The corners of the little room split from the main house. Flames from the raging inferno a few feet away glowed through the gaping walls.

"Oh, God! Oh, God!" Don shouted above our terrified screams. I dashed from the door and sprang onto the bed with the others.

"Get back!" Don yelled at us. "Get away from the window!"

We screamed, cried and huddled, broke free, and ran back together. We clung to each other. Pushed away screaming, then rushed back shrieking. Terror ripped through us in savage bolts. I felt it myself, I saw it in the others.

The room glowed red and yellow from the fire. The roar filled the night, muting our cries. Searing heat reached through the wall, swirling around us, creating a prickly static in the air.

Mason ran to the door.

"Get away from there!" Don screamed at him. "Help me get the bed away from the window!"

Mason hesitated, his eyes wild with fear. Then he bounded across the floor and onto the bed with the rest of us. He and Don shoved us back and grabbed the iron bedstead blocking the window. They both jammed a foot against the lower railing.

"On three!" Don yelled.

We clutched each other and watched.

"One! Two! Three!"

With one fierce yank, they broke the bedstead at the railing. The slats and mattress crashed to the floor. We screamed and watched as Don grabbed a pillow to protect his arm and smashed the glass. He knocked the jagged pieces out then grabbed at us.

Mason ran back to the door.

"Don't open that!" Don's face twisted in fear. "Go out the window!"

Mason's eyes were filled with terror as he yanked open the door. Kerosene and fire swept across the floor. Billowing smoke swirled around us. We coughed, sputtered, and cried. Mason glanced back once then plunged headlong into the fiery living room.

"Mason!" With Mason's name still crying from his throat, Don grabbed Amy and pitched her out the window. He turned to Jenny and tossed her out. Just as he reached for me, he glanced back at the door, where flames roared in like an open furnace. "Mason!" I heard in his cry the hopeless sense of horror that I felt, that it was too late.

I landed hard on the frozen ground, almost on top of my sisters. Their legs felt hot in the frigid air. We clutched at each other, grappling to get up.

Thurmond hit the ground beside me. His blonde hair gleamed in the red light of the burning house. Don's large, strong body leaped out beside us. He frantically scooted us away from the house. "Get back! Get over there! Othello, you're in charge of the others!"

As quickly as he appeared, he disappeared around the side of the house. I knew he went to get Mason or Gordon. Jenny and Amy clung to me. Thurmond hovered close to us. We didn't cry but watched, slack-jawed, as the fire ate at the house.

The back door, off the kitchen, suddenly burst open. A burning, screaming figure stumbled into the night.

Thinking it was Mason because I had seen him plunge into the fire, I cried out his name again and again. "Mason! Mason! Someone help Mason!" I wanted to run to him, to try and help, but was bound by terror. I had to stay put. To watch the others.

Thurmond cried and leaned into the metal clothesline pole, his mouth open with his wails, his eyes riveted to the burning figure. The sky glowed an eerie reddish-orange as wild, frenzied flames licked into the surrounding night.

Then Daddy burst from the back door, ripping off his burning shirt. "Help your mother! Help your mother!" He screamed. Strange figures seemed to appear from nowhere. I felt disoriented, confused.

Momma? Was she still in the house? No, she couldn't be burning up in the house! Daddy wouldn't come out without her!

"Don! Get a blanket from the truck!"

Don dashed toward the front of the house.

The burning figure flopped and rolled, crying and screaming, but everything seemed slowed and dimmed and somehow unreal because the fire, the smoke, and the roar of the burning house had suddenly created another world.

"Mason! Get a shovel! Pitch dirt on her!"

"My babies! My babies!" Momma cried.

Mason ran for the shed. *Mason ran for the shed? Mason? Then who…? No. No . . . it couldn't be . . .*

Daddy flung himself down on the burning figure, tried to hold it still, to smother the flames. He couldn't hold her. She tore away, kicking and fighting, rolling and screaming.

Was it really Momma on fire? But . . . it couldn't be. Not Momma!

"My babies! Get my babies!" I heard her say it again. I wanted to scream, "I've got 'em! I've got 'em!" but I couldn't say it. To say that would have meant admitting to myself that it was my mother who was burning. I couldn't do that.

Thurmond's mouth is stuck to the clothesline pole . . . the pole is frozen and his wet mouth is stuck there . . . he's crying . . . howling because he can't move. His mouth is stuck to the clothesline pole and his eyes are stuck on Momma.

I wanted to help Thurmond but I couldn't. I couldn't move. I had my job. I couldn't put Amy down on the frozen ground. I had to hold her so she wouldn't freeze and so Jenny had someone to cling to.

Oh, but it hurts so bad to see it . . . to know it . . . to feel it. It hurts so bad to think it . . . to think that my Momma is burning up!

Mason jabbed the shovel at the ground. It skidded on the hard surface. He tried again and again, jumping onto it with both feet. "It's too hard!" he cried.

Throwing the shovel aside, he ripped off his shirt and ran toward Momma.

"Save my babies!" The cry came again and my heart seemed to stop beating. *Where is Gordon? Is he still in the house?* "Mason! Daddy! Someone get Gordon!"

Don bolted into the yard, yelling hysterically. "There's no blanket! No blanket!" He pulled off his shirt and ran to Momma. The three of them tried to hold her, to smother the flames with their shirts, but couldn't. Wild with pain and panic, she flung herself about, a torch refusing to be extinguished.

They threw themselves on top of her, again and again. They pressed their bodies against her, but couldn't hold her still.

"Where's Gordon?" I sobbed. "Somebody get Gordon!"

Jenny and Amy began to cry, calling for their little brother.

In her confusion, Momma continued to kick and scream and roll. Hysteria propelled her with incredible strength. Powerless against her flailing, Don, Mason, and Daddy continued to struggle.

"Gordon!" I screamed. "Someone get Gordon!"

It went on forever. A frigid night heated by the roar of a burning shack. The three of them running every which way, screaming and yelling at each other, the four of us huddled together, our skin pink in the glow of the fire, cold on one side and scorching on the other. Everyone locked in anguish and grief too torturous to express.

Confusion and despair fed on itself. Reality warped and twisted and disappeared into even greater confusion.

Momma did not stop burning until an ambulance arrived and the attendants smothered the flames with heavy blankets. When at last they removed the smoldering, smoking blankets, the charred and blackened figure that they lifted onto the stretcher bore no resemblance to my Momma.

Only then, as they carried her to the ambulance, did I become aware that strangers had stopped to gape. The hatred I felt for them paralyzed me with rage. *Why hadn't they tried to help? They were wearing coats!*

I mourned two losses as I stood there, still holding Amy securely in my arms, Jenny clinging to my side. I thought that Gordon had died in the fire that still raged as they carried Momma away.

Thurmond sat on the ground beside me, his head bowed low and his cries hoarse and deep. I didn't know when he had torn his mouth from the clothesline pole, but I knew without looking that it was raw, swollen, and bloody.

The shack's skeleton glowed in the darkness as the wind continued to whip evil tongues of fire into the night. When the fire truck finally arrived, it seemed unimportant. Everything had burned.

I didn't move from my spot, nor set my sister down, nor run screaming after the ambulance, as I wanted to do. I saw it well enough, though. I heard Don crying and begging God to let him die instead of Momma. I saw them all crying, shaking, and huddling with fear. Like confused, terrified animals, unable to mask their pain, they howled and cried into the wind. And I loved them so much I could have died from the ache of it all.

I didn't leave that spot for a long time. I didn't leave it until two boys about Mason's age walked past, and one of them said to the other, "Well, we was hoping to see a show tonight. I guess we seen one."

I wanted to kill him but I had to hold my sister. Trembling, I tried to stare my hatred into his back.

"Ya'll come on," I said to Jenny and Thurmond.

Just then, warm and gentle hands touched my shoulders. I looked back to see a woman who I recognized as a neighbor from down the road. "You kids are gonna spend the night with me," she said.

A new threat rippled through me. I didn't want to be separated from the family.

"No!" I said. "We're staying with Daddy."

She shook her head patiently. "You can't, honey. He's gone to the hospital with your mother. Don and Mason's gone with him."

A second fear caught me. *When* had they gone? Only seconds ago they were standing across the yard! I frantically searched for them in the milling crowd of strangers.

"Gordon died!" Thurmond gasped and began to cry.

My strength suddenly vanished. I almost dropped Amy.

"No, no!" the lady said. "Gordon didn't die. Mason saved him! He put him in the truck!"

"He's alive?" My heart leapt at the news. For an instant, I loved the lady.

The lady patted Thurmond's head. "Yes, Gordon's fine. But, my goodness! What's this?" She stooped to examine Thurmond's torn mouth.

Thurmond repeated through his tears and swollen, bloodied mouth, "Gordon's alive?"

"He's fine. Mason saved him." Then she said, "Here, let me take Amy."

"No!" I clung to her protectively. "I've got her. Don said I was in charge."

The lady nodded. "I just wanted to help."

We all stood there staring at the last of the fire. Its fury spent, its havoc wrought, the firemen spurted streams of water into the hissing, charred remains.

"I'll make you some hot cocoa," the lady said, nudging me to move so the others would. "Gordon's already at my house."

Her words encouraged me. It would feel good to actually see my baby brother. Slowly, I began to walk, hanging onto Amy, Jenny clinging to my arm.

"Gordon's alive?" Jenny asked me.

"She says so," I nodded toward the neighbor.

We said nothing else during that long, cold, dreary walk to the lady's house. The icy wind never stopped blowing and Thurmond cried openly, all the way, while I tried to think of something that would make him feel better. Poor Thurmond. Maybe seeing Gordon would help.

That night Gordon slept with the neighbor lady. The rest of us clung to each other and whispered concerns for Momma as we lay on palates in the middle of an unfamiliar living room floor. The smell of smoke in our clothing, and flecks of ash and soot in our hair, kept the horrible scene alive in our minds.

"Do you think she's hurt bad?" Jenny asked.

Thurmond sobbed aloud. "She was black! Burned black!"

"Don't cry," Virginia whispered, her own voice quivering. "You'll make your mouth bleed again." She and I put our arms across his chest.

Amy burrowed next to me under the quilt and shivered. I needed more hands and arms.

I awoke with a start the next morning and listened for sounds of someone moving about. Hearing nothing, I disentangled myself from our mass of arms and legs and crawled from the pile. I tiptoed across the room to look out the window. The sun wasn't up yet but there was enough light to see so I quickly grabbed the neighbor lady's sweater from the back of a chair. The sweater reeked of smoke and hung almost to my feet. After pushing up the sleeves to free my hands, I opened and closed the door quietly and ran out to the road.

The blackened frame rose from the earth like charred bones as I approached. The porch and front of the house remained standing but the rest of it was so burned out, in places I could see through to the field on the other side.

The stench of scorched, wet wood made me nauseous as I neared the porch. Streaks of dark soot reached out the open door, and thick, gray ash blanketed the porch and yard. Gingerly, I stepped onto the porch then carefully moved to the door. There, I hesitated, shocked at what I saw. The ruins of our life sprawled before me like a corpse. For a moment, I couldn't move. My heart beat against my ribs and pulsed in my ears.

Warm, stinking puffs of steam belched through the floorboards when I stepped inside. The piano, which stood against the front wall beside the door, was still there. Its finish had crinkled from the heat and the keys were dirty from smoke and soot, but it had survived. The green chair was gone except for the seat springs, and the bed was burned down to the frame. The slats had burned and given way, dumping the springs, which now slumped crookedly to the floor.

I had just turned my eyes toward the kitchen when someone yelled, "Hey, get out of there! You could get hurt!"

I whirled around and saw two men in the yard.

"Come on! That's dangerous! That floor could collapse!"

I had been aware of danger since I first stepped onto the porch, so I felt relieved to be ordered out. Stepping as gently as I could, I retraced my steps to the front yard and then looked back. The sun was almost up now and in its harsh and unforgiving glare the grim, ugly truth was so magnified it took my breath away.

"You one of the kids that lived here?" the older man asked.

I nodded.

He shook his head soberly then spat tobacco juice onto the sooty ground. "Damn shame," he said, wiping his hand across his mouth. "A damn shame."

The younger man moved to the porch and craned his neck to see inside. "I think the porch is safe," he said as he crossed to the door. Leaning inside as far as he could, he glanced around. "Good God! It looks like the belly of hell!"

The tobacco spitter couldn't resist the urge to see it for himself. "You stay here," he instructed. "That's no place for little girls." Then, cautiously, the older man moved to the door and peered inside. "Damn shame," he repeated. "A damn sh—well, I'll be damned! Look at that!"

The young man tried to see. "What?"

"That piano! That's what! That's the piano that was stole from the Baptist church!"

"Naw!" the young man said in disbelief. "How'd you know?"

"Cuz I helped move the damn thing twice! Then it was stole! Stole right out of the church!"

My face grew hot. I wanted to argue with him but was afraid. Insulted and embarrassed, I turned and ran. *How could he say that? My daddy wouldn't steal a piano—not from a church . . . would he?*

Chapter 7

When Momma Died

Momma lived a few days after the fire, and during that time I was allowed to see her only once. Someone had braided my hair so tightly that my scalp burned as I sat in the hospital lobby with Jenny. Daddy had told us to wait there until a nurse came for us, then he turned and walked down the long hallway, which we assumed went to Mamma's room.

Jenny turned to me, a pale, sick look on her face. "What smells so bad?"

I had overheard my aunt talking about the "stench of the burn ward" and now that I knew what she meant, I wanted to spare Jenny. "It's just the way hospitals smell. I think it's medicine."

She looked away, grimacing. "It makes me sick!"

"Breathe through your mouth," I instructed. "Then you can't smell it so much."

A fat, grim-faced nurse waddled toward us. Without speaking, she pointed to Jenny and motioned for her to follow. Jenny glanced apprehensively at me.

"Go on," I whispered. "We have to go one at a time. Daddy told us that."

Blinking back tears, she slid off the smooth bench and followed a step or two behind the fat nurse, whose shoes squeaked like tortured mice with every step. I watched them moving slowly down the long hall, until they turned and disappeared from my sight.

Alone, I continued breathing slowly through my mouth, sitting perfectly still, my back stiff against the wall. With my legs straight out before me, I stared at the scuffed, brown shoes that I'd never seen before today. With no idea who they belonged to, I hated them and hoped Momma wouldn't notice how ugly they were. She knew I wanted shiny shoes.

Eventually, the nurse led Jenny back to the bench and nodded for me to follow. I looked at Jenny to read her face and know what to expect. Crying silently, she wiped her eyes and I hated to leave her there alone.

"Can she go with us?" I asked.

The nurse shook her head. "No. But I'll send someone to stay with her."

Jenny, too lost in her grief to care, crawled onto the bench, curled up, and cried.

The nurse had already turned and was walking away.

"I'll be back, Jenny. Don't cry!" I yelled back as I followed the nurse in the squeaking shoes.

My heart pounded until I could hardy breathe. The idea of seeing Momma excited me, but not knowing what to expect created a dread and resistance that made my movements wooden and stiff. Remembering Jenny's tears, I gulped at the hard, salty lump in my throat that wanted to choke me.

When the nurse hesitated outside the door and stepped aside so I could enter, I stopped. I wanted her to lead, to show me the way.

She nodded toward the room. "She's in there. Go ahead."

Taking a deep breath, I stepped inside the room and immediately felt confused. A bed stood in the center of the floor, but it wasn't just a bed. A large, curved metal frame rose from one side, arched up two feet over the bed and sloped down to the other side. A sheet covered the frame.

I couldn't see Momma.

"Stand on the box." I heard Daddy's voice but didn't see him.

Afraid, I stood motionless and waiting.

Then Daddy moved around from the other side of the bed. "Stand on the box." He pointed to a box about the size of the orange crate near the head of the bed.

Grasping the edge of the bed, I pulled myself up. What I saw only confused me more. This wasn't Momma. There was nothing about this person that looked like her. The head on the pillow had no face, only swollen, lumpy blisters, weeping and as raw as uncooked meat. The bubbled flesh puffed and creased but it had no eyes, no nose, and no mouth. Only black, ragged lines where bubbles pushed out and joined, swelled against each other, some as large as eggs, others the size of walnuts.

"There's my little China doll."

The words seemed to come from the swollen, lumpy head but it didn't move and it didn't sound like Momma's voice. I wanted to look away and scream, "This isn't Momma!" but I couldn't stop staring, trying to find something to recognize.

"Don't be afraid," the strange voice spoke again.

I looked up at Daddy who now stood on the other side of the bed. "It don't sound like Momma," I whispered.

He nodded. "Her vocal cords are burned. That makes her voice sound kind of high and soft."

"Othello," the voice said, and for the first time I saw a tiny movement in the area where her mouth should have been. "Are you taking care of everything?"

That she called me by name removed some of my doubt, made me want to trust. "I—I, well, we ain't all together. I'm staying with Aunt Ruby. Jenny's with Aunt Maudine. And I don't know where Amy and Gordon's staying, so . . . so I'm not doing too good a job taking care of 'em." I felt guilty and wanted to change the subject. "What's this thing over your bed?"

"It keeps the sheets from touching her," Daddy answered.

"It's my playhouse," Momma said. "Remember your playhouse in the backyard tree?"

I saw a glint of light sparkle between the puffy folds of raw skin where her eyes were buried. My heart fluttered. Seeing a tiny slit for eyes made a great rush of hope wash through me. "I remember."

"Well, this is mine. I'm laying here playing like I'm not here. I'm playing like I'm home fixing supper and singing songs with you."

"When'll you be home?"

"Before Christmas."

"But that's a long time."

"Just six weeks. But I'll be home. I wouldn't let you have Christmas without me."

I instantly pictured a Christmas tree grander than anything we had ever had and imagined her rushing through the door in a burst of cold air, all well and smiling, happy to be home again.

"In the meantime," she said in her high, whispering voice, "you've got to set a good example. Do you hear?"

"Yes, ma'am."

"Whatever you do, the others will do. So you've got to be extra good so they'll be good, too. Understand?"

"Yes, ma'am. And you'll be home for Christmas?"

"For Christmas. We'll have the best time we ever had."

I smiled. "I'll have everything clean and neat. You won't have to do nothing. Remember how good I was when you had Gordon? I made you something to eat and brought it to you. I set it on a box by your bed and put a fork by your plate?"

"I remember."

"Was it good?"

"It was very good."

"Well, I'll do better when you come home at Christmas. I'll do better even than that. You won't have to do a thing. Nothing!" Suddenly, I couldn't stop the tears that burned to be cried and rushed down my cheeks while I talked.

The nurse took hold of my arm as if to help me down. I jerked back, not ready to leave Momma's comfort.

"We've got to let her rest now," the nurse said.

"Othello?"

The nurse loosened her grip and I turned back, starved for another word. "Yes, ma'am?"

"I love you."

"I love you, too, Momma! Please hurry and get well!"

With a firm tug, the nurse urged me off the box. I glanced back and saw Daddy standing near the window, his face red, his cheeks wet from crying. He ducked and turned away so I wouldn't see his tears.

I don't remember who took us back to the various relatives where we stayed, but I do recall having one wonderful, happy thought to cling to: *Momma would be home for Christmas*.

Two nights later, as I tossed and turned between cold, stiff sheets and tried not to disturb my cousin, Patsy, who slept with me, the phone rang. I heard Aunt Ruby, in the next room, get up, grunt as she put on her slippers, then scuff down the hall to the phone just outside our door.

We had never had a telephone and I had never been in a situation to overhear a conversation before, so I listened intently.

"Hello? Yeah, this is Ruby. Who? Russell? Okay. Go ahead. Hello! Yes, well, they're all okay. Uh-huh. Uh-huh. Oh, Lord! I hate to hear it. I hate to hear it! Yes. Yes. Okay. Sure, I'll do that. Oh, I'm so sorry. So sorry. Whatever I can do—yes. Okay. Goodbye."

She hung up and immediately started to cry. "Oh, sweet Jesus, what're we gonna do? Sweet, sweet Jesus! Help us. Help us, now."

I held my breath as I listened to her footsteps whisper back down the hall. "Clyde," I heard her say before she closed her door. "Clyde, wake up—"

The sheets just wouldn't get warm. Their slick stiffness made me shiver as I fought the uneasiness that tried to spoil the only thought that brought me comfort. Because I had heard Aunt Ruby mention *Russell*, I began to dread that something had happened to Daddy. But that was too horrible to think about. If something happened to Daddy, then we wouldn't be perfectly happy at Christmas, and we *had* to be happy at Christmas because Momma would be home.

I pushed it all from my mind and moved as close to Patsy as I could without touching her. Somehow when Patsy slept, she grew all warm and toasty, and she hated it when I touched her. So I inched as close as I could and shivered against a deep and lonely coldness that wouldn't go away.

The next morning, I awoke and dressed for school before I went into the kitchen. Aunt Ruby looked soft and round in her pink terry cloth robe as she stood at the stove warming milk in a pan. Patsy had brushed her red hair back and clipped it in place with two white barrettes. Even though she was only a year older than me, somehow she always seemed very adult.

"How about some hot cocoa, Othello? Would you like that?"

I nodded and scooted a chair from the table. I watched her carefully to see if she was going to mention the telephone call last night.

"Hot cocoa and Cream 'o Wheat. Keep you warm on the way to school." Her voice sounded kind of pinched and funny.

She dished up the cereal, poured the cocoa into cups, and said, "How about some marshmallows, Othello? Would you like some marshmallows in your hot cocoa?"

A terrible dread began to build. Aunt Ruby was being too nice, way too nice. She had never paid special attention to what I wanted, until this morning.

"Yes, ma'am. I'd like marshmallows."

She dropped two large white marshmallows into my steaming cup. I eyed her suspiciously but couldn't see any reason to be suspicious, except that she was being too nice.

Nothing else was said. Aunt Ruby left the kitchen and we ate as if there was nothing else in the world to do. Minutes later, our coats buttoned up to our chins, scarves tucked in and stocking hats pulled over our ears, we stepped outside into the freezing Oklahoma wind. When we reached the end of the walk, I looked back and saw Aunt Ruby standing in the open doorway. Her round belly bumped the screen as she stood there in her robe, ignoring the cold air that had to be rushing over her and chilling the inside of the house.

"I got this terrible feeling," I told Patsy as we carefully picked our way along the frozen dirt path toward school. Ice crystals formed at the edge of mud puddles, reddened by the clay. "Something ain't right."

"What?" asked Patsy, her breath fogging out when she spoke. "What ain't right?"

"Something. Something's terrible wrong. I can just feel it. I feel it something awful."

"I don't know about nothing being wrong," she said.

I looked to see if I could determine if she was lying but her scarf and hat almost hid her face.

We had walked several blocks and were just coming into the school yard when I couldn't stand the sense of dread building inside me. "Something's wrong, Patsy! Something's terrible wrong! I ain't going to school today! I cain't!"

Abruptly, I turned and ran back down the path toward her house.

"Wait!" Patsy ran after me. "Don't go back!" she panted. "We've gotta go to school!"

I ignored her and kept running. I slipped and slid on icy spots but regained my balance and kept running. Patsy matched my stride step for step until we approached her front yard, then she dashed ahead and beat me to the door. She flung it open, rushed inside, and yelled, "I couldn't stop her, Momma! She said she knew something was wrong!"

Uncle Clyde sat in a chair near the window, his round belly resting on his knees and his hands folded affectionately on top of it. He watched our noisy entrance with a crease between his brows, and his fat lips pulled to one side. "Close the door, Patsy."

Aunt Ruby entered the room from the hall, her arms and hands hanging limply at her sides. A heavy weariness deepened the lines of her face and darkened the area beneath her eyes, which were red and damp, as if she had been crying.

"I couldn't help it," Patsy explained again. "She said she just had this feeling . . . "

"It's okay," Aunt Ruby assured her, although she kept looking at me. "Go on back to your room."

Patsy left immediately and Aunt Ruby looked at me a long time before she moved or spoke. Suddenly, I wished I hadn't come back.

Moving slowly to a chair near the kitchen, Aunt Ruby sat and motioned for me to come to her. Hesitantly, I did. She pulled me onto her lap and I felt an icy wall of distrust stiffen my spine, protecting me from whatever she was going to say. I had never sat on her lap before and I didn't like it. Nothing good was going to happen here, and I knew it.

"Othello, honey, I have to tell you something." She sniffed and rubbed a handkerchief under her nose. "I don't know how to tell you, except to just say it."

My ears rang, trying to stop the sound of her voice because I knew I had never heard anything as bad as she was going to say.

"But . . . well, Sugar, your mother died last night."

I didn't answer. I didn't move. The explosion that erupted within me paralyzed me with hate. I hated Aunt Ruby. I hated Patsy. I hated everyone in the world. But mostly, I hated Aunt Ruby for lying to me. Why would she tell such a hideous lie? My Momma wouldn't die! She wouldn't! She said she would be home for Christmas, so she would. Nothing else could be true. I had no idea why Aunt Ruby wanted to lie to me, but I also had no intention of asking.

Slowly, deliberately, I scooted off her lap and went to sit in a chair that faced the big picture window. Uncle Clyde pushed himself out of his chair and left the room. I didn't see anything else in the house for the rest of the day. From that chair, I stared out at the gray sky, the gray naked trees, and the gray dead grass on the frozen ground. I watched a single sparrow hop around in a thin patch of snow beneath the leafless tree. Every once in a while, it would stop as if listening to something, and seemed to look up at me. Then, without warning, it flew up to the window sill as if I had called it. It looked at me and cocked its head this way, then that, as if wondering why I wouldn't let it come in where it was warm.

I wondered why the little sparrow hadn't flown away for the winter. Why hadn't it gone where it was warm, where it could be with the other birds? Now, alone and cold, it might never find its way to where it belonged, might never be warm again. I cried for that sparrow for a long time, and as I did, I wondered if birds cry.

I didn't think about Aunt Ruby's lie because it hurt too much. But she had lied, and secretly, I hated her for it, although I would never let on. It wouldn't be nice to let her know I hated her, but I hated her just the same.

The sparrow left the window sill while I was looking at something else, and I felt ashamed when I realized it had gone. I wondered if it left because I had quit watching it, and the thought made me cry again.

"Othello," Aunt Ruby said, "come on, now, and eat some supper."

Keeping my eyes straight ahead so she wouldn't know how much I hated her, I said, "I'm not hungry. I just want to sit here some more."

"I let you sit here and miss dinner," she replied patiently, "but you've got to get up and eat some supper."

The sky had gone from gray to darker gray but nothing else had changed outside. It seemed to me that nothing at all had happened except that the poor little sparrow had been stranded in the cold without a friend anywhere in sight.

The Funeral

On the day of the funeral, only a few ladies were at the church when we arrived. Our family took up a whole pew, and I sat directly in the middle. Jenny and Thurmond, on either side of me, cried the most, and the sounds of their crying twisted my heart with such pain I could hardly stand it. All I could do to help was hand them tissues and pat their arms and hands. The big coffin in front of the church wouldn't let anyone forget, even for a second, what we were there for.

The church began to fill with other people and ladies started singing from behind the baptistery wall.

In the sweet by and by, when we meet on that beautiful shore . . .

I had heard Momma sing those words many times and I hated their singing it now. It seemed wrong, like everything in the church seemed wrong. The music made everyone cry harder and I couldn't look at my brothers and sisters without crying for them. It was wrong! The ladies should shut-up!

Daddy suddenly leaned forward, elbows on his knees, and cried so hard his shoulders shook and shuddered, but he didn't make a sound. I wanted to reach out and touch him, but he was too far away.

Don and Mason, faces red and pinched, clenched their teeth and stared straight ahead, untouched tears dripping from their chins. I knew they wanted to burst, to explode with their pain, but they sat silently, as stiff as statues, their eyes fixed straight ahead.

When the roll is called up yonder . . . the ladies began another song as soon as they finished the first.

Why is this happening? Why are they doing this? It isn't real! Momma isn't dead! She'll be home for Christmas. Didn't she tell anyone else? Was I the only one who knew? And who were they burying, and why were they saying it was Momma?

Confused and tormented by my own questions, I struggled to do as Momma had instructed, to take care of my brothers and sisters, to be a good example, to show them all how to behave. Poor, poor things . . . they were all sad about Momma being dead when she wasn't. They didn't need to be here, to see this terrible thing, to be hurting this way. They were crying over a lie!

A preacher in a black suit and black shoes slowly walked to the coffin. He said something that I didn't listen to because I knew he was telling lies. Instead, I patted and comforted Jenny and Thurmond and kept watching Don and Mason. It twisted up my insides to see them cry without making any sound at all.

Suddenly, we were standing and walking past the coffin, Thurmond in front of me, Jenny behind me. Just as Thurmond past the coffin, he turned away and covered his eyes, crying. Aunt Maudine, standing nearby, grabbed Thurmond's head and forced his face down, inside the coffin. "Look at her!" She whispered sternly! "For God's sake, look at her! That's your mother!"

Thurmond cried out, jerked away, and ran out past everyone, and I stared at Aunt Maudine, horrified by what she had done. Why wouldn't everyone just leave us alone?

I glanced nervously into the coffin. First, I saw her hands, which, somehow, didn't look real. They were too perfect, one hand resting on the other, just below her breasts.

My eyes traveled slowly upward to her neck, her chin, mouth, and nose. I stared. This looked a lot like Momma but it wasn't her. This lady was never anyone's mother because this wasn't a lady. It was a doll, like in the stores . . . a mannequin . . . a dummy! I could tell by the nose. Its nostrils weren't hollow. I could see where putty or something had been rounded out, and the rest of her face looked as hard as a doll's.

Momma had real skin and this face wasn't made of skin! It didn't have any scars or blisters on it, and it never could have. It was a fake lady!

A wonderful comfort came to me. Soon the others would be happy again because they would see it, too; but even if they didn't, Momma would be home for Christmas. Then they'd know!

On the way to the cemetery, I wondered why everyone wanted to lie to us and pretend that Momma was dead, and why they insisted on keeping her away. The only good thought I had that day was knowing that she would, somehow, find a way to come back.

As we stood at the open grave with the coffin hanging suspended above it, icy wind picked up dirt from the freshly turned earth and whipped it about our faces and legs. The smell of the newly dug grave made my stomach roll and turn. I knew what was going to happen and I didn't want to see it.

Aunts and uncles clutched their coats and cried, leaning on each other for comfort. The preacher in the black suit and shoes mumbled a few words in a low, sorrowful tone, and the coffin was lowered into the grave. Mesmerized by the gruesome scene, I watched in horror as two men picked up shovels.

The saddest sound I ever heard was dirt falling onto that coffin. The last glimmer of hope that the nightmare would end, died, and in its place, despair, confusion, and a sense of utter hopelessness filled me with a black, suffocating pain.

Remember . . . it isn't real. They're burying a dummy . . . not Momma.

In Daddy's bed

There were three rooms and three beds in the shabby little house that had become our new home. Jenny, Amy, and I slept in one bed, in what was probably a dining room, while Mason and Thurmond slept together in the only real bedroom, and Daddy had a bed in the living room. Don had returned to Colorado to work and was no longer with us, and Aunt Lola Mae had taken Gordon to her house.

The evening after the funeral, we were all exhausted. After Jenny and Amy had cried themselves to sleep beside me, I laid awake, staring at the light underscoring the door to Daddy's room. I could hear him moving from time to time and kept listening to see if he was up.

After awhile, he opened the door to our room and stared in at us for a moment, then moved over to our bed. He was naked except for his shorts.

"You awake, Othello?"

"Yes."

He picked me up and hugged me with trembling hands and, crying, he buried his face against my neck. I patted his shoulder and back. "It'll be okay, Daddy. It really will."

Turning slowly, he carried me back to his bed and laid down beside me. It hurt me to see him grieve and I could tell from the way he smelled that he had been drinking. "It's okay. Momma ain't really dead."

"Of course she is," he said. "What kind of silly talk is that?"

"No," I assured him. "She ain't really dead. That wasn't her today. I could tell. I could tell by the way the skin was. It wasn't really skin!"

"That was your mother." He sounded tired and impatient. "That's just the way they fixed her up for the funeral, to hide the burns. Now, hush that crazy talk."

He snuggled close against me but the smell of whiskey made me scoot away and turn my back to him. Again, he pulled me close and this time, he pushed something hard between my thighs. I knew what it was because I had seen my brothers and the guilt I felt exceeded any I'd ever experienced.

All I could think of was Momma and how horrible she would feel if she knew what he was doing. This was grownup stuff, meant for her, and I didn't like it.

"Daddy, don't!"

He ignored me and jabbed at me several times, hurting and confusing me. I shoved away and climbed outside the covers. He fumbled drunkenly, unsure of what had happened, then untangled himself from the covers and laid on top of them with me.

I cringed when he pulled me close and pushed himself between the top of my thighs again. "Stop it! Don't do that!"

Scrambling off the bed, I stood trembling and staring at him, knowing he was drunk and confused, and feeling guilty because I thought I had hurt his feelings.

"Come 'ere!" He lunged for me but I jumped back. Arm outstretched, he sprawled half off the bed. When he didn't move or come after me again, I knew he had passed out. Shivering from the coldness of the floor and the air, with hot tears spilling down my face, I pulled the blanket over him and went back to my bed with Jenny and Amy. Once in bed, I became aware of something cold, wet, and sticky. Disgusted, I wiped myself with the blanket and cried. I cried about anything and everything, but mainly because I sensed that nothing would ever be the same again.

The house wouldn't be the same. The family wouldn't be the same. Even Daddy's hugs wouldn't be the same because I knew I would never trust him completely again. With that realization, my loneliness sank to a deeper, blacker depth.

Christmas without Momma

As Christmas approached, so did my excitement. Certain that Momma would be true to her word, I wanted a gift ready for her to open. On Christmas Eve, I found the perfect gift half buried in the mud in the gutter of the street. A little scratched but otherwise perfectly beautiful, I had found a red bead and was convinced it was a ruby.

I doused it in the rain barrel several times and poked a straw through the hole to clean it out, then hunted down a piece of twine to string it on. The tiny hole was hard to thread but I licked the string, twirled and pinched the end repeatedly until I finally rolled it small enough to fit through the hole. After tying the dirty ends together, I held it up to the sun to see it sparkle. Sure enough, it was a ruby! It had to be.

The others told me I was silly to think Momma was coming home for Christmas, so I kept my comforting information to myself. They would find out soon enough.

I wrapped the ruby necklace in plain white paper and tied it with string, then hid it under the back edge of the sheet under the little Christmas tree. Only a few ornaments hung from the dry, thin branches but when the sun came through the window, they glinted and glistened like stars.

"Ain't it pretty?" Amy kept asking. "Ain't it?"

"Yeah," Jenny agreed. "'Specially if you squint and look at it cross-eyed. See? Try it."

Amy imitated Jenny, wrinkling her nose and crossing her eyes. "Ooooo! Yeah!" Amy swooned. "It's even prettier!"

Convinced it might be worth a try, Thurmond joined them in making the Christmas tree prettier, but it didn't have the same effect on him.

"Gaw!" He backed away, holding his stomach. "It makes me wanna throw-up!" He went back to scooting a little rubber car across the floor. "I wanna gun for Christmas. I hope somebody gets me a gun."

We stared at the Christmas tree, and the four colorfully wrapped gifts beneath it. Aunt Lola had brought them over that afternoon and grinned when she said, "Now, don't you kids touch these! Understand?"

"What's in 'em?" Amy asked.

"Well, you'll have to wait and see."

Aunt Lola Mae, Daddy's sister, wasn't much bigger than Thurmond, but she always seemed in control of everything, so we knew she was an adult. She laughed and joked with us more than anyone else but there was never any doubt that she was in charge, wherever she was. She even scolded and bossed Daddy when she came over.

Her eyes sparkled now, as she stood in the door ready to leave. "Who's gonna touch their present? Tell me now and I'll go ahead and give you a lickin'!"

We kept our hands to our sides and our mouths closed, even though we knew she was teasing.

"Good. I'm gonna trust you. And you prove me right. Okay?"

We nodded, casting quick glances toward the presents.

She laughed and closed the door. Had it been anyone other than Aunt Lola Mae, we might have disobeyed. The closest we came, since none of us could read, was pointing and guessing which belonged to us.

I wondered if anyone had found my hidden gift. I wanted to check, but didn't want to give away my secret, in case they hadn't already discovered it.

Daddy and Mason both worked at the body shop and Don was gone so the house seemed particularly hollow during the days. Daddy and Mason picked up Gordon from Aunt Lola's house sometimes and that livened the house for awhile as we dragged him around, tickling him and handing him back and forth like a puppy.

Thurmond eyed the gifts longingly, especially a long, thin box. "Think I'll get a BB gun?" he asked.

Jenny, who busied herself rearranging the ornaments on the tree to suit her, said, "I dunno. I wanna doll with hair to comb."

"Me, too! Me, too!" Amy squealed. "I wanna doll."

"What do you want, Othello?" Thurmond ran the rubber car over my foot.

"Nothing."

"She wants Momma home, huh?" Amy nodded sympathetically as she spoke. "Huh?"

Not wanting to argue about it again, I didn't answer.

"Then nothing's what you're gonna get!" Thurmond shouted, tears building in his own eyes. "Cause she ain't coming back! No matter how bad we want it! She ain't coming back!" Tormented by his own words, he whirled and left the room, crying.

On Christmas Eve, I refused to go to bed. I could think of nothing worse than Momma trying to come in, with everyone asleep, and no one hearing her or knowing that she came. After all the lights were out, I sneaked behind the Christmas tree, retrieved my secret gift and sat on the couch, waiting. I propped myself in the corner so that I would be sitting up, even if I fell asleep, and Momma would see me the minute she opened the door. With the treasured ruby squeezed tightly in my fist, I stared at the door. She had never lied to me. It was Christmas Eve and sometime soon, she would come.

I awoke with Amy patting my leg. "Open your present! Open your present!"

My heart sank for a moment, then realizing that Momma still had a whole day to be true to her word, my hope returned.

Thurmond and Jenny ran into the living room, shouting, "Daddy! Mason! Get up! We wanna open our presents!"

I stayed on the couch so I would never lose sight of the door. When Daddy and Mason came into the living room, the mood abruptly changed.

"Pipe down!" Daddy yelled, "Or I'll throw the presents in the trash right now!"

Mason went to the tree and handed out the gifts. "Let's see . . . " he considered the first tag. "This one's for Amy and it says it's from Santa."

"Whose she?" Amy asked.

The rest of us laughed. We had a vague idea about Santa, but had never had the luxury of believing in him.

"A fat man," Thurmond answered.

"Who looks a lot like Aunt Lola Mae," Mason chuckled under his breath.

Amy eagerly took her gift. "Where's he live?"

"At the Salvation Army." Thurmond laughed as hard at his own joke as the rest of us did.

Daddy made coffee and carried a cup into the living room with us. "Will you pipe down?" He sat at the table in the corner and rubbed his forehead.

Aunt Lola Mae had bought tea sets for both Jenny and me, no doubt to cut down on the squabbling over who had the better gift. I didn't care because there was only one gift I wanted, and it was yet to come, but Jenny's disappointment mounted by the minute. When Amy opened her gift and it was a doll, Jenny threw the tea set down and ran from the room, crying.

"I'll take it," Amy said, which was enough to bring Jenny rushing back to protectively claim what she didn't want.

"It's a gun!" Thurmond said breathlessly, tearing the wrapping paper away. "It's a—"

"A pop gun," Mason finished. "Shoots a cork. See?" He showed Thurmond the cork, which was fastened to a three-foot-long string.

Thurmond seemed impressed enough until he shot it a few times and the cork bounced back without hitting anything. "I need to get it off this string," he said thoughtfully, putting the string in his mouth and chewing at it.

Then the knock came! I bounded across the room and flung open the door with all my strength. "Momma!"

Two ladies I'd never seen before jumped back in surprise and glanced uneasily at each other.

"Oh." I stared at them. "I thought you was Momma. She's coming today."

The ladies smiled but it looked as though it hurt them to do so.

"Ah, we have some presents from the church," one of them said.

Only then did I notice the gifts piled high in their arms, each wrapped in bright paper and tied with shiny bows.

Everyone suddenly clamored to the door. I moved back to let Daddy open the screen. "Thank you," he said. "I appreciate it."

"Did you pass Momma on the way here?" I shouted. "Do you know who she is? What she looks like? She's real tall and pretty and—"

"Shut-up!" Daddy snapped. "Stop talking crazy! Folks will think you don't have good sense!"

He turned back to the startled women. "Much obliged. Much obliged."

I went back to the couch and took my place in the corner. I had no interest in the new presents, but I was willing to wait for what I wanted.

The day came and went, and I kept waiting. Daddy gave up arguing with me late in the afternoon and said I was crazy, but I knew I would prove him wrong. She would come.

Long after dark, I continued to sit on the couch, clutching the sacred ruby necklace and expecting her any second. Even after everyone had gone to bed, I stared at the Christmas tree and clung to my hope. When, eventually, I could no longer keep my eyes open, I didn't move. I couldn't bear the thought that she might come and I would miss her.

Chapter 8

Abandoned

My heart beat so fast I could hardly breathe as we entered the admissions office of the Baptist Home for Children. With no idea what to expect, Jenny, Amy, and I stayed close to Daddy and none of us made a sound. Thurmond, however, cried in loud gut-wrenching sobs, begging and pleading with Daddy not to leave him. Pulling at his arm, Thurmond gasped and repeated, "I'll be good, Daddy. I'll be good! Please don't leave me here! Please!"

Daddy ignored him and walked straight ahead, his eyes darting into open doors, searching for help.

A man in a gray suit rushed from an open office and extended his hand. "I'm the Superintendent. May I help you?"

Daddy gave a short, quick nod.

"No!" Thurmond screamed, his face red, splotchy, and wet with tears. "I'll be good, Daddy! Honest, I will! Don't leave me! Please don't leave me here!" He grabbed Daddy around the waist and buried his face against him.

Jenny, Amy, and I drew back, clinging to each other. The man put his hand on Thurmond's shoulder. "It'll be all right, son. It's not as bad as you think."

Thurmond shuddered, clung tighter, sobbing as though he knew he was about to die.

"You're Russell James?"

Daddy nodded. "I called yesterday."

"Yes." The man nodded. "I recall, now. Three girls and a boy."

Daddy pried Thurmond's arms from his waist. "Now, stop it! I don't have a choice. Settle down!"

Thurmond coughed, backed away, and doubled over with grief that he couldn't silence. The strangling noise broke my heart. I was scared, too, but I knew I couldn't show it. At least, not now. Not while Thurmond was having such a hard time, and not with Jenny and Amy watching. If I cried, they would feel worse.

A woman came out and stood by anxiously, as if waiting for directions.

"Clara, please stay with the children while I talk with Mr. James in my office."

Clara smiled and nodded. She reached to comfort Thurmond but he jerked away and ran to a chair across the room. Pulling his legs onto the seat, he buried his face against his knees and cried.

Clara turned to the three of us, while Jenny and Amy clung to me so tightly, I couldn't move. She knelt in front of us and smiled at Jenny and Amy. "My, aren't you the prettiest things! Pretty as dolls! Every one of you." She lifted Amy's chin. "What's your name?"

After a few minutes, Jenny and Amy warmed to Clara and although they never turned loose of my hands, they did begin to smile a little and answer questions. As long as I could touch them, I felt they were okay, and turned my attention to the Superintendent's office and listened for Daddy's voice.

"We have lots of little girls your size . . . ." I could tell Clara was trying to be nice but I wanted to hear what was being said behind the closed office door. I heard voices but not the words because Clara kept interfering.

" . . . and your brother will be okay, soon, too. We have . . . ."

After a moment, a chair scraped the floor, as if someone stood. Maybe Daddy had changed his mind. Maybe the meeting was over and he was going to take us back with him. The thought made my heart quicken.

" . . . good food. Toys. Swings and teeter-totters . . . ." Clara kept talking.

My senses narrowed until I saw only the office door. I felt my sisters' hands, heard my brother crying, and strained to listen for Daddy's voice. When, after several minutes, I realized I hadn't heard anything in a while, a heavy dark feeling overtook me. Why weren't they talking? Were they just sitting there, staring at each other?

Then a pair of large hands touched my shoulders. Startled, I whirled around to find the Superintendent smiling down at me. Two older women stood behind him, both smiling.

"Where's Daddy?" I glanced back toward the office. "Where's Daddy?"

My question prompted Thurmond to stop crying and look up.

"He left," the man said. "We felt it was best that he leave through another door."

"No!" Thurmond screamed.

I pulled away from Jenny and Amy, ran to the office, and opened the door. The chairs were empty. "I wanted to say goodbye!" I turned and ran back to the other room.

My heart almost stopped. Jenny and Amy were now separated, crying, and being led in opposite directions. The superintendent stood beside Thurmond, gently urging him up by his arm. He turned to me and said, "Go with Clara. She'll show you to your dorm."

"I wanna be with my sisters!" I screamed. "Let me be with them!"

Clara reached for my hand. "We'll try to do that, but it can't happen today. Today, we have to put you where we have room."

I felt sick for Jenny and Amy and worse for Thurmond. At least, I might be with my sisters soon, but Thurmond would be all alone. One by one we were led into different areas of the building, everyone crying except me. I couldn't cry yet. That would only make it worse.

Spiders and Fire Snakes

Once I had been delivered to my dorm, a girl about ten years old approached me. "My name's Twila. I'm supposed to show you around."

"Can I see where my sisters are?" I asked.

"No. We can't leave the dorm, but I'll show you everything here."

My tour began on the second floor—one long room, bright with sunlight from many windows, and filled with small beds. Different colored spreads covered the beds and the waxed tile floor shone in the afternoon light. Beyond the sleeping area, an L-shaped dressing area filled with green lockers disappeared around a corner.

"I don't know which locker will be yours," Twila said, "but they're all alike. And you can't open someone else's locker or you'll get in trouble."

A little further down the hall, Twila said, "These are the toilets and bathtubs. We bathe every night before supper."

The huge blue-and-white tiled room had two tubs set up on a tiled platform at the back of the room. Four ceramic tiled steps led up to the platform. I couldn't wait to bathe in the white, shiny tubs. Short toilets squatted on one side of the room and low sinks ran along the other.

A few minutes later, I followed Twila downstairs to a dining room with two tables, each with ten chairs. The surface of the dark wood shone like none I had seen before. I ran my fingers over it as I passed.

"This is the kitchen," she announced, disappearing through another door. "That's Margaret and that's Barbara." She pointed to two older girls in aprons whose hands were covered with flour as they rolled out dough on the counter.

"You're cute," Barbara smiled. "Have you got an older brother?"

I nodded. "Thurmond."

"How old is he?" She asked.

"Almost ten."

She laughed. "Ten's a little young. Got one about fourteen?"

I nodded. "Don. He lives in Colorado."

She waved a flour-covered hand at me and threw fine white powder into the air. "He won't do me any good."

Twila motioned for me to follow her further and we moved behind a large stove where a man in a tall white hat and white apron carefully eased a large pan from the oven. He placed it on a wooden table and then turned to us. When he saw me, he smiled, leaned down and touched my cheek. "What a beautiful smile you have," he said. "It lights up the whole room!"

Stunned to hear such wonderful words said about me, I didn't know what to say. I wanted to hug him but didn't move. Maybe this wouldn't be such a bad place after all.

"Come on," Twila said. "I'll show you the basement." She led me out of the kitchen, back through the dining area and across a hall, to a door beneath the stairwell. She hesitated a moment, then slowly opened the door. A cool dank odor crept out over us.

"There's nasty things down there. Spiders and fire snakes." She seemed none to eager to go down.

"Fire snakes?" I asked. "What's fire snakes?"

She frowned. "It's a snake that when it bites you, you catch on fire. It burns and leaves big blisters on you!"

I remembered Momma's face. "Let's don't go down there."

"You have to," Twila said, turning on the light outside the door. "I'm supposed to show you everything." She took a long breath and let it out slowly before taking the first steps. "Come on."

Hesitantly, I followed, careful not to touch the wall. Even with the light on, it was hard to see. A yellow glow spilled from the top of the stairs and faded as it neared the bottom. We moved slowly, neither of us eager to descend.

"Is there another light?" I asked, afraid something horrible would jump out once we reached the bottom.

"Yeah. If it's not burned out."

I thought of Jenny and Amy and hoped they weren't having to go down into a spider-and-snake-filled basement.

When Twila's foot touched the basement floor, she leaned around the wall and flipped on another light. I was surprised to see a huge room, filled with cardboard boxes, broken chairs, and things I didn't recognize. To the left, there was a smaller empty room with a closet, its door ajar. I stared into the closet for a moment and turned to leave, but something on the shelf caught my eye. I glanced back. A huge spider crawled to the edge of the shelf and stopped, as if deciding whether or not to jump on me.

My heart hammered in my ears. I tried to move but couldn't. "Twila!"

Twila ran into the room.

"Look!" I gasped. "Is it gonna jump on me?"

Twila moved to the closet and stared at the spider. "It's a tarantula," she said calmly. "Tarantulas won't hurt you. It's black widers and fire snakes you gotta watch out for."

Horrified at the tarantula's ugliness, I bolted out of the room and headed for the stairs.

"Wait!" Twila yelled. "There's one more room. The laundry room." She pointed to a closed door. "That's it. You need to know it because we help with the laundry."

"Okay."

"Let's go." Twila flipped out the light. "I hate it down here."

"Me, too!"

Just before we closed the door to the basement, I glanced back to make sure that no spiders or fire snakes had followed us up, and shuddered from the feeling that I had narrowly escaped some unimaginable horror.

Outside, in the sunshine, Twila ran around the edge of the building with me following close on her heels. It was exhilarating being out of the basement and in the fresh air again. She led me to a playground where several tall swings moved in the breeze and teeter-totters rested with one end in the air. "You'll get to play here tomorrow for awhile."

"Can we swing now?" I moved toward a swing.

"No. It's time to go upstairs again. We've got to get our baths before supper."

Remembering the shiny, white tubs, I didn't mind following her back inside to the dressing area where several girls hurriedly grabbed things from their lockers. The lockers banged loudly and echoed off the walls.

Brothers and piss ants

"Othello?"

The adult voice made me spin around and look up. A tall, dark-haired woman about thirty looked down at me with a pleasant expression. "I'm your house mother, Miss Hornaby. Will you come into my room please?"

Without answering, I left the other girls and followed Miss Hornaby into a small room with a bed, dresser, chest of drawers, and a big chair.

From her window I could see the swings moving restlessly in the wind, as though crazy ghosts were trying to swing.

Miss Hornaby sat in the chair and sized me up like she was thinking of buying me. Her eyes moved from my hair and face, down my body, and to my feet. I shuffled self-consciously, afraid she wouldn't like what she saw.

"I hear you have older brothers." She looked directly into my eyes and smiled, almost as if she were teasing me.

"Three of 'em. Don . . . Mason, and Thurmond."

"Who's the oldest?"

"Don."

"How old is he?" She crossed her legs and rubbed her thigh.

"I'm not sure. Fifteen or sixteen"

"Is he handsome?" She rolled her head to one side, a funny, sort of sick smile on her face.

I nodded eagerly. "Yes ma'am. He and Mason are the handsomest men in the whole world."

She laughed in a low, husky voice and watched me closely. Uncomfortable, I looked away and stared at the floor where I saw a line of tiny ants crawling from the edge of the door and disappearing under her bed.

"Piss ants!" I shouted. "There's a line of piss ants going under your bed!"

She grimaced, glanced down, and then looked sharply at me. "You can't say that!" She sounded angry. "Don't use that word again!"

I didn't know which word she meant.

"Those are sugar ants."

"No, they're not. They're piss ants. I've heard 'em called piss ants all my life. My daddy calls 'em piss ants. My brothers call 'em piss ants. My sisters—"

She catapulted out of her chair and clamped her hand over my mouth. In a low voice, she allowed her words to escape one at a time. "I . . . said . . . those . . . are . . . *sugar* . . . ants!"

When she finally took her hand off my mouth, she pointed at the ants and asked, "What are they called?"

"You call them sugar ants," I said. "But they're—"

Her hand came up threateningly.

"—sugar ants."

She smiled and withdrew her hand. "That's right. Now, go get ready for your bath. We always bathe before supper."

Man in the Bathroom

I left her room and followed the noise at the end of the hall. There, in the large bathroom, a dozen girls were either naked or undressing. Squeals and laughter bounced off the tile walls and the warm steamy air smelled of soap.

I stared at the scene. Girls were lining up on the right, standing on the steps that led up to the tubs of sudsy water. Older girls, maybe twelve or thirteen, stood at each tub, helping smaller girls into the water. They quickly ran washcloths over faces, arms, backs, and scrubbed knees. Once washed, they walked to the other side of the deck and waited in line, their bodies still dripping sudsy water. One by one, they walked to a smiling middle-aged man with a stack of towels, who dried them.

I loved the smell of the room and the steamy air but felt self-conscious about undressing in front of the man. When, finally, I decided to ignore him and follow the lead as I saw it, I discovered that I loved the smooth slippery tubs and the mounds of frothy bubbles.

The only thing I didn't like was the man being in the room, but since no one else seemed to mind, I said nothing. However, when it was my turn to be dried, I reached to take the towel from him. He reached for me at the same moment and I jumped back. "I can dry myself," I said, holding my hands to hide myself.

"It's okay," he said, "I won't hurt you."

"I ain't afraid of you hurtin' me," I said. "I just want the towel 'cause I can do it myself!"

He smiled as though he were amused and handed me the towel. I quickly wrapped myself in it and left the room. I heard him laugh but I didn't care. I wanted to dry between my legs without him watching. When I tossed the towel back into the bathroom, he didn't notice because he was busy drying off someone else.

A few minutes later, Miss Hornaby gave me a pair of pants and a matching blouse. She tapped on a locker and said, "This one's yours," then disappeared down the hall. All of the girls were dressing so I put on the pants and the blouse.

Someone laughed and said, "Dummy! You can't wear your pajamas to supper."

I turned to see who she was talking to, surprised to find all eyes on me. "What?"

"Why'd you put on your pajamas? You can't wear them down to supper."

I glanced down at my new clothes. "Why?"

"Because you can't! You've got to get dressed!"

I suddenly realized everyone else had put on a dress. "Oh."

"Pajamas are for sleeping, stupid!"

Amazed to learn there were "sleeping clothes," I did my best to hide my ignorance and embarrassment. "I know it," I lied, as I opened my locker and took out one of the three dresses hanging there. "I just forgot about supper."

Locked in the Basement

Minutes later, we walked single-file downstairs to a meal of peanut butter, jelly, and bread—something I had never eaten. I watched carefully as the other girls made their sandwiches. When the jar was passed to me, I smelled it and then spread a thin layer over my bread. My knife didn't come away clean, so I licked it.

"We don't eat with our knifes," Miss Hornaby snapped.

"I wasn't eatin' with it," I explained. "I was lickin' it." To me, there seemed a definite distinction.

"Don't sass me!" She glared at me from the end of the table.

"No, ma'am, I wasn't. I was explainin'."

She lowered her eyes but her face didn't get any sweeter.

My first bite of the peanut butter and jelly sandwich lifted my spirits immensely. I loved the way it stuck to everything in my mouth and took forever to swallow. As soon as I finished the first sandwich, I quickly began to build another. Unfortunately, when I reached the point of having a dirty knife that needed licking, I licked it again.

"We don't eat with our knives!" Miss Hornaby shouted, scooting back her chair and jumping up.

"I wasn't eatin' with it!" I tried to make her understand. "I just licked it to get it clean."

"That's it!" She yanked my chair away from the table and lifted me out of it. "Follow me, young lady! I'll show you what I do to girls who eat with their knives and talk back!"

She grasped my braids with one hand and shoved me forward. I stumbled ahead of her, not sure where we were headed.

"Down there!" She opened the basement door. "You can just stay down there and think about what you've done!"

I froze and stared down into the darkness. "I-I won't do it again!" I gasped. "I won't!"

The hand on the back of my head shoved me forward and I was suddenly teetering on the top step.

"I know you won't!" She slammed and locked the door, plunging me into the darkness that hid fire snakes and tarantulas ready to crawl out of the basement and get me.

Too terrified to move, I pressed my back against the door and eased myself down on the top step, where I cringed, afraid to open my eyes. If the spiders and fire snakes came to get me, I didn't want to watch them coming. Elbows on my knees, I pulled myself into a tight ball and covered my eyes with my hands. I listened to sounds of talking and chairs scraping the floor, dishes clattering and laughing, all the while hoping and praying that Miss Hornaby would come back and get me.

I stayed perfectly still. Maybe if I didn't move, the spiders and fire snakes wouldn't know I was there. I let my breath out gently and evenly on my hands. Keeping my eyes covered, I tried not to exist.

Sometime later, Miss Hornaby yanked opened the door and I spilled out onto her feet. At that moment, I became even more terrified. I had imagined that I heard talking and chairs and sounds from the kitchen, but when I opened my eyes, the hall was dark and the dining room cleaned and silent. Every chair was placed under the table and all the lights were out. It horrified me to know she had left me in the basement so long—where I must have gone to sleep—and could have died from spiders and fire snakes!

"What do we do with our knives?" Miss Hornaby asked.

"We don't eat with 'em."

"That's correct. Now, go upstairs, get into your pajamas, and go to bed."

I ran up the stairs ahead of her, fully aware that I didn't know which bed was mine, and at the moment, I didn't care. I just wanted to get as far away from the basement as I could, so I ran into the dimly lit locker area, found my locker, undressed, and put on the pajamas.

Miss Hornaby waited to point me to the only empty bed in the dormitory. Once I had pulled back the covers and crawled under them, she turned out the hall light and went into her room. When she closed her door, all light vanished from the dormitory except the soft moonlight filtering through the windows. I pushed myself up on my elbows and glanced up and down both sides of the dorm. There was a small lump in each bed, and everyone appeared to be asleep.

I stared out the window and felt so lonely I thought I would die. I wanted to be near my sisters, to sleep with them as we always had, and I didn't even know where they were. I had heard they were in another part of the building and that I would get to see them occasionally. I fell asleep thinking of their faces, pretending they were snuggled against me.

"Don't suck your thumb!" The words screeched through my head as my covers were yanked back. Before I could comprehend what was happening, Miss Hornaby slapped the side of my face.

"Don't suck your thumb!"

I put my hands between my knees, trying to ignore my stinging cheek.

She leaned over my bed and hissed, "I come around and check! Anyone sucking their thumb gets slapped!" Her eyes blazed with anger.

I stared at her, afraid to move.

"Do you want me to tell everyone you suck your thumb?"

Unable to imagine why anyone would care, and thinking that perhaps that would end the slapping, I said, "Okay."

Frustrated, she groaned and bolted away.

The nightly slapping continued until I thought perhaps I *should* want to quit sucking my thumb, even though I didn't. So one night, I prayed for God to strike me dead if I ever sucked my thumb again. Certain that God had heard me and would do it, I was never even tempted after that. However, afraid that I might forget and stick my thumb in my mouth while I was sleeping, I slept on my back with my hands tucked under my butt, palms down. I wasn't sure if God would know the difference between deliberate thumb-sucking and an accidental suck or two, and I didn't want to find out.

Chapter 9

The Cheater

I hated school. I hated it for lots of reasons, but mostly because I couldn't read. When forced to sit in the semi-circle of chairs with the teacher and other kids, the giggles and laughter humiliated me, making me hate my classmates, too. I marveled at the way some kids knew what letters formed which words, and I tried to figure it out as they read, but was never sure I was looking at the right letters. And when it came my turn, I never had the slightest idea what to do. Usually, the teacher prompted me with the first word. I would repeat it, not knowing which group of letters she was referring to. Then she would go to the next and the next . . . saying each word . . . until everyone in the circle was laughing.

At night, I longed for my sisters until my heart felt like it would explode from the pain. I rarely even saw them and never got to speak to them. So when the longs days of school and trying to read ended, all I could think about was Momma and my sisters. I wanted to sit on Momma's lap and have my sisters beside me with everyone laughing and singing again.

Spelling was equally painful. In the second grade, knowing I would miss every word on the spelling test if I didn't cheat, I copied the spelling words on a narrow piece of paper and hid it in the folds of my dress, between my knees. As the words were called, I peeked down and copied. Since I didn't know which word she had called, I copied any word and hoped she wouldn't notice or wouldn't remember the order. It worked the first week, so I did it again the second. However, about two words into the second test, the teacher, Miss Billings, said, "Othello, come to my desk, please."

My heart sputtered with panic. I squirmed, wondering what to do. If I removed the list while she was watching, I'd be exposed; and if I stood, she would see it fall. I hesitated, hoping she would look away and I could snatch it and put it away before she noticed.

But she wouldn't stop staring at me.

"Othello? Did you hear me?"

"Yes, ma'am."

I had no choice. I had to stand and hope she wouldn't notice the paper fluttering to the floor; but because I was sitting in the front row, I knew she would.

"Othello?"

I stood. My heart hammered in my ears and my face burned with embarrassment as the paper dropped and scooted toward her desk.

She noticed.

"Want to bring me that?" She nodded toward the paper.

"No, ma'am." I stood still.

"Bring me that." Her tone hardened.

Feeling the gaze of the other students, I picked up the list and took it to her. She glanced at it, then at me, her mouth puckered to one side and her eyebrows raised in question.

I volunteered nothing.

Without a word, she stood, walked around to my desk and pulled it out of the front row and over near her desk, then turned it to face the other students. She pointed to it and I sat. Embarrassed until I could hardly think, I kept my head down and with each word she called after that, I labored over drawing letters, hoping some of them were correct.

They weren't. Not one of them.

When everyone else handed their papers to their neighbors for checking, the teacher took mine. Large blue check marks signaled every word was wrong.

She kept my chair beside her desk, and when the bell rang, ending the day, I, like everyone else, rushed to leave.

A hand on my shoulder stopped me. "Othello, please wait."

Again, my heart hammered against my ribs as I stared into Miss Billings' face. Was there a basement in the school, too, filled with spiders and fire snakes?

When the last students left the room and it was quiet, she turned to me and said in a kindly voice, "I think you might do a little better if you practiced more. So I'm giving you special homework. I want you to write every word ten times every day, until the test."

I could tell from her expression that she wasn't being mean and that she really did want to help me, so I accepted the assignment and took the spelling list and sheets of paper.

I meticulously copied each word ten times every day, and while I loved drawing the letters, they meant nothing to me. I learned their names and recognized them but that was the extent of it. Trying to remember which letters formed a word remained a mystery. They were nothing more than drawn marks on the page.

Eventually, as an incentive to help all of the weak spellers in the room, Miss Billings said that everyone who scored 100 on the next test could go to the park on Friday. I practiced extra hard, writing every word fifteen times a day, trying to associate the letters in a way that made sense, but when Friday came, I failed again.

Miss Billings came back to my desk and knelt beside me. Tears floated on her lower lids as she stroked my hair. "Would you like to draw while we're gone?" I nodded, and she brought me a tablet of bright yellow construction paper and a box of colored pencils. "You're not alone," she assured me, "other classes are still here. If you get scared, just go sit in another class. The teachers know you're here."

I said, "Okay," but knew there was no chance I would prefer another class to drawing. When she hesitated again, I felt guilty for letting her down. "I'm sorry, Miss Billings," I said. "You tried really hard."

She stood and blinked back tears. "So did you."

Her kindness at that moment meant more to me than a thousand trips to the park. I drew her six pictures, and when the class returned, I'd been so engrossed in my drawing that I forgot I was alone. Miss Billings rushed back to my desk, knelt down, and smiled. "I meant to tell you," she began, touching the sleeve of my dress, "you're wearing my favorite colors . . . red and yellow. And they look very pretty on you."

I gave her the pictures and she acted as if I'd given her diamonds. She held them up for the whole class to see and taped them to the top of the blackboard.

Numbers and lines made sense to me, like the piano, so drawing was easy, but reading and spelling remained a mystery. In the fall, the school held a contest for the best drawing of an Indian. I drew braves dancing around a fire, tomahawks raised and braids flying, and won first place, salvaging a little of my ego.

My sisters, Jenny, and Amy, lived in the same building I did, but I saw them so occasionally that loneliness never left me. Occasionally, their dorms would be in the play yard the same time as ours, or we would pass each other going to and from the dining room, so they never knew my drawing won first place.

Thurmond's misery

I saw Thurmond a few times on Sunday evenings, the only night the dormitories didn't serve full meals. On those occasions, I was sometimes allowed to carry sandwiches to his dormitory. When I saw him, I always felt sad and wished I could be with him and make him feel better. When I did sometimes manage a short conversation with him, he always talked about running away.

One Sunday evening, as I approached with the sandwiches, I found him sitting alone on the steps leading into his dorm. His red-rimmed eyes told me he'd been crying, and he didn't smile when he saw me.

"Thurmond!" I called, still several feet away.

He only looked at me.

"I'm doing it tonight," he whispered when I got near enough to hear him. "I'm gettin' out of here."

"Is Daddy coming for you?" I clung to the box of sandwiches.

"No. I'm just going."

"Where? Do you know where Daddy is?"

"It don't matter!" His eyes narrowed and he glared at me. "I can't stand it here! I get a whippin' almost every day—and I hate it!"

I envisioned him running from town to town and house to house looking for Daddy and tears suddenly slipped down my face. "Don't go! Please, don't go!"

"You won't miss me," he said. "Not after awhile, you won't."

"I will, too!" I snapped. "And you better not do it because if you do, I'll run away and look for you!"

"Don't be stupid. You'd never find me." He brushed blonde curls off his forehead.

"Yes, I would!" I tried to get a better grip on the box of sandwiches.

Just then, the door opened and another boy started to come out but stopped when he saw me. His eyes lit up when he saw the sandwiches and he yelled back over his shoulder, "They're here now! We can eat!"

He dashed down the steps and I gave him the box, which he quickly carried inside.

"I mean it," I said to Thurmond. "I'll come after you. I told Momma I would watch you, and I'll find you!"

The door opened again and Mrs. Green, Thurmond's matron, stuck her head out. "Thurmond! Come eat."

"Don't do it," I warned under my breath as he stood to go inside.

That night I prayed a long time, telling God that I was sorry I couldn't do what Momma asked. I told Him I was trying, but that I wasn't sure Thurmond was going to listen.

The next morning, as all the kids in grade school walked to school, I rooted my way past the others in my dorm and through the line of kids in the next dorm, until I got close enough to see the boys in Thurmond's dorm. I wasn't supposed to walk with the boys so I kept bobbing this way and that, looking for Thurmond's shiny blonde hair. When at last I saw him trudging miserably along, hands stuffed in his pockets, his head down, my heart leaped with joy. He hadn't run away!

Relieved, I allowed the other kids to pass me until my dorm caught up with me, and I finished walking to school with them.

Nightmares

Shortly after arriving at the orphanage, I began having nightmares that left me so horrified, they stayed with me all the next day. I was always trying to escape some horrible thing but couldn't because my feet were stuck in mud, and I couldn't scream because the scream wouldn't come.

But one recurring nightmare made me afraid of even going to sleep. I was always alone in a dimly lit house and no matter where I turned I couldn't find a door that would let me out. I sensed that behind one of the doors a terrible evil lurked, waiting to pounce on me, so every door I opened, looking for escape, terrified me. Too frightened to stay in the house alone, I had to keep looking, and invariably, I would stumble into a room where the door would slam shut behind me. At that moment, I knew it was too late. *This* was the room I didn't want to find.

The first time the door closed, I had just climbed a flight of narrow stairs. When I tried to open the door and couldn't, I turned to see what was in the room. It smelled more like a dark, damp basement than an upstairs room. In the center of the floor were two sawhorses, supporting a huge, long box. On the other side of the room, a dirty window promised possible escape.

Taking slow, cautious steps, afraid something would jump out of the shadows and get me, I started across the room. I wasn't particularly curious about the box, but as I tiptoed beside it, I glanced inside, and froze. Inside, lay my mother, her eyes open, staring at the ceiling. I wanted to run away and felt guilty for it, but I couldn't force my eyes away.

Then she blinked and turned her head to look at me.

The wretched, evil terror that tore my mind apart jolted me awake. I sprang up in bed, my hair and neck drenched in sweat. I looked around the dorm, reassured to see the familiar beds and sleeping girls. Panting, pulling at my sweaty pajamas, I was afraid to lie back, for fear of going to sleep again. I never, ever wanted to see that room again.

But the nightmare returned again and again. Sometimes, it was varied just enough that it seemed like a different dream for awhile. But always, I found myself in a house or a room, alone, trying to find a way out. As time went on, my mother was replaced by a doll, with teeth and ratty, tangled hair. The doll would always be between me and the escape route, and although it looked only like a forgotten doll, tossed in the middle of the floor; when I tried to walk around it, its eyes opened, its head turned, and it smiled and said something. Once it said, "You'll never get beyond me." Another time, it hissed, "You can't get away from me!" In one dream, when the door closed behind me, I instantly recognized the smell. It was the heavy, earthy odor of a freshly dug grave. The room was only a few feet wide, like a large crate—not much bigger than a coffin—and when I saw the doll, I knew I had to get past it.

I hesitated and then began to crawl over it. I was almost over it when it screeched, jumped up, and bit me. I knocked it away, smashing it against the wall of the box-size room, but it only laughed. I tried to get out a tiny window at the end of the crate, but it was stuck; and when I looked back, the doll was getting up. It laughed, showing all its teeth, its matted hair tangled about its head. I fought with the window. "Leave me alone!" I screamed. "I'm getting out of here!"

"Over my dead body," it answered.

"I am!" I whirled around and picked up the hard, screeching and squirming doll and threw it out the tiny window. Glass shattered. The doll screamed. I saw it arc away from the crate and heard it hit the sidewalk below. I waited and listened, afraid to look, at first. When, finally, I found the courage, I looked out and realized the crate was high up in a tree, like a tree house, and the doll lay sprawled and broken on the concrete below. Its arms and legs twisted at awkward angles and its head was broken into three pieces. Between the pieces lay the eyes attached by the wire that made them blink.

"It's gone," I thought, finally daring to believe the ordeal was over.

Then the eyes, still loose from the head, blinked. The section of the head that had the mouth laughed and said, "Oh, it's not over."

Stunned awake, I gasped, cringed, and cried. Why wouldn't it leave me alone? Sometimes, for days or weeks, I awoke recalling only ordinary dreams, but eventually the doll would return to trap me in one grave-smelling place or another. We fought viciously, more from my terror than any belief that I would actually win. So I often, and deliberately, guarded my thoughts before I went to sleep, trying to guarantee I would dream about good things and keep the doll away.

The Problem with Liver

One evening, as we went into the dining room, I was delighted to learn that the little girls in Amy's dorm were having supper with us because their matron was sick. Thrilled at the sight of Amy, it was all I could do to sit in my chair and eat my own food. I wanted to touch her, talk to her, and play with her.

Long curls fell around her face and her wide brown eyes peeked up at me over a grin that made me happier than anything I'd felt since coming to the home. We teased each other with looks and giggles, but we knew better than to talk. The dining room was supposed to be a quiet place. Only eating happened there.

Bowls were passed and we served ourselves, always under the watchful eyes of Miss Hornaby, who determined if we had taken too much or not enough. A plate of fried liver moved slowly because Mrs. Hornaby kept saying, "Take more!"

I, like almost everyone else, had learned to eat liver while holding my breath. Quick, small bites, chewed rapidly and gulped down, and quickly followed by a gulp of milk was the only way to handle it.

However, as I watched Amy struggling to get her mouth closed around the small piece of liver on her fork, I knew she was in for trouble. Three or four times she lifted the fork, wrinkled her nose, blinked back tears, and set the fork down.

"Amy!" Miss Hornaby snapped. "Liver is good. Now, eat it."

"You like it?" Amy asked, staring in amazement at the thought.

"I love it!" Miss Hornaby took an extra large bite of liver and smiled as she chewed.

"You can have it." Amy lifted her plate.

Miss Hornaby's smile disappeared. She swallowed quickly, wiped her mouth and said, "Young lady, you will eat your liver just like everyone else at this table. It's good for you. Now, lift that fork and eat!"

With slow, jerky movements, Amy brought the fork toward her mouth, then moved it back and shuddered. Miss Hornaby glared menacingly. Amy tried again. As the fork neared her mouth, her lips closed tighter and tighter until her whole chin dimpled and turned white.

Miss Hornaby couldn't stand it. She jumped up and stormed around to Amy's chair. Amy cowered, afraid she was going to be hit.

"I said, eat it!" With that, she grabbed Amy's hand, lifted the fork, and plunged it toward her mouth. Amy opened her mouth and took the liver.

"Now chew!"

I stared, horrified, as I watched my little sister cry and chew, then try to swallow the liver. Miss Hornaby repeated her actions. Amy shivered, chewed and swallowed, tears streaking her cheeks.

After two or three more bites, Miss Hornaby dropped the fork and strode triumphantly back to her chair. "There!" she gloated. "Now, we can all finish our supper."

The words were hardly out of her mouth when Amy suddenly heaved the liver and everything else she had eaten, onto her plate and the table around her.

Everyone moved back a few inches, but Miss Hornaby jumped up again and rushed back to Amy. "I said you will eat your liver—and you *will* eat your liver! Even if you vomit it up!"

Grabbing a spoon, she ran it through the slimy, regurgitated food and forced it back into Amy's mouth. At that point, we all gagged and threw up in our plates. The sound was as disgusting as the sight of it.

"Stop it! Stop it!" Miss Hornaby screeched, racing back and forth, her hands flying above her head as if she was being attacked by invisible birds.

Several of the girls ran out of the room and up the stairs. Miss Hornaby turned and fled into the kitchen. The rest of us saw our opportunity to leave. I ran around the table, grabbed Amy's hand and hurried her up the stairs.

"I didn't mean to," she cried. "I couldn't help it!"

"I know." At the hallway that separated our dorms, I urged her to hurry. "Get cleaned up before your matron sees you!" I warned. "Wash your face and hands and throw your dress down the laundry chute. Get in your pajamas! Act like it didn't happen."

Her head bobbed as she absorbed the instructions, tears still wetting her cheeks. When we heard Miss Hornaby's voice rising from the dining room, we both turned and ran.

"Good Lord!" I heard the cook say as I dashed down the hall. "What on earth happened?"

"Just clean it up!" Miss Hornaby's shrill, trembling voice was the last thing I heard as I joined the others in the bathroom to wash my own face and hands.

I guess Miss Hornaby reached her limit with us that day because she walked straight into her room, slammed the door, and didn't come out all night. We cleaned ourselves, got into our pajamas, and played Jacks and Old Maid until it was time for "lights out."

Two days later, when Twila and I were sent down to the basement to sort the soiled laundry, I almost threw up again. The dozen dresses splattered with vomit were now covered with white, squirming maggots. Repulsed at the thought of getting one on me, I lifted every piece with a broom handle and placed them all in the hamper. Twila gagged, ran upstairs, and left me to finish the job. I knew I should report it, but I wasn't about to. With my luck, I'd be sent back to pick the maggots out, one at a time. So I left the problem for someone else to discover.

Poster Kids

One Saturday afternoon Miss Hornaby called me into her room and closed the door. "Othello, I want you to get your bath now but be careful not to get your hair wet."

"Why?" Taking my bath early, and alone, made me suspect I was in some kind of trouble.

"Just do it. I'll send Leta in to help. And when you're through, come back into my room."

Reluctantly, I headed for the bathroom. Leta, an older girl who frequently helped with our baths, hurried in behind me. "Know what's gonna happen?" she asked, her voice echoing off the tile walls.

I shook my head no and started unbuttoning my dress.

Leta turned on the tap and poured bubble bath into the water. "You're going to get your picture taken."

I relaxed. "What for?"

Leta swished the water to make suds. I dropped my clothes and stepped into the tub.

"Wait!" she said, grabbing a towel. "Let me put this on your head to keep your hair dry." She quickly wrapped the towel around my head. "We don't want a picture of wet hair, now, do we?"

"What's the picture for?" I asked again, secretly hoping it was to send to Daddy.

"For the home stationery. They're going to use a picture of you and your sisters on the letters and envelopes."

My heart sputtered with excitement. "Jenny and Amy?"

She nodded and smiled. "Lift your knees so I can scrub them."

I could hardly contain my excitement. The idea of seeing my sisters pumped new energy through me because I couldn't remember the last time I saw Jenny.

Miss Hornaby dressed me in a new dress, one I had never seen. Then she brushed my hair, herself, something she had never done. "Be still," she said repeatedly. "You have to be still!"

Jenny and Amy were already in the room with the photographer when I arrived. "Jenny! Amy!" I grabbed them and hugged them so tight it hurt my arms. They squeezed back just as fiercely.

The photographer, amused at our long and passionate greeting, allowed us time to hug and kiss again and catch our breath before posing us for the picture. We were in a bedroom I had never seen before, with a large window near the foot of the bed.

"Here," the photographer urged, "You—" He pointed to me. "You sit on the edge of the bed . . . " I sat where he indicated. "And you—" He pointed to Jenny, "sit on this little chair in front of your sister." He placed the chair in front of me and Jenny sat. "And you, sweetheart," he took Amy's arm and placed her in front of Jenny's chair, "you sit on the floor, right here." Amy sat with her back to Jenny's knees.

Just then, Miss Hornaby entered the room, still carrying the hairbrush she had used to brush my hair. Seeing the photographer, she smiled quickly, kind of giggled, and then played with the sting of beads around her neck. "Hello. I'm Helen. Helen Hornaby." She extended her hand and he shook it. "Ah . . . how long have you been doing . . . ah, been a photographer?"

"Eight years." He moved his equipment where he wanted it and peered at us through the lens. We giggled and squirmed, patting each other, whispering, "Whatcha been doin'?"

After a moment, the photographer looked up at Miss Hornaby. "Could I borrow your hairbrush for a moment?"

Miss Hornaby looked at the brush as if she was startled to see she had it. "Oh! Yes, of course." She smiled and handed it to him.

"And could you get me another one?" he asked. "I think that would be a great shot, if they were brushing each other's hair."

Miss Hornaby seemed flustered. "Yes. Yes, of course." With a glance back and an uncomfortable smile on her face, she left the room. In the meantime, Jenny, Amy, and I shared every secret we'd been saving for each other.

"Here you go." Miss Hornaby hurried back into the room and handed the photographer the brush, which he handed to me.

"Now," he studied us for a moment and gave Jenny the other brush. "I want you—you, on the bed—to be brushing your sister's hair, and you—on the chair—to be brushing your little sister's hair. Okay?"

He should have only known how much Jenny loved his instructions. I remembered how, before Momma died, Jenny had always loved to brush Amy's hair.

Several pictures were taken that day, and I left the room feeling more satisfied than I had felt since we arrived at the home. The few minutes it took to photograph us was the longest period of time we had spent together.

No one showed us the picture; but one day, when a woman from the office came to our dorm, she had letters in her hand and I saw it.

"Why'd they do that?" I asked. "Why'd they put our picture on the paper?"

She looked from me to the stationery. "Oh! It *is* you! Well, I guess because you're all so cute . . . and it will help us raise money."

"People will send me money?"

"Not to you, but to the home."

"Why not *us*?" I asked, resenting her answer. If people sent me money, I could send it to Daddy and we could go live with him. He always said when he had enough money, he would take us again.

The woman walked away from me. "Sorry. That's not the way it works."

I brooded all evening, thinking of people sending money to the home because of our picture, and we wouldn't get any of it.

Baptized!

I loved church because it reminded me so much of Momma and because I got glimpses of Thurmond through the shoulders of those in front of me. The preacher's yelling and screaming reminded me of Grandpa Birdwell and the sermons Momma had listened to on the radio, so I began to listen and try to understand what all the yelling was about.

One Sunday morning, when I was eight, while the whole congregation stood and sang, the minister hollered over the microphone, begging for someone to come forward and be saved. "Open your heart to Jesus!" he repeated in a loud whine. "Open it up and let the Lord come in. Jesus stands and knocks at the door of your heart! Open it now, and let Him in!"

I tried to imagine my heart having doors, and suddenly it felt as if my whole chest opened, like the doors of a church, and rushing inside was an urgent feeling of wanting to be good, to be the best person who ever lived.

The choir sang and the minister kept begging, "Come forward and be baptized today! Let not another day pass without accepting Jesus into your heart!"

The song went on and on, and my eyes were fixed on the pleading minister. He raised his arms, the Bible in one hand, and prayed, "Send them forward, Lord! Some have felt the door of their hearts open! Give them the courage to step forward and be baptized!"

That was it. As far as I was concerned, he was talking directly to me, so I stepped out into the aisle and walked to the front of the church, and with every step gained confidence in my decision.

The minister's eyes widened when I reached the front pew. He rushed over and clasped my hands in his, his smile strained and his eyes darting nervously back down the aisle. He sat me on the front pew and when the singing stopped, he stood beside me and announced, "A child has come forward, and well, she's so small, I'm not sure . . . " Then he sat down beside me and whispered, "Honey, why did you walk up here?"

"I wanna be baptized."

He smiled and patted my hand. “Do you know what it means to be baptized?”

“You said Jesus would come into my heart. And I felt the doors open. I’m ready.”

He took a deep breath, swallowed, and stood. “This little girl . . . what’s your name, honey?”

“Othello!”

“She says her name is Or-thello—”

“No, I never!” I corrected him. “I said O-thello.”

“Oh. O-thello. O-thello!” The people behind me chuckled. “And,” the preacher continued, “she says she felt the doors of her heart open and she wants to be baptized so Jesus will come inside.” He paused and chuckled nervously. “I, ah, well, I think maybe we should vote on this and see how the rest of you feel.”

A rush of indignation swept through me. How could *they* decide? They hadn’t felt my heart!

He then asked for a show of hands, to determine if, in fact, I should be allowed to be baptized. The vote was overwhelmingly in my favor and I was taken back to the dressing room where I undressed and put on a white robe, so long I had to hold it up to walk. Again, singing filled the church as I descended the steps into the baptistery.

Apparently, I disappeared from the congregation’s sight.

“She’s still here,” the preacher assured them, as I walked slowly, the water creeping up over my mouth.

He put one arm on my shoulder, raised his other arm high into the air and said, “I baptize you in the name of the Father, the Son, and the Holy Ghost.” He sort of pinched my nose closed, tilted me back, and dunked me beneath the surface.

The whole congregation broke into a joyful song and I suddenly felt as pure as an angel. I had done a good thing. God was pleased, and I felt genuinely happy to know it.

Chapter 10

Leaving the Baptist Home

Finally, a year and a half later, Daddy came and took us—rejoicing!—to live with him. He moved us to Lubbock, Texas, and put us in a small one-bedroom apartment that he said was once a motel. I stopped dead in my tracks as I ran through the apartment the first time and saw a picture of Momma on the dresser. Her eyes seemed to be looking directly at me and my heart pounded hard as I studied her beautiful face. Each of us stopped and reverently touched the picture when we first saw it.

We learned that Don was still working in Colorado, and Mason, who was now fourteen and working with Daddy at the paint and body shop, would be with us in the evenings. Our baby brother, Gordon, lived in Oklahoma with Aunt Lola Mae, so we wouldn't be able to see him for awhile.

The bed in the living room, jammed into the corner and against the wall, took up most of the floor. A small brown couch and a torn blue chair, with stuffing bulging from the arm, sat against the other walls.

Too excited to sit down, we explored every inch of the place. The kitchen, just wide enough to move and maybe six feet long, had a counter running along one wall, with a sink below a window. A short refrigerator stood in the corner opposite the counter, rust spreading down from the top and up from the bottom.

The floors were bare except for gray-and-white-flowered linoleum that had a well-worn dark path running from the front door, through the living room, the dining area (which also had a bed in it), and into the kitchen. A dinette table stood in the center of the dining area, making the edge of the bed a place to sit while eating. I could see this was necessary since there were only four chairs to sit around the table.

The only real bedroom had a full-size bed on one side and an Army cot against the other wall. The cot was designated as Thurmond's, which he thought was great because he liked sleeping by himself.

Jenny, Amy, and I did not share his passion for sleeping alone and were happy to learn that we would be sleeping together in the full-size bed in the dining area. The only novelty in the apartment was the shower. I had never seen one and had no idea how it was used.

"You just turn the water on," Daddy said. "Right here." He turned a handle and water spurted from high overhead. We squealed and jumped back. "This is hot, over here; and this is cold, over here." He cranked the handle from side to side. I tried to pay attention, knowing this was important information he wanted me to remember.

The shower walls, finished in a gritty, tan color that looked like cement, darkened when water hit it, and a bar of green soap on the floor of the shower melted a little more.

Daddy turned off the shower. "You kids come into the front room for a minute."

Eager to please him, we hurried ahead of him and found seats on the bed and floor. "I'm not going to be staying here with you," he began. "I'm . . . well, I'm going to be staying a couple miles away . . . but Mason will be here with you at night."

I glanced around and saw that the others felt as disappointed as I did.

Daddy lit a cigarette and sat down in the chair. "Othello?" He exhaled smoke from his nose. "You're big enough to keep things going here during the day, aren't you?"

I nodded, but felt a little frightened to be left in charge. "I'm eight-and-a-half."

"Well, I'm counting on you. You said if I took you out of the orphanage, you'd make me proud of you."

I nodded again. "I will, Daddy."

"Well, good. 'Cause I don't want no trouble from neighbors complainin' that you kids are botherin' them."

My chest felt tight, making it hard to breathe.

"Like I said," Daddy went on, "Mason'll be here at night."

Thurmond sat up straight, his eyes narrowed, his eyebrows pinched together. "How come you're leaving her in charge? I'm older!"

Daddy took another drag on the cigarette, squinting against the smoke curling up toward his eyes. "Because you're going to work with me."

Thurmond's frown gave way to a wide, happy smile. "No kiddin'?"

"Why in hell would I leave a healthy kid like you home when you can be making money?"

Thurmond laughed, flattered at the thought of working with Daddy. I'm sure that the others felt a little jealous, as I did, but I also wondered about school. "Daddy?" I spoke softly, not wanting to interrupt the laughter he and Thurmond were enjoying. "Daddy?"

Holding the cigarette close to his mouth, he glanced at me. "Yeah?"

"Well, I was wondering . . . what about school?"

"What about it? You'll go when it starts."

I looked toward Thurmond, then back at Daddy. "Does he have to go?"

He shook his head, lowered his eyes, and sucked on the cigarette. "Naw. He's too big. He needs to be workin'. It's gonna take every cent we can make to keep you kids in food and clothes."

"Oh."

"Food don't just jump up on the table. Someone's got to buy it and put it there."

Jenny laughed. "Food jumping on the table!"

"It's hard earning money. And you kids cost a lot to feed. It won't be easy. But if you'll take care of the house and watch your sisters, between Thurmond, Mason, and me, we'll make the money." He stubbed out the cigarette.

I felt guilty about making Daddy and my brothers work so hard but before I could think of how to talk about my feelings, the door opened and Mason stepped inside. He had grown a head taller than Daddy and his arms were thick and strong looking.

"Mason! Mason!" We were all over him, hugging and clinging to him. He laughed, dropped to the couch, and let us maul him.

Daddy stood. "Well, I'll be going now."

The laughter stopped.

"When'll you be back?" I asked.

"Few days. I'll be by with some food." He gestured toward the kitchen. "There's stuff in there, now. Just don't eat it all at once, okay?"

"Okay." We nodded and waved as he put on his cap and left.

For several minutes we stayed near Mason, asking him questions about everything imaginable. Thurmond wanted to know what it was like to work in the shop.

"It's work. That's all."

"I'm glad he's letting me go!" Thurmond's grin widened his cheeks.

"That won't last long." Mason scoffed. "In a couple of weeks, you'll wish you were in school. I know I do."

"Why?" Thurmond looked confused. "Isn't making money better?"

"If you could keep it, it might be. But he won't let you keep a goddamn nickel."

Jenny leaned around to look at Thurmond. "It goes for food."

Mason raised his eyebrows and shrugged. "Sometimes."

Later that evening, I climbed on the kitchen counter and looked through the cabinets to see what food I could find. There were two boxes of cereal, a package of elbow macaroni, several cans of Vienna sausage, and a loaf of sliced bread. The refrigerator held a new package of baloney and an opened package of goose liver sandwich meat.

For supper, we feasted on Vienna sausage and bread, washed down with glasses of tap water, and savored every bite and every word of conversation. Jenny and I sat at the table, on the edge of the bed, holding hands most of the time. Amy, Thurmond, and Mason sat in the chairs, with Mason overseeing the whole situation.

After we ate, we went outside to play while Mason worked on his car. Thurmond quickly abandoned us in favor of leaning under the hood, beside Mason, staring at the engine.

The motel-turned-apartments was a three-sided structure, stretched out in a horseshoe shape with a gas station in the center, near the street. The gravel drive bit into our bare feet as we sneaked around the gas station, peering into the windows, familiarizing ourselves with everyone and everything in sight.

A fat lady a few doors down from our apartment, sat outside her door in a metal chair, watching us. "You kids come 'ere!" She yelled. "Come 'ere a minute!"

Jenny and I looked at each other, then back at Mason. Apparently, he hadn't heard her. He and Thurmond, both, leaned under the hood of the car, working on something.

"Come 'ere!"

I took one of Jenny's hands and Amy took the other. Wincing with every other step across the gravel, we slowly made our way to her, halting a few feet short of her chair. Large eyeballs protruded from their sockets and soft wrinkled bags of darkened flesh draped beneath her eyes and sagged like pillows onto her cheeks. Gray, faded pupils stared out from the yellowish white of her eyes.

"Ya'll Russell's kids?"

We nodded. "Yes, ma'am."

She rubbed the rounded belly that rested on her thighs as she continued to stare at us. "The little 'un here—" She nodded toward Amy. "I'm 'sposed to watch her while you two go to school. That right?"

I shrugged. "I dunno."

"Well, I am," she said, still absently rubbing her stomach.

Just then a swift breeze rushed over us and the fat lady's gray hair, which had been fanned out in limp little curls around her head, suddenly stood straight up. She laughed and we saw that she had only two teeth.

"No!" Amy cried. "I don't want to!"

I put my hand over Amy's mouth. "Shhh!"

After the breeze passed, the fat lady's hair settled back into limp little curls again. "Amy? Ain't that what your daddy said your name is?" She peeked around at Amy who was now hiding behind me.

Amy didn't answer.

"You gonna have a baby?" Jenny asked.

The fat lady's eyes widened and she barked a quick laugh. "Lord, I hope not!" She turned in her chair and hollered into her apartment. "Lloyd! Get out here and see these cute kids!"

A skinny man whose scalp showed beneath oily dark strands of hair combed sideways over his head, suddenly appeared in the doorway. He leaned against the doorjamb as if he were tired. His face hung in folds, a thousand lines wrinkling his cheeks, and when he sucked on his cigarette, the whole bottom half of his face seemed to collapse. "Russell's kids?"

The fat lady nodded. "That one—" She pointed a stiff swollen finger at Jenny. "She asked if I was gonna have a baby and I told her—" She yelped another laugh, "I told her, God I hope not!"

The man laughed with her. Jenny and I laughed too because, between them, they had only three teeth.

That night after we were in bed, I stared at Mason, sitting in the living room writing something on tablet paper. When I was sure Jenny and Amy were asleep, I slipped out of bed to sit with him. "Whatcha' doing?"

"Writing my girlfriend, Annette."

"What's she like?"

He stopped writing and rested his head on the back of the chair and stared at the ceiling as he talked. "Well, she's got kinda blonde hair. And she's real pretty. I'm gonna marry her some day."

"Where's she live?"

"Right here, in Lubbock. In fact, she's Irene's daughter."

It took me a minute to remember that Irene was the woman Daddy lived with. Mason went on to tell me that Irene worked as a short-order cook in a coffee shop, and that Annette worked as a waitress in a restaurant across the street. He said that he loved being with Annette more than any person in the world because she made him feel so special.

As I listened, I was aware of feeling happier at that moment than I had been since Momma died. Just being with Mason, and knowing I would see Daddy every few days, gave me a sense of belonging that I had missed so much in the orphanage. In my heart, I knew that this was the way families should be—together and talking, learning things about each other—and never feeling alone.

Empty Stomachs and Cupboards

Two days later, I woke up to a fight between Jenny and Amy, and Sugar Crisp cereal strewn all over the floor. Amy clung to an empty upside-down box and Jenny, inches away, yelled in her face, "Now, see what you've done!"

Since the cereal was all that was left of our food—with the exception of the elbow macaroni that I had no idea how to cook—I scrambled out of bed and stood there staring at the mess. It was seven o'clock, so I knew Mason and Thurmond were gone already.

"We'll just have to pick it up," I finally said. "It's all there is."

Amy squatted where she was and picked up the pieces around her feet. Those she didn't eat immediately, she dropped into the box. Jenny looked irritated. "I'm not picking it up! It wasn't my fault! She grabbed the box from me."

"Then you're not eating any, either," I said. "We'll pick it up and eat it all ourselves."

Amy grinned, liking my solution.

"I don't need any." Jenny turned and left the room. "It's dirty anyway!"

Amy and I ate our way over the floor, one Sugar Crisp at a time, content to let Jenny go hungry. In all, there probably weren't two cups of cereal in the box, so picking up our breakfast didn't take long.

Later in the morning, I stared at the bag of macaroni and wished I could read. I had eaten macaroni before and knew I liked it, but as I stared at the uncooked version—and the words printed on the bag—I knew someone would have to read it and tell me what to do. So I took it to the fat lady with bulging eyes.

Minutes later, I dashed back and put a pan of water on the stove to boil.

This tiny bit of information gave me a great sense of liberation. I could cook something besides fried potatoes! (I was sure I could fry potatoes because I had watched Momma do it hundreds of times.)

Daddy came by that evening and brought two bags of groceries. Pork 'n beans, more Vienna sausage, two loaves of bread, more macaroni, and a length of baloney. We clamored around him, as glad to see him as the groceries.

"Daddy! Daddy!" We tugged and pulled on him, urging him to play.

"How's it going, Othello?" He sat down and lit a cigarette.

"It's okay, 'cept we need more food. We get hungry in between."

He nodded. "You're not wasting it, are you?"

I shook my head "no," but Jenny said, "Amy dropped the box of cereal and spilt it all over the floor!"

Daddy frowned. "I'd say that's wasting it!"

"No," I told him quickly, "we ate it anyway."

He sat quietly for a while then turned to me. "I'm expecting you to take care of things. Don't let me down."

"I won't." I glared at Jenny for making him think I wasn't doing a good job.

"Schools gonna start in a couple of weeks," he said. "I've made arrangements for Amy to stay with a neighbor."

Amy puckered up to cry. "Her teefs gone!"

Daddy chucked. "Then she won't bite you. Right?"

I laughed, Jenny rolled her eyes in disgust, and Amy cried harder.

Daddy continued to drop by with food just when it seemed we were going to starve to death. One evening, he took us to Irene's apartment where we met Annette, who smiled and patted our heads as if we were puppies. Irene, on the other hand, never left her place in front of the stove where she was cooking. A large woman, taller and heavier than Daddy, she had big yellow, gaping teeth. Most of the time, however, a cigarette dangled from her lips, making her teeth less noticeable.

Whatever she was cooking smelled wonderful and I kept trying to peek into the pan, but Daddy repeatedly warned, "You kids stay out of the kitchen."

"Can we eat here?" Jenny asked.

"No," Daddy said. "I've got to take you back now so I can go to work."

"But you already worked today," Jenny whined, "and I'm hungry."

Daddy jerked his head toward the door. "I'll get you something on the way home."

Something was Peanut Patties and orange soda pop, and we ate and drank with gratitude and gusto, sure we had the best dad in all the world.

The Good Witch

The remaining week before school started, we ran wild up and down the street. We often played around the gas station, talking to motorists who stopped, or striking up conversations with Ralph, the man who ran the station. Eventually, though, he'd say, "You girls go on home, now. I've got work to do," and, reluctantly, we'd leave. The alley was another of our favorite haunts, looking into boxes and trash cans that overflowed with promising treasures.

About two streets away, we happened upon a trailer park, and walked through. "Pretend we live here," I instructed. "No one will know the difference."

In one small trailer, a small silver-gray thing, rounded on both ends, the door stood open, tempting us to look inside.

"Hello, girls," a soft, shaky, old-woman's voice called.

We strained to see who had spoken, but the brightness of daylight didn't penetrate into the darkened trailer, except to reveal a couple of little jumping flames that appeared to be candles.

"Would you like to come in?"

I looked at Jenny.

"Sure," she encouraged me. "Let's see what it's like."

Not as brave as she, but being oldest, I stepped inside first. Jenny and Amy followed, standing close to my back. It took a moment for my eyes to adjust to the darkness, and then I saw a tiny, wrinkled old woman, sitting on the edge of a small bed.

"I'll bet she's a hundred!" Jenny whispered next to my ear. I thought she might be right.

"What's your names?"

I introduced myself and my sisters. The old woman said her name but it was something foreign-sounding and I knew I would never remember it.

"God is taking care of you," the old woman said. "He loves you."

We stood before her, mesmerized by her age, her piercing dark eyes, and the jumping flames of the candles beside her.

"I was baptized." I thought it was important she should know.

She smiled. "Just remember, God is taking care of you."

She stretched a skinny arm from beneath her shawl and thrust a bony, gnarled hand toward us. "Take my hand."

I knew from Jenny's expression that she wasn't even going to consider it, so I took the old woman's cool, soft fingers.

"Remember this," the old woman leaned forward, her voice just above a whisper, "I'm here if you need me."

Jenny pushed around me in the tight, confined space, and stared at the old woman. "How do you know God is with us?"

The toothless old mouth smiled as the woman withdrew her hand and sat back on her small bed. "I know a lot of things most people don't know."

Jenny pressed. "Like what?"

"Well, I know your mother is dead. I know you live by yourselves."

Jenny and I looked at each other, impressed.

"How'd you know that?" I asked.

She smiled again, a twinkle in her eye. "Here . . . " She removed the long, black-beaded necklace she wore. "This is called a rosary. It's a way to talk to God."

Jenny took the necklace and we studied it. "How's it work?" Jenny asked.

"Just hold it when you say your prayers. God will listen carefully, if you do."

The gnarled hands reached toward a small table and picked up another rosary. "Here's another one. Both of you should have one."

I glanced at Amy to see if she was going to object because she didn't get one but the look on her face told me she wanted no part of this old lady and her necklaces.

"Keep the rosaries with you. Hold them when you say your prayers at night." She held up a misshapen, bony finger. "Will you do that?"

We nodded.

"And come back to see me if you ever need anything."

"How do you think it works?" Jenny asked, the minute we were out in the bright sunlight, heading down the alley again.

I shrugged and examined the strand of beads, wishing I understood. "I dunno."

"I wanna know things," Jenny said. "I wanna know things other people don't, like that ugly old lady. Do you think she's a witch?"

Amy struggled to keep up with us. "She's scary! Let's go home!"

Jenny and I laughed, feeling we held some mysterious treasure in our hands, and glad that Amy didn't want one.

Lying to the School Nurse

We hated school. Each day began by dressing ourselves in whatever clothes were least wrinkled and dirty and then we took Amy to the big-eyed fat lady where she stayed until we returned from school. Rarely was there breakfast food in the house, so we ate bread and baloney, if we had it, and if not, we went to school without eating.

Other kids with full lunch boxes and pretty clothes made us hate being there. I particularly hated it when it was time to read out loud, so I frequently pretended to be sick, and spent most of the day lying on a couch in the "sick room."

After several "sick" days, the school nurse asked me what I had eaten for breakfast. That day, I hadn't eaten anything but I knew I shouldn't say that. I knew Daddy would probably get into trouble and we'd end up back in the orphanage. So I lied.

"I had oatmeal, toast, peanut butter, jelly, and milk." I named the foods I recalled eating at the orphanage.

"Oh, really?" The nurse sat back, folded her arms and stared at me. "That's strange. Your sister is in the other sick room and when I asked her what she had for breakfast, she said she had eggs, bacon, biscuits, and gravy."

Stunned to realize Jenny was playing the same game, I just stared at the nurse.

"Can you explain that?" the nurse asked.

"Yes," I spoke as calmly as I could. "I don't like those things so Daddy didn't make them for me."

She rolled her eyes and made a hissing sound. "I think I'll call your father."

"Why?"

"Because something's not right here. I'm beginning to suspect that you girls aren't being cared for."

Panic clawed through me. "Yes, we are! We are! We have a good home! Lots of food! Tons of toys!"

She stared at me another minute, sighed, and said exactly what I hoped she would, "You and Jenny might as well go on home. You're not going to learn anything as long as you're *sick*." She stood. "I'll call your father to pick you up."

Sensing our world was about to fall apart again, I begged her not to call Daddy. "He's at work! He can't leave! We can walk home. We know the way."

Finally, she relented, made some notes on a pad, and told us to go straight home.

For the next several weeks, we played hooky more than we went to school but we always took Amy to the fat lady. We also knew we couldn't stay home or roam the streets because someone would see us and report us. Generally, we sneaked down the alley, scavenged for "good stuff," then climbed a tree behind our apartment and sat in its shade through the hottest part of the day.

One morning when we happened to find a book of matches, we both decided it was time we learned to smoke. We picked up butts in the alley and carried them up to the roof, where we coughed and gagged until we finally got the hang of it.

One afternoon, I remembered my promise to Momma to always be a good example and decided that even though I couldn't teach Jenny to read, I should at least teach her the arithmetic that I understood. So the next day, I took a pencil, several sheets of paper from Mason's tablet, and did my best to help her understand numbers. She didn't seem to mind my instruction, and learned everything I knew in an afternoon, but when she decided it was time to quit working and draw pictures, she threw a fit because I wouldn't let her go down to get more paper.

"Someone will see you!" I tried to explain. "And then, we'll be back in the orphanage!"

She went down anyway.

The Warning

That evening Daddy showed up with sacks of groceries and a ten-pound bag of potatoes. "I got a call at the shop today," he said to me as he dropped the potatoes on the counter. "It didn't make me happy."

I just stared at him. There were so many things I'd done lately that wouldn't make him happy, I decided I'd better let him talk first.

"You know what I'm talking about, young lady?"

"No."

"Well, the school says you and Jenny ain't been there for over a week."

I lowered my eyes and stared at my bare feet. "School's dumb. I hate it."

"Well, I'll tell you one thing for sure, Miss Smarty Britches! If you don't stay in school, the state will take you away from me! Is that what you want?"

My heart raced. I felt hot. My legs felt rubbery. There was no good way out of the mess. I hated, hated, *hated* school! I felt stupid there. And I hated the girls who had pretty dresses and shoes and ribbons. Just being in the same room with them was bad enough. Then, when they laughed because I couldn't read . . .

But I hated the idea of the orphanage worse. The basement . . . fire snakes creeping up the stairs . . . never, never getting to see Jenny and Amy!

For a moment, I thought I would throw up.

"Are you listening?" Daddy snapped.

I nodded. "I'm listening."

"You want me to whip your tail right now to make sure you go to school tomorrow?"

I shook my head. "No. I'll be there. So will Jenny."

"Good. Now—" He stopped and lit a cigarette. "Mason and Thurmond are out front working on a car we drove home. You're gonna fix dinner for us. I bought some taters and bread and baloney. Can you cook the taters?"

I nodded.

After he left the kitchen, Jenny asked, "Want me to help?"

"No. There's only one knife to peel taters."

For the next several minutes, I struggled futilely to peel the potatoes. The dull blade exhausted my fingers, the potatoes slipped from my hands, rolled off the counter and onto the floor. Finally, when I realized I was defeated, I searched through the drawer and found a butcher knife which made the job easier. I chopped off four sides and two ends, and after using the whole bag of potatoes, I dumped the peelings in the trash.

I opened the small can of lard Daddy had brought, lit the burner under the cast-iron skillet, and felt like a contributing member of the family again. While the lard melted in the skillet, I washed the peeled potatoes, whacked them up into bite-size pieces and put them in the heating grease. Daddy also brought a can of black-eyed peas and some canned green beans, and I opened both to serve with my first, real supper.

When we finally all sat down, everyone's eyes danced over the choices. We dragged the skillet of potatoes from one end of the table to the other and everyone dug in. Thurmond and Mason both smiled and heaped potatoes, peas, and beans on their plate. Jenny brought the loaf of bread to the table and everyone took a slice.

I kept waiting for Daddy to say how good everything tasted. It seemed especially important that he should like it. When he didn't say anything for the longest time, I decided I should impress him with how grown up I had become in the last two hours.

"You're sure right about how 'spensive it is to feed us, Daddy."

He glanced up and then went on eating.

"It took that whole sack of taters to make supper tonight."

His fork stopped midway between his plate and his mouth. He didn't look at me immediately, just stared at his fork. Finally, he said, "The whole ten pounds?"

I nodded. "All of 'em."

He suddenly jumped up, walked around the table and into the kitchen. Oblivious to any notion that he might be upset with me, I went on eating. Seconds later, I almost choked when he stormed back into the room, holding up one side of a potato that I had whacked off.

"What the hell is this?" he shouted.

"A tater peeling."

"Hell, it ain't no peeling!" He wagged it in the air. "It's a third of a tater!"

He carried it to the table, shouting and waving the peeling in the air. "I'm wasting my time on you, Gal! Wasting my time! You kids is eating me out of house and home, and wasting half of what I haul in!"

"I couldn't cut 'em littler, Daddy. The knife hurt my hand!"

"Well, I'm gonna whip your tail as soon as supper's over and you've got that mess in there cleaned up! Then you'll learn the difference between this—!" He held up the piece of potato "—and a peeling!"

The rest of my grand meal was eaten in silence and every bite tried to stick in my throat. Jenny helped me clean up the kitchen, and for sure we stretched the job out as long as we could because we knew that Daddy would follow through on his promise to "whip my tail" the minute we finished.

Once the dishes were washed and put away, we decided to sweep and mop the floor, hoping to impress him so that he would forgive me.

It didn't work. Before the floor even dried, Daddy came inside. "All right," he said, unbuckling his belt, "let's make damn sure that don't happen again."

"It won't, Daddy! It won't!"

"You're damn right it won't!" He grabbed my right arm just above the elbow to hold me and brought the belt down against my thighs with a sharp smacking sound. Each hit stung and burned. Screeching and yelling, I twisted and pulled to get away.

"Think you'll remember?" He huffed, winded from his effort.

"Yes!" I cried. "I would've remembered anyway!"

Thurmond had come in to see the whipping, and left as soon as it was over. Through the window, I saw Mason out by his car, his arms crossed, staring into the distance.

Jenny and Amy watched me closely as I stood and wiped my eyes.

"It still hurt?" Amy asked, raising my dress to look at the welts.

"Not too bad." The truth was, the whipping hadn't hurt nearly as much as Daddy's anger. I knew the belt's hurt would stop, but the hurt from him believing I was stupid felt like it might never go away.

That night, I lay awake a long time, dreading going back to school.

Humiliating Haircut

My feet simply didn't want to go. Each step toward the school building made them heavier, and I could tell it affected Jenny the same way. We ate bread before we left for school and stuffed bread in our pockets for lunch, but we knew we would eat it long before the lunch bell rang.

At one point during the day, the teacher, Miss Langley, stopped at my desk and whispered, "Tell your mother to cut your bangs."

I just looked at her. Part of me wanted to tell her that I didn't have a mother . . . while another part refused to admit my mother was dead . . . and still another part warned me that saying anything would probably mean going back into the orphanage. So I only stared and nodded.

Days later, as I suffered through more endless hours of feeling stupid—and *hungry*—Miss Langley stopped by my desk again. This time, she didn't whisper. "Othello. Why didn't you tell your mother to cut your bangs?"

"I forgot."

"Don't forget tonight."

Unfortunately, I did. It wasn't until I went to bed that I remembered the instruction, and then it was too late. With everyone asleep, I couldn't get up and search every drawer for scissors, and as far as I knew, we didn't have any.

The next morning, my choice was to go back to school with my bangs hanging in eyes (which didn't bother me in the least, and I couldn't figure out why it bothered Miss Langley, either!) or go back to the orphanage. Hoping she wouldn't notice, I took my seat and tried to appear absorbed in a book.

"Othello?"

I raised my eyes.

Miss Langley's blue eyes twinkled beneath her own shortly cropped bangs. "Will you come up here, please?"

I did as instructed, stopping just short of her desk.

"Now—" She stood, lifted a pair of scissors from her desk and walked around to where I stood, smiling all the while. "If you can't remember to tell your mother to cut your bangs . . . and your mother hasn't noticed they need cutting . . . "

She turned me to face the class. " . . . then I'll cut them!"

The class laughed and squealed.

"I can't stand to see them hanging in your eyes one . . . more . . . day."

The laughter continued as she placed one hand on top of my head to hold it still, raised the scissors, and began cutting. Too humiliated to cry or protest, I closed my eyes, cringing as the hair fell onto my cheeks and to the floor. When she finished, she blew in my face to remove the hair that had stuck. Her sour breath went right up my nose.

"There!" She stepped back and smiled, proud of herself. "That looks much, much better! Now you can see to read!"

For a moment I froze, terrified that she would put me to the test on the spot, but the words had no sooner left her mouth than the fire alarm sounded.

Miss Langley jumped and turned toward the class. "Fire drill! Fire drill! Line up by the door!"

Once outside, it was easy to slip away from the group. Our class walked, two-abreast, to the far side of the playground, and stood next to the hedge, as other classes hurried out and stood together. Even though no one left their groups, everyone was talking and yelling at other kids in other classes.

By the time the last class left the building, it was time for the first class to go back inside. When it was our turn to leave, I waited until Miss Langley turned her back to lead the class toward the building, and I dived for the hedge and scooted back up against the fence. From there, I saw all the classes eventually go back inside. Then, I slipped out of the hedge, hurried off the playground, and went home. I ate the two slices of bread in my pocket and waited on the roof of the apartment until I thought it was about time for school to let out; then I walked back to wait for Jenny, and walked home again with her.

Chapter 11

Hunger, Guilt, and Lemon Pie

It was a Saturday and we were out of food again. Mason and Thurmond were working on a car (as they always were), and Jenny was busy washing and combing Amy's hair, so I decided to walk over to Irene's apartment to find Daddy and tell him to bring us some groceries.

I knew I would recognize the building when I saw it, and I remembered that it was on a corner. The only thing I felt uncertain about was the distance. The further I walked, the more I started to doubt my decision but when I'd gone a dozen or so blocks, I knew I had to be closer to their apartment than ours, so I kept moving.

My stomach growled and my knees felt shaky by the time I saw it but I climbed the steps with renewed hope, glad I had come.

"Good Lord!" Annette said when she opened the door. "Did you walk all the way here?"

I nodded, pushing past her. "I need a drink."

"Well, I guess so! That's over a mile! And you shouldn't be crossing those busy streets by yourself."

I gulped down two glasses of water and wiped my mouth. "Is Daddy here?"

"No. Why?"

"Cause we're hungry and there's nothing to eat."

Annette's eyes softened. "I'm sorry. He and Mom left about twenty minutes ago. I don't know where they went."

I felt my shoulders slump. "They didn't say how long they'd be gone?"

She shook her head. "But here!" Her eyes lit up. "We have some lemon meringue pie. You can have a piece of that."

I glanced at the pie and noticed two pieces were already gone. My mouth watered. Lemon meringue was my favorite. I wanted to say "Yes!"

but the image of my hungry sisters at home created a horrible guilt. "No, thanks," I finally managed.

Annette looked confused. "Why?"

"Cuz Jenny and Amy won't get any, and they're hungry, too."

Reluctantly, I moved to the door.

"You've gotta be kidding!" Annette stood near the table, arms outstretched and palms open to the pie. "Your dad ate a piece just before he left. He eats here every day."

Almost out the door, I stopped and looked back. Her words created a heaviness inside me that threatened to make me sick. How could he do that? How could he eat when we were hungry?

Too disturbed to say anything else, I closed the door and left. All the way home, I tried to understand how he could do that. For some reason, I had always believed that he ate when we did . . . not before and not in between. This unsettling information threatened to topple my image of him. And I wasn't sure which I hated more—knowing or not knowing, the truth. Either way, I felt like a fool.

By the time I reached our apartment, Daddy and Irene were there with bags of groceries, so it was easy enough to dismiss my misgivings and wrap myself again in the sweetness of blind love.

The Daddy I Didn't Like

One evening, about dusk, Daddy stood outside in front of the apartment, talking with Mason and Thurmond. After a few minutes, I heard Mason yell, "You can't do that!"

Seconds later, I saw Mason get in his car, slam the door, and drive off without looking back. Daddy opened the front door and said, "Othello. Jenny. Come out here with me and Thurmond."

Amy followed us to the door.

"No, you stay inside, Amy. You can watch through the window."

We gathered around Daddy as he squatted in the middle of us. "Thurmond says he stole some ice and a pop from the gas station tonight."

We looked at Thurmond, waiting to hear what his punishment would be.

"Now, there's candy, gum, peanuts, and all kinds of stuff in there," Daddy continued. "And if you do it right, and if you're smart enough and don't get caught then there's no reason why you should ever go hungry."

I laughed, thinking he was joking.

"That's right," he said. "I'll teach you how to steal it and not get caught."

It took a moment to make the transition from "That's wrong" to "If it's okay with Daddy, it must be okay." But what had been unthinkable only minutes ago, began to emerge as a viable solution. Why should we be hungry when the gas station had plenty of pop and candy?

"When cars are out front and you see him talking to customers . . . that's when you go in. There's nobody else working there. Just him." He hesitated and smiled. "See?" He pointed to Ralph who was washing somebody's windshield. "He's busy now. Come on. I'll show you how to do it."

I couldn't make myself move. Neither could Jenny. Thurmond, on the other hand, followed Daddy to the back of the gas station where they slipped into the shadows. We saw them enter the back door. My heart sputtered as I watched Ralph talking to the customer and taking his money.

Seconds later, Daddy and Thurmond sneaked back out and ran to us, laughing under their breath and showing us handfuls of candy bars.

I stared at Thurmond and wondered if he remembered the whipping Momma gave him for stealing the cardboard skeleton from the drugstore, and how she marched him back to the store, saying, "I'm not raising a bunch of liars and thieves!"

Daddy's lesson didn't "take" for Jenny or me. Neither she nor I ever mentioned it again and I often wondered if she felt the same as I—too ashamed of Daddy to admit he had done it.

Then, a few days later, Daddy did something that left me limp inside. There was almost nothing I wouldn't have done for him, but there were also times when my love and my loathing created a vicious tug-of-war with my emotions, I wasn't sure what to feel.

It had rained all day. The front door was opened several times for one reason or another, and probably left ajar longer than it should have been, and at one point, a pregnant cat, unnoticed by any of us, slipped inside and hid in the closet.

The next morning Daddy came by early for something. He yelled at Mason and Thurmond to get up and opened the closet door. "Well, I'll be goddamn!" he yelled. "There's a cat in here!"

The mother cat hissed and cried but Daddy yelled and stomped until she fled. "Open the door!" he shouted. "Get her out of here!"

The poor tormented cat ran outside but stayed near the door, yowling and crying in the rain. What Daddy did next made me hate him, at least for that moment. He kicked the baby kittens all the way through the bedroom, the living room, and out the front door. One at a time, he kicked them out into a puddle just beyond the door. The mother cat cried and dashed to save them. She picked up one, carried it out of the puddle and dropped it; then she ran back and got another, and another. The third one must have died because she picked it up, shook it, then dropped it and ran back to the two she had rescued. She carried one kitten around the edge of the apartment and hurried back for the second. As I watched her frantic efforts through the window and stared at the kitten lying in the puddle, the rain falling on it, I thought I might never forgive or love Daddy again.

Letting Mason Practice

Thurmond had gone to a friend's house and Jenny, Amy, and I were playing outside early one evening when Mason called me into the apartment.

"Sit down on the bed a minute." He gestured toward the bed in the living room and sat down in the chair. Lowering his eyes, he said in a quiet voice, "I want to ask you something."

"Okay." I wiped sweat off my face and scratched a mosquito bite on my elbow.

Mason sighed and reached into his shirt pocket. "Do you . . . do you know what this is?"

I stared at the long clear balloon and nodded. "It's a balloon. Jenny and I find 'em in the alley sometimes."

He shook his head. "No. It's not a balloon, and don't ever try to blow one up."

I shrugged. What could it hurt? We had already done it several times.

Mason squirmed uncomfortably. "It's called a rubber." He stuffed it back in his pocket. "It's something boys use when they . . . when they . . . do it to girls."

We stared at each other.

"Do you know what *do it* means?"

"I think so." I remembered Thurmond saying those words in the tree house when he told me he'd give me a rubber doll if I'd let him *do it* to me. I also thought of Daddy poking himself at me the night Momma died.

"Well," Mason said in a shaking, low voice, "big people do it to people they love. And the man puts a rubber on his . . . his thing . . . so the woman won't get pregnant."

"You and Annette are in love. You mean people like you?"

He nodded, seeming relieved to have a reference point. "Yeah, except we haven't done it yet. She said she won't until we're married. And then, she doesn't want any kids for a long time."

"Why?"

He frowned. "She just doesn't want any kids for a long time."

"No, I mean why doesn't she want to do it before you're married."

He looked at me as if I had no brains. "Because that's the way it's supposed to be! You're only supposed to do it if you're married."

I thought of Daddy again. "If you're married, does it matter who you do it to?"

"Of course it does! You're only supposed to do it with the person you marry!" He looked at me and laughed nervously. "So . . . " He drew the word out slowly. "I'm telling you all this because I've got a problem . . . a problem you can probably help me out with."

"Okay."

"I've never . . . never done it before, and . . . " He hesitated and cleared this throat. "So, I'm afraid I won't be any good doing it, and I was wondering—"

Just then Jenny and Amy ran up to the screen. "Othello! Come out and play!"

I slid off the bed, ready to join them.

"Wait!" Mason held up his hand. "I'm not through talking to you."

"In a minute!" I yelled at them. "I'll be out in a minute." Wishing he would hurry up and say what he had to say, I sat back down on the bed.

When Jenny and Amy ran back to their game, Mason took a long breath and said, "I need to practice."

I just stared at him, not sure what he meant.

"Practice doing it. And I was wondering if you would . . . if you would . . . let me practice . . . using the rubber . . . with you."

I looked at Mason a long time. The last thing I wanted to do was let him down. I loved him far more than I loved Daddy. He never raised his voice . . . he was always gentle and kind . . . and I knew he wouldn't ask me if he could have practiced with someone else. So, finally, I asked, "Will it take long?" I honestly resented losing playtime for such a dumb thing.

"I don't think so."

Grudgingly, I said, "Okay."

A few minutes later, I gritted my teeth against the pain. I wanted to help him but I could only stand it for a few seconds. "Stop! You've got to stop!" I gasped. "It hurts!"

He stopped instantly. "I'm sorry," he said. "I didn't mean to hurt you." He quickly left the room and came back with his pants zipped and his belt buckled again. Sitting beside me, he took my hand. "I'm really, really sorry."

"It's okay." I ignored the stinging. "Can I go out and play now?"

"Of course. But . . . are you all right? You're . . . you're not bleeding or anything are you?"

I didn't know; I hadn't looked.

"I'm okay!" I snapped. "I just want to go play!"

He nodded. "Go ahead."

I felt no resentment for the physical pain. I knew Mason had not intended to hurt me, and I knew he wouldn't have asked me if Annette had let him practice.

Neither Mason nor I ever mentioned his "practicing" but sometimes when he looked at me I thought he was still sorry he hurt me.

Days seemed chaotic and sometimes exhausting but I thought life would have been bearable if we could have skipped school. Day after day of humiliation and grumbling stomachs made it too miserable to remain in class. Jenny and I began feigning sickness again, and playing hooky every time we thought we could get away with it.

Then, one day, without planning it, we both ended up in the "sick room" together. This time, the nurse called Daddy. Terrified of the outcome, we waited silently as the principal talked with him.

Minutes later, as he drove us home, he said, "Well, I don't know what I'm gonna do. I'm not too worried about you, Othello, because you're almost grown. In a couple of years, you can go to work as a waitress. You don't need schoolin' for that, but Jenny . . . I don't know about her. She's still got a ways to go."

For the first time, I knew that Daddy was wrong about something. Even though I hated school, I knew I should be there, at least trying to learn. I couldn't think of what would make it tolerable, but I knew it was the right thing to do and I was ashamed of Daddy for not knowing that.

Don Corners Daddy

It was a Saturday and I was wondering what to do when Thurmond shouted, "Don's home! Don's home!"

We rushed to the door, then ran out to the car that had pulled up to our apartment. Don got out, smiling, and grabbed each of us as we piled on.

We clung to his hands and arms and stared in amazement at his grown-up size.

"Look at those muscles!" Thurmond said. "They're like Popeye's!"

Don laughed, asking each one of us what we had been doing. "You doing okay in school?"

Jenny and I glanced at each other. "Yeah," we lied.

"That's good," he said. "Momma would want you to do your best, you know."

Guilt swept through me, almost making me sick.

"Hey, Mason," Don slapped his brother on the shoulder. "Got any beer in there?" He inclined his head toward the kitchen.

"Shit, I wish. There ain't nothing in there except maybe some cereal and baloney."

"Then let's get some!"

"Can we go? Can we go?" We chorused.

"Sure, come on." He herded us out to the car. "Girls in the back," he said playfully as he, Thurmond, and Mason slid onto the front seat.

An hour later we were home again with six bags of groceries and beer for Don and Mason. It wasn't until we were putting away the food that Thurmond said, "It's a good thing you weren't here last year, or you'd of been sent to the orphanage, too. And you'd of hated it as much as me, I bet."

Don stared at him. "The what?"

Thurmond repeated, "The orphanage."

Don's face paled. His lips pressed together and his dark eyes narrowed. Then his expression eased a little. "Oh, yeah?" He looked at Mason and nodded toward the door. "Let's go outside a minute."

Mason immediately got up. The rest of us went into the kitchen, climbed over the counters, and put away the rest of the groceries.

It was after dark when Daddy came by. He opened the front door and stepped inside, asking, "Whose car—?" He stopped short when he saw Don. No one spoke because we all knew, by then, why Don's mood had gone sour. For the past two years, while he had been working in Colorado, he had been sending most of his paycheck to Daddy, to help take care of us. He had no idea we had been put in the orphanage.

"Hello, Don," Daddy said as he closed the door and started across the room, his eyes down, avoiding all of us.

"You want to talk—outside?" Don asked.

Daddy stopped. "About what?"

"About me sending home almost every cent I made to take care of these young'uns, and they were in an orphanage the whole damn time!"

Daddy almost smiled. "So now you know."

Don stood. "Why, you sorry—"

"Go ahead and hit me!" Daddy yelled. "I know you want to. Go ahead! Hit me!"

Don took a step forward, then stopped. After a moment, he said, "No. I'm not gonna hit you. I'm not gonna be the excuse for your next drunk."

"Go ahead! Hit me!" Daddy yelled. "I can take it!"

Don grunted a scoffing laugh. "You also ought to know that I stopped in Altus on the way here. I was looking for you. Thought you still lived there." He made no effort to disguise his contempt. "And guess who I saw? Ol' Doc Mabrey. He walked right up to me and said, 'Aren't you Russell James' oldest son?' and when I nodded, he said, 'Well, I was the one who delivered you, and your daddy's not paid me yet. Maybe you'd like to do it.'"

"Shee-it!" Mason groaned.

Don kept his steady, angry gaze on Daddy. "You know . . . it's a sorry day when you gotta pay for your own ass being brought into this world."

Daddy chuckled and Don's face and neck flushed. He strode away from Daddy and stared out the window. "You'd better leave until I'm gone."

Daddy gave a short, quick nod, turned, and left. For a moment, I felt sorry for Daddy. I wasn't sure I understood all the reasons Don was angry, but I was so happy to be with him, it didn't take me long to forget Daddy. Within minutes, Don and Mason relaxed, talking and laughing like they had before Momma died.

When we crawled into bed that night, Don came over and sat with us for awhile. "You girls be good," he said, patting our hands and faces. "I'll be gone in the morning when you get up, so I want you to know before you go to sleep . . . I love you. And I always will."

We promised our undying love, and Don was gone when we woke up the next morning.

The Awful News

Ralph at the gas station saw Thurmond running out the back door with candy. He yelled, but Thurmond kept running. We all thought he got away with it until later that evening when Daddy came over and said, "All right, you kids. Get in here, we've got to talk."

We gathered around, wondering what had happened. Daddy had never called us all together except to lay out the rules when we first left the Baptist Home.

He lit a cigarette, sat on the edge of the bed, and said, "This afternoon, someone from the City called me. He told me that I have to put you in an orphanage or get someone to take care of you, and I don't have the money for that."

Everyone except Mason started to cry. He just sat there, an angry look on his face as he stared at Daddy.

"Othello?" Daddy said, "This is more your fault than anyone else's. You let me down. You didn't take care of things the way you said you would."

"I tried!" I wailed. "Gimme another chance! I'll do better."

"Your Momma told you to take care of the little 'uns. I heard her."

For a moment, I felt such shame and cried so hard, I thought I might throw up. When I looked at Daddy again, he was crying, too, and the guilt I felt for making him cry was worse than I had ever felt. When I couldn't stand it anymore, I tried to comfort him. "It's okay, Daddy. We want to go back."

He looked up. "What?"

"I said . . . it's okay. We . . . want to go back."

Daddy's tears dried so quickly, I felt betrayed, as if he was just waiting for me to say something that would take the blame off him.

"No!" Thurmond screamed, "I'm not going back! I'm not! I hated it! Hated it!"

"Okay," Daddy said, "You can stay and work at the shop."

His tears now dried, Daddy said, "All right, you kids get in the car. We're going to call *the orphanage*."

Mason didn't move. "I'm not," he said. "I'm not going to be part of this."

"Then you stay here and watch Amy."

Jenny, Thurmond, and I got in the car and Daddy drove us to the corner to a pay phone. He handed me a piece of paper with a number on it and said, "That's the number to the Baptist Home. Call it and tell them you want to come back."

My stomach knotted at the thought of it. I looked at the phone booth and felt as if I were betraying Jenny and Amy. I got out of the car but my feet and legs didn't want to move. Finally, I made it to the phone booth. I took the receiver off the phone but wasn't tall enough to talk into the mouthpiece. Daddy sent Thurmond to hold me up so I could dial the number and talk.

When a female voice answered, I told her my name and said that Daddy had to bring us back.

"Othello! I remember you! What did you say? Your Daddy wants to bring you back?"

"Yes, ma'am."

"Well, where are you living now, Othello?"

"In Lubbock, Texas."

"Oh." There was a long pause. "Well, dear, you tell your Daddy that we can't take you back. We only accept children who reside in Oklahoma."

My heart skipped a joyous beat. We couldn't go back! I heard her say that, but I wasn't sure what she meant. "Ah, what's reside?"

"We only take children who live in Oklahoma."

"Oh, thank you! Thank you!" I slammed the phone down and Thurmond dropped me back to the floor. "We don't have to go!" I yelled. "They won't take us back!"

I dashed to the car, bubbling over with the good news. "They won't take us, Daddy, because we live in Texas! They only take kids from Oklahoma!"

"Shit!" He glared at me. "Get in the car!"

Jenny and I held hands and smiled at each other even though Daddy didn't say anything on the way home. Once we were inside the apartment, he yelled and swore about the home's stupid, goddamn rules.

Practically holding our breaths, we went to bed sooner and more quietly than ever before. None of us wanted to rile him further. Maybe if we just went to bed and stayed quiet, he would calm down and tomorrow everything would be better.

From the dining room, where we slept, I heard Daddy hounding Mason. "Didn't you tell me about an orphanage you saw near Altus?"

"No. I don't think so."

Daddy stormed across the room. "Don't lie to me, boy! I know goddamn good-and-well, you told me you saw an orphanage just on the other side of the Red River last year!"

Mason stared straight ahead. "Must've been someone else."

"Dammit! It was you! I remember. Where was it? Somewhere over in Tillman County. Right?"

Daddy kept yelling until Mason cried, and said, "It's in Tipton."

"Tipton. That's right. All right. We'll get their things together in the morning and leave by noon. You'll drive."

Jenny and I both heard the horrible news and cried ourselves to sleep, clinging to each other.

The next morning, the strange old woman who lived in the tiny trailer, sent a neighbor to tell Jenny and me to come visit her. Daddy didn't care; he wanted us out of the way. "Don't be gone long!" he barked.

The trailer was as dark and scary as it had been before. "Come in! Come in!" she urged as we pressed our noses against the screen. We climbed inside to find her sitting exactly where she had been before, on the small bed against the wall.

"I know you're going away." She took our hands. "And I wanted to say goodbye."

Jenny and I glanced at each other. We hadn't even thought of her—or the rosaries—since the day she gave them to us.

"Do you still have the rosaries?"

We nodded.

"They're in a safe place," Jenny volunteered. "With our special things."

"Good. Keep them with you at all times. Use them to pray and God will hear you."

"We're going to another orphanage," I said, hoping that telling her would somehow break the curse that forced us to go.

She nodded, her eyes shiny with tears. "I know. Just remember to pray. Pray a lot. You'll be okay. That much I know. It won't be easy, but you'll be okay."

In the distance, we heard Thurmond calling us. "Come on! We've got to go!"

She nodded, reached to touch our hands, and said, "God speed."

From that moment on, there was no time to discuss the old woman or her strange accent and words. Daddy told us to put our best clothes in a bag and to get ready to go.

The rosaries, with their mysterious power, were the first things packed.

Chapter 12

The Separation

The trip to the Tipton Orphans Home was an endless nightmare of sadness and crying. Mason drove, tears occasionally wetting his cheeks and his jaw muscle working in anger and frustration. Daddy sat in the passenger's side of the front seat, staring straight ahead except for occasionally yelling back at us, "Stop the goddamn crying! I can't hear myself think!" Thinking there might still be some hope that he would change his mind, I tried to set a good example, and although I couldn't stop the tears, I swallowed the sounds the best I could. Jenny and Amy sobbed endlessly. Depressed beyond words, I stared out at the miles and miles of lonely, country roads, feeling as though we were being dumped off the face of the earth.

When, at last, Daddy folded a map and said to Mason, "Should be just a few miles up the road," my senses sharpened to all the details of the countryside. I wanted to remember, to know how to escape if I had to.

When Mason turned onto a sweeping U-shaped gravel driveway and stopped, we stared up at an imposing red-brick, two-story building with huge columns supporting a porch. From the backseat of the car, I saw huge letters carved into the top of the building. Intimidated by their size, I asked, "What's it say, Mason?"

"Tipton Orphans Home." His voice cracked as he read.

"Come on. Get out." Daddy opened our door. Fresh tears flowed quickly as we slid across the seat and climbed out.

Mason didn't move from behind the steering wheel. When Daddy leaned down to look at him, Mason said, "I can't go in there. I can't watch this."

"Mason! Mason!" We ran to him for goodbye hugs. His cheeks were warm and wet. "Be good." He whispered. "I love you."

Our steps crunched across the gravel driveway. The towering door seemed heavy for Daddy to open and the vast lobby and offices of the empty Administration building echoed with our footsteps. Eight vinyl chairs faced each other, four on either side of a fireplace at the back of the room. These, and the water fountain were the only items in the room, except for pictures of a deer and a rabbit painted on the wall.

Daddy pointed to the chairs, telling us to sit, and we did.

"Please, Daddy, we'll be good. We'll go to school." Jenny reached out, trying to touch him.

"I'll keep the house clean. I won't cut the taters too thick! Please, don't leave us!"

When he wouldn't look at us, and there was nothing to stop the pain, we ran to him, clinging, hugging, and sobbing. "Don't leave us, Daddy! Don't leave us again!"

"Sit down!" He pushed us away, "I've got no choice! Don't you understand!"

We didn't sit down. "Just give me another chance," I begged. "I can do better. I know I can."

He shook his head and blinked back tears.

"Momma wouldn't want us here, Daddy! She wouldn't!" I hoped I could shame him into listening to us. "Please, don't do this!"

Suddenly, he pushed us back more forcefully. "Can't you see I don't want you? I don't want you!"

His words took my breath away. Overwhelmed by the sudden hopelessness of the situation, I stopped begging. I told myself that he didn't mean it, because otherwise he wouldn't be crying, but deep down in a small part of my stomach, I knew he meant it. Despair deepened until there were no thoughts of hope left.

Amy continued to cry and Jenny kept trying to reason with Daddy, making promises no one could keep. "I'll never do anything wrong again! I'll never lie. I'll never skip school. Please, Daddy . . . !"

Two women appeared from different directions, entering through doors that led into hallways. The gray-haired woman looked stern, big, and slow. The other, younger and stronger looking, smiled, exposing teeth too big for her mouth. Terrified, we clung to each other. "No! No! Don't let 'em take us, Daddy! Don't let 'em take us."

"Good afternoon," the older woman said to Daddy. "I apologize. We were in the dining room and didn't know you were here."

Daddy followed the older woman into an office and the younger one sat in a chair facing us. "Hi. What's your names?"

We didn't speak. This time we would be wiser. We wouldn't let them separate us.

The woman kept asking questions. "How old are you? Who's the oldest? What grades are you in?"

Silently, we clung to each other, afraid to divulge anything.

She pointed to the pictures behind us. "Did you see the murals of Bambi and Thumper?"

Jenny and I looked at each other, no idea what she meant and no interest in anything she had to say. My eyes darted frantically toward the office where I had seen Daddy disappear because I didn't want him slipping out the way he had at the Baptist Home. This time, at least, I wanted to say goodbye.

Just then, Daddy and the older woman appeared and I felt better.

"Hello, girls." She smiled at us and spoke in a happy voice, as if we would be glad to see her. I glanced at Daddy, who turned quickly and headed for the front door, his face scarlet and twisted in pain.

"No! Daddy! Don't go yet! Don't go!"

Frozen in horror, we clung to each other.

"Come on, girls." The women approached us. "It's time to go meet some of the other children."

We refused to budge. They put their hands on our shoulders and gently tugged. We clung to each other.

"Girls . . . now, it doesn't have to be this hard," the toothy one said. "You can't just stand here, crying."

Their fingers pried and pulled at our shoulders and arms. When we felt our grips loosening, we screamed each other's names.

Amy was the first to be separated. Screaming and crying, she tried to run back to us. Another woman appeared and Jenny and I were pried apart, our wails echoing off the vacant lobby walls.

Confused and sick to my stomach, I thought about Daddy and how he had been crying as he hurried out, and I couldn't understand why he would leave us if it hurt him. It wasn't right. It just wasn't right.

Behind the Administration building, eight or ten long, gray buildings sat on the sprawling dead-grass campus. As I was led to the one where I would live, I wondered if I would ever see Jenny and Amy again.

I later learned that the gray, slate-tiled buildings were W.W.II Army barracks. Rows of bunk beds stood on either side of the long dormitory and every girl was assigned a wooden footlocker at the end of her bed. There were also foot-wide metal lockers in the dressing and shower area, where we hung our clothes. This time, at least, I knew what pajamas were.

The campus seemed huge and barren, with a few trees to break the monotony of the landscape. Only the barracks and a half dozen trees scattered over the campus interrupted the view of the never-ending Oklahoma flatness. A bell tower in the center of the campus rang three times a day, calling us all to the dining room. A "kitchen girl" pulled the rope that sent the message to every dorm.

Jenny, Amy, and I were separated by distance as well as walls, and it was days before I even learned where their buildings were. Knowing, gave me a little sense of security, but we weren't allowed beyond our own dorms, except to go to the dining room. Only there could I catch glimpses of Jenny as her dorm filed in, but Amy was placed in the nursery, which had its own kitchen and dining room.

Unlike the first orphanage, there were no swings, slides, or playground equipment, and very few toys. Cleaning consumed much of our time, as did braiding rugs and pot holders from long strips of rags. The only outside games were jumping rope or spontaneous games of tag.

We went to church, in town, Sunday morning, Sunday evening, and Wednesday evenings. We sat still through chapel services before school and through Bible study classes on Monday evenings. Only Saturday was free from any kind of religious service. The first week I sat through each, oblivious to what was being said from the pulpit and praying that God would somehow intervene and rescue us. At night, I sneaked my treasured rosary from its hiding place and prayed the same prayer.

Orphan's Haircut

Eight days after I arrived, an older girl approached me and said, "Time to get your hair cut."

"I don't want my hair cut."

"Doesn't matter. Follow me."

Knowing it was useless to argue, I followed her to a small building near the laundry. Once she had opened the door, the girl left. A plump woman with bluish hair and a matching mustache stood behind a barber chair, clipping another girl's hair into a "Buster Brown" bob.

"So you're Othello." The woman glanced at me, then went on clipping. "I'm Sister Wellington, the Superintendent's wife and the Dean of Girls."

Her introduction meant nothing to me. I was only aware of the lack of warmth in her voice.

"I was gone when you arrived, and Brother Wellington is still out of town."

I sat in one of the wooden folding chairs. "Do I have to get my hair cut?"

"Everybody gets their hair cut," she said, whisking the cape off the girl in the chair. She ran a brush over the girl's neck and said, "Off you go! Back to work!"

While I submitted to Sister Wellington's Buster Brown specialty—the only haircut worn by girls under fourteen—she explained how the home "worked." Her husband was boss, she was the next boss, and all the matrons were bosses. Kids older than ten were expected to work at some job and she assigned the jobs, which included working in the kitchen, the laundry, the dormitory, or the office. "Only the older girls work in the office," she added. "And since you're only nine, you won't have to work for another year.

However, you'll still be expected to help out in your dormitory. Everyone does what they can."

"Why can't I live with my sisters?" As I waited for her answer, I stared at the piles of hair on the floor.

"Because," she finally said, "we've found that it's best to keep families separated. That way, there's lots less trouble."

"Whatta ya mean?"

"I mean scheming . . . plotting . . . and planning mischief together. When you live in different dormitories, none of that goes on."

I wanted to like this woman and to have her like me, but her emotionless voice implied she didn't like me, and everything she said made me like her less.

Your Mother Went to Hell

Later that week, two matrons sat on a bench, watching the girls in my dorm play outside while killing the last few minutes before supper. Waiting for the kitchen girl to ring the bell, some involved themselves in a game of tag while others of us just stood around and watched.

"I heard your momma died," a girl named Julie said.

Still unable to admit that Momma was dead, I neither denied nor confirmed it.

"What church did she belong to?" Julie asked, pushing herself further into my space. Her demanding tone forced me to take a step back and prompted two other girls to step closer to see what was happening.

"Baptist," I said. "We went to the Baptist church."

"Then when she died, she went to hell!" Julie's triumphant tone enraged me as much as her words.

"No!" I stepped back. "That's not true!"

Julie pressed closer. "She's burning in hell right now!"

"You don't know my momma!" I yelled. "How can you say that?"

"Cause I know!"

"Yeah!" another girl taunted, "We all know! Because she wasn't a member of the Church of Christ!"

I stared, dumbfounded. "What?"

"Only members of the Church of Christ go to heaven!" Julie taunted. "So your momma went to hell. She burning up right now!"

Memories of seeing my mother writhing on the ground, engulfed in flames, made me cringe.

"Say it!" Julie shoved me. "Say my momma went to hell!"

All I could do was scream, "No! Get away from me!" then turn and run, crying at the horrible images filling my mind.

"Say it! Say it!" They ran after me. "Say my momma went to hell!"

I ran around a small tool-shed near our dormitory, aware that the matrons were sitting on the bench and could see and hear us. Gasping, running as fast as I could, I hoped one of them would intervene.

"Say it! Say it!"

Someone threw a rock and hit me in the head. The gang—which had grown to four girls—tackled me. I fell hard, face down. While they held me down, they all screamed and chanted, "Say my mother went hell! Say it! Say it!"

Twisting my face off the ground, I spat dirt and dead grass and looked between their legs to see the matrons sitting on the bench. I had hoped for help but instead, saw the matrons watching and laughing. At that moment, my dread intensified. There would be no help. No protection. I was truly on my own.

Wincing against the bony knees pinning me to the ground, I cried and begged God to forgive me for the lie I was about to tell. I knew Momma wasn't burning in hell. In fact, in the most secret place of my heart, I still believed she was alive. Why she didn't come home from the hospital, I wasn't sure . . . but the mannequin they buried certainly wasn't her. I didn't know why someone was keeping her from us, but I knew for sure that she wasn't in hell. None of that mattered at the moment, however. I had to say it.

"Say it! Say it!"

The yelling continued. Other girls had come to watch.

Would it do any damage to Momma when she got to heaven if I lied? Would God remember my lie and punish her for it?

"Twist her arm! She'll say it."

The instant before someone grabbed my arm and twisted it behind my back, between their skinny legs I saw a kitchen girl about to ring the supper bell.

"My momma went to hell." Strength slipped away and I stopped struggling.

"She said it! She said it!"

My guts heaved. I knew I would never say uglier words or tell a more horrible lie . . . and I hated them for it. My hatred for the girls, however, paled in comparison to my hatred and distrust of the matrons on the bench. As the bell sounded, they stood, pulled at the seat of their dresses and laughing, waved for us to form a line to walk to the dining room.

Everyone scattered. The entertainment had ended. I moved to the back of the line. I had to get out of this horrible place. If God wasn't going to answer my prayers and send someone for us, I'd just have to think of a way to do it myself.

Unable to turn my back on the advice of the old woman in the trailer, I couldn't resist one more attempt to solve my problem with the rosary, so after supper, I sneaked it out of its hiding place and carried it outside. With no one around to disturb me, I tried to recall the old woman's words. *Run your fingers over the beads as you pray. God will hear you.*

I closed my eyes, let the beads play through my fingers, and thought the words of my prayer carefully as I whispered them to myself. "Please let someone come and get us. Please don't make us stay here."

"What's that?" The matron's strident voice interrupted my prayer, and before I could look up, she yanked at the rosary.

I held on with both hands. "Just beads!" I said. "Just a necklace!"

"Where did you get that evil thing?" She screeched as though I were holding a snake. "Give it to me, right now!"

I jerked away but she grabbed it. We both tugged. It broke in two places and beads bounced on the concrete.

"That's evil! Evil! Where did you get it?"

I wasn't about to incriminate the nice old woman who gave it to me. "I found it."

"It's the devil's tool! Don't touch it! It's going into the trash, right now!"

Her hysteria confused me.

"It's not evil! I was talking to God!"

"Ha!" She picked up the beads and dropped the whole thing in her pocket. "You weren't talking to God with this! You were talking to the devil!"

That night, in bed, I knew that without the beads, I didn't stand a chance of rescue. There was only one option. I had to figure out a way to get out—and take Jenny with me if I could. There was no way to take Amy because I never saw her, but there might . . . just might be . . . a way to contact Jenny if I really thought about it.

Running Away

Church provided more time to think than any other place. At least there, I could ignore what was being said and think my own thoughts. So, it was there that I plotted our escape.

The only opportunity would have to come in the dining room because that was the only place I saw Jenny. We were still new enough that most of the kids and matrons didn't know our names, so I had to take advantage of the situation, somehow.

For the plan to work, it had to involve the matron because, without her permission, there was no way I could talk to Jenny.

The rosary. I would use the rosary to get the permission I needed.

The next Sunday, after church, as we lined up to go to the dining room, I hurried to get in front of the line, so I could talk to the matron. Timing was everything, so I had to plan carefully. There would only be two or three minutes from the time we entered the dining room until we were expected to be standing quietly behind our chairs waiting for the blessing to be said.

"Miss Sharply," I said in my friendliest voice as we neared the dining room. "I'm glad you told me about the evil necklace."

She raised a skeptic eyebrow.

"Really!" I added. "I am! I'd hate to go to hell because I didn't know about it. It's evil powers and all."

"Good," she said, warming a bit. "I only did what any good Christian would do."

"Well, I feel better knowing the devil won't get me through the necklace. And I just wanted to thank you."

"You're a smart girl to understand so quickly." She pulled herself up, pleased with the good she had done.

We rapidly approached the entrance to the dining room. "But you know what, Miss Sharply . . . my sister, Jenny, has one, too. I don't want her to go to hell, either, so I wrote a note telling her all about it."

"Good. Good."

Other dormitories converged on the entrance, as we did. My moment of opportunity would come inside, in the confusion, as the dining room filled with 180 kids and twenty-five or thirty matrons. That few minutes of noise and commotion were my only hope.

I waited until we had moved halfway down the dining room toward our table before I reached in my pocket and grabbed the piece of paper I had put there. "I'll run give Jenny the note before we sit down!" I moved away as I spoke.

Bodies pushed toward tables, voices rose, kids bumped each other and in the midst of the confusion, Miss Sharply gave a quick, irritated nod, and I disappeared into the crowd. When I reached Jenny, I grabbed her hand and said, "Follow me."

Without a word or a moment's hesitation, she gripped my hand and we wiggled our way through the larger bodies and sneaked out the door. "Don't run," I whispered. I dropped her hand. "Just walk natural. Like we've been sent to go somewhere and do something."

Two or three of the older kids looked our way and cocked their heads curiously, but no one made a move to stop us. By the time the prayer was said and kids sat down to eat, we had made it safely off the campus where we broke into a run.

"Where we going?" Jenny asked.

"To Altus. To Daddy."

"You know how to get there?"

"Yes."

Actually, I wasn't sure Daddy was there, but I knew Aunt Lola Mae would be, and she would help us find him.

"There's a car coming! Get in the bushes!" I pushed Jenny toward the growth along the road. "Stay down."

We squatted and hid, waited for the car to pass, then got up and started running again.

We made it, unnoticed, to the highway, where I knew we had to turn. It didn't take long to trot past the few houses and be in the clear again. Soon, on either side of us, cotton fields stretched as far as we could see.

"My side hurts!" Jenny complained. "Let's stop awhile."

We ran between rows of cotton and sat down. It took us several minutes to catch our breaths. As we rested, Jenny began to cry. "I hate the home!" she said. "I hated it the first day we got there."

"Me, too."

She wiped her eyes on the hem of her dress. "The very first day, when they took me to my dormitory, there was girls in the hall, just sitting there, with panties on their heads. Dirty panties. They said the matron made them sit there with the dirty side of their panties on their heads because they forgot to wash them the night before."

"Do you have any nice kids there?"

She didn't seem to hear me. "And there's dolls, real pretty dolls, but we can't touch them."

"Why?"

"I don't know. They're up on a high shelf by the ceiling."

"That's stupid."

A few cars and pickups passed but we were out of sight. "We've got to keep going," I said. "I don't know how long it'll take us to get to Altus. It might get dark."

She nodded, wiped her eyes on her dress, and we ran back out to the highway. The flat terrain allowed us to see cars coming long before they reached us, giving us plenty of time to dart back into the cotton patch and hide. I wasn't too concerned about cars coming into Tipton, only the ones heading out of town - who might be looking for us.

"See that house up there?" I pointed to a farmhouse up the road.

"Yeah."

"Well, if anyone stops and wants to know who we are, say we live there."

"They won't know, huh?" She smiled.

The chance to test our story came almost immediately. We saw a blue and white sedan, heading into Tipton, so didn't worry too much about it. Then, as it approached, it began to slow and a man about fifty, in a white shirt and tie, stopped in the middle of the road. He didn't get out of the car but yelled, "Where are you girls going?"

"Home. We live over there." We both pointed.

He shook his head. "I don't think so."

"Yes, we do!"

"Why don't you get in the car and let me drive you home?"

"No!"

He opened the door and got out. "Well, I can tell from your haircuts—"

"Run, Jenny! Run!" We dashed into the cotton field, pushing our way through the weaker plants, snagging our dresses and legs. The man walked to the edge of the field and stood with his hands on his hips.

"Keep running!" She followed me like a shadow. After we had made it back several rows, I said, "Now, get down!" We fell to our knees and crawled. "He can't see us now. He won't remember where we were. Keep crawling!"

I peeked up occasionally to check on the man's whereabouts. He stood with his hands on his hips for several minutes, staring after us, then got into the car and drove off.

"He's gone!" I said. "But he'll tell someone else and they'll come looking for us!"

We looked down the long rows of cotton, which seemed to run to the edge of the earth, and ran as fast and hard as our legs would take us. Sweat and red dirt collected on our faces, hands, and legs.

"Wait!" Jenny suddenly stopped, panting. "We can't go down there! There's bulls down at the end!"

Gasping, I stopped and stared toward the end of the field. "That's not bulls! It's cotton pickers!"

"No!" She shook her head. "They're bulls!

I looked again. "Cotton pickers! They won't hurt us! Come on! We've got to go!"

"No! I'm not going to no bulls!"

Frantic about what to do, I looked in every direction. We couldn't run in another direction. It was either straight forward . . . or back, and that was unthinkable.

Then I saw two pickups pull to the edge of the field and stop. "Get down!"

We both dived to the ground. "They're coming for us! The old man told!"

"I don't wanna go back!" Jenny cried. "I ain't going back!"

"Hide!" I yelled. "They can't be sure where we are! They're out by the road."

"Hide, where?" She cried.

"Get up under the cotton! Far as you can. And don't cry! Be quiet!"

No more than ten feet in front of her, I followed my own directions. The scratchy plants caught on my clothes and dug into my arms and legs but still I scooted as far under them as I could.

Neither of us made a sound. The field fell silent except for the wind rushing through the plants, whipping fine dirt against my skin. I buried my face against my arm, listening for voices or footsteps.

Finally, I heard footsteps. I held my breath.

"Well, looky here." It was a man's voice. He sounded amused. I froze.

Then Jenny screamed. "No! No! Leave me alone!"

The man laughed. More footsteps hurried closer. Other men laughed.

"I got me one, too!"

I opened my eyes just enough to see the toes of boots standing only inches from my face. I cringed. Something horrible happened inside me—something like falling and knowing I was going to die.

"Come on, now." Huge hands pulled at my arm.

"No! Get away! Get away!" As the words left my mouth, I was lifted into the air, kicking and screaming, and held at arms length.

"Ain't she a feisty little thing!" the man laughed. "Come on, now. Settle down. No one's going to hurt you."

I wasn't afraid of being hurt. It was the dread of going back to the orphanage that made me fight. I flung myself about, trying to break his grip.

"If you'll stop kicking, and promise not to run, I'll put you down," he said.

"She won't get very far," another man laughed.

I knew it was true. They weren't going to let us go, and the realization sickened me. Jenny and I cried as they walked us to the edge of the field, where Sister Wellington waited beside a car, the back door open.

Beads of sweat clung to her bluish mustache. "Where were you girls going?"

"To Daddy. In Altus. "

"Well, get in the car."

We both dropped to the ground, crying. "We don't want to go back to the home. We want to live with Daddy!"

"If you get in the car, I'll take you there."

As her words sunk in, we looked up and wiped our eyes and noses. "You'll take us to Daddy?"

"If you get in the car."

The men who had caught us turned and left, laughing and talking.

"Do you know where he lives?" Jenny asked.

"I can find him, I'm sure. Now, get in the car."

A rush of excitement brought us to our feet. We brushed ourselves off and climbed into the backseat. Both of us gave Miss Wellington all the information we had about Aunt Lola Mae's house and explained that she would know where he was.

"It's a white house with big trees on the street."

"It's called Live Oak!" I suddenly remembered.

"I'll know it when I see it!" Jenny assured her.

Then Miss Wellington turned the wrong way—back toward the orphanage.

"You lied!" I screamed. "You lied to us!"

Miss Wellington didn't look back.

The sinking, falling feeling grew worse. It wasn't just in my stomach, but my mind and someplace so deep inside it made my whole body tremble and sweat. Again, as on the day the matrons had watched while I was pinned to the ground and forced to tell the worst lie ever told . . . I realized that no one could be trusted. They either did nothing to help or lied and promised to help, but didn't. They just tricked us to get what they wanted.

Our dread deepened and our tears continued as we approached the orphanage. Once inside the Administration building, we were both spanked, and Jenny's matron came and walked her to her dormitory. Mrs. Wellington walked me down a hall to a long, skinny closet where two long racks of dresses hung.

The stuffy, overheated room smelled of mothballs and there was hardly room to move. Mrs. Wellington took a stack of clothes from a chair in the corner and sat down. "I want to tell you a few things, Othello."

I could tell from her voice that she wasn't angry anymore, but my depression held my eyes focused on the floor.

"First," she continued, "I want you to know that if you run away again, you won't get to go to Bible camp and you won't get your vacation with your clothing people."

When I didn't move or respond, she asked, "Do you know what clothing people are?"

I shook my head, no.

"They're members of the Church of Christ. Nice people who send you clothes. We don't have clothing people for you yet, but we'll have them before long. Anyway," she said, waving her hand as if she knew I didn't really understand, "kids who do what they're told and don't run away, get a week or two off during the summer to spend with their clothing people."

I shrugged. I didn't want clothes. I didn't want clothing people. I wanted to leave the home.

"So . . . since you don't have any clothing people yet, I brought you in here to let you pick out a new dress. You need a nice church dress." She stood. "Go ahead and look them over . . . here, in this section . . . these should fit you."

"I don't care if I have a nice dress."

"Well, you need one. So—" She gestured toward the section of smaller dresses.

"You pick," I said.

Mrs. Wellington pulled several dresses off the rack, held them up to me, then hung them back. She could have handed me a gunnysack as far as I was concerned.

"Okay." She handed me a red and white striped dress. "I think you'll like this."

I knew she was trying to be nice and one side of my mind felt ashamed that I couldn't be nicer myself, but the best I could do was take the dress and walk to the door to leave. To me, the dress was ugly, but so was everything I saw.

My matron, Miss Sharply, didn't seem happy to have me back. "Go clean up. You're a filthy mess!"

I hung the new dress in my locker and took off my dust-covered clothes. When I found the note in my pocket—the one I had used to trick Miss Sharply—I opened it and smiled. It was blank. I had made her think I could read and write, and I almost got away! Realizing I had pulled off *that part* of my scheme flawlessly, I used my time in the shower to begin planning my next escape.

More School Problems

The home had its own elementary school and I was put in the third grade, where I suffered daily because I couldn't read and was too ashamed to admit it. I had no particular trouble with the arithmetic, but felt completely lost with anything to do with reading and spelling.

I listened closely to what was read, however, so that I could answer questions now and then. I also paid close attention to which seats were empty each day so that when I returned from my well-timed trip to the bathroom—a trip I always took just before it was my turn to read—I could sit in one of them. I never knew if the teacher didn't notice or didn't care, but it worked.

Our teacher, Mr. Bunt, was a grouchy, round bellied man with a bald head and glasses. He never smiled. At least, not at us. He did, however, have a terrible limp (for some reason I never knew) and we could hear him ker-thumping down the hallway in plenty of time to get in our seats. Usually. When someone didn't make it, the day turned bad.

After a red-faced lecture, someone was usually bent over Mr. Bunt's desk. Sometimes he used a paddle and other times a thin rubber hose he carried, coiled up, in his back pocket. I was told that it was the kind of hose used on air conditioners—but that wasn't what he used it for.

I didn't care how it was used, as long as it wasn't used on me. Terrified that I would get a whipping or *worse*—that one of my sisters would—I tried to follow the rules.

A *Real* Orphan

"There are only two real orphans here," I overheard someone say. "The Whiteheads."

I knew Leanna Whitehead, a beautiful girl with dark curly hair, and smaller than me.

"She's got a picture of her dead parents."

Without waiting to hear more, I located Leanna and asked her about the picture, saying I would like to see it.

"Sure. It's in here." She opened her locker and pulled out a small box containing several photos. After shuffling through them a minute, she handed me a brown and white snapshot. Expecting to see a picture of her parents as they were alive, I stared in amazement at two open coffins (with corpses in them!) propped up against the side of an old weather-beaten house.

Dumbstruck and embarrassed, I looked from Leanna to the picture several times. Eventually, I realized there were other people in the picture and finally found my voice to ask, "Who are these people?"

"Aunts and uncles."

Handing the picture back, but unable to take my eyes off it, I asked, "How did they die?"

"My momma kilt my daddy then kilt herself," she said.

"Did you see it?"

She nodded, her huge violet eyes widening as she remembered.

"How'd . . . how'd she do it?"

She blinked several times, found a steady voice, and said, "She kilt him in the back with an ice pick, then got a gun and kilt herself in the head."

"You—you saw it?"

She nodded and put the picture back into the box. I wondered if her memories were worse than mine were. I decided they had to be. She saw *both* her parents die.

The photograph lingered in my mind, and I was impressed that Leanna could always be so pleasant and smiling. Her older sister, Lilly, who worked in the office, was also very tiny and beautiful. She laughed and smiled as if she was the happiest person on earth. She had a high, clear voice and sang solos in the home chorus.

From that point on, whenever I saw Lilly, I studied her, wanting to be like her someday.

Chapter 13

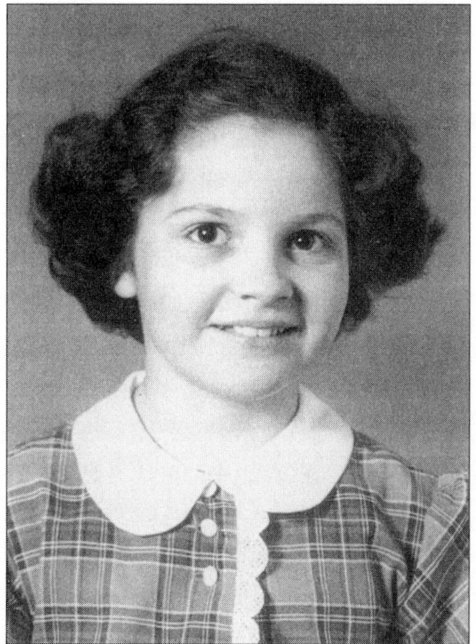

Othello, third grade

Nightmares of Momma

Shortly after seeing Leanna's picture, my nightmares returned. I kept dreaming of being locked in a room with an open coffin, with Momma's body in it. When I looked, it wasn't really Momma but a doll that looked like her. The doll would always open its eyes or start to sit up and I would wake up so terrified I couldn't breathe.

Then, I began to dream about little dolls again. They would come alive and want to bite me. As in the Baptist Home, in every dream, I was in a small place, hardly able to move, when I would see a stringy-haired, dirty doll. It would open its eyes, sneer, and say something terrifying, such as, "You'll never get out of here alive."

I would lie awake, staring at the ceiling, trying to stay awake.

Running Away Again

Two months after running away, using the plan that had almost worked before, Jenny and I slipped from the dining room ran away again. This time, though, we were spotted as we approached town. A pickup with two men inside pulled up behind us, and one of the men yelled, "Hey!"

Instantly, we ran toward a gas station on the corner, but the truck swerved around us and cut us off. We doubled back, but not before one of the men jumped out and grabbed us both.

We resisted less, but our depression deepened. We were put into the truck between the men and driven back to the home. Holding hands, we stared at each other and I saw the same hopelessness in Jenny's eyes that I felt. This time we hadn't even had a chance to talk to each other and find out what had been going on. Now, we wouldn't see each other again for months except for glances across the dining room.

This time, however, we were taken to Brother Wellington's office. As he stared at us across his desk, I recalled the first time we saw him. He was the man who stopped on the road when we first ran away.

"You gonna whip us?"

"No." He rolled a pencil between his hands as he talked. "But you will get a whipping. We can't have you girls running off every other week."

"But we don't wanna live here!" Jenny slumped in her chair. "We want you to take us to live with Daddy."

"He brought you here."

"Well, we hate it!" I said. "We hate everything about it!"

Mrs. Wellington stepped into the office and stood just inside the door. "Come with me, girls." Her mouth was a tight straight line beneath her mustache.

In her office, she took a long thick paddle from a cabinet, turned slowly, and said, "You know there will be no Bible camp and no vacation, now."

I didn't care about that. I still planned to get away from the home long before those things happened, but I did care about the paddle. She carried it around her desk and stood in front of us. "Jenny, bend over."

Crying, Jenny bent over the desk. I gritted my teeth and flinched each time the paddle fell and Jenny cried out. I thought I would go crazy before Mrs. Wellington finally stopped and Jenny dropped to the floor, rubbing her thighs and butt. Then, afraid she'd be hit again, she scrambled to the other side of the office.

I tried not to cry as I leaned over the desk and I held out as long as I could, but by the fourth hit, the pain erupted involuntarily through my mouth, and I cried out with every whack after that.

I was still rubbing the lumpy welts on my own butt and legs when Jenny's matron, Miss McGregor, came to get her. At the same time, Mrs. Wellington put the paddle down and said to me, "Go back to your dorm. You're in trouble. Big trouble."

My First Job

Miss Sharply waited for me outside the door, watching to make sure I didn't run away again. Once inside, she told me to go into her room. I stood just inside while she sat down and stared at me, her arms crossed, her mouth puckering, relaxing, then puckering again.

"You're going to start working tomorrow. In the laundry."

"I thought you had to be ten to work in the laundry or kitchen."

"Not in your case. You're a troublemaker. We'll all be better off if you're busy." Then she added as an afterthought, "You won't have time to be thinking up mischief. You'll start in the morning. I'll get you up at six."

I went to bed that night, glad to be assigned a job. I wanted to get out of the dormitory more and have more chances of seeing Jenny and Amy.

The laundry was a single-story building with twelve ironing boards, two long folding tables, and two large dryers that became so hot they "browned" the underwear and sheets.

A machine called an "extractor" spun the water from clothes and stood near a large wooden washing machine with a huge, single barrel that rolled over and over, slobbering suds and dribbling water into a concrete trough.

Two galvanized tubs of starch stood next to the extractor and two more tubs sat against the far wall, with rub boards for scrubbing extra dirty collars and socks.

The warm, moist laundry air smelled of soap and starch, and the constant activity of twelve or fifteen girls ironing, starching, folding, and scrubbing excited me. I recognized Elaine, the young, plump woman in charge of the laundry, as one of the women who separated me from my sisters when we first arrived. In the laundry, however, she didn't look so menacing. Instead, she smiled, her teeth still too big for her mouth, and introduced me to the other girls, all older than me.

I soon learned that Elaine and her family lived in town, which is maybe why she laughed more than the other matrons. Her husband also worked for the home and sometimes came in to talk to her. The first time I saw him, my knees went weak because he was the man who picked me up in the cotton field, the first time I ran away. Thankfully, he never mentioned it.

The best part of working in the laundry was that we were allowed to carry the clean clothes to all of the dormitories, and sometimes see our brothers and sisters.

On one trip to Jenny's dormitory, I walked in with a basket of clean sheets and caught Miss McGregor slapping Jenny repeatedly on the face and shoulders.

"What happened?" I yelled, dropping the basket. "What happened?"

All the girls in the dorm crowded around, thinking they were going to see a fight. Miss McGregor immediately stopped hitting Jenny, and panting and yelling, shooed the others toward the back of the dormitory.

With Miss McGregor out of the room, Jenny, still crying, tried to explain what happened.

"She thinks I stopped up a toilet but I didn't! It wasn't me!" She rubbed her face and arms. "It was Patsy Duvall. She makes big hard turds that won't go down!"

"Really?" I would have laughed but Jenny was too upset.

"She's 'spose to cut 'em up to flush 'em down," she continued, "but this time she didn't."

"Cut 'em up?"

"Yeah."

"With what?"

"A big ol' knife Miss McGregor has."

Finally, I laughed, imagining it.

"And Pasty didn't ask for the knife," Jenny continued. "She tried to flush it. Then when it stopped up the toilet and water started comin' up, Patsy ran! And I was just standing there staring at it! I don't even know how she did it! It looked like a brown baseball! And wouldn't go down!"

"That's enough!" Miss McGregor scolded, rushing back to Jenny. "Get back there with the rest of the girls! And you—!" She pointed at me. "Pick up those sheets, put 'em where they go, and get out of here!"

Later, I heard two stories about Patsy Duvall dying from something called "locked bowels." One person told me that she had run away and was found dead in a field and that she had died of "locked bowels." Someone else said she died in the hospital while they were operating on her for "locked bowels." I never knew which was true.

The Lost Arm

We worked in the laundry an hour before breakfast, then after school until supper. Two or three weeks into my job, I had learned the basics and worked all the jobs except ironing, a job done only by older girls.

Although I was the youngest, there were other girls just a year or two older than me who also sorted clothes, loaded the huge bubble-belching washing machine, took dripping piles of wet laundry and transferred them to the extractor, scrubbed filthy socks and stained collars on rub boards, dunked and starched what needed starching, loaded the dryers, folded hot clothes, and carried them to the dorms. When we weren't busy doing those things, we mopped the concrete floor because it became slippery from splattered sudsy-water and starch that had been tracked into the walkways.

Glenda Faye Hathaway, a year older than me, had a twin sister named Linda Mae. Glenda Faye worked in the laundry with me and Linda Mae was a "house girl" who cleaned the dormitory. Although not identical, the two looked enough alike that it was hard to tell them apart. Their blonde Buster Brown haircuts curled softly around their faces and their wide blue eyes danced when they laughed.

Glenda Faye and I would, every chance we got, move over to the extractor and watch the machine spin water out of the clothes. The machine's lid was rarely closed and the blur of spinning colors swirled like a kaleidoscope. The high-pitched screeching motor, exposed beneath the extractor's tub, added to the excitement. Hot air rushed over our legs when we walked or stood near it and when Elaine saw us leaning on the edge of the machine, watching the clothes spin, she would shout, "Get away from there!" At least once a day she warned us, "That thing would yank your head off!"

A few days later, as I stood at the starch tubs and dunked white shirts in thick, heavy starch, Glenda Faye hurried past me, bumped my shoulder, and whispered, "Hurry up! There's more where that came from!"

Although I knew she was joking, I groaned. My arms ached from lifting one starch-drenched shirt after another and I wasn't anxious to do more. Just as I glanced back to say so, she slipped on the wet floor, beside the extractor. It happened so fast, I couldn't move or speak. Her right arm went directly into the whirring, screeching machine. It yanked her forward, headfirst, then just as abruptly, she jerked back, flinging blood in a high arc across the room.

The machine screeched. Girls screamed. Paralyzed, I held a white shirt frozen in my grip above the starch tub. Glenda Faye dropped to the floor and fell toward the extractor's spinning belts and whirring motor.

Elaine raced toward the machine and yanked Glenda Faye back. "Turn it off! Turn it off!"

Lottie, an ironer, ran behind me and flipped the switch.

Elaine dragged Glenda Faye toward the dryers and propped her against the wall. Only then did I see that Glenda Faye's arm had been torn off at the elbow. The bone protruded from flesh and muscle twisted off almost to her shoulder and poured a steady stream of bright red blood onto the floor.

"Arland! Get Arland! And give me a belt!" Elaine screamed.

The screams brought several older boys into the laundry. "Arland's coming!" One of them yelled. "And here's a belt!" He ran forward, pulling his belt off as he moved.

Arland, Elaine's husband, rushed through the side door. He saw the situation and immediately took over, yanking the belt tight around Glenda Faye's arm. All the while, Glenda Faye's head slumped to one side.

"Help me get her to the truck." He spoke to the boy beside him. Between them, Glenda Faye stumbled along, trying to raise her wobbly head and open her eyes.

When the commotion died down, I stared at the blood, ashamed of myself for not being able to move. Seeing that I was still grasping the dripping white shirt, I dropped it back into the tub of warm starch.

A few minutes later, Harold Bree, a good looking teenager, entered the laundry carrying a gunnysack. "Gimme back my golden arm!" he yelled. "I came to get my golden arm!"

The older girls groaned. Elaine frowned. "Shhh!"

Harold laughed. "I'm supposed to bury an arm." He nodded toward the extractor. "I heard it's in—" He peered inside the machine. "Hey! I found my golden arm!"

Still standing at the starch tub, my hands raw, my fingers too feeble to squeeze, I watched in horror as he lifted the mangled arm from the extractor. Torn, stringy tissue hung from it, the chalky white skin dotted with dozens of tiny purple spots from the holes in the extractor.

"Gonna bury my golden arm in the field!" Harold let out a loud sinister laugh.

"Get out of here!" Elaine yelled. "Get out! Get out!"

That night, guilt kept me awake. I should have done something, or at least, tried.

A few days later we were told that Glenda Faye wouldn't be back for several months. She was at a hospital where she would learn to use an artificial arm. For months I had dreams about her severed arm digging its way out of the field and crawling back to strangle me because I had just stood there, too scared to move.

The Meanest Matron of All

"Othello, you and Letha take this load of clean rags over to the kitchen."

Elaine scooted a large galvanized tub toward us.

Letha, almost twelve, grabbed one of the handles and between us we carried the tub of clean rags toward the kitchen. It was Saturday, the only halfway relaxed day of the week, so as we followed the sidewalk around the campus we guessed what we might be served for lunch.

This was my first trip into the kitchen and I was startled at all the activity. Older girls rushed about, working with dough, frying and cooking things, lifting large rectangular pans of hot biscuits from tall ovens with six or eight racks and doors.

Two large wooden tables stood on either end of the kitchen. A huge stove with a dozen burners and a large griddle squatted in the center of the floor. Behind that, more tables were piled with long pastry pans. Metal racks hung from the ceiling above the wooden tables, draped with pans of every shape and size. Two large walk-in refrigerators took up one side of the back wall and smaller refrigerators sat on the opposite wall. To the far left, several deep metal sinks and a long drain board ran the length of the kitchen.

Miss Polk, the kitchen matron, stood at the stove, stirring a tall, deep kettle with a long wooden paddle that looked like an oar. I had heard about Miss Polk since the first day I went to work in the laundry. Everyone was afraid of her.

"She's the meanest person here!" Someone said every time her name was mentioned, so I watched her out of the corner of my eye as we carried the tub of rags across the kitchen and dumped them into the rag bin. Short and stout, with a square, masculine jaw, she eyed me with suspicion, too. Strong muscles in the back of her legs looked tight and hard and tapered to thin ankles and small feet, clad in ugly brown shoes and no socks.

"Don't dilly-dally!" She barked in our direction as we slowly made our way back across the kitchen. "We're busy. Don't need gawkers gawkin' at us!"

Letha picked up the pace. As we left the kitchen, I noticed a long pass-through bar where food was dished up and scooted out to the "dining room girls" who served the tables. It was too early for the dining room girls to be working but the kitchen girls were already pushing bowls of mustard and ketchup through the pass-through windows.

"Wait!" I whispered to Letha when I thought we were out of Miss Polk's sight. "I love mustard!" Veering to the left just far enough to run my finger through one of the bowls, I licked my finger, closed my eyes and smiled.

"I saw that!" Miss Polk yelled.

I almost spit out the mustard.

"Do you think I'm blind or stupid?" Her heels cracked against the floor as she strode toward us. "I saw you run your dirty finger through that bowl! Are you an idiot, or what?"

She hovered inches from me. Both Letha and I backed up. The tub banged the wall.

"Get out of my kitchen!" She yelled in my face, pointing through the dining room. "Get out! Get out! I hate sneaky people and I've already heard about you!"

I blinked rapidly, trying not to cry.

"You're the one with ants in your pants. Keep running away!"

I tried to get past her but my stiff legs would hardly move.

"Go! Don't ever come in my kitchen again!"

My ears rang, my heart raced, and my breath seemed to disappear. When Letha and I finally made it to the back door of the dining room, we both gasped and ran outside.

"She's the meanest person in the world!" Letha cried as we ran back to the laundry.

When we breathlessly repeated our experience, everyone in the laundry laughed, including Elaine.

"You don't want to fool with her," Elaine said. "And if she said get out and don't come back . . . you'd better not go back. I'll send someone else next time."

The following Monday morning, Elaine met me at the door of the laundry. "Come here, Othello." I followed her around to the side of the laundry. "I have some bad news. You're going to a new job."

Disappointment sapped my energy. I liked working in the laundry.

Elaine hesitated and smiled sympathetically. "Sister Wellington called me this morning and said she had heard about what happened in the kitchen the other day . . . and she thinks it'll be good for you to work in the kitchen with Miss Polk."

My heart pounded. "Oh, no. Not that."

She nodded sympathetically. "She said you need to learn to mind, and Miss Polk will teach you that."

"No . . . please, can you beg her to let me stay in the laundry?"

She shook her head. "She's the boss. And you're supposed to go there today, after school."

I gripped my hands in front of me, trying to accept it.

"And remember," she cautioned, "you'll never get moved from a job unless you get along with the matron. That's true for everyone. You have to work there until you can get along. Then you can get transferred if someone else wants to change."

As the day wore on, my dread deepened and I might as well have missed school because I heard and learned nothing.

At four-thirty, I followed the older girls toward the kitchen, hoping I would be hidden and go unnoticed but the minute we walked through the door, everyone scattered in different directions, leaving me standing alone, not knowing what to do. Miss Polk stood a few feet away, pouring a jar of canned tomatoes into one hand, squashing them between her fingers, and letting them drip and fall into a pan.

"So there's the trickster! Antsy Pants, who runs away." She squashed more tomatoes, pouring and squashing without even looking, her eyes fastened on me. "Well, let me tell you something, Miss Tricksy, I don't want you in my kitchen but there's nothing I can do about it. So you better watch yourself."

"Yes, ma'am."

"See those ice tongs hanging up there?" She looked in the direction of the rack hanging over a table. "You'll do as I say or I'll put those things in your ears and swing you around the kitchen until your neck's a foot long! You got that?"

I nodded stiffly, hardly able to make my head move.

"Good. Now . . . " she turned and yelled over her shoulder, "Joline! Joline! Get in here!"

A plump red-faced girl with short dark hair hurried from the back of the kitchen, her breasts jiggling as she ran. "Yes, ma'am?"

"Take Miss Tricksy, here, and give her some cereal to get ready for tomorrow's breakfast."

"Yes, ma'am." Joline nodded breathlessly and motioned for me to follow. Relieved to get away from Miss Polk, I practically ran. Joline led me toward the back of the kitchen and into a pantry where shelves lined three walls, all filled with boxes of cereal. Every size and color, some opened, some new, filled the disorganized shelves.

She asked my name, then said, "Okay, Othello, here's what you have to do. Take all the open boxes that are alike and carry them out to the long pass-through counter. Some of them will have a lot in 'em and others won't. You need to pour them together so we can see how many full boxes we have. We need at least forty boxes for breakfast."

"Forty!"

She nodded. "Well, there's two hundred people to feed . . . ten people at each table . . . and each table gets two boxes. That's forty boxes." She handed me four opened boxes of cornflakes. "Go set these on the counter and come back. I'll give you more."

I made several trips back and forth, each time having to pass Miss Polk, feeling as if she wanted to reach out and trip me as I carried one armload after another to the counter.

"If you have several boxes with just a little in them, pour them together. Wheaties, Cornflakes, Raisin Bran . . . it doesn't matter. There's always several junk boxes that have to be served."

Remembering the times our dormitory had been given "junk" boxes, I knew exactly what she meant.

At the counter, knowing my every move was being scrutinized by Miss Polk, I peeked into each box. I found two half empty boxes of cornflakes and began pouring one into the other. Inch-long cockroaches suddenly ran out of the box, scattered over the counter, and fell to the floor. I screamed and jumped, flinging cereal everywhere. Everyone, except Miss Polk, laughed.

"Stop it!" she barked. "Stand still! They'll leave."

By the time the words were out of her mouth, the roaches had disappeared into nooks and crannies around the counter. "Look at the mess you've got to clean up now!"

She told me to get a broom from the back, sweep up the mess, and finish the cereal job. "And don't throw the cereal on the floor the next time you see a roach. Otherwise, they'll be no breakfast tomorrow."

I could hardly make myself look into the next box but when I did, all I saw was cereal. Once again, however, when I turned it upside down, roaches ran out, scattered over the counter, and fell to the floor. The second time, I didn't scream or move. I cringed and shivered at the sight—and the thought of eating the cereal—but I stood still and silent.

"Well, Miss Tricksy, at least you're not stupid. Apparently, you can learn."

When all the cereal boxes had been consolidated and put back on the shelves, I understood why cereal was served to the dining room tables in large bowls—to give the roaches a chance to escape so no one would know.

Everything that happened, I wanted to share with Jenny, even though I couldn't. In a way, it was good I couldn't tell her about the roaches because she would have never eaten cereal again; and on mornings when there was nothing else for breakfast, she would have gotten in trouble by refusing to eat it.

Still, I wanted to talk with her and constantly rehearsed imaginary conversations because it helped relieve the loneliness, especially at night. Nights were the hardest because I worried about Amy, too, and cried to see my brothers. Sometimes I prayed for them and sometimes I felt like prayers were stupid. If God really listened and cared, we wouldn't be in the Tipton Orphans Home.

Spelling *Fern*

Mr. Bunt took a whole hour to explain how important it was to write our names clearly so that everyone could read them. "Half the time I don't even know whose paper I'm grading!"

I found great comfort in his words. Even though I couldn't write anything else without copying, I could write my first and last names, and write them neatly. Then he went on to discuss signatures, autographs, and "John Henrys."

I had learned to write my first and last name before Momma died, but when Mr. Bunt asked us to write our middle names on our papers, too, I suddenly realized I couldn't spell "Fern." I had seen it written before and knew it had four letters but because letters made no sense to me, I couldn't remember their order. I played with several combinations and each looked as right—and wrong—as the last. Eventually, I settled upon a combination and turned it in.

The next day, Mr. Bunt ker-thumped his way between our desks and handed back our papers. In blue pencil, he had written "SP" above my middle name, which I had spelled: "Enrf." For several days, we received the same "full name" instruction and I experimented with other combinations: *Rfne, Fnre, Nref, Fner.*

Too embarrassed to admit I couldn't spell it, each time I handed the paper in, I hoped he would correct it and spell it for me so I could memorize it and know it forever. Instead, he continued to write "SP" in blue pencil. Then it occurred to me that I might be wrong about it having four letters. Maybe I confused it with something else. Maybe Mr. Bunt was trying to tell me that "SP" spelled Fern!

Hoping I was right, the next day, I wrote Othello Sp James. This paper came back with three blue question marks over my name. Finally, I decided he couldn't spell it either, so I stopped worrying about it.

A few weeks later, however, a new girl came to the home and was introduced to our class as Clarita Fern Garrison! Thrilled by this wonderful stroke of luck, I rushed up to her at recess, thrust a pencil and paper at her, and asked, "May I have your autograph, please? Your whole name?"

She smiled and nodded as if she frequently got such requests and a few seconds later, my problem was solved forever.

Dear Santa Claus Commission

As the first Christmas approached, a deepening sadness began to overtake me. Although I didn't say it, I secretly hoped Momma would magically appear. In the evenings, I found myself staring out the window, hoping to see her emerged from the darkness, walking up to the dormitory.

In early December, Miss Sharply called the whole dormitory together. "It's time to write letters to the Santa Claus Commission," she announced. She then held up a paper and said, "I'm going to pass around two pieces of paper. This is one of them. It's from the Santa Claus Commission." She waved the paper in the air with her left hand. "And this," she picked up another paper with her right hand, "this is a blank sheet of paper. I want you to look at the list of toys in the letter . . . " She waved her left hand, "and write down what you want on this sheet." She waved her right hand. "If the letter says you can have a yo-yo, jacks, a bracelet, hair barrettes, a puzzle, and a hair brush . . . you choose three things and write them down on this sheet of paper." She wagged the sheet in her right hand again. "Put your name at the top of your list so we know who wants what."

I hadn't the foggiest idea what she was talking about.

She read the whole list of possible gifts from the sheet in her left hand. "Those are the things you can get from the Santa Claus Commission. Now, does everybody understand?"

I raised my hand. "What's a Commission?"

"It's a group of people working together." She handed the letter and paper to the girl nearest her.

"Are they real?" I asked.

"What do you mean?" she said irritably. "Of course, they're real."

"Well, Santa Claus isn't real, so I thought maybe the commission wasn't real, either."

"You're right. Santa Claus isn't real, and Christmas isn't Jesus' birthday, either. It's just another day. Even if it was his birthday, the Bible says we shouldn't make any religious holidays, so we don't. So . . . Christmas isn't real. Santa Claus isn't real. But the Santa Claus commission is real."

I hoped so. I wanted a bracelet.

The Nice Matron

Miss Sharply left the home in the middle of December and Mrs. Harrison, a new matron, took over our dorm. A sweet-faced woman who smiled at us and spoke in a soft voice, we all liked her immediately. However, because she was very tall and broad-shouldered, we were also timid about approaching her. She wore her dark silver-streaked hair swept back in soft waves and fastened in the back with pins.

It was a Saturday, and she had been our matron only a few days when she came to the back of the dormitory where several us were talking, pointed to me, and said, "You're Othello, aren't you?"

"Yes, ma'am."

We all grew quiet, wondering if I was in trouble.

"Will you come into my room, please?"

I glanced around. Everyone was as scared for me as I was.

Mrs. Harrison closed the door behind me and sat in a chair by her bed. "I've been listening to all of you talk for several days."

My mind raced, trying to remember what I had said that would get me in trouble.

"And . . . " she smiled, "I want you to know that I think you're a very smart little girl."

Afraid I had misunderstood, I stared in silence.

"But what I've heard you say . . . several times . . . concerns me."

I wasn't sure what she meant by "concerns me" so I didn't smile or move. Adults were always full of tricks.

"Come a little closer." She reached out and took my hand and I edged nearer. "Several times I've heard you say, *I'm so stupid* . . . or *I'm so dumb* . . . and you say it like you really mean it."

Was I in trouble for *that*?

"Why do you say that? You're not stupid or dumb. I think you're very clever. I like the way you see things, and you express yourself very well. That tells me you're intelligent. Clever. You can do great things with your life."

Her words sounded wonderful but also made me a little apprehensive. Was it a trick?

"So why do you think you're stupid or dumb?"

I thought about not being able to read but knew if I told her, she wouldn't think I was smart anymore, so I shrugged and stared at the floor.

She squeezed my hand. "Please don't say it anymore. Okay? It makes me sad to hear such a bright girl saying things like that."

I nodded. "Okay."

A Letter from Korea

I didn't know my brother, Don, was in the Navy until I received his first letter from Korea. He had written it in cursive so I wasn't too embarrassed to ask Mrs. Harrison to read it to me. When I took it to her twice more, she read it again.

Dear kids,

Aunt Lola Mae sent me your address so I could write to you. I hope all of you are doing fine. I like knowing you're safe and being cared for. Even though you might get lonely there, do your best to be happy and obey the rules.

What's going on here is not good but I would rather fight a war here than to have our own country experience this. I see the little kids here and it breaks my heart, and I'm glad you're safe from it.

Please remember I love you and as soon as I get home, I'll come to see you.

Love, your brother, Don

I slept with the letter under my pillow for several weeks, until he wrote again.

Chapter 14

From back left: Jenny and Othello, Amy and Gordon

Brothers Coming and Going

I didn't know when our brother, Gordon, was brought to the home nor who brought him, but Jenny, Amy, and I had been there about a year when one of the office girls said, "You've sure got a cute little brother."

"You saw him? How? When?" I thought maybe Daddy had come for a visit and they wouldn't let him see us. That had happened to other kids.

"I don't know who brought him but he's in the nursery, now."

My spirits soared, nearly lifting me off my feet. "I want to see him!"

"You know you're not supposed to go over there."

Gordon was four and knowing he was close but not being able to see him created a restlessness that disrupted every other thought. I wanted to look at him, to touch him, to let him see me and tell him that we were there, and that we loved him. I had to find a way to get to him.

Asking wouldn't help because Sister Wellington was the only person who could give permission, and I knew how she felt about families visiting. That wouldn't stop me from it, though. I just had to think of a way.

In the kitchen, Miss Polk and I had learned to endure each other. She yelled at me sometimes, but she yelled at everyone so I didn't feel like she hated me any more than the others. Mainly, I tried to stay out of her way and asked the older girls if I could help them. Most of them said, "Just stay out of my way," but usually I could find one who really needed help or was willing to tolerate me.

Two days passed before I overheard my opportunity being presented to Miss Polk. Penny Ann Brinks, one of the office girls, came to the kitchen and said, "You're supposed to send whatever extra pot holders you have to the nursery. And Miss Brannon is sick and wants some soda crackers."

Miss Polk resented special requests. "Always somethin'!" She waved her hand impatiently at Penny Ann who stepped back. "Go on!" Miss Polk snapped. "I'll send the things when I have time. I'm tryin' to cook supper right now."

Penny Ann tugged at the bottom of her sweater, obviously uncomfortable to leave empty-handed, but nonetheless not willing to argue with Miss Polk.

I went to the rag bin where assorted pot holders could generally be found. If I planned it well, I might be able to see both Amy and Gordon today because Miss Brannon was Amy's matron.

A few minutes later with six pot holders and a half box of crackers, I stood by Miss Polk and watched her pour coffee into a large gray mug.

"I found some pot holders." I spoke as nonchalantly as I could. "Would it help if I took them to the nursery and then took Miss Brannon the crackers?"

Miss Polk lifted the mug, held it just off the stove, and said, "You think I don't know your little brother came to the home this week?"

My heart sank.

"And do you think I don't know you have a sister in Miss Brannon's dorm?"

I just stared at her, clutching the pot holders and crackers to my chest.

"Pssst!" She waved me away like a pesky fly and turned on her heel. "Go on! Take 'em! You can't do anything else worthwhile!"

I ran all the way to the nursery. Not only was I going to see Gordon and Amy, but I had permission!

I knew Gordon wouldn't recognize me because he hadn't seen me for so long, but I didn't care. I swept him up in a big hug and kissed his face and neck and arms! He laughed at first, then pulled back, frightened.

The other kids in the nursery, maybe twenty all together, ran up wanting hugs, too. Clinging to Gordon, I touched their faces and ran my fingers through their hair, knowing they wanted to see their brothers and sisters, too, but couldn't.

"I'm your sister!" I kept telling Gordon. "I'm Othello! Oh, you're so cute!"

I swung him around, held him upside down, tickled his belly, and kissed his face a hundred more times before his matron said, "All right. Don't get him so excited he won't settle down."

I knew that Miss Polk didn't expect me to be gone long, so I hugged him one last time. "I'll be back," I whispered. "As soon as I can."

Amy's dorm was in a wing of the Administration building. I climbed the steps and entered the glass doors into a dimly lit hallway. The matron's room was straight ahead, the dormitory just around the corner.

I knocked softly on Miss Brannon's door.

"Who is it?" She sounded weak.

"I brought you some crackers from the kitchen," I spoke to the closed door.

"Oh." Momentarily, I heard movement inside the room and the door opened. Miss Brannon, her red-rimmed eyes droopy and her cheeks sagging into folds beside her mouth, took the crackers and shut the door without even looking at me.

Stepping around the corner, I saw Amy playing with several little girls in the middle of the floor. In a loud whisper, I called her. "Amy! It's me!"

Her round face popped up, her brown eyes wide and excited. "Othello? Othello!"

"Shhh!"

She ran to me and grabbed me in a strong hug. "Whatcha doing here? You runnin' away again?" She looked worried.

I laughed. "No. Not today. I just brought Miss Brannon some crackers."

"She's sick," she said soberly. "So we've got to be quiet."

We talked about everything we could within the five minutes or so that I thought I could spare without getting in trouble.

"I wanna see you more," she whispered, tears building quickly. "I wanna see you and Jenny."

"I know. Me, too. How's Miss Brannon? Is she nice to you?"

She scrunched up her nose and shook her head. "She whips us a lot."

I hugged her. "We'll get out of here someday."

"Is Daddy coming?" She gripped my arm, waiting for the answer.

We hadn't seen him since he left us so I didn't feel good about lying to her. "I don't know. But somehow . . . we'll get out of here. Right now," I kissed her forehead, "I've gotta go."

She clung to my arm, her dark eyes pleading with me. "You'll remember me?"

"Of course, I will! I'll always remember you!"

"Don't forget me," she cried. "Please don't forget me, Othello!"

I cried so hard when I left, I couldn't hurry back to the kitchen. Instead, I walked all the way around the back of the kitchen and stood in the warehouse a few minutes to dry my eyes. There, among the long shelves stacked with dusty jars of home-canned fruits and vegetables, I thought about Momma and how happy she had been when Thurmond and I discovered some jars of canned fruit buried in the backyard. As we kept digging and finding more, Momma realized we had found a caved-in cellar. Remembering made me feel better.

"You were gone long enough," Miss Polk said when I went back into the kitchen. "I don't suppose anybody said thank you, did they?"

"No ma'am."

She grunted. "They never do. I'm nothing to them."

I felt honored that she shared her complaint with me.

"Now, go on. Aggravate someone else."

The Lobby Piano

Cold, blustery wind swept through the campus as I ran toward the Administration building. Clutching the envelope Miss Polk had instructed me to deliver to Brother Wellington, I struggled to open the heavy glass door. Once inside, I shuddered as the warm air engulfed me.

I had never been sent on an errand to the main office before, so I walked quietly, listening to voices filtering into the hall. When I entered the lobby, I stopped and smiled. A piano had been added, placed against the far wall. It was all I could do to remember my mission.

Brother Wellington stepped into the lobby, headed for another office, and saw me. "Is that Miss Polk's papers?"

"Yes, sir." I hurried toward him, my hand outstretched.

"Did she sign them?"

I shrugged. "I guess."

"Thank you." He took the envelope. "Now, hurry back to work."

The wind didn't feel nearly as cold as I trudged against it, taking my time returning to the kitchen. Thoughts of the piano filled my mind. Somehow, I had to get over there and play it, if only for a few minutes. I felt sure I could remember the songs Momma had taught me.

I began to scheme and wait for the opportunity, which came the following Saturday evening. It had been a warmer day than usual and Miss Harrison allowed us to play outside until dark. Taking advantage of the commotion of twenty running, jumping, squealing girls, I sneaked away and ran over to the Administration building.

The offices were closed and dark except for a dim light in the lobby. As quietly as I could, I scooted out the bench and sat down. The first several notes sounded so loud I worried that someone would hear. But moments later, unable to resist testing my memory, I worked my way through the several songs I knew. I played some of them two and three times and had just decided I should leave, when a huge towering figure appeared in the doorway leading to one of the offices.

Suddenly, Brother Haster, the home's bookkeeper, stood with his hands in his pockets, smiling at me. Knowing I was in trouble, all I could say was, "Hi, Brother Haster." I scooted the bench under the piano and closed it up.

"I enjoyed that," he said. "You play very nicely."

Relieved that he wasn't angry, I smiled, said thank you, and ran for the door, praying he wouldn't tell on me. I made it back to the dormitory just as the other girls were going in for the night. Miss Harrison hadn't noticed I was gone.

The next Friday, I was called to the office and introduced to a smiling older woman in a pink hat. "I'm Miss Felty," she grinned. Although I had never seen her before, I knew who she was. She gave piano lessons to ten or twelve of the kids in the home who had sponsors for their lessons.

"I understand you're quite a piano player," she said.

"I know the songs my momma taught me."

She nodded politely. "Well, Brother Haster has agreed to pay for your piano lessons, dear. Would you like that?"

"Yes! I would love that!"

A time was arranged and I left feeling as if I owned the world. I had to pass Brother Haster's office to leave the building, so I stopped and told him how happy I was.

He put down his pencil, closed a large ledger, then folded his hands over his enormous belly and smiled. "You're welcome. I'm sure you'll do very well."

Miss Felty turned out to be as sweet as she looked. Each week, she played the songs she wanted me to learn. Sometimes I would ask her to play them several times. I watched intently, memorizing as much as I could, and the next week I usually played the song well enough to move to the next piece. Because I could watch and listen, I never bothered to learn how to read music. I only wanted to play, and was not above doing it the easiest way.

There were three pianos at the home but not one in our dorm. I was assigned the piano in the third-grade classroom, and allowed to practice for half an hour, three times a week. It wasn't enough to satisfy my love for sitting there and making music, though, so I took every opportunity to sneak away and practice, sometimes getting into trouble because I was supposed to be somewhere else.

Lonely Sundays

Sunday afternoons were "visiting days" for our relatives, consequently, they were also the longest and loneliest hours of the week. I never gave up hope that Daddy would come visit us, and generally I waited the whole afternoon, wishing he would show up.

After two years, when I'd almost given up hope, he came but we weren't allowed to see him. One of the office girls told me the next day.

"He was drunk!" Her face reflected her disapproval. "They're not gonna let him see you if he's drunk!"

Disappointment and doubt filled me. "How'd they know he was drunk?"

"He smelled like whiskey."

In his defense, I argued, "That's just the way Daddy smells!"

Miss McGregor, Jenny's matron, was standing nearby and overheard me. "You need to forget about your father," she snapped. "He's just a no-good-drunken-bum."

Shocked and indignant at her intrusion, I frowned. "How can you say that when you don't even know him?"

She grunted, shook her head, and stared at me as though I were an idiot. "The sooner you accept it, the better off you'll be."

The idea that she would condemn someone she had never met or seen infuriated me and deepened my resentment.

Jenny's New Job

Shortly after Jenny's tenth birthday, she was assigned to work in the dining room. Both of us were thrilled, fantasizing about all the talking and giggling we would do.

"Do you think I'm stupid?" Miss Polk asked when I volunteered to work the pass-through counter where food was dished up in the kitchen and scooted out to the dining room. "Do you think I don't know your sister is out there?"

"She *is*?" I feigned ignorance.

"Don't gimme that, you little trickster! Get over there and baptize a few biscuits! The last thing I need is for you two to start plotting and scheming on my watch!"

I shrugged and sauntered over to the table near the large ovens. "Baptizing biscuits" meant sprinkling water on leftover biscuits before reheating them for supper. The Church of Christ believed that true baptism involved being dunked, so sprinkling the biscuits and calling it baptism was our way of mocking "the sprinklers."

In spite of her best efforts, though, Miss Polk wasn't able to keep me away from Jenny. We met almost every day for a few seconds, never long enough to talk, but long enough to smile and say hello.

Thurmond Joins Us

I waited at the supply hut for a gallon of disinfectant to take to the kitchen. The boy ahead of me, also waiting, looked back and said, "Did you know your brother, Thurmond, came to the home last night?"

Immediately, I was torn between being sad for Thurmond and happy for myself. Remembering how he hated the Baptist Home, I was sure he was angry and depressed.

"Where is he now?" I asked.

"In our dormitory."

"Can you get him?" The boys had much more freedom of movement than the girls and I thought there might be a chance I could talk to him.

"I think so." He took the jar of green liquid being handed him and left quickly. "I'll tell him to hurry!"

Thurmond looked every bit as miserable as I expected he would. We sneaked behind the supply shed to talk. He talked rapidly, trying to fill me in. He said that Mason and Annette had eloped and married, and when Irene (her mother, and Daddy's girlfriend) found out about it, she had the marriage annulled. Mason became so enraged, he got a gun and shot at her. He didn't hit her, but he had been sent to prison for attempted murder.

"He went to Huntsville prison in Texas." Thurmond's anger reddened his face. "Mason was only sixteen and Daddy wouldn't even go to court and say something good about him. He just let him go. To a *real* prison!"

"For how long?" I struggled to hang on to the gallon of disinfectant.

"Four years."

That was the only conversation I had with Thurmond before he ran away, three weeks later. I felt tremendously sad that I wouldn't see him again for a long time, but secretly hoped he would get far away and be very happy.

I wanted to write my brother, Don, about Thurmond and Mason, and see what else I could find out but I couldn't unless I could get someone else to write the letter for me. Sue Ann Davis seemed the most likely person to do it. She worked in the kitchen, too, and was a couple of years older. She rarely said anything but she had always been nice to me.

"I'll do something for you, too," I bartered. "Just tell me what."

"Help me scrape pans. I've got about a dozen to do."

Like everyone else, scraping pans was my least favorite job, but I agreed and Sue Ann wrote the letter.

When Don responded, Miss Harrison read the letter to me.

July 2, 1953
Hi, Kids-

How are all my sisters and one little brother getting along? Fine, I hope. Well, kids, I got your nice letter yesterday and was really glad to hear you are all well. I hated to hear that Thurmond didn't come back but I guess he's doing what he thinks is right. If he was only old enough to know just how wrong it is, I'm sure things would be different. I hope and pray that he will be okay and that none of you will ever get the idea that you should do something like that. Please, please don't. Stay where you are. Write me and promise me that.

I've been in Wansan, Korea, for the last two months. It isn't a job with much fun attached to it, but it's a job that has to be done.

And there is not much anyone can do about it except get it finished and over as soon as possible. I hope it never happens to anyone else.

Remember, kids, don't do what Thurmond did. You're much better off where you are, and I'll come see you just as soon as I get back.

Well, kids, guess I'd better close this for now, things are getting mighty busy around here.

Love, your brother, Don

I had the letter read to me dozens of times by anyone I could find to do it. I tried hard to remember exactly what Don looked like, and wondered if he would still love me if he knew that I had already run away twice.

Daddy's Second Visit

When the girl from the office stuck her head in our dorm and said, "Othello, your dad is here," I catapulted off the chair. The only thing that could have made me happier would have been hearing, "Your dad is here to take you home with him."

Daddy got permission to take us to the park in town and we exploded with shrieks of joy. At the park, Amy and Gordon ran to the swings and teeter-totters. "Come on, Daddy!"

Jenny and I hung back, wanting to talk to him more than play. He sat at a table and lit a cigarette, watching Gordon and Amy.

"We want to live with you, Daddy." Jenny said it first.

He nodded.

"Come swing!" Amy called.

Daddy looked at Jenny. "I'm working on it."

We moved closer, not wanting to miss a word.

"Things are working out for me better, now. Pretty soon, I'll have a big white house with a swimming pool and everything, and you can come and live with me then."

"Really?" We looked at each other and smiled, never doubting a word of it.

"When?" I pressed. "How long?"

"Not long."

"Daddy!" Amy called, "Come over here and swing!"

He got up, walked to the swings, took hold of an empty one and grasping a chain in each hand, slowly lifted his feet off the ground and turned himself upside down. Like a gymnast, his legs straight up in the air, he laughed at our shock as all the change rained down from his pockets.

I was impressed that he could do that but I was also embarrassed and a little ashamed of him. I knew that Amy and Gordon wanted him to play with them, and instead, he entertained us.

Before he took us back to the home, Jenny and I pressured him for specifics. "How long till you come for us?"

"Next week. Have your bags packed."

"When? Which day?"

"Sunday," he said. "Sunday night."

"What time?"

"Eight or nine o'clock."

Jenny and I laughed and hugged each other. I explained to him that Amy and Gordon wouldn't be able to get out of their dorms, and he said, "We'll come back for them."

At that moment, it occurred to Jenny that she couldn't leave her dormitory at night without being seen. Miss McGregor always left her door open and Jenny had to pass it to get to the front door.

"We'll come back and get you the next week," Daddy said. "Othello knows the home. She'll be able to do it."

I agreed, even though I had serious doubts at that moment.

"Pick me up in front of the Administration building," I instructed Daddy as we got out of the car, "I'll be hiding in the bushes. Right there." I pointed to show him the exact spot.

The whole week was spent plotting and planning every step of my escape. By the time Sunday night arrived, I had every last detail memorized, and managed to be hidden and waiting in the bushes well before eight o'clock.

In the dark, with the bushes scratching my legs and arms, I squatted and watched the road for cars. My greatest concern was spiders, and hoping Daddy would come before a spider bit me.

Crickets chirped. The wind blew. My legs cramped and every time I moved, the noise of my own movements frightened me. No one came in or out of the building and only a few cars drove down the road. Still, my hopes ran high.

Then a pickup pulled into the drive and its lights shot right over me and the bushes. I ducked. Elaine, the laundry matron, got out. "I'll just be a minute." she said to someone in the truck.

My heart jumped until I could hardly breathe. What if Daddy drove up right now? We'd be caught!

She unlocked the front door, disappeared inside, and the only sound I heard came from the pickup's radio. I waited, praying that Daddy wouldn't come until they left.

Moments later, Elaine came out and locked the door. She held a stack of papers under her arm. "It's only nine-fifteen," she said as she opened the door to the truck. "We still have plenty of time to get there."

Tires crunched over the gravel as the truck backed up then pulled onto the road.

Her words rang in my ears. *Nine-fifteen?* The sinking feeling in my stomach made me nauseous. Daddy wasn't coming. He probably never meant to come. He just said what we wanted to hear . . . to shut us up.

Aware that I only had a few minutes until "lights out," I crawled out of the bushes and ran back to my dormitory, checking at every corner to make sure no one would see me. Thankfully, Miss Harrison was in her room when I slipped back inside.

All the other girls were bathed and ready for bed, so I headed straight for my locker and changed into pajamas.

"Where've you been?" one of the younger girls asked.

"Shhh!" I spat the words at her. "No where!"

My tone was threatening enough that she moved away quickly and I made it back to my bed just as Miss Harrison said, "Okay, Girls. Time for prayers."

As always, she prayed out loud that God would keep us safe then turned out the light.

How could he tell me he would come and then not do it? Maybe something happened. Maybe his car broke down. Or . . . maybe he just lied. I didn't want to believe that but I suspected it was the truth. He probably didn't even have a house with a swimming pool.

Maybe he got sick and couldn't come.

I wrestled with my disappointment, refusing to believe any of the "reasons" I could imagine.

The next morning, when Jenny saw me, her eyes widened in surprise, then closed in disappointment. For a moment, she frowned, trying to accept the obvious truth.

"Couldn't you get out?" She whispered.

"He didn't come. I waited and he didn't come."

Panic flitted across her face, as if to say, "Now, what will we do?"

Class Whipping

The year I entered the fifth grade, the teachers were shuffled around and Mr. Bunt moved up to teach fifth and sixth. All of us groaned when we found out. He disliked us as much as we disliked him so the instant he left the room, it exploded with paper wads, eraser tossings, and imitations of his gimpy walk.

Fatter and balder every year, with wire-rimmed glasses on the end of his nose, he yelled at us constantly. He still carried the thin, coiled hose in his back pocket on most days, but generally preferred using the paddle when the boys got out of line. Girls who acted up, he sent to Sister Wellington for spankings.

One warm spring day, Mr. Bunt was late returning from lunch and by the time we heard him ker-thumping down the hall, the blackboard was speckled with spit wads and rectangular patterns of chalk dust, indicating where the thrown erasers had landed. We all made it back to our seats a split-second before Mr. Bunt entered the room, but just as he stepped inside, a paper wad sailed past his face, missing him by inches.

He stopped dead in his tracks and glared at us. "Who threw that?"

No one moved or spoke.

"Who threw that?" He leaned into his yell; his face reddening.

Again, silence.

"All right! Then you'll all get a whipping! Then, whoever did it will get their socks beat off by the rest of the class!" He ker-thumped to the desk and stood there staring at us, searching our faces, trying to determine who the culprit was.

"One last time . . . *who threw that?*"

A pale, skinny arm went up and Kenny Holister's quivering voice said, "I did."

A bird-like kid with skin as white as his hair, Kenny was about half the size of the other boys in class. Now, with Mr. Bunt glaring at him, Kenny's eyes glistened as he sank lower in his chair.

"Come pick it up!" Mr. Bunt's rage made his arms twitch as he pointed at the paper wad beside the wastebasket. "Get up here and pick it up!"

"Am I gonna get a lickin'?" Kenny stood slowly, holding his bottom in anticipation of the paddle.

"Yes! That's what happens to boys who throw paper wads!"

Kenny cried openly as he reached down to pick up the wadded sheet but before he straightened up again, Mr. Bunt kicked him to the floor. He yanked the rubber hose from his back pocket and hit Kenny across the back. Kenny screamed and dodged, squirming around on the floor. He tried to get up several times but Mr. Bunt kept kicking him down and hitting him again.

The beating lasted several minutes as we sat dumbfounded, too scared to move or speak. When Mr. Bunt finally stopped and stomped out of the room, Kenny couldn't get up. Puffy red welts streaked his arms and neck as he rocked back and forth, holding his sides and moaning.

Kids in the front row rushed to help him.

"What on earth happened?" Miss Wheeler, the third grade teacher, stood in the doorway, her eyes wide, her mouth open.

"He got a whippin'."

"Here . . . here. Get back. Let me see . . . " She moved over and knelt beside Kenny. Kenny continued to whine and cry.

Miss Wheeler glanced back at us. "You're dismissed. Go back to your dormitories. I'll take care of Kenny."

As we filed out of the room, one of the boys said, "I wonder what David will do about this?" David was Kenny's older brother. He was also pale and blonde, but not small or skinny. He worked on the home's farm and was known for his temper. We separated for the day and walked to our dormitories, hoping David would take care of Mr. Bunt.

Kenny wasn't in school the next day, or the next. Three days later when he returned, he moved slowly and stiffly, his ribs were taped and black and blue marks covered his arms. Mr. Bunt didn't return for a week and when he did, blue and yellow bruises discolored the left side of his face. He also had new glasses. None of us saw it happen, but it looked like David got pretty mad about what happened to Kenny.

New Shoes and Mannequins

There were no shoes in the stockroom that fit me so Sister Wellington took me to Altus to buy some. Butterflies filled my stomach because I thought I might see Daddy or Aunt Lola Mae, and because it was the first time I had ever been in a shoe store. Not knowing what to expect, I found it painfully embarrassing for a strange man to hold my foot and put shoes on me. Had they been pretty shoes I might not have objected so much, but all Sister Wellington would allow me to try were brown shoes with laces.

"I need to go across the street," she said, once the shoes were in a bag. Never having been inside a department store, my eyes roved the racks, walls, and ceilings as she shopped. At one point, I stepped back and bumped something.

"Excuse me!" I turned, hoping it wasn't a person, and my knees suddenly felt weak. A mannequin stared vacantly above my head as chills rushed up my spine. The hard plaster face reminded me of the way Momma had looked in the coffin. I quickly glanced around the store and saw others, all seemingly aware of me, no matter where I stood.

"Can I wait for you at the door?" I asked. Sister Wellington nodded.

As I walked toward the door, I took care to avoid the mannequins, panicky when I was forced to walk near one.

The experience prompted a return of the horrible nightmares—seeing Momma in a coffin. She always opened her eyes and each time, I awoke, afraid to go back to sleep.

Grandpa Birdwell

I untied my apron and slipped it from beneath my coat as I left the kitchen and walked toward my dormitory. Although our aprons were washed frequently, they always smelled of onions and grease and we couldn't wait to get them off. I rolled the apron around my hand and saw Brother Wellington and a tall gray-haired man coming from the Administration building. Brother Wellington frequently showed guests around the campus—usually members of the church—so I thought nothing of it. However, as I reached my dormitory and opened the door, Brother Wellington called my name. I hesitated until they came closer.

"Wait a minute, Othello."

The two men walked purposefully in my direction and as they neared, I realized I'd seen the other man before. He carried his large broad shoulders erect, as the wind whipped his white hair over his head. A long dark coat flapped about his legs with every step.

"Your Grandpa Birdwell has come to visit you." Brother Wellington smiled. "He's only passing through and can only stay a few minutes."

"Grandpa Birdwell?" I squinted, squeezing my memory for a time past when I knew him better.

When Brother Wellington turned and left, I stared up at the tall old man, not sure what to say. I had an urge to scream at him and ask, "Why didn't you take us? Why did you let us come here?" but I only looked at him.

He smiled broadly, his square, strong jaw reminding me of another life . . . another place . . . when Momma played the piano at the tent revival and he preached and yelled at us like the devil was just outside the tent.

He leaned down and gave me a hug. "You're the image of your mother, and I'm sure you'll grow up to be as fine a woman as she was."

We walked to a bench by the sidewalk—where the matrons had sat four years ago and laughed when I was forced to say my Momma went to hell. We sat and stared uneasily at each other. He seemed so far removed from my reality that I couldn't decide what to say and found myself trying to remember Grandma's face.

"I don't remember Grandma," I confessed. "Is she nice?"

"Most of the time." He didn't smile, but looked at me intently as if seriously considering my question. Then abruptly, his face lit with a warmth and sparkle. "You've grown so much!"

"I haven't seen you since I was seven. That's why."

"Yes, yes. And how old are you now?"

"Almost twelve."

"Twelve! And you're a lovely young lady, too!"

"Thank you." I stuffed the apron in my coat pocket so he wouldn't smell it.

"Are the other children okay, Othello?"

I nodded. "Are you going to see them?"

He shook his head. "Don't have time. I just wanted to stop and check on you children, and see you if I could, since you're the oldest and all."

He stood then, took my hand, and walked me back toward the dorm.

His warm hand wrapped completely around mine and I loved the feeling of being close to him . . . to family. He paused as we neared the door and leaned down close to my face, his gray hair catching the afternoon sunlight as it whipped about his head. "Do you write poetry?"

I shook my head no, mesmerized by his hair, the width of his shoulders, and the feel of his hand. I wanted him to hug me.

"Your mother did, you know." He pulled himself up and stared at the sky as if remembering, then smiled and said, "She was a fine writer. Published, you know."

"I remember."

"Yes . . . yes . . . you would, I suppose. We used to work on her poems and stories . . . when you were just a little tyke."

I thought about the house that burned and all the mornings that I had awakened to see her sitting in the kitchen, writing by the light of a coal oil lamp.

"Well, I'd like to quote a few lines of one of my favorite poems, if you don't mind." He looked deeply into my eyes, as if trying to reach some hidden part of me. Then in a deep, resonant voice, pausing for emphasis every few words, he said, "If I should live to be the last leaf upon the tree in the spring, please don't smile as I do now, at the old forsaken bough where I cling."

He kept looking into my face, as if trying to memorize it.Then he pulled himself up again, patted my shoulder, and said, "It's good to see you again." Because I had to look up to see him, his head and shoulders were set against the sky. Clouds moved behind him, the wind whipped his thick white hair, and I wondered if he looked a lot like God. Then he turned and strode away toward the Administration building. The words of the poem and the timber of his voice rang in my ears as I watched him go, his long coat blowing around his legs, his hair alive in the wind. For a moment, I felt as though I had slipped through a small crack and entered another world.

He didn't walk back through the Administration building but around it. As he disappeared, I doubted I would ever see him again.

She'll Go Places

"You're gonna sit at the birthday table!" Jenny whispered in the "glass room"—where all the cups and glasses were stored.

"Yeah. I hate it."

"Wish I could wait on your table."

"Othello!" Miss Polk's voice penetrated the wall. "Get back in the kitchen!"

Birthdays were celebrated once a month, and everyone who had a birthday in that month sat at the same table. In previous years, I had enjoyed it but as I turned twelve, I was too self-conscious to want to sit with boys so I tried to think of a way to get out of it.

"You have a birthday this month, don't you?" Miss Polk stopped me when I went back into the kitchen.

"Yes, ma'am."

"Well, you'd better go get cleaned up."

While I changed from my work dress into school clothes, I thought about playing sick until I remembered that we had a better than usual meal—and cake—something usually reserved for Sundays, when we had visitors.

It felt strange entering the dining room with all the other kids. I hadn't done that since my last birthday. From the kitchen, the whole arrangement looked different with the boys sitting on one side of the long dining room, and the girls on the other. From the kitchen, I could only see the first tables, filled with little kids.

Brother Haster, who sponsored my piano lessons, sat at the head of the birthday table. Each month, a different adult sat there. As always, we stood behind our chairs until the blessing was said; and during those few minutes, I glanced around to see who else had a March birthday. Two teenage boys, opposite me, smiled when I looked at them and I immediately glanced away, wishing I had played sick.

Once we sat, bowls were passed with few words as we served ourselves. I stared at my plate, embarrassed to look up. In the past three years, I had eaten in the presence of boys only twice before—both times at the birthday table. It hadn't bothered me before, but this time, I couldn't have been more embarrassed if I'd been sitting on the toilet. And I hated it! Several of my favorite foods filled my plate and I couldn't make myself pick up my fork.

"Aren't you eating, Othello?" Brother Haster asked.

"Ah—I'm not feeling very well."

"It's very good." He waved his fork over the table. "If you can force yourself, try a few bites."

When I glanced up again, the boys grinned awkwardly. One of them had started to take a bite of green peas but when our eyes met, the peas slipped off his fork. He glanced down, tried to smile, then put down his fork and picked up a biscuit. After that, I didn't feel quite so bad. The boys felt stupid, too.

"Attention! Attention!" Brother Haster stood and clanked his spoon against his glass. "It's time to read the birthday names."

The room quieted as he read off our names. Each kid stood, received applause, than sat down again. Every name was called except mine and I hoped no one would mention it. Brother Haster sat down and took a sip of coffee.

"Psst! You forgot Othello!"

Brother Haster glanced at me. "Oh, so I did." Scooting his chair back a second time, he clanked his glass again and said, "Now, I want to tell you about someone special. This young lady is intelligent, talented, and frankly, I expect great things from her."

I tensed. My mouth went dry. Every kid was going to hate me, now! Didn't he know that?

"Othello James," he shouted as if announcing it to ten thousand people, "stand up and take a bow!"

Everyone laughed as they applauded and I was too embarrassed to stand immediately.

"Get up, O Talented One!" An older boy yelled from the back of the dining room, creating a new round of laughter.

Brother Haster gestured for me to stand and my quivering legs finally pushed me up, but only for a few seconds.

Everyone sang "Happy Birthday" to us and the ordeal ended. The room broke into its usual chaos and noise and although I expected to suffer teasing and insults for several days, I was also grateful for Brother Haster's praise.

I felt guilty, convinced that I had somehow tricked him into believing I was better and smarter than I was, but before I left the table, I said, "Thank you for saying such nice things about me."

He nodded and smiled. "I meant every word of it."

Chapter 15

Othello, sixth grade

Amy's Punishment

The commotion and noise level in the kitchen peaked at mealtime. Heaping bowls of food were placed on the dining tables before the kids were seated, but keeping the bowls filled required an organized and coordinated effort between the kitchen and dining room.

The busiest station was the "food hole"—the pass-through window where dining room girls slid empty bowls into the kitchen to be filled and waited until they were scooted back out. A second window a few feet away kept plates of bread sliding back and forth.

Working the food hole meant standing at the pass-through window and plunging quart-size dippers into fifteen-gallon pots and kettles, filling the bowls, wiping off the drips, and pushing them back through the window. Meat, generally cooked in large pans, sat on the stove a few feet behind us, requiring extra steps and movements.

A twenty-gallon milk container with a spigot stood beside the counter. Dining room girls refilled the pitchers for their tables but spills and mishaps occurred frequently because the pitchers were heavy and the girls were small. These messes, too, were handled by the person working the food hole.

We ate as we worked, standing at the window and grabbing a bite when there were a few seconds' break. The rest of the kitchen girls ate quickly, too, keeping the windows supplied with large containers of food and doing whatever they could toward preparing the next meal.

Regardless of the hectic pace (which happened three times a day, including our one-hour lunch break), I preferred working at the food window because it allowed me to peek out occasionally and see Jenny, Amy, and Gordon—when he outgrew the nursery.

One evening, as the pace began to let up a little, I looked out and realized that Amy wasn't at her table, so the next time Jenny brought me an empty bowl, I whispered, "Where's Amy?"

"I dunno."

I filled the bowl and gave it back to her, then glanced back to see if Miss Polk was watching. She wasn't. "See if you can find out."

"I already did, but nobody knows."

"You talked to the kids in her dormitory?"

She nodded, turned, and left.

A terrible uneasiness disturbed me for the rest of the day. At four-thirty, when we went to the kitchen to start supper, Miss Polk said, "Othello, tonight you're gonna pick beans with Joline and Laverne." She pointed to the table in the corner where Joline was already sorting through a pile of dried pinto beans.

My heart sank. If I didn't work the food hole, I couldn't find out what happened to Amy. I put on my apron, scooped out a dipper of beans, and poured them on the table. Somehow, I had to figure out a way to talk to Jenny.

"You don't like pickin' beans?" Joline glanced at me, a hint of a smile on her lips.

I shrugged.

"I like it," she said. "It's quieter over here in the corner. Sometimes I can't hear myself think over there." She nodded toward the center of the kitchen.

"How come we're pickin' beans now? We usually do it on weekends and have 'em on Monday." I ran my finger over the spotted beans, watching for rocks. When I found a rock, I scooted it aside then swiped the handful of beans off into my apron and spread another handful for inspection.

"Miss Polk said we didn't get a meat delivery yesterday, so we're having beans twice this week." Her fingers worked swiftly, examining, discarding rocks and sweeping the sorted beans into her apron.

The sounds of the kitchen coming alive as the other girls started preparing supper filled long, silent minutes. Pots and pans clanked and scraped across burners. Refrigerator latches popped and snapped with repeated openings and the deep thud of the walk-in refrigerators' doors punctuated the other sounds like a giant exclamation mark. A dozen pairs of feet moved incessantly over the clean concrete floor, which we swept and mopped after each meal, and scrubbed with brooms and hot soapy water every Saturday afternoon.

"Get down from there, Lulu!" Miss Polk's voice rose above the noise. "You're gonna fall and break your neck. Let someone taller get that!"

I knew without looking that Lulu was standing on the top rung of a step ladder, trying to reach something on the top shelf, far beyond her reach. Miss Polk had yelled at me for the same thing at least a dozen times.

"You mad about something?" Joline asked.

"Kinda. My sister, Amy, wasn't at breakfast this morning and no one knows where she is."

"Maybe she ran away."

I dismissed the thought out of hand. "Not Amy. She's too scared . . . and too little to even think of that."

Joline emptied her bean-filled apron into a crock. "How old is she?"

"Eight."

She grunted and laughed. "I ran away before that."

"I'm afraid she's sick or something and they're not telling it."

"The kids would tell you that."

Laverne Carson, a slim, athletic girl with dark penetrating eyes and black hair approached the table. She tied an apron around her small waist and sat down. Half Cherokee, her olive-colored arms looked even darker when she sat next to me.

She dumped a pile of beans on the table and spread them out. Then, without taking her eyes off the beans, she said, "Amy ran away last night with her friend, Jan Stodder."

"*What?*"

"I told you!" Joline whispered. "When someone's suddenly gone, that's usually what happened."

"They caught 'em this morning. In town." Laverne kept her voice low and her eyes on the beans.

"Where are they now?"

"Dunno." Her fingers hurried over the beans, flicking rocks aside.

"How'd you find out?"

"Jenny told me—just now—when I came through the dining room."

Miss Polk walked up behind us, took a wide stance, and planted her hands on her hips. "You three planning to be here all night jawin'? You're not leaving till it's finished, you know."

We nodded and kept working, and Miss Polk turned and walked away.

I liked Laverne, as almost everyone did, because she could be trusted with any secret and paid no attention to gossip. She rarely talked, but when she did, it was worth hearing. Her lean strong muscles and alert, quick responses gave her an edge in any physical game, and unlike most of us, she was a serious student. Both she and her brother, Roy, paid attention to details and made better grades than the rest of us.

She defended herself and her friends against any kind of attack, and occasionally laid in wait to retaliate against those who had hurt or insulted someone she cared about.

Joline, on the other hand, befriended everyone. Soft and emotional, she stood by comforting, long after others wandered away.

"Did Jenny say anything else?" I asked.

Laverne shook her head. "Didn't have time."

The next forty minutes dragged by. The clanging and banging in the kitchen rose, the nearer it came to supper time. Miss Polk barked orders behind our backs, and girls rushed about to keep up. Beans accumulated in the crock as we emptied our aprons time and time again.

"Othello!" Miss Polk shouted. I glanced around to see her standing near the ovens, then emptied my apron and went to her. "You want to ring the bell?" she asked.

"Yeah, but it's Mattie's turn." I glanced around for Mattie. We all liked to leave the kitchen and walk out to ring the bell.

"Well, Mattie just burned her arm and everyone else is busy, so you can do it."

Because Miss Polk had taken over Mattie's job of removing large pans of biscuits out of the oven, I knew how Mattie burned her arm. I had burned my arms so many times, reaching to remove large pans from high racks, I had a ladder of scars running from my elbows to my wrists. Usually, we just ignored the burns, so I knew that Mattie's burn had to be pretty serious.

As I walked through the dining room, Jenny was setting plates on her tables, with the dining room matron hovering at her shoulder. I kept moving, hoping to catch her on the way back. Outside, I scanned the campus, looking for someone who might be walking my way—someone who would know something about Amy.

No one was out. The buildings stood silent and separated by wide expanses of sunburned grass. I reached the bell tower and grabbed the rope, still hoping to see someone. I yanked hard and the bell, some fifteen feet over my head, clanged, swung down and around, and lifted me off my feet as it always did. I rang it several times, then feeling disappointed, went back to the kitchen.

The next morning, there was still no news about Amy and because Mattie's arm was too sore to ring the bell, I did it again.

Three days later, as school let out, I saw Amy walking toward the barber shop. She spotted me at the same time and we ran to each other, "Where have you been?" I asked.

"Upstairs, in the punishment room."

"When did you get out?" I asked.

"Last night."

"How long were you up there?"

"Three days." We walked slowly toward the barber shop. "I saw you ring the bell," she said, her eyes welling with tears. "I screamed and screamed to you but you couldn't hear me."

My heart ached, wishing I had heard.

"But some angels came," she said. "They came and talked to me."

I didn't believe that angels talked to her but I didn't care if she believed it.

"They asked did I want to live a short and happy life or a long one, and I said long." She looked at me and smiled. "They said okay."

When we reached the barber shop, we held hands a minute before she went inside for her haircut.

"I'm sorry I didn't hear you calling me. I love you."

"I love you, too."

A deep sadness welled up within me. The "punishment rooms" were upstairs, over the Administration building. I had been locked there only once—when I was caught plotting to run away for the third time. The room itself wasn't bad; it was just a room with a bed, a nightstand, and a small bathroom. A single window overlooked part of a black-tarred roof of the Administration building's back porch and out over the center of the campus. From there, all the outdoor activity of several dormitories and the dining room could be observed.

Knowing that Amy had seen me ringing the bell . . . but I hadn't heard her screaming my name . . . created unbearable pain.

Saved! (Again)

Sometimes on warm summer evenings, the whole orphanage lined up by dormitories, two abreast, and walked a mile into town, to church. Along the way, we passed homes where "normal" people lived, and invariably, some would be sitting on their porches, in their rocking chairs.

I dreaded the walks because it never failed that someone would yell from their porch, back into the house, "Hey! The orphans are going by! Come watch the orphans go by!"

The younger kids, at the front of the line, waved and smiled at those on their porches, but I and many others stared straight ahead, wishing we could evaporate into the air. It didn't matter to me that we were all dressed in our best clothes and had our hair combed, or that we walked as quietly and properly as we knew how. The words, "Hey! Come watch the orphans go by!" meant the same as, "Hey! Come watch the freaks go by!"

I despised it.

As far as I could tell, The Church of Christ taught one message: "We're the true church and if you don't accept that and be baptized by us, you're going to hell."

After four years, I began to wonder if God would be better to me and my family if I were baptized into the Church of Christ. Maybe they were right and everyone not baptized by them would go to hell. Maybe God was mad at me for not being a better example. In my heart, I wanted to always do what was right but I couldn't. I couldn't keep from getting angry when I saw little kids being whipped for dumb things that didn't hurt anyone—like throwing paper wads.

However, determined as I was to make things right with God and cover all bases as far as my soul was concerned, I told Sister Wellington I wanted to be baptized.

"You're not ready," she said.

"How do you know?"

"I just do." She moved away from me, but I pursued her.

"What will make me ready?"

"Study the book of Acts for three months. Read it over and over again. Then you might be ready."

I couldn't bring myself to admit that I still couldn't read, so I walked away feeling worse than before I asked. I did love God and I wanted to go to heaven . . . and just in case the Church of Christ was right . . . I didn't want to miss out.

As it turned out, it didn't matter that I couldn't read. Joyce Johnson and Frieda Hale also wanted to be baptized and Sister Wellington put us all together to study. We met in a corner of the dorm, twice a week, for three months. The first night I asked, "Would you mind reading out loud? I remember it better when I hear it than if I read it."

Frieda, a freckled-faced red head, nodded quickly. "I don't care. I like to read out loud."

"Me, too." Joyce smiled at me. "We'll read. You listen."

At the end of the three months, Joyce, Frieda, and I knew every missionary journey, where it started and ended, who believed, who didn't, and why we ought to be baptized. We told Sister Wellington that we were ready and she took each of us, separately, into her office and asked us questions about the book of Acts.

"How'd you do?" We asked each other after the quiz, and we all felt certain we had passed the test.

Being dunked a second time didn't have nearly the thrill I experienced the first time, but then, the first time I was certain that I'd felt the big church doors of my heart swing open when the preacher begged, "Open the door to your heart and let the Lord come in!"

The second time felt more like a "back up" in case the first one wasn't acceptable to God.

My Play

Toward the end of the sixth grade, I wanted to write a play but I couldn't spell well enough to do it. I thought about it for several days and decided to ask Joline to write it for me. I promised her that I would polish her shoes and clean her room for her if she would write down every word I told her.

We sat on her bed to talk about it.

"What kind of play?" She eyed me a little suspiciously.

"A funny one."

"About what?"

"Well, I was thinking it would be funny if the matrons were the actors. I'd have them say some of the dumb things they say to us."

She laughed, not at the idea, but me. "You mean you want them—the matrons—to be in your play?"

I nodded. "Why not?"

"And you'll have them saying dumb things?"

"Yeah."

She rolled her eyes and mocked me. "What makes you think they'll do that?"

"'Cause it'll be funny."

"Funny to you, maybe. But probably not to them."

It hadn't occurred to me that they might not think it was funny. "Really? Why?"

Turning her palms up, pleading with me, she said, "Can't you see?" Then she dropped her hands. "Okay. Wait. Tell me some of the lines."

My enthusiasm returned because she was going to listen. "Well, ah . . . ah . . . they're always telling us dumb things . . . like . . . pick up this room!"

She stared blankly.

"Don't you think that's funny?"

"No."

Frustrated, I got off the bed. "Well, no one can pick up a room!" I squatted and grunted as if trying to pick up something heavy.

"Oh! That kind of pick up this room. Oh!" She chuckled. "Yeah, that's sort of funny."

"And they say . . . they say . . . Sweep up this floor!"

She frowned. "Yeah?"

"Well, they don't mean that! They mean sweep up the dirt but they say . . . sweep up the floor! And what about this? This is one of the dumbest things they say . . . They say, Pick up your feet when you walk! You can't pick up your feet if you're using them to walk!"

She laughed. "You think like a crazy person. Everyone knows what they mean."

"Remember the day Miss Polk told us to wash the wall down? The wall would be gone if we'd of done what she said."

Joline, now sitting cross-legged on the bed, nodded, slowly accepting. "I didn't hear it that way but . . . you're right. That's what she said."

We went over more of the lines I wanted to use, and the more I talked, the more Joline liked it. "I want the matrons to play the part of the kids, and for kids to play the matrons. That'll make it funnier."

"I'm not sure they'll do it, but I'll write it down for you. Maybe they will . . . and maybe not."

Joline also wrote a letter to the matrons telling them about the play, and I had one of the laundry girls take it to Elaine, first. I thought she was the most likely to agree, and if she would do it, some of the others might.

The report came back positive: "She laughed when she read it, and said she'd like to do it."

"Really?" Excitement rose quickly. "Tell her I said thanks."

I went to the kitchen early that day and gave the letter and the play—about a dozen pages all together—to Miss Polk. "Elaine said she would like to do this, if you would."

Miss Polk's eyes narrowed. "What are you up to now? More tricks?"

"No! No. Just read it. It's something funny for matrons."

Miss Polk wiped her hands on her apron and carried the pages to a table where she sat down. I stood nearby, wanting to see her reaction.

"This is the kitchen," she groused. "You work here. Remember?"

Since none of the other girls had arrived yet, I moved to the far side of the kitchen and started drying a stack of dishes left on the drain board, never taking my eyes off Miss Polk. She sifted through the pages for a minute then set them aside. I sighed, disappointed.

Laverne and Joline came through the back door followed by half a dozen other girls. They each grabbed an apron and tied it on.

"Come here!" Miss Polk waved them over and thrust the papers into Laverne's hands. "Read this and see if you girls think it's funny."

"Read it now? Out loud?" Laverne looked confused.

"Yep. Right now. I want to see what *you* think."

As Laverne read the cover letter, everyone laughed at the idea of the matrons doing a play, and Joline and I exchanged nervous glances and laughed as if we'd never heard it. During the six or seven minutes it took to read the whole play, the rest of the kitchen girls arrived and stopped, listened, and laughed.

When Laverne finished reading, Miss Polk looked at me. "This is your doin', isn't it?"

Had she not had a grin in her voice, I might have denied it. "Yes, ma'am."

"I don't know," she said. "I never done such a thing."

"Do it! Do it!" The others encouraged.

"Stop it!" she barked, snatching the papers back from Laverne. "Go on! It's time to get supper started." She waved us away and we scattered to our assigned jobs.

I didn't know until the next birthday celebration that several of the matrons and one teacher had agreed to do my play, and that they had been rehearsing with some of the fourth-graders. When it was announced that everyone would go to the gym after the birthday dinner to see a play written by Othello James—and that it would be performed by the matrons—Jenny ran back to the food window to tell me.

The ten minutes it took to perform the skit went so fast I could hardly stand it. The kids howled and laughed from the opening curtain to the end. The idea of fourth-graders "bossing" matrons delighted everyone.

I expected my play to win me approval from the matrons and the kids, but except for Brother Haster, no one mentioned it again. He, however, remembered it every time he saw me. "I told you . . . you're going to go places!"

While his words always made me feel good at the moment he said them, as I walked away, shame quickly replaced the glow. I felt sure that if he had known I hadn't actually put the words on the paper, he would have felt differently.

Each time I saw him, I spent more time studying words in the books, trying to figure out how the letters made words—and how other kids knew what those words were. Some of the three-letter words I had memorized but anything beyond that was an impossible puzzle.

The No–Good Bum

I never stopped wanting our family to be together and I longed for Daddy to come visit us again, but when he didn't, I began to look elsewhere to find the acceptance and feeling of belonging that I craved. Sometimes, even with Sister Wellington, who I had the hardest time respecting because she had lied to me, I fantasized about being hugged and feeling her approval. My fantasies expanded to matrons, including Miss Polk. Although I was still afraid of her, and she frequently punished us more harshly than any other matron, I respected her fairness.

Finally, however, it occurred to me that my life might be easier if I made a few concessions with some of the matrons. Miss McGregor rarely saw me that she didn't mention Daddy and say, "You'd be better off to forget that no-good worthless bum." So as the long, lonely years passed, and Daddy didn't come to visit, it began to seem more realistic to have a matron's approval than none at all.

My opportunity to concede came late one afternoon, on my way to the kitchen. Miss McGregor and a new matron, whose name I didn't know, stood visiting on the sidewalk near the kitchen. I approached tentatively and waited to be recognized. When finally Miss McGregor acknowledged my presence with a curt nod, I said, "I've been thinking about what you said about my Daddy, and well, I . . . I've decided . . . you're right."

Miss McGregor stared at me, as if waiting for me to continue. "You're right about . . . about my daddy." The words stuck to my tongue. "Ah, my daddy is a . . . ah, no-good worthless bum."

Both women gave me a quick, approving nod and slight smile.

I swallowed at the lump in my throat that suddenly wanted to choke me. I had sold him out. Betrayed him.

"Good!" Miss McGregor punctuated her remark with a sharp nod. "It's always good when we see the truth."

Her words burned my ears and my mind, prompting a dark despair and sense of desperation because *at that moment* I realized that *if Daddy is a no-good worthless bum, then I'm no better. I came from him. I'm worthless and no good, too.*

As I stood looking into their smiling, nodding faces, the feelings of acceptance that I had hoped for were replaced by biting, raw hatred. First, I hated Daddy for being no-good and worthless, then I hated myself for being like him, but at that moment—more than I hated Daddy or myself—I hated Miss McGregor for pointing out the horrible truth.

Turning quickly, I left, crying, despising myself for betraying Daddy, and wondering how I would ever accept this awful new awareness of myself.

Gimme Something

Toward the end of the sixth grade, new cinder block dormitories were built, replacing the old Army barracks that had housed us, and the home suddenly looked bigger. My new dorm and several others sat out beyond the circular road that ran around the home, and the new arrangement stretched the distance between me and my sisters.

One icy, blustery evening as I darted from the kitchen to my dorm, I saw Amy huddled against the wind, heading toward her dormitory. I yelled at her but she couldn't hear me over the wind, so I ran halfway across the campus and caught up with her. I knew I could get into trouble, but I hadn't seen her in months.

"Othello! Othello!" She jumped up and down, thrilled to see me. "Othello, gimme something! I've gotta have something."

I didn't know what she meant. "Like what? What do you want?"

"Something. Just something," she tugged anxiously at my sleeve. "Something of yours, to keep."

"I'll see what I have—"

"I don't care! Just something that's yours so I can hold it and it's mine."

Braced against the wind, we walked toward my dorm, arms around each other, talking as fast as we could. When we reached the road, where the sidewalk ended, I said, "Wait here." Had she gone any further, we would both have been in trouble, if caught.

I ran inside, rummaged through my locker and tried to find something to give her, but I had no trinkets. Nothing pretty. Nothing she could keep with her, just to have. My locker held only the bare essentials—a comb, brush, and toothbrush.

Frantic because I knew she was freezing, I glanced out the window as I rummaged through the little desk drawer that held scissors, pencils, and lined school paper that belonged to my roommate, Carla Jean.

When I glanced out the window again, I saw that it had started to sleet. Amy hugged her coat, her face red and wet, her dampened hair plastered to her head on one side and whipping in the air on the other. My heart seemed to crumble into a thousand pieces and I cried for her, pitying her as she refused to move, waiting for something that belonged to me.

Finally, I yanked opened Carla Jean's locker and grabbed an empty nail polish bottle on the top shelf. Then, running as fast as I could, I took it to her. Shivering uncontrollably, she looked at me with warm, grateful eyes, took the bottle, and hugged me tightly. "Oh, thank you! Thank you! I need it for when I can't see you!"

Before that moment, I hadn't realized the depth of her loneliness or her extreme sense of isolation. My own life involved many activities every day, some fearful, some ordinary, but all kept me busy, and beyond them all, I still carried warm and loving memories of Momma to keep me going. Amy had none of that. Her life was filled with endless days of isolated sameness and loneliness, and she probably had no memories to sustain her.

That night I prayed long and passionately, begging God to rescue us, to let us leave the home and live together again . . . somewhere . . . somehow.

Scandal of Bible Camp

My continual plotting to run away kept me from summer vacations and Bible camp during July and August, almost every summer. With many of the kids gone throughout those months, the home felt deserted as only a few of us continued with the daily activities, such as laundry and cooking.

Then, the summer between the sixth and seventh grade, I was allowed to go to Bible camp, run by new adults called "counselors." I ran, screamed, and played beneath the canopy of trees as I had never played before. I loved the cabins crowded with giggling girls I had never seen before, the dining lodge where I didn't have to cook—and most especially, the pond where we swam almost every day.

But I also loved the daily Bible study classes. I seriously studied, wanting to know what God was like, and how to make Him like me—and I wanted to know every detail of what I should do, say, and expect, so I wouldn't let Him down.

After one class, I felt so moved by what I had heard and learned, I didn't want the class to end. I felt as though I was on the brink of some new understanding and wanted to study more, so when the class broke for the day, I asked a girl named Kathy, who also seemed interested in the studies, if she would like to spend her "free time" with me, talking about God.

She smiled and picked up her Bible. "Yes."

Although we had only known each other a few days, we wandered away from the main part of the camp and through the trees to an isolated spot by the stream that ran through the camp. There, we sat on the bank, tucked our dresses under our thighs, and put our feet in the water.

"I like this part," she said, opening her Bible. "I'm not sure what it means but when I read it, it makes me feel good." Her marked and underlined pages told me she had been in many Bible classes. "It says . . . love understands all things." Holding her finger on the passage, she looked at me. "Does it make you feel good?"

I nodded. "Yeah. Sorta."

"Do you know what it means?"

I thought about it for a few seconds and shook my head. I loved Daddy but I didn't understand why he took us to the home.

"Then—!" she flipped through the pages again. "I like this one, too!"

For the next hour or so Kathy's long blonde hair fell across her face as she read various scriptures to me and we tried to understand them. Once, she said, "Oh, this one's scary! Listen to this . . . " And I cringed as she read about dead people coming out of their graves and the streets running red with blood.

"What're you two doing?" Two older girls, walking barefoot in the stream, approached us.

"Talking." Kathy pulled the hem of her dress over the Bible. We both knew they would tease us about extra studying. "Just talking."

They looked at us suspiciously as they waded on by but didn't say anything else.

Kathy told me how much she wanted to be a kind and helpful person, maybe a nurse, and I told her I wanted to be a famous singer or piano player. We spent a wonderful hour together and walked back holding hands. When we got back to our cabin, two counselors, moving quickly and brusquely, approached us.

"You come with me." One of the counselors took Kathy's hand and led her away and the other counselor said to me, "Follow me," and led me to the empty dining lodge, where all the long wooden tables had been cleaned for the next meal. We sat in the corner, at the end of the last table.

"We heard what you and Kathy were doing."

I didn't respond because I wasn't sure what we had done wrong, but her tone and sharp gestures told me she was angry.

"I should have known when you went sneaking away that you were up to no good." Disgust tightened the corners of her mouth and sharpened her glances.

I felt confused and a little sick.

"We were just—"

"I know what you were doing! Two older girls saw you! You had your skirts up and were doing nasty things to each other!"

"Wha—?" I couldn't imagine what she meant. "We were just—!"

"I don't want to hear it!" She stood, scowling at me as though I revolted her.

Two hours later, Kathy's mom arrived and took her home. I wasn't allowed to put on a swimsuit or swim again, and a camp counselor stayed near me at all times. I replayed the incident a thousand times, trying to understand why anyone would have thought we were doing something bad. Since the counselor had said our skirts were up, I guess she meant we were looking at each other—an idea that didn't even make sense to me. We were both girls, we knew what the other looked like!

It angered me that the wonderful hour Kathy and I had spent together was turned into something ugly and stupid, and there was nothing I could do about it except glare hatefully at the two older girls who made up the story.

Chapter 16

New Teachers–New Life

Every few months, roommates were split up and new assignments made, in an attempt to keep us from forming close bonds and friendships that "could lead to no good," as Sister Wellington put it.

Most of us harbored enough ill-will and skepticism that "best friends" rarely remained in that category for more than a few days. Our single, lasting bond was allegiance to each other as a group—us against the matrons. Although a particular grievance might consume us for a few hours, or even days, we realized that we were all in the same situation and that no one was treated better or worse than anyone else.

The idea of being "picked-on" never entered our minds. Some days it was "your day" and other days, not. Personal grudges found sympathetic ears and individual stories remained in our hearts and minds, but "sisterly closeness" didn't develop. Those sacred feelings were reserved for our "real families," even if they were only memories. We all longed to recapture that closeness and prayed constantly that God would mercifully intervene on our behalf and "make it happen."

So the week before starting the seventh grade, when my roommate, Carla Jean, was transferred to a room down the hall, I helped her move, dreading the unknown person who would take her place. I hoped it wasn't Glenda Faye because her artificial arm and hand still scared me half to death.

"Joline? Really? Joline?" I couldn't believe my luck. Joline was two years older than I, so it was unusual that we were put together.

Eager to please her, I helped put her things away.

"Are you ever gonna grow?" She asked as I stretched to put a shoe box on top of her locker. "You haven't grown an inch this year, have you?"

"Nope."

She sighed. "I hope I'm through growing. I'm five-eight." She placed her hands on plump hips and stared down at her feet. "I probably wouldn't mind so much if I didn't look like a baby hippo. I can't even see my feet. My boobs are in the way!"

"I can see 'em. I'll let you know if you forget your socks or something."

She laughed and plopped down on her bed. "You start seventh grade tomorrow, don't you?"

"Yeah."

"Excited?"

"Yeah. Scared, too."

"Why?"

I wanted to tell her how hard it was to cheat and not get caught, but I hadn't actually admitted (out loud) that I couldn't read, so I said, "I just am."

"You'll like Town school. It's a lot different than school here at the home. It's bigger. You'll have different teachers . . . and, of course, there are some cute boys, there, too."

"Have you got a boyfriend?"

"Me?" She made a scoffing sound. "I'm bigger than half the football team!"

Tipton Junior High and Tipton High School shared the same building and together, had perhaps 200 students, half of those from the home. The first week seemed more like good-natured confusion than school as we hurried back and forth down the halls, changing rooms and giggling with new classmates from Town. Most of the teachers laughed and joked with us, something I hadn't experienced before, so for awhile, every day felt like a holiday.

"Home kids" and "town kids" all knew who belonged to each group but it didn't seem to make much difference to any of us.

Mrs. Hayword, the English teacher, loved poetry and Shakespeare and read for us with such passion that I could hardly wait for her class each day. Sometimes she would close her eyes and repeat long sections from plays and books, and occasionally cry when the words touched her deeply. Most of the boys rolled their eyes and took advantage of the opportunity to aggravate the girls next to them.

The Oklahoma history teacher, Mr. Allen Taylor, was a young, good-looking man with reddish-blonde hair and a strong athletic body. He was also the assistant coach for the Tipton Tigers, our football team. The first day, when Mr. Taylor took attendance in his class, I was drawing in my notebook. He stumbled when he called my name. "O-Oth-el-lo James?"

I raised my hand. "Here."

He shook his head soberly. "Is that really your name?"

Everyone laughed.

"Yes, sir."

"Well, kid, with a name like that you'd better get famous or join a circus."

More laughter.

"You don't mind if I call you James, do you?"

"No, sir."

Mr. Taylor leaned against the corner of his desk and stretched his neck to look at me. "What's that you're doing?"

"Drawing."

"*Drawing*? This isn't an art class! Put it away. This is a history class."

I put it away, but what Mr. Taylor didn't know was that every class was an art class as far as I was concerned. And for the first week, every time he entered the room, he yelled, "James, stop drawing and get out your history book."

On Monday of the second week, he did the same thing. "James, stop drawing." Reluctantly, I put away my paper. "No! Wait!" he called, holding his hand up. "On second thought, let me see that. I don't want it on my conscience that I thwarted a budding artist's career." He came back to my desk and picked up the picture. "Hmmm. That's pretty good." He held it up for the class to see. "I could never draw anything but flies."

The kids laughed and he handed the picture back to me. "Tell you what, James," he threw the words over his shoulder as he walked toward his desk. "I'll let you draw all you want, on one condition . . . you listen to everything being said while you're drawing . . . and participate in the discussions . . . and at the end of the semester, for your final test, you turn in the best drawing you can do." He picked up the history book, leaned against the desk, and smiled at me.

"Yes, sir!"

Some of the kids laughed and others hooted as if to say "unfair!"

"Hey!" Mr. Taylor said, "I'm the teacher! I call the shots! I mean, after all, James has a really unfortunate name. Somebody's got to help her out, some way."

That seemed to satisfy everyone, especially me.

From that point on, I spent all of Mr. Taylor's classes drawing with a clear conscience, listening and participating in discussions. And at the end of the year, I turned in the best picture I could draw. I received an A on the picture and a C on my report card.

I liked all of my teachers but my favorite was Don Royal who substituted occasionally when our math teacher was out, and taught US history in high school. He was also the head coach of the football team and brother of Coach Darrell Royal of The University of Texas.

"Coach" had an easy and unhurried way about him, and a smile for everyone who entered the classroom. Nothing seemed to rattle him and, perhaps because of his obvious physical strength, boys who angered other teachers, rarely acted up in his classes.

Several weeks into the first semester, on a cold afternoon when the wind threatened to blow the coats off our backs, I skipped study hall—time I usually used to copy someone else's homework—and went for a walk around the school. As I neared the football field, I heard Coach yelling at the team and decided to walk over to watch them practice.

After a few minutes, Coach Royal moved over to the bleachers and sat on the third tier while Coach Taylor stayed on the field with the team. A few seconds later, I climbed up and sat down a few feet from Coach Royal.

"What's up, Kid? Aren't you supposed to be in class?"

"Just study hall."

He smiled. "Do you already know everything?"

"No, sir. Do you care if I sit with you?"

Elbows on his knees, he kept his gaze on the team. "I guess not." Then he jumped up and shouted, "Come on, West! Get the lead out!"

I wondered what it would be like to have a father like Coach—someone so smart and respectable. I waited for him to sit down and said, "Could I ask you something?"

"Sure." He still didn't look at me.

"Well, I was wondering . . . the matrons have always told me my daddy is a no-good. But my brother, Thurmond, who was in the home for awhile . . . well, he didn't really agree with them. He said Daddy is a good person most of the time."

"Yeah?" He finally glanced at me then looked back out at the team.

"Well, I was wondering who I should believe."

His eyes followed the plays on the field. Grunts and the crack of shoulder pads filled the silence. I had decided that he hadn't heard me, when he asked, "Did you ever hear the expression . . . there's honor even among thieves?"

I admitted I hadn't.

He nodded. "Well, think about it. It might help."

The growl of bus engines behind us told me to get up. The school bell rang and the wind almost blew the sound away.

"Thanks for talking to me."

A hint of a smile touched his mouth. "You bet."

I had no time to think about his words for the rest of the day but when I went to bed that night I mulled them over in my mind, trying to figure out what he meant, but thinking about it didn't help. I couldn't figure out who the thieves were—Daddy and Thurmond or the matrons.

Bartering for Homework

Trying to complete reading and writing assignments required constant alertness, creativity, and a lot of bartering.

"I'll polish your shoes if you'll read this to me."

"I'll mop your floor if . . . "

"I'll clean your bathroom if . . . "

Those who liked to read would generally do it. Even when someone read the material aloud, I wasn't able to turn the information into written words, so the bartering accelerated because I needed to actually copy. For this, I agreed to wash socks and underwear, clean rooms, and run "sneaky" errands.

Then, one evening, when Joline was fussing with her hair, I volunteered to set it for her.

"Why not?" She dropped the comb in defeat. "No matter what I do, it just looks stupid."

She handed me a box of bobby pins and a comb. "How do you want it to look?" I ran the comb through her wet, jaw length hair.

She told me and then slumped in the chair, as if knowing I would make it worse. I, on the other hand, understood lines and movement and didn't have the slightest doubt that I could do it. I had never done it before but as I listened to her describe what she wanted, I felt sure I could pin the curls in a way to do it.

From that one evening, I never had to barter for readers or homework to copy. Half the girls in the dorm wanted me to set their hair. Some evenings, after we finished in the kitchen, two or three girls came to my room, hair pins in hand. Two of my classmates even offered to copy their homework for me if I'd do their hair first, but I knew that wouldn't work. I should at least take the time to copy it in my own sloppy handwriting.

After setting their hair, I would take my shower and get into bed by "lights out," then sneak into the bathroom, shove towels against the bottom of the door to block the light, and laboriously copy pages due the next day.

My Secret Adviser

On another afternoon, planning to run away again, I sneaked out of study hall and went out to sit on the bleachers, hoping Coach Royal would come talk to me. He was on the field with Coach Taylor and when he saw me, he gave a little wave then came off the field. He climbed to the bleachers and sat down, leaving enough space for someone else to sit between us. The wind gusted occasionally, whipping my hair across my face.

"You know everything again today? Don't need study hall?"

"No. No. I, well, I came to tell you I'm going to run away. But this time I'm not getting caught."

He raised his eyebrows and cocked his head a little. "You going to any place in particular?"

I nodded. "Altus. To live with Daddy."

He shrugged and looked back at the team as they took turns slamming into each other. "Do you know he's there?"

"I heard he is. Thurmond told me."

He nodded. "This is the brother you told me about?"

"Yeah."

He turned to look at me, his face serious, but his penetrating gaze revealed nothing. After a moment, he took a deep breath, exhaled slowly, and said, "You really hate it at the home?"

My head bobbed. "A lot. But mostly I'm lonely. I want to see him."

He nodded again and stood. A gust of wind billowed his wind breaker behind him. I stood, too, knowing our conversation was ending.

"Tell you what," he said, thrusting his hands into his jacket pockets and looking me squarely in the eye. "This isn't something you're planning to do tonight or this weekend, is it?"

"Yes, sir. You won't tell, will you?"

"No, no." He shook his head. "That's not why I'm asking. It's that . . . well, there's supposed to be a big storm coming in tonight. It's gonna be nasty all weekend. I'm, well, I'm thinking you'd better wait."

"Oh." Weather had never concerned me. We heard no reports and had no newspapers to read, so whatever we woke up to, we accepted. "Oh. Okay."

He patted my shoulder and smiled. "In fact, I think it would be a good idea for you to check with me before you do it. There's no sense walking into problems that you can avoid."

"Okay."

"Go on, now." He nodded in the direction of the school building. "I've got work to do."

As I walked back to the building, I felt considerably calmer. The urgency to leave that night, or even that weekend, diminished considerably. Just knowing Coach Royal cared enough to warn me about the weather dissolved a lot of my loneliness and took away the necessity to leave immediately . . . to reestablish a sense of belonging. The weatherman must have been wrong, though, because it didn't even sprinkle that weekend.

Daddy Wants Sex

A few weeks later, Sister Wellington came to our dormitory and called me into the matron's room. She said that Daddy had come to the home earlier in the week and asked to take us to Altus for the weekend.

My heart raced as I listened. I couldn't imagine how wonderful it would be to have a whole weekend to visit with him. Surely, he had missed us as much as we'd missed him.

Sister Wellington and I stood in the middle of the room, her face pinched with disapproval. "It's you I don't trust," she said. "So before I let you go, I want a promise that you won't do anything foolish, like trying to run away or disappearing when it's time to come back."

“I promise.” The promise sounded silly. She had to know I would have promised anything for this opportunity.

“You’ll set a good example for your sisters and brother.”

“Yes, ma’am.”

She sighed. “Well, we’ll give this a chance and pray that it works out. Your father will be here Saturday morning and bring you back Sunday by five P.M.”

This was Daddy’s third visit. The first time he had been drunk and we weren’t allowed to see him. The second time he had taken us to the park—and lied about picking me up the following Sunday night.

Now, however, as he drove toward Altus, all of our hopes and dreams of a wonderful life with him rekindled and burned as fiercely as before. We talked incessantly, bombarding him with questions.

“Do you have the big house yet?”

“Does it have a swimming pool?”

“Will Thurmond be there?”

“Where’s Mason now?”

“Will Don be there, too?”

Daddy grunted and nodded most of his responses, smiling and teasing us occasionally. As we drove into Altus, Jenny and I searched for familiar buildings, saying, “I remember that! Oh, I remember that!”

Then he pulled up to a small, old, and unfamiliar house. “I want you to come in and meet my mother,” he said as we trampled across dead, wet grass, the frigid winter air taking our breaths away.

The porch, almost as big as the house, blocked the sun and darkened the small front room. My eyes had to adjust to the darkness before I saw the frail old woman sitting in the corner. Deep within the shadowed corner, her almost black hair, skinned back from the bony structure of high cheekbones and deep-set eye sockets, gave the impression of a skeleton. Wrapped in a gray-fringed shawl, her black eyes sparkled like marbles as she looked us over.

“You probably don’t remember her,” he said to me.

I shook my head. “No.”

He then pointed to each of us and told his mother our names. She continued rocking ever so lightly in the rocking chair and offered only the slightest nod to indicate she understood.

"She's half Cherokee," Daddy said. "And she doesn't talk much."

Uncomfortable, because she looked so old and frail, we backed away and sat on the couch.

"You kids wanna go to a movie this afternoon?" Daddy asked.

"Yeah!"

He moved toward the door. "Well, I'll be back in a few minutes and take you down to the cafe for a hamburger. Then, we'll go to the movies."

When he left, we talked excitedly for a few minutes about how great it was to see him . . . how wonderful it would be to taste a hamburger . . . and marveled at the idea of going to a movie—something we had never done.

Soon, though, our conversation thinned because he didn't return right away and the old woman in the chair didn't move or speak.

"Maybe she died," Jenny whispered. "Ohhhh! What if we're sittin' here with a dead old Indian woman!"

We took turns peeking at her, making sure her eyes were still open.

The little house with its few furnishings offered nothing in the way of interest for any of us, especially Gordon, who began to fidget and kick the sofa. Finally, he got up and began inspecting everything. A picture of Jesus on the wall seemed to stare down at him. Gordon glanced from the picture to the old woman, as if wondering why the two were in the same room. He continued making his way around the room until he stood directly in front of the old woman. Hands hanging at his side, he stared right into her face for several minutes and she stared back, neither of them speaking. Finally, he shrugged and sat down again.

"She dead?" Jenny whispered.

He shrugged. "Can't tell."

"She breathing?"

He shrugged.

Just then, loud footsteps sounded on the porch and Thurmond burst inside. We exploded with happiness and relief. "Come with me," he said, "I'm taking you to the cafe and to the movie!" Then, he turned to me, "All except you, Othello. Daddy will be by after while to pick you up. He told me to take everyone else right now."

I asked him a few questions before he left and learned that he was working for the same paint and body shop where Daddy worked. I asked him if he was happier now and he said he was. Then, they all piled into the car and left.

I went back inside the dark little house to sit with the old woman.

"Can you talk?" I finally asked.

She didn't answer.

Thinking that maybe she only spoke Cherokee, I asked, "Do you speak English?"

She just stared at me, then slowly got out of her chair, pulled her shawl about her thin shoulders and shuffled into the tiny kitchen. From where I sat on the sofa, I saw her take a cold biscuit from a pan on the counter.

She stood by the window, slowly breaking off small pieces of the biscuit to eat. As she chewed, I realized she had no teeth, and the biscuit must have been hard because every tiny bite took great effort to soften and swallow. Her thin hunched shoulders made her appear to be a hundred years old, and in the light from the kitchen, the few silver hairs mingled with the black, shone like polished silver.

Hungry, I probably would have asked for a biscuit, except I knew Daddy was coming to take me to the cafe and movie. The old woman finally returned to her chair and we resumed our silent waiting. I waited for Daddy to pick me up and I didn't know what she waited for . . . maybe just for the afternoon to pass . . . or for us to leave so she could be alone again.

I guess I fell asleep because when I heard a car pull up in front and ran to the door, I was surprised to see that it was almost dark. My heart sank when I realized it wasn't Daddy, but Thurmond, returning with the others.

"Didn't he come yet?" Jenny asked.

"No."

Thurmond scooted Gordon and Amy inside. "Well, don't worry. He'll be here."

Almost an hour later, while Jenny and Amy were bathing, and I sat in the front room with the old woman, Thurmond, and Gordon, we heard footsteps on the porch and Daddy opened the door.

"Ready, Othello?"

So hungry I could hardly think of anything else, I grabbed my coat and said "Goodbye" to Thurmond, and ran out of the house. "We gonna eat?" I asked as soon as the car door closed.

He nodded and pulled onto the street. "In just a minute. I've got to make a quick stop in town."

"Good. My stomach's growling."

He nodded and assured me, "This'll just take a minute."

He wound his way through several streets, then turned down an alley between two brick buildings and parked. "I just need to run upstairs for a second. I'll be right back."

When he turned out the headlights, the alley fell dark and the winking neon across the street, at the end of the alley, cast an intermittent yellow-orange glow over the hood of our car and the four or five others parked in the alley.

He closed the door and climbed a flight of stairs that led to a second floor landing. Light spilled out for a moment when he opened the door, then disappeared as it closed.

The neon blinked. The darkness between the blinks was like going blind every few seconds. I shivered from the cold, pulled my coat closed, and waited. He didn't come down right away. My stomach growled and my feet grew cold inside my shoes.

When I saw a man come stumbling down the alley, headed in the direction of the blinking neon, I slumped down in the seat, hoping he wouldn't see me. His footsteps echoed down the alley as he passed and I breathed a sigh of relief when he crossed the street and opened the door beneath the blinking sign.

Minutes later, Daddy came down the stairs to the car. I sat up, anxious to go. He opened the door and leaned inside. “I’ll be back in a minute. I can’t leave right now.”

“Why?”

“I’m in the middle of a shuffleboard game, and I’m winning. I can’t leave now.”

“But I’m hungry!”

“I’ll be right back.” He closed the door and went back upstairs. I had waited all day for him and suddenly felt resentful. I didn’t know, and didn’t want to know, what shuffleboard was. I just wanted to eat.

Sullen, now, I slumped against the passenger door, staring at the wall. What was the point of coming to visit him if he wasn’t even going to talk to me? Or spend any time with any of us? What was he doing up there? I wanted to go up the stairs, open the door, and find him but I was too afraid that someone else might come stumbling down the alley.

Once in a while people would come out of the door across the street. I watched them walk to cars and drive away. Suddenly, a man’s face appeared outside the driver’s window. He blinked and stared at me. My heart pounded. Waves of heat engulfed me.

“You Russell’s kid?” he yelled.

I nodded and he opened the door. He thrust his hand inside and I jerked back.

“Here. He said for you to take this dollar and get something to eat.”

I stared at his hand. “I don’t know anyplace to eat.”

He waved the dollar. “Here. Take it.”

I took the money and he gestured across the street. “There’s a cafe over there. Your daddy said for you to go over there and get a hamburger. He’s gonna be a few minutes longer.”

I didn't respond, so he leaned down a second time. "You understand? Go over there . . . " He pointed over his shoulder. "That's a cafe. Get something to eat."

As I watched him climb the stairs, an unfamiliar panic gripped me. I had never been in a cafe or restaurant and I had no idea what to do. Afraid to move, I sat staring toward the neon, the dollar rolled and squeezed in my palm.

Finally, I decided to do it. If I could get something to eat, I would feel better—and maybe not so afraid.

Slowly, looking behind me, searching for some unknown danger, I walked down the alley, across the street, and stood outside the door.

Daddy called it a cafe so it had to be okay.

My hand shook as I reached for the door. I swallowed hard, took a deep breath and then opened the door. Immediately, I wished I hadn't. I wanted to vanish but felt too embarrassed to run or move. The six or eight people inside stared at me as I tried to figure out what to do. Three men sat on bar stools on the left side of the room, where mirrors and bottles filled the wall behind the bar. Two couples sat in the booths on the right. The backs of the booths were low and every head turned to watch me.

"Come in, little lady," a man seated at the bar yelled.

Reluctantly, I stepped inside and let the door close behind me. Not sure where I was supposed to sit, I took two or three steps and stopped.

An older woman with blonde curls piled high on her head, smiled, and asked, "Whatta ya want, hon?"

Humiliated that everyone kept watching me when I was so uncertain, I took several wooden steps toward the bar and awkwardly pushed myself up onto a stool.

The woman came closer. "What can I get'cha?"

I couldn't remember the word *hamburger*. My mind had locked in a place where I suddenly couldn't think at all.

"Want some water?"

Did I have to pay for it? If I did, would I have enough money to get something to eat?

Still, everyone stared. I glanced around, tormented that I couldn't think and didn't know what to do. Finally, I choked out the question, "What's it cost?"

She raised her eyebrows and put her hands on her hips. "Water?"

I nodded.

The room erupted with laughter.

I gulped back tears, knowing I looked like a fool, but not sure why.

The man who had yelled for me to come in, now got up and carried a glass of beer to the next bar stool and sat down. "Relax, sweetheart. Water don't cost nothing."

He put his arm around my shoulder and leaned toward me. When I looked directly at him, I smelled his breath and saw he had no teeth. "Don't worry, lil' lady. I'll take care of you."

My stomach rolled. Waves of heat tried to suffocate me beneath my coat as I watched the woman behind the bar get a glass of water and set it in front of me.

"It's free." She and those in the booth behind me laughed again.

I took a sip of water, still unable to think, to remember any word that would take care of my hunger.

"Can I get'cha somethin' else?"

"No, thank you." The feel of the man's arm on my shoulder and the sour smell of his breath propelled me off the seat. I whirled around and hurried for the door, hearing the laughter long after the door closed behind me. I ran for the safety of the car.

When Daddy finally came down from his game of shuffleboard, he woke me and handed me two bottles of beer. "Hold these," he said, "till I back out."

Already cold, the icy beers made me shiver. I didn't want to hold them and I didn't want him to drink them. I just wanted to go back to the house and go to bed.

Once on the street, he took one of the beers. "You can take a few swallows of that if you want." He nodded to the beer in my hand. I held the beer for a couple of minutes, then rolled down the window and threw it out.

"What the hell—? Did you throw that beer out?"

"Yes. I didn't want it."

"Well, goddammit! *I* did."

I didn't care. My hands were freezing. He had a beer and I just wanted to get to the house and go to bed. "I wanna go home."

"Goddammit! Waste a good beer! Do you think money grows on trees?"

We rode in silence for several minutes and suddenly I realized we were no longer in town. He was driving down a muddy little road between two open, muddy fields.

"I wanna go home!" I said, impatiently. "Why are we out here?"

"Now, just settle down." He didn't sound angry now. His voice carried an unfamiliar sweetness that made me uneasy. Then he stopped the car and the fear I'd felt in the alley returned. "Let's go, Daddy."

"We'll go in a minute, sweetheart." He scooted across the seat, put his arm around me and tried to kiss me on the mouth. I pulled away. "No, Daddy! I'm cold! I wanna go!"

He moved away. "Like I said . . . we'll go in a minute. Right now, I've got to pee." He opened the door and got out. I cringed, afraid, ashamed and sick with guilt. I loved him . . . didn't want to hurt him . . . and I hated the feeling of being trapped, forced to decide between loving and hurting him.

I glanced out the rear window, and in the faint moonlight saw him standing, facing the open field, and realized at that moment that his pants would be unzipped when he got back in the car, and I would have to fight him off.

Frantic to think of a ploy, create a plan to stop him, I took off my coat and threw it onto the floor of the backseat. I hoped he wouldn't remember I'd worn it.

I sat rigidly against the passenger door as he scooted beneath the steering wheel. He didn't move to start the car but slid over against me and put his arms around me again. "I just wanna tell you how much I love you."

His disgusting breath forced me to turn my face.

"Here," he coaxed in the soft, patient voice. "Hold my hand." He found my hand and held it for a minute. "I miss you something terrible, Othello. Something terrible."

"Let's go." I tried to push him away. "I'm cold."

"I'll keep you warm," he chuckled, rubbing my upper arm with one hand and my thigh with the other.

"I just wanna go, Daddy. Let's go."

"Well, wait a minute, sweetheart. Just wait a minute. I wanna talk to you a minute. I never get to talk to you."

So where were you all day? I couldn't make myself say it.

Then he moved my hand, and just as I suspected, his pants were unzipped. I jerked my hand back and shoved him, hard. "Don't, Daddy, don't! I'm cold! I want to go! I'm freezing! Freezing!"

Startled, he seemed disoriented. "Well—well, goddammit, where's your coat? Don't you have enough sense to wear a coat?" He scooted back behind the steering wheel and relief weakened me. "Huh?" he yelled. "Are you too stupid to wear a coat when it's freezing outside?"

I hated what he said and that he yelled it, but I didn't respond. I just wanted to leave.

He revved the engine and pressed the accelerator but the back tires spun in the mud. He pressed harder but the car only rocked forward and slipped back.

"Dammit! Now, look what you made me do! We're stuck in the mud and it's all your fault!"

I had enough wits about me to know I wasn't to blame for the car being stuck in the mud but it didn't make me feel better because he kept yelling and swearing.

After several unsuccessful attempts to get unstuck, he got out of the car, slammed the door, and went back to open the trunk. For a moment, I didn't know what he was doing. Then, when he slammed the trunk, I saw that he had several gunnysacks in his hands. He stuffed them under the rear tires.

Back in the car, he wiped his muddy hands on a rag and tossed it onto the backseat. For a moment, I cringed, afraid he would see my coat, but he didn't.

Finally, the car pulled forward.

"It's the goddamnest thing I ever saw," he complained as he drove home. "A daughter who won't even let you love her! Who won't even treat you like you're important to her." He turned and glared at me. "You're no better than me, Miss High and Mighty!"

I let him yell, sometimes feeling guilty, sometimes justifying my actions. All the while, I watched him smoke, flipping the ashes out the vent window, opened a couple of inches.

"Why, I'd give my right arm for you!" He growled. "I'd give my right arm for you! And what do I get in return? Nothing. Absolutely nothing."

His words rang in my ears as I watched him flick the ash from his cigarette . . . with his left hand. His left hand. Until that moment, I had forgotten it, but suddenly I remembered . . . he was *left-handed*! The impact of his words . . . "I'd give my right arm for you—" and the fact that he was left-handed, impacted every cell of my being. For a moment, I wanted to laugh. The realization instantly liberated me from all guilt and shame.

He had spoken a truth that even he didn't recognize. He didn't love me at all. He might give up his right hand for me . . . a statement I seriously doubted at this moment . . . but not his left . . . not the one used to feed himself, to smoke, to drink his beer.

Until that moment, I had often felt I would have given anything—both hands probably—if I could make his life better and make him love me. After that moment, I realized that what I longed for all of my life was impossible. It didn't exist. I wanted him to love me. Really love me. But what I wanted and what he was willing to give were two different things.

He ranted and raved all the way home, telling me how much I disappointed him. "It's all your fault your mother died!" he raged. "If you'd been more responsible . . . helped out more . . . she wouldn't be dead today. So don't tell me how much you hate the orphanage! It's all your own doing that you're there! You're the one who even said you wanted to go!"

Too stunned to respond, I tried to recapture the feeling of liberation I'd had a few minutes ago. What he was saying now couldn't be true. It just couldn't!

"So I took you to another orphanage—like you said you wanted!—and I was all alone again! Now, this is how you treat me!"

My ears rung, my head reeled, and my stomach churned. *How could he turn everything around this way?*

When finally he parked in front of the house and got out, I reached around and grabbed my coat. I slipped it on as he marched across the yard ahead of me, and waited for me at the door. He didn't notice the coat as I approached.

"I still love you." It surprised me that he was using his "sweet" voice again. "In spite of the way you treat me. I still love you."

I shivered from the cold, the exhaustion, and a thousand confusing feelings. "I love you, too." As I heard the words leave my mouth, I recognized the change in my voice. The warmth was gone.

Later, safely in bed with my sisters, I recalled his "right arm" remark and again tried to reclaim the sense of freedom it had first given me. The day had been hideously long and draining, and I still hadn't eaten, but I had learned something that would forever take the guilt and sting away when I thought of Daddy. I wasn't nearly as important to him as he had been to me, and the new perspective, while it brought no comfort, it did end my impossible struggle for something I could never have. There was no sense grieving for love that didn't exist.

The scene in the car played through my mind hundreds of times in the next few days as I went to and from school and work. Several times I laughed out loud when I recalled the line . . . "I'd give my right arm . . . " and each time I remembered, I felt a little more liberated, a bit more removed from the pain of missing him, of wanting something I couldn't have—a love that didn't exist.

Chapter 17

"Fun Day" was one day a year kids were allowed to gather in the yard and play with brothers and sisters. Jenny and Amy had a hard time having fun only one day a year.

The Camera

Various congregations of the Church of Christ volunteered to accept responsibility for clothing one or two children. The congregation that sponsored me the year I turned fourteen was the Tenth and Broad Church of Christ in Wichita Falls, Texas. Lewis and Lou Ellen Foster, a couple from that church, sent me a Brownie camera and several rolls of film for my birthday, and I treasured it. Since I rarely saw Jenny, Amy, and Gordon, I carried the camera everywhere, hoping to see them and take a picture. Finally, one Saturday, Jenny and I sneaked out of the kitchen and dining room and took pictures of each other.

I still didn't have a picture of Amy or Gordon, so I continued to take the camera wherever I went. It was the best gift I had ever received and I proudly showed it to everyone.

Late one afternoon, as I walked out to ring the supper bell, I spotted Gordon and several other boys playing in front of their dorm. I knew I was too far away to get a good picture, but at this point, any would do. I snapped the shot, wound the film to the next picture and dropped the camera back into my pocket.

"Give me that!"

I spun around to find Sister Wellington walking hurriedly toward me.

"I saw what you're doing!"

"What?" I protected the camera. "I just took a picture of Gordon."

"You're taking pictures of boys!"

Furious, I turned to the bell tower and rang the bell. The instant I dropped the rope, Sister Wellington grabbed the camera from my pocket. "I said give me that!" She held it with both hands.

"Why?" I pleaded, "I was just taking a picture of Gordon!"

"I know you!" Her tone implied she knew a disgusting monster. "You can't be trusted! Always sneaking! Always thinking about boys!"

My temples throbbed, my arms twitched at my sides, my hands itched to hit her. "Those were little boys. Gordon's age!"

"I'm sure you've been taking pictures of boys at school. Nasty pictures!"

"I have not! Develop the film! See for yourself!" I waved wildly toward the camera.

"I intend to, young lady! And I'll not abide your sassing me this way!" Her mouth hardened into an angry line, her brows knitted together and pinched her forehead. She turned in a huff.

"When can I have it back?"

"I don't know." She didn't look back.

"Sister Wellington! *When*?"

"Two weeks." She threw the words over her shoulders.

Two weeks came and went. I asked for the camera every time I saw her, and each time she said, "Maybe later." My anger seethed and strengthened. After six months, I knew I would probably never get it back but that didn't stop me from asking each time I saw her. Finally, she only smirked, not bothering to answer, and that day, as I watched her walk away, I realized that the blistering rage pumping through my veins was raw, savage hate.

Learning to Read

Two weeks before the end of the eighth grade, most of the kids were filled with the energy and anticipation that came at the end of each school year. I was not. Again, I had sufficiently cheated my way to another grade level, still unable to read. Throughout the year, I had written spelling words on the insides of my sleeve cuffs, in the palms of my hands, between my fingers, and every other conceivable hiding place.

With only ten school days left in the year, I finally didn't care if I was caught. The night before the test, I copied the spelling words with a dark pen onto another piece of paper, intending to place a clean sheet over it and simply copy them. I knew they wouldn't be in the right order, but I was beyond worrying.

I walked to the pencil sharpener and ground my pencil to a fine point then took my seat. Miss Morse stood near the window, her list hidden behind a notebook, waiting for everyone to get out a single sheet of paper. I carefully lifted the two loose sheets of notebook paper, hiding my cheat sheet.

When the room finally settled, Miss Morse raised her chin and spoke precisely. "Chattel." She hesitated and repeated it again. "Chattel."

I pressed the top sheet firmly and searched for something I thought might be the correct word. I copied, c-h-a-t-t-e-l, with no confidence that I'd made the right selection.

Miss Morse lifted her chin again. "Chicory . . . chicory."

I ran my eyes and finger down the words dully visible beneath my sheet. I chose a second time and copied, c-h-i-c-o-r-y. Afraid I'd selected incorrectly, I glanced over the other words.

"Chieftain . . . chieftain."

Pencils pecked against thin sheets of paper as others wrote. Erasers rubbed out mistakes and breaths blew eraser crumbs away.

I searched for another word. Maybe it's . . . I considered the options. I glanced over all the words. The words chattel and chicory still rang in my head. Now, chieftain . . . The first two words I'd chosen began with "ch." I saw another one beginning with "ch." I heard the similarity of the beginning sounds . . . . cha . . . . cha . . . if I had guessed correctly the first two times, then chieftain had to begin with ch, too. I copied the only word left that began with ch . . . c-h-i-e-f-t-a-i-n.

I stared at the three words. Miss Morse's voice echoed in my head. "Chattel . . . chicory . . . chieftain . . . " Each word started with the *same sound*! I had found three words beginning with the same letters! That was it! That was the key! The secret that everyone else knew! *Letters had sounds assigned to them!*

The wave of energy that swept through me left me tingling and breathless. I didn't care if I passed the test. It didn't matter about the rest of the words. I had discovered the secret! *Letters had sounds assigned to them*! It was nothing more than that. All these years, the torture, the struggling . . . how did I *not* know? Wasn't anyone supposed to tell me, too?

Maybe they did tell me and I was too dumb to understand. Or maybe many people didn't know. Maybe other students, like me, cheated. Whatever the reason—I didn't care! I had broken the code and revealed the great secret of the universe. God didn't matter as much as this. Life and death didn't matter as much as this. Nothing was more important, anywhere, anytime, than this moment! I had broken the code and understood what others knew . . . letters . . . stupid markings on a page . . . had sound assignments! What a great idea!

My heart beat erratically and I grew warm with excitement. Now, I had to start at the beginning, like a first grader, but that didn't matter. I would teach myself.

Let's see . . . let's see . . . I know the letters in my name. I looked at my name written on top of the sheet. I sounded them out in my head. I counted them. *Thirteen in all. And ch, too. Fifteen out of twenty-six. A good start. I can do it. Using only these letters, I can figure out other sounds, trying every sound I'd ever heard until the words in a sentence made sense.*

I wanted to jump up, shout, and dance. To scream, "I know the secret! I can read, too! I know I can! Just wait and see! I know I can!" but instead, I trembled silently, so excited I could hardly sit still.

With a headiness I'd never experienced, I waited breathlessly for class to end so I could rush to the library, check out a book, and prove to myself that I could read. *The library*. Prior to this moment I had never *wanted* to go into the library. It served no purpose in my life except to humiliate and torment me.

"I wanna check out a book," I said excitedly to the librarian.

"Which book?" she asked.

Stumped, not knowing a single title, I gaped stupidly at her. I knew that I probably shouldn't check out a "thick" book, so I said, "Oh, ah, about a second-grade book, I think."

Without further questions, the merciful librarian disappeared between the few rows of shelves that comprised our small library and soon returned with a book entitled, *The Mystery of the Little Green Turtle*.

Embarrassed to be seen with a "baby" book, I hid it quickly inside my notebook.

Back at the home, I tried to hide my excitement as I quickly changed clothes and hurried to the kitchen. *The book* was all I thought about. I had it hidden under my pillow and I knew I could read it! I could figure it out! So, while everyone was busy during dinner, I slipped out to the warehouse and took the flashlight that hung inside the door, then hid it until we had finished cleaning the kitchen, then I sneaked it to my dorm.

Later that night, after the lights were out, I eased the book and flashlight from under my pillow, pulled the covers over my head, and began to sound out my first words. I didn't know the sounds for all the letters, but I had a running start on it. Ch was "Cha" and with the letters in my name, I knew half of the alphabet already—and almost every word in my book had one or more of those letters.

Oh, the joy! The freedom! I grunted silently, painstakingly uttering idiotic sounds in my head, until words that I had heard . . . and which made sense within the context of the sentence . . . began to form complete thoughts and pass information to me. Ink markings on a page began to talk to me and create pictures inside my head! They told me things I had never thought before. Things about a little green turtle. Who could have imagined that I would have cared? And yet I did. I loved that little turtle—and he was missing! Where did he go? Did someone steal him? Was he lost forever? Oh, how I wanted him found!

When I finished the book, I lay enthralled. I had reached a high beyond anything I had ever experienced. So *that* was why people read—to find the turtle!

I could hardly wait until I could return that book and check out another. Having now read *The Mystery of the Little Green Turtle*, I thought I was prepared to read anything. So the next day, I hurried back into the library and announced, "Now, I want a high school mystery."

"Which one?" the librarian asked.

"I don't know. You choose," I said.

The librarian turned back to her beloved shelves and brought me Daphne DuMaurier's *Rebecca*. This time, I proudly carried my *thick* book out of the library.

Later that night, huddled under my covers, I reverently turned to the first page. My initial response was horror, but not the kind Ms. DuMaurier had in mind, I'm sure. All of my newfound pride vanished as I stared at the multi-syllable vocabulary.

But I wanted the thrill back. I wanted the sense of pride and accomplishment I had felt last night, because for those few hours when I thought I could read, I felt like a different—and better—person. So, sound for sound, syllable for syllable, and eventually word for word, I worked at it. Many nights later, when words finally became sentences, and thoughts were being communicated to me, I was overwhelmed with another realization. Words not only passed information—they created feelings. As the words passed through my mind, I grew afraid because the thoughts were frightening!

There was this poor scared lady in this big spooky house and her new husband seemed kind of cold, like he didn't love her much, and there was this scary, awful housekeeper who kept creeping all over the place and she reminded me of the matrons and . . .

The words, and the ideas they expressed, had created my fear, and the realization astounded me. This was priceless information—maybe even the most important information in the world!—because with it, I could literally change my feelings any time I wanted, and maybe change my life. Knowing I had discovered something of great value, I considered it carefully, determined to remember and use it.

At the end of the year, I kept the copy of *Rebecca* and continued to struggle with it. I knew I wasn't really *reading* it. Some of the words and phrases just wouldn't make sense, and I wanted to know them, so I hid it under my mattress, not caring if I ever returned it. I would read it again and again until I had sucked every juicy word off the page and felt it in my mind and body.

Each time I set it aside, I felt better, smarter, more deserving of being recognized as a real person. A person who could read. Sometimes, when I would put the book away, I actually felt taller.

Letters from Don

Within days after finishing *Rebecca*, I received a letter from my brother, Don, and carried it to my bed to savor every word. He said that when he got out of the Navy, he had gone into the Air Force and was now stationed at Altus Air Force Base. It excited me that he was so close. He also said he had married a woman named Mary, that they had a baby, and they would be coming to see us soon.

Because I could read, I wanted him to describe every detail of Mary and the baby but all he said was, "She's anxious to meet all of you because I've told her all about you."

When I went to put the letter away, I couldn't resist reading his previous letters again, this time, by myself. When I finished, I put them under my pillow, hoping that would make me dream about him and bring back some of the warm loving feelings that I hadn't felt in so long.

Scalded with Oil

We rarely prepared fried foods except on Saturday because it was too time consuming. On Saturday, however, we frequently breaded and fried round steak, then covered and baked it on Sunday morning while we were at church. "Smothered steak" was a favorite with everyone.

One hot Saturday, Joline and I were the "fryers." Using two pans approximately eighteen inches long, twelve inches wide, and eight inches deep, we fried enough steak to feed 200. We had been working since seven A.M. and the stoves had created a furnace inside the kitchen. Everyone wanted to leave but no one could go until every job was finished, so the other girls hurried us. The floor still had to be scrubbed with soapy hot water and brooms, and the two large kettles of water boiling on the stove now added sweltering steam to the insufferable heat.

When the last pieces of steak were fried and our grease had stopped sizzling, I grasped the corners of my pan with pot holders then carefully and slowly moved to the five-gallon "used grease" cans in the pantry. I had blistered my thumbs on many occasions, so I moved with extreme care, tilting the pan ever so slightly to pour the hot oil. Solid, grayish-white fat melted instantly when the hot oil hit it, boring a hole that deepened and widened as I poured.

As the last drops dribbled from the pan, I turned and saw Joline lift her pan off the stove. She took no more than two steps when the pan slipped and fell. Scalding grease splattered down her side. The pan hit the concrete floor, flinging hot oil over her arm and neck. She gasped, screamed, and tried to turn but slipped and fell. Screaming, writhing, she brushed at her legs, trying to brush off the blistering oil.

The kitchen erupted with sympathetic screams and cries as we all rushed to help. Miss Polk threw rags on the floor to soak up oil so she could get to Joline without falling. Grabbing Joline under her arms, she pulled her back and dabbed at her blistered skin with clean rags.

"Get to the office! Tell them to call a doctor!"

Two of the older girls turned and ran from the kitchen while the rest of us hovered close, wanting to help. Joline sobbed and trembled, her eyes rolling back, her teeth chattering.

"Get back!" Miss Polk shouted, sitting on the floor, Joline propped against her. "Start cleaning up the mess!"

We rushed to the rag bin, grabbed handfuls of rags, and soaked up as much of the grease as we could. Through Joline's cries, we heard the clatter of milk cans as the farm boys delivered milk to the back of the kitchen.

"The milk boys are here!" We looked to Miss Polk, not sure how significant their presence was.

"Good." She held Joline's jerking, trembling body. "Tell 'em to get over here."

"What's happening?" Calvin, an eighteen-year-old senior, carried a ten-gallon milk can through the kitchen's back door.

"Come here!" Miss Polk shouted. "We need your help!"

The can whacked loudly against the concrete as Calvin set it down and hurried to Miss Polk. "Oh, boy." He stared at the white loose skin pushed into wrinkled bunches, exposing shiny, raw tissue below.

"Who's with you?" Miss Polk asked.

"Richard."

"Get him."

Calvin turned and ran to the truck.

"Take her to her dorm." Miss Polk instructed when they returned.

"Yes, ma'am." Both boys circled Miss Polk and Joline, looking for a way to lift her.

"I don't think the back of her legs are too bad," Miss Polk said.

Joline, who was now silent except for occasional involuntary shudders and teeth chattering, trembled as Calvin and Richard slipped their arms beneath her and lifted her up.

"Take her to her dorm and put her on her bed." Miss Polk got to her feet, her dress soaked and darkened with grease. The rest of us watched in silence as Calvin and Richard carried Joline out.

"All right," Miss Polk instructed, "I'm going to change my clothes. You know how to clean up this mess."

She was hardly out the back door before we were throwing hot sudsy water on the grease and scrubbing frantically with brooms, pushing the water toward the drain in the center of the floor.

By the time we finished, we were all exhausted but ran to the dorm to check on Joline. She was stretched out on the bed, her body glistening with some kind of oil. Our substitute matron, Miss Sally, and several girls hovered outside the door.

"What's all over her?" I asked.

"Butter." Miss Sally's voice held a note of disgust. "That's what the doctor said to do."

"Butter?"

"In this heat, I can't imagine the pain she's in. She kept begging me to put her in the shower, under cold water." Her frown increased as she talked. "I was tempted to do it but the doctor said no . . . rub her down with butter!"

Joline trembled and shook for two days. The skin on her legs and side bubbled and broke and wept a pinkish water. The relentless sun bore down on our window from noon until sundown and although I tried to keep the curtains closed, the sun occasionally streamed in around the edges. When it did, the rays tortured Joline like hot knives.

No doctor ever came to see her and she was never taken to one. For awhile, I thought she would die from the pain of it. Her legs swelled and the burned wrinkled skin eventually sloughed off. A crust formed over some of the areas and it, too, eventually healed. The new bright red skin beneath the scabs remained too sensitive to touch or for her to shower. For weeks I helped her with sponge baths and continued to lubricate the tight new skin with butter.

By the time school started again, she was able to hide most of the scarring with clothes.

Can I Live with You?

I sang in the home's chorus and the girl's sextet, often traveling by bus to neighboring towns to perform at churches in Oklahoma and Texas. These were generally day trips used to promote the home, solicit donations, and find clothing sponsors for new kids. We were also asked to perform at funerals and weddings in nearby towns.

At one funeral, a fifteen-year-old girl had died in a plane crash, and I watched the heartbroken parents as the minister spoke. I was fourteen at the time and seeing the depth of their grief, I couldn't help but cry as I sang.

I didn't get a chance to talk to the parents, but later that night, I tried to imagine having parents who cared and would miss you when you died. They seemed to miss their daughter as much as I missed my mother, and the more I thought about it, the more reasonable it seemed that perhaps we could solve each other's problems. Maybe they would like to have another daughter as much as I wanted parents. It might mean a better life for all of us.

Deciding to take action, I slipped out of bed and into the bathroom where I wrote them a letter.

Dear Mr. and Mrs. Amberson,

I sang at your daughter's funeral today. It made me cry to see how sad you were. I'm sorry she's gone and I know how much you miss her. I know, because my mother died a long time ago and I'm still sad. I've lived at Tipton Home for six years.

If you would ever like another daughter, I would like to be her. I wouldn't try to take your daughter's place, but I would be good and never cause you any trouble. I'm a good worker and I know how to cook and clean, too.

Please let me know. I'm fourteen. Maybe we can help each other.

Love, Othello James

I gave the letter to a Town girl named Dottie Clinton, who promised to mail it for me. I addressed it to "general delivery" and prayed they would get it. I waited for several weeks but never received an answer.

Defending Gordon

The blistering sun had overheated the kitchen and dining room until we all tugged at our sweaty collars and groused at each other. Someone else rang the supper bell so I couldn't enjoy even that short reprieve. Through the pass-through window, I watched the kids enter, all of them noisier and grouchier than usual. Eventually, the dining room filled and the noise level grew until everyone was standing behind a chair, waiting for the prayer.

I happened to glance at Gordon's table just as his matron, Miss Diggs—a short, fat woman with huge breasts—moved behind him to serve green beans onto his plate. He shook his head, wrinkled his nose, and shuddered. She whacked him hard on the head with the serving spoon and he grabbed his head and ducked, crying.

Enraged, I tore out of the kitchen and ran to her table. "Don't you ever hit him again!" I yelled in her face.

Startled, Miss Diggs stepped back. Still holding the bowl of green beans, she said, "Do you want to fight me?" Her nasty smirk challenged me.

"Yeah! Come on!" I turned and headed for the "glass room," where all of the cups and glasses were stored. Waiting for her to follow, I paced restlessly. Seconds later, she stepped inside the small room, her hands behind her back.

"I know you've got a board or rubber hose," I said, "but you're not gonna hit me with it!"

Her breasts heaved dramatically with each breath as she eyed me, waiting for the perfect moment to land her hit. I stared, tensed and alert, ready to protect myself.

Finally, she stepped back toward the door. "I'll report this, you know."

"I don't care. Just don't hit Gordon again!"

She glared at me for a moment, still breathing heavily, then turned with a snort, and left. I knew my moment of triumph was just that—*a moment*—but I enjoyed it immensely.

Fortunately, Joline had rushed to cover for me at the food window and Miss Polk hadn't noticed my absence.

It was months later before I saw Gordon alone, and then, just for a few seconds on the campus sidewalk.

"Othello!" He laughed as he ran to hug me. "She didn't hit me again! Never. Miss Diggs never hit me again. She said she thinks you're crazy!" We both laughed and he waved excitedly as he ran off toward his dorm.

Letters for Miss Polk

Learning to read changed my life in numerous ways, including my relationship with Miss Polk. After circling each other like suspicious dogs for years, we both accepted a silent truce and even shared a few moments of laughter now and then.

Occasionally, she caught me sneaking a cup of coffee, and only gave me a long disapproving look as I walked away with the cup. I wasn't sure how or why our silent pact evolved, but I gratefully accepted it. Unlike most matrons, she handled the discipline problems without calling in Mrs. Wellington. For that, we were all grateful because the punishment ended immediately instead of following us for weeks to come.

Lying, stealing, and cheating sent her into a screaming red-faced rage, and if the guilty party couldn't be identified, she wasted no time with hell-fire-and-damnation lectures. Instead, she punished all of us.

"All right! Line up! Every one of you! Get over here right now!"

Groaning, we reluctantly formed a line in front of her. "You probably all know who did this, so you're all going to get popped!"

We stilled ourselves and tensed, dutifully stepping forward when it was our turn, submitting to a jarring, jaw-throbbing, ear-ringing slap. Still, as much as we hated it, we preferred it to long-winded lectures about hell, and days of strung-out punishment.

Generally, "pops" were handed out at the end of the day, just before we left the kitchen, so we dreaded them for an hour before they happened, then walked back to our dorms rubbing our faces and complaining, and glad it was over.

One evening, as we finished scrubbing the kitchen floor and mopped the last puddle dry, Miss Polk shouted, "Othello, I want you to stay when the others leave."

My heart sank. No doubt she'd seen something or overheard me saying something that she wasn't going to ignore.

A few minutes later, when the kitchen was straight and everyone had left except me, she poured herself a cup of coffee, walked to the table that was "her place" and sat. Not sure what kind of trouble I might be facing, I waited for her to speak.

For the longest time, she rotated her coffee cup slowly, as if inspecting it for flaws. "Sit down."

I sat.

Finally, she stopped turning the cup and sat back. "Last June when you told me your secret . . . that you had figured out how to read . . . you said that I was the only person you told. Is that true?"

"Yes, ma'am."

"Have you told anyone since?"

"No, ma'am.

She nodded, slowly lifted the cup, and took a sip of coffee. Then, just as slowly, she returned the cup to the table. "Does that mean you can also write?"

"Yes, ma'am." She picked up a dried pinto bean from where it had slipped between the table and the wall. She studied it with the same intensity she had studied the cup. "Well, then, what I want to know is . . . will you write some letters for me if I tell you what to say?"

Relief loosened my neck and shoulders. "Yes, ma'am."

She leveled hard gray eyes on me. "I can't read or write, either, but you'll keep it to yourself."

I nodded, amazed at her confession and honored by this confidence.

"You can keep your mouth shut?"

"Yes, ma'am. Did you tell anybody about me?"

"'Course not! It wasn't nobody's business."

"I can keep it shut for you."

"All right. Go on. Get out of here. If anyone asks you why you're late, tell 'em to talk to me about it." She waved her hand for me to go. "I'll probably want you to write a letter for me this weekend."

"Yes, ma'am."

I didn't hurry back to my dorm. That she had shared this confidence created an unaccustomed and pleasurable sense of pride—pride, that she, the "meanest" but fairest matron in the home, had trusted me with such a huge secret. And no one knew better than I the magnitude of that secret and the importance of respecting it.

Except for outward appearances, Miss Polk and I had a different relationship from that day forward. I wasn't exempt from rules or granted any special privileges, but when I stayed to write her letters every couple of weeks, we grew more and more comfortable with each other.

One day, after I had written a letter for her, I asked if she had ever been married and she looked away quickly. "I was in love, once."

"Why didn't you marry?"

"He was killed in the war."

"You never fell in love again?"

"Nope. Didn't want to." She blinked at suddenly watery eyes.

"Do you still love him?"

"What kind of question is that? He's dead! What good would it do?"

I shrugged. "Well, I just thought maybe—"

"Stop thinking. It's none of your business."

I knew she wasn't angry. That was just Miss Polk. She couldn't talk about things that made her cry. "May I go now?"

"Go! Get out of here!"

I started across the kitchen, headed for the back door.

"And listen to me, young lady!" She yelled after me. "I know how much coffee you're sneaking! You're not putting anything over on me."

I smiled and nodded, knowing it was her way of saying, "I still like you."

Being alone with Miss Polk gave me the same deep satisfaction I felt with Coach Royal. I couldn't really describe it but it had something to do with trust . . . knowing you could be honest and have a secret, and not be punished for it.

Only once was I privileged to be inside Miss Polk's little apartment, a tiny room behind the kitchen, connected to the kitchen and the warehouse by a concrete loading ramp. In the few minutes that I stood in that warm little room, I basked in a sense of intimacy and marveled at the neatness and softness of her belongings. Unlike her gruff "matron" demeanor, her little room with its simple furnishings was filled with quiet pastels, pictures in ornate frames, and antique lace on every pillow.

I longed to know *this* Miss Polk . . . the one who lived in a gentle room with soft, feminine things, but I knew I never would. As I turned to leave, I saw a picture on the table beside her bed—a black and white snapshot of a young soldier smiling at the camera, his foot propped on the running board of an old car.

I reached to pick it up.

"Come on." She stopped me. "If the others see you in here, I'll have to give tours."

Her dead lover was never mentioned again.

Chapter 18

Don and Mason, 1956

My Hero Returns!

We had been at Tipton Home almost seven years and hadn't seen Don or Mason once. I had seen and talked with Thurmond only one time, the day after he came to the home and just before he ran away a week later, so when on a Sunday afternoon I was told that Don had come to visit, I yelped excitedly, quickly changed my clothes, and ran to the Administration building.

Jenny and Amy were already there, perched on the edge of aqua blue chairs near the fireplace, laughing and giggling with Don and Mary. I could tell from Amy's expression that she probably didn't remember Don, but when she saw me, she squealed and ran for a hug. The truth was, I was almost as glad to see her, as Don.

Disentangling myself from her excited hug, I ran to Don's open arms. After a long, sweet embrace, I studied his strong handsome face, trying to etch it into my brain. He didn't look much different than I had remembered, just a little older.

"How've you been?" He squeezed me tightly.

"Okay." Even as the word left my mouth, I wanted to scream, "That's not true! Take us out of here! We hate it here!" But I knew there was nothing he could do.

"This is Mary." He turned me in the direction of a thin, dark-haired woman, holding a baby. "And that's William. We call him Billy."

Mary smiled and talked with us, as we gathered around to inspect the baby. "I'll be able to come see you kids every few months." Don held my hands. "When I joined the Air Force, I requested duty at Altus, so I could be near you kids." He smiled as he talked, his large brown eyes sparkling and gentle. "And the Superintendent, Brother Wellington, said I can take you for a weekend once in a while."

"Really?" The idea of spending time with him and each other thrilled us.

"Can we see Daddy?" Jenny asked. "He lives in Altus, don't he?"

I no longer shared Jenny's enthusiasm for wanting to be around Daddy, but somewhere in the back of my mind, I still loved him and wanted him to love me. That logic had entered into the picture hadn't erased the desire, it only reminded me that what I wanted couldn't be found in Daddy.

Don's smile faded. "Well . . . we'll see. I . . . well, Mary and I live on the base, so . . . . we'll see."

Then Gordon's matron brought him into the room. Eight years old now, he grinned when he saw all of us.

"Hey, kid!" Don laughed. "Remember me?"

Gordon kept smiling but shook his head. "I know you're my brother, Don. The matron told me."

Don and Mary laughed and Don tousled his hair. "Yeah. I'm your big brother. But you were just a baby with poopy diapers the last time you saw me."

Gordon, embarrassed, rolled his eyes and we all laughed.

"Sergeant James?" Brother Wellington came out of his office and walked toward us. "It's time for everyone to go to the dining room. Would you like to stay and eat with us?"

"Thank you, ah—" He turned to Mary and she nodded. "Yes, sir, we'd like that. Thank you, sir."

For the next hour, we lived in a fantasy world, the six of us at a table, eating together like a family. Don laughed and teased Gordon for eating so many canned, sliced peaches. "This is the visitor's table," Gordon whispered. "I can have all I want!"

"Oh." Don nodded, suddenly aware that his presence provided us special consideration. "Then let's get more!"

Four times, the bowl was filled with slippery, sliced peaches and Gordon ate until he couldn't force another bite down. Then he sat back, grinned, and rubbed his stomach. "I like peaches."

We walked back to the lobby, one big, almost happy family. As the minutes passed and we realized only a few minutes remained, a sense of urgency created a confusing energy. Amy tugged at me, giggling, then Jenny began to laugh and tickle Amy. I pulled Gordon down on the chair beside me and teased him. For a few minutes, we totally forgot our visitors and used the opportunity to play with each other.

When I became aware that Don and Mary were sitting quietly, waiting patiently for us to stop playing, I felt embarrassed. "I'm sorry," I said.

He smiled. "I'm glad to see you enjoy each other's company so much."

I knew he couldn't understand how starved we were for each other, and for him, too—but there wasn't enough time to go around. And I also thought I shouldn't tell him. In every letter he had written me, he mentioned how lucky we were to be in the home, so I knew he didn't know we never got to see each other.

Don and Mary stayed until Billy began to cry and fuss. I tried to tell them how much their visit meant and how ashamed I was that we behaved the way we did, but Don kept interrupting. "It's all right, Sugar. I'll be back. And you can come visit me, too. We'll start seeing each other now."

As the door closed, dread began to replace our joy. We stared at each other, knowing we wouldn't be together again until he came, and we had no idea when that would be.

Dive into Embarrassment

"Come on! Jump!" Dozens of eager voices encouraged me as I trembled on the high dive at the Altus Air Force Base. Don had taken us for the weekend and the summer heat sent us to the base pool.

"Jump! Jump!"

At fifteen, I stared down at the handsome young airmen and wished I hadn't allowed the others to talk me into this. The pool looked small from the high board.

"Dive! Other people are waiting!" Don yelled.

I glanced back at the line ascending the steps and the young man waiting behind me.

"Want a push?" He smiled and I realized he was staring at my breasts. Embarrassed that he stared so obviously, I turned back toward the pool and tugged modestly at the single strap around my neck. Then, holding my hands over my head, my thumbs locked, I sprang off the board as high as I could.

No sooner had I left the board than I knew it had been a mistake. I felt my legs trailing awkwardly behind me, uselessly kicking the air. I hit the water hard and thought I would drown before I stopped descending and started a slow return to the surface. I burst up gasping and spitting, flinging my hair out of my eyes. I sank and surfaced again, still gasping and spitting.

Then I heard the laughter. It came from both sides of the pool, from overhead, from everywhere. Did I look that stupid?

Sputtering and coughing, I tried to stabilize myself, to stop dipping and bobbing about. I looked for Don and saw him laughing, too, an instant before he dived into the water. The laughter grew louder as he swam toward me and I continued to gasp and bob in the pool.

"Hey, little sister," Don swam within inches of me, and still laughing, said, "You lost your suit!"

"What?"

"Your strap broke!"

I looked down at my naked breasts bobbing in the water. Horrified, I ducked beneath the surface, scrambling for the strap. I thrashed frantically but couldn't catch it.

Don grabbed my arm and pulled me up with one hand, grabbing the front of my suit with his other hand. With one solid yank, he tugged it up.

The laughter became hoots. Someone yelled, "Boo! Leave her alone!"

Don, still laughing, pushed me forward until I had secured enough footing to stand, then handed me the strap. Fumbling awkwardly, I tugged on the suit until I was completely covered again.

"I think I'm in love!" an airman shouted as I climbed out of the pool and hurried for the shower. At that moment, I wished I had drowned. At least, then, there would have been some sympathy to accompany the laughter.

Killing Jo Ann

Jo Ann, a dull-eyed ten-year-old, struggled to speak around a thick tongue and full slack mouth. I rarely understood her mumbled complaints. She shuffled along behind other girls in her dormitory and we all knew there was something "wrong" with her, so most of the kids tolerated her, giving her what she wanted.

The dining room was short-handed one evening, so I was sent out to wait tables. Miss Gillion's dorm of eight- to ten-year-old girls included Jo Ann. I wasn't aware of this when I was assigned the tables, and would have thought nothing of it later, had Jo Ann not died that night.

Miss Gillion, as many of the matrons did, served her girls' plates while they stood behind their chairs waiting for the blessing to be said. Each girl moved aside as Miss Gillion spooned portions onto plates.

I had just walked up with a last-minute plate of hot biscuits when Miss Gillion approached Jo Ann with a bowl of spinach. Jo Ann frowned and put her hands over her plate. "Nnnn! Nnnnn!" She shook her head, her eyes wide and panicky.

"Stop that!" Miss Gillion snapped. "Move your hands or I'll make you eat the whole bowl!"

"Nnnn! Nnnnn!" Jo Ann jerked her head from side to side.

Miss Gillion slammed the bowl down, slopping spinach on the table. Jo Ann leaned over her plate, guarding it with her arms. "Nnnn! Nnnn!"

Miss Gillion slapped the back of her head! "You're evil! An evil child!"

She hit her again, this time on the side of the face. Jo Ann jerked back, stumbled, then twisted and fell. She jerked about unnaturally, making a strange growling, sputtering sound.

The girls moved back. Other matrons ran to see.

Jo Ann twisted and jerked, her loud strange noises pushing the other girls farther back.

"She's possessed!" Miss Gillion shrieked. "Look at her! The devil's got her!" She kicked at Jo Ann's twitching, jerking body.

The matrons pressed closer. Miss McGregor gripped her paddle with both hands, staring wild-eyed at Jo Ann.

"Hit her!" Miss Gillion screamed. "Hit her! She's possessed!"

Miss McGregor raised the paddle and the matrons moved in so closely I couldn't see Jo Ann actually being hit but I saw the paddle rise and fall and heard its thudding blows. Jo Ann yelped and groaned as she thrashed about. The matrons shrieked, jumping back as if Jo Ann would contaminate them.

Then the gagging and moaning stopped. The dining room fell motionless and silent for several seconds.

"Get back! Get back!" The matrons yelled at those closest.

"Let's get her out of here!" Miss Gillion ordered. "While she's quiet."

Miss McGregor and Miss Gillion each grabbed a foot and dragged Jo Ann around the table, down the middle aisle of the dining room, and out into the catwalk. Her legs in the air, one shoe missing, Jo Ann's dress rode up to her waist, exposing her panties and the welts on her buttocks and thighs. Once she had been pulled out of sight, Miss McGregor closed the door and came back inside.

"Stand behind your chairs!" She snapped at her ashen-faced girls. "Get back behind your chairs! It's time for the prayer."

Whatever happened in the catwalk, none of us saw. We didn't know who came to take Jo Ann but by the time the meal was finished, she was gone. Miss Gillion didn't come back into the dining room that night, and the next morning in chapel, Brother Wellington stood before us for a full minute before he spoke. With his fingertips pressed together and his palms rounded as if holding an invisible ball, he began in a somber tone. "I have a sad announcement. Jo Ann died last night."

Our collective gasp rose through the room.

"She died of an epileptic seizure."

Ice formed in my heart.

"Her parents are to blame," he said in a soulful tone. "When we called them last night, we learned for the first time that Jo Ann was an epileptic. And because they didn't tell us . . . well, Jo Ann died as a result."

The ice spread through my mind and body. *She died because crazy matrons thought she was possessed by the devil. All of us knew there was something wrong with Jo Ann. Why couldn't the matrons see it?*

The ice burned as it thickened, forming a solid wall between Brother Wellington's words and what I knew was the truth. In an effort to absolve the matrons and the home, he talked for twenty minutes about her shameful parents hiding the truth from them and how the only information they had on any of us was what our parents told them.

Anger stiffened my back. Any sane person could tell something wasn't right with Jo Ann. Prior to Brother Wellington's lengthy description of epilepsy, I had never heard of it, and learning about it only heightened my rage. How could such a sickness be called demon possession? And why, if the kids knew something wasn't right with Jo Ann, didn't the matrons know?

I seethed all day because there was nothing I could do to bring Jo Ann's attackers to justice. Then, after supper, just before I went to bed, Sister Wellington came to our dormitory and called six of us into the matron's room.

She looked at each of us. "You'll be singing at Jo Ann's funeral."

Before that moment, I hadn't realized she had assembled the girl's sextet. Still upset over the death, which we all agreed was caused by the beating, we listened sullenly as she told us the songs to rehearse.

The funeral, itself, sickened me further. We crowded in a small dark hallway of a house, hidden behind a door opened only a few inches so we could be heard, and five or six adults sat in folding chairs in the living room. Jo Ann's coffin blocked the door that hid us from their view. All the while, my stomach churned. Singing for Jo Ann was an honor, but the circumstances of her death not only dishonored her, they dishonored all that we'd been taught about truth, goodness, and holiness.

That day, our Christian examples toppled from their pedestals—pedestals that I suddenly realized had been built *by* and *for* themselves. Their lofty perches created only an illusion of goodness, an illusion they honored only when convenient.

That night as I stared at the cinder block wall beside my bed, and ran my finger along the rough mortar separating the blocks, I wondered what it would be like to live in a good family, like some of the Town kids had. What did it feel like to love and know that the ones you loved, loved you? What kind of difference would it make when it was time to fall asleep, to know that the adults in your life could be trusted to defend you against harm?

I doubted that Jo Ann ever asked herself those questions, yet I felt certain that every hour of her life had been more frightening than mine. Now, the only "goodness" that remained for her was the fact that nothing could threaten her.

Lesbian Encounter

I awoke in the middle of the night, stumbled groggily into the bathroom and stopped, confused by what I saw. Two girls, at the far end of the bathroom, were embraced in a strange, tangled position. One sat on the lavatory, wearing only her pajama top, and the other, naked, was crouched between her legs. They looked up, startled, then turned their faces.

For the briefest of moments, I tried to comprehend what I was seeing, but confused and afraid, I spun around and left immediately. The image haunted me for several days as I tried to understand what I had seen, and was very glad that I wasn't awake enough to recognize them.

The next Saturday, when Miss Polk asked me to stay and write a letter for her, I found the courage to tell her what I saw.

She barked a short scoffing laugh and asked, "Who was it?"

"I don't know," I said. "I was too sleepy. I mean, I couldn't even understand what they were doing."

She laughed uncomfortably. "Doesn't matter. I'll bet I know who they were."

"Well . . . what I don't understand," I began tentatively, "were they . . . were they—? *What* were they doing?"

"They're lesbians!" She said as if I should have known.

"They're—? What?"

She looked away and shook her head.

Embarrassed that I didn't know what she obviously thought I *should* know, I said, "Well . . . what—? Can you explain it?"

Impatiently and a little embarrassed, she said, "Some girls like girls. Some boys like boys."

"Like?"

"Well, some girls like girls the same way most girls like boys."

I squinted at her. "You mean . . . they like 'em like a boyfriend?"

She nodded. "That's what I mean."

I tried to imagine two girls kissing and trying to "do it," both frustrated because neither had a penis, and I began to laugh. Uncontrollably. "But how . . . how—?" I couldn't stop laughing.

Miss Polk laughed as hard as I did.

"What good does it do?" I finally managed.

Still laughing, she wiped her eyes. "I don't have all the answers. Somehow, I think they work it out so they're happy."

I squinted at her. "How?"

"All right, that's enough about that." She wiped her eyes again. "I just know some girls like girls and some boys like boys. And I think I know who you're talking about."

I didn't ask who she thought they were because I didn't want to know. The idea of bumping pelvis bones made me laugh so quickly and easily, I knew I would burst out laughing every time I saw them.

Entertaining Angry Lions

We were not allowed to have radios because the music and lyrics were "sinful" and would tempt us to dance. In the ninth grade, however, when some of my classmates started driving, they roared into the parking lot, their car radios blasting. The music was so much different than church songs—which were the only songs I knew—I listened in awe. I loved what I heard and decided the matrons might be right for the first time—that music just might tempt me to dance.

When I heard Debbie Reynolds sing *Tammy*, I thought her voice was the sweetest sound I had ever heard. I hummed the song all day, trying to memorize it so I could pick it out on the piano. For a week, every chance I got, I slipped off to a piano and worked on it.

Then, at school, I heard that the Tipton Lions Club was looking for entertainment for their next meeting. I cornered Jenny in the hallway between classes, told her about it, and asked her if she would sing *Tammy* if I accompanied her. She thought it sounded like fun, if in fact, we were allowed to do it.

Since Jenny and I had never been allowed to be together, to work or play, and we were surprised when Sister Wellington said she would check and see if the Lions Club would let us entertain, and even more surprised when they agreed.

The week prior to the performance we were allowed to practice a half hour each day in one of the home's classrooms. Those were the sweetest moments we had spent since arriving at the home, seven years earlier—and definitely the most time we had ever spent together during those years.

When the day arrived, we left school on our lunch hour, knowing we had to be back by our first afternoon class. At the Lions Club meeting hall, we waited patiently to perform while the men argued over the price to sell brooms at an up-coming fund-raiser.

"You sell 'em for that and we'll lose money!"

"Yeah! This is a fund-raiser. Not the Salvation Army!"

Our excitement and anxiety mounted as the argument continued . . . and continued.

When, finally, they stopped and gave us a nod to begin, every man sat with his arms crossed, scowling, making us even more nervous. I played the introduction and when Jenny sang, I could hardly hear her. I dampened the piano with the soft pedal but I still couldn't hear her.

We struggled through all the verses, acutely aware that not one man in the audience had changed his defiant posture or released his frown.

When at last it ended, the feeble applause lasted maybe five seconds before the men in the front row turned and began arguing with those behind them again.

Jenny and I scooted out the side door, laughing and running to get back to school. "Can you believe that?" she said. "They were so mad they couldn't listen!"

"I know! It was horrible!"

We mimicked their scowls and arguments, yelling and jabbing our fists at each other. "We gotta charge more!"

"This is a fundraiser! Not the Salvation Army!"

Just doing something together made us heady. The stupid old men at the Lions Club couldn't argue us out of that. For a whole hour we had been together, publicly, as sisters, an experience we never wanted to forget.

All Together . . . Once

It had been almost eight years since Momma died, and eight years since I had been with all of my brothers and sisters. Then one Sunday, Don brought Mason and Thurmond to visit and my excitement soared to new heights.

From left: Gordon, Thurmond, Jenny, Othello, Amy, and Don. Mason took the picture.

Amy and Gordon didn't remember Mason and Thurmond, and only knew Don because of his recent visits. They, however, were so starved to see Jenny and me that they bounced around like puppies romping between us.

Thurmond, now in the Army, strutted proudly in his spotless uniform, while Don sat comfortably talking to whoever sat nearest.

It was Mason, however, that fascinated me most that day. The tallest of the three, he spoke quietly and touched us gently when we approached. I hadn't seen him in seven years and couldn't take my eyes off his handsome face. Although he smiled constantly, softly joking at what we said and did, the pain in his eyes hurt me.

I knew that his experience in prison probably caused it and I sensed it was too raw and sensitive to mention, so I asked, "What are you doing now?"

"Well, Sugar, I'm working for GM . . . and . . . and well, I've got this little band and we play at some clubs on weekends."

"Do you sing?"

He shook his head and chuckled. "Naw. I play guitar."

"Really? Did you bring it?"

He glanced around the lobby and laughed quietly. "Well, I doubt that would be appreciated here, Sugar. It's electric. I don't think anyone but you would like me playing it here."

They stayed for two hours, visiting with us in the lobby, and when they left I began to count the months, days, and hours until I was eighteen, when I could leave and be a part of their lives again.

Bible Class Beating

"All right! Come in. Sit down. And be quiet. Sit over here."

Between fifteen and twenty teenage girls entered the gym and sat on the bleachers in front of Joe Bard, our new Monday night Bible teacher. Three or four of us sat on the front and lowest bleacher, just a few feet from where he stood.

For two days we had looked forward to Joe teaching our Bible class because he was about thirty, handsome in a Rock Hudson sort of way, and was the PE coach for the home's athletic program. Girls were sometimes allowed an hour to play basketball on Saturday afternoons, but there were no girls teams.

"Open your Bibles to First Corinthians," he said.

Several of the girls behind me continued to shuffle and whisper but I didn't think anything of it. It generally took us several minutes to settle down, and tonight would probably take longer because we all wanted Joe's attention.

"Sue Ann," Joe said firmly. "Stop whispering and open your Bible."

"Yes, sir." I glanced back and saw her flipping through pages, trying not to giggle because she had been singled out.

Joe had us each read three or four verses, then asked us to explain what they meant. A few tried to impress him with their understanding, others with wit, but we were all eager to impress him. When, occasionally, he smiled at someone, we were all jealous.

About halfway through the class, Joe said, "Sue Ann, this is the second time I'm telling you to stop talking. If I have to tell you a third time, you'll be given an assignment you won't like." Neither his voice nor his words sounded particularly menacing, until he added, "You don't talk in my class, unless I call on you!"

We hushed.

"Yes, sir." Sue Ann turned scarlet and lowered her eyes.

Toward the end of the class, as he flipped back and forth through pages, telling us which scriptures to read before next class, we started to murmur and whisper again as we flipped through the pages, trying to keep up.

"What'd he say?"

"What verse was that?"

"I said four and five! Four and five! And Sue Ann! You're talking again!"

"No. No, Joe, I wasn't. I was just asking—"

"Talking! That's what you were doing. So . . . let's see . . . for next week, Sue Ann, your assignment is to bring me one hundred verses that call Satan by the name Lucifer. Have you got that?"

"Yes, sir. May I use a concordance?"

"If you want." Then he smiled at her. "Class dismissed. Good night."

It wasn't my assignment so I didn't think about it again until the following week, after we had assembled on the bleachers and Joe said, "Sue Ann, did you complete the assignment?"

"Ah, no . . . sir. I didn't because . . . because there aren't one hundred scriptures that refer to Satan by the name of Lucifer."

"I know." He carefully set his Bible on the bleacher and picked up a paddle from the floor. We gaped at it, not convinced he would really use it. About twenty-inches long and a half-inch thick, it had nickel-size holes drilled every couple of inches. "Now come down here. I'm going to demonstrate what I do to girls who talk in my class. That way, there will be no talking in my class."

Over the years, I had heard the boys at school occasionally talk about these paddles but I had never had one used on me. I knew they did a lot more damage than regular paddles, so I held my breath as Sue Ann slowly descended the bleachers.

A thin girl with short, blonde hair, Sue Ann halted about two feet from him. Tears streaked her cheeks at the thought of what was about to happen. "I'm sorry, Joe. I won't talk again. Ever."

It was as if he didn't hear her. "Turn around."

"Please . . . "

"Turn around."

So stiff she could hardly move, she slowly turned her back to him.

"Now, grab your ankles."

Without another sound, Sue Ann leaned down and grabbed her ankles.

The gym fell completely silent. Then Joe hit the back of her thighs so hard he sent her sprawling, face down.

"That's what I do to talkers!" he yelled, hitting her again and again as she tried to get up or away. "And this! This! And this!"

She screamed and twisted, raised her arms, but he didn't stop. Skin popped from the holes in the board, leaving bloody wounds in her thighs and legs.

We cried and screamed, huddled together. Sue Ann had stopped moving but Joe kept hitting her, yelling, "This is what I do to talkers! This!"

Two teenage boys ran into the gym. "What's all the—? Good God!" They ran at Joe, shoving him aside and knocking the bloody paddle to the floor.

Joe didn't seem to know he had been shoved aside. His back to us now, he kept screaming, "And this! And this! And this!" He flailed at the air.

"Let's get her out of her." The boys lifted Sue Ann's unconscious body and carried her out of the gym. We ran out after them, leaving Joe still crazed and shouting, and beating the air. The boys carried Sue Ann halfway across the campus, to the "girls' side," then gave her to us. Four of us half-dragged and half-carried her to the dorm.

Miss Carter had been our matron only three weeks and when she saw Sue, I thought she was going to faint.

"Oh, dear God! Oh, dear God, forgive me!" Her hands trembled at her mouth. "He told me he was going to paddle her . . . I just . . . didn't know . . . Oh, God, forgive me!" Frantically, she turned to us for help. "Get some water and washcloths! Oh, God, is she conscious?" She leaned down to peer more closely. "Is she even breathing?" She picked up Sue Ann's bloody wrist and felt for a pulse. "Someone go call Brother Wellington!"

While we waited for Brother Wellington, Miss Carter directed us as we gently laid cool wet cloths on Sue Ann's bruised and beaten body.

Sue Ann regained consciousness just as Brother Wellington arrived. He knelt beside the bed, frowned, and called her name. Sue Ann slowly lifted her eyelids until she could see him.

I couldn't hear what he said but after a few minutes, he and Miss Carter walked back to Miss Carter's room and shut the door. He left a few minutes later, and it was clear Miss Carter had been crying.

The rest of us went to our beds quickly, without talking. The next morning Sue Ann's swollen face and body, blackened with bruises, was hardly recognizable. We left for school thinking that she would probably be taken to a hospital, but when we returned she was still in her bed, looking as if she hadn't moved.

Miss Carter sat beside her, encouraging her to take sips of water and broth. Sister Wellington came by in the evening, two days later, and studied Sue Ann as she slept. "I think she'll be okay," she said. "Let's just leave her be."

"But I'm not even sure she's conscious half the time!" Miss Carter said, panic raising her voice.

Sister Wellington glanced around to see who might be listening. "Let's go into your room."

We heard their voices rise and fall behind the closed door but couldn't hear specific arguments. However, when the door opened, it was obvious that both women were angry.

The next afternoon, when we returned from school, another new matron greeted us when we came in. "I'm Miss Gladden," she said. "I think we'll all get along fine. I used to work at Boles Home."

We all knew that Boles Home was another Church of Christ-sponsored orphanage because other matrons from Boles had come to work at Tipton. The rules were apparently similar between the homes because the matrons seemed to have no trouble adjusting.

Sue Ann didn't get out of bed for a week. When she did, two of us helped her get to the bathroom and back, and it was another week before she moved about slowly on her own. We knew she had never seen a doctor, and figured that was why Miss Carter had left. Not only had she thought the beating was excessive, but she wanted Sue Ann to be taken to a hospital or doctor.

Joe didn't leave the home right away, but we were assigned another Bible teacher, which helped us relax a little because none of us wanted to look at Joe again.

"Why wouldn't they take her to the doctor?" I asked Joline one night after we were in bed. "It doesn't make sense. She could've died."

"Probably because a doctor would have hospitalized her and the home doesn't want that kind of publicity. The home would lose lots of donations if the churches knew things like that happened."

It had never occurred to me that the church members would have cared. I always assumed that because the home was overseen by the Elders of the Tipton Church of Christ, probably all the members knew and agreed with what went on.

Teaching Gordon to Sing

At church, the home kids filled half of the pews. Most of us liked going to church because it gave us a chance to peek at, and wave to our brothers and sisters. When Gordon was about ten, his dorm filled the pews behind our dorm. He sat directly behind me most of the time, and listening to him sing gave me immense pleasure.

The Church of Christ doesn't use instrumental music in their worship services, so most of us learned to harmonize at an early age. Gordon's matron, a strong alto, ran her finger along the music line as she sang and Gordon followed along. Over the months I heard his confidence grow, and because I now played the piano well enough to accompany him, I asked if I could teach him to sing a few songs that could be sung outside of church.

Eventually, my request was granted and I worked with him after school once or twice a week, using the old piano in the fifth-grade room. He loved singing and I loved the time I had with him. A few weeks later we performed at the monthly birthday assembly.

His quick smile and unusual confidence made him fun to watch, and the larger the audience, the more comfortable he became. He sang three songs and everyone applauded enthusiastically.

A few weeks later, although Gordon was only ten, he was asked to lead singing in chapel, and then in church. A few weeks after that, he was asked to speak, to actually present a lesson. Quoting scriptures and flipping through his Bible like a miniature minister, everyone watched, mesmerized by his presentation. Too small to use the podium, he stood beside it and spoke with more ease and charm than most of our ministers.

Soon, he was asked to speak at the Wednesday night church service in town, prompting other invitations to speak at Churches of Christ in neighboring cities. A perfect representative for the home, by age twelve, Gordon enjoyed more travel and celebrity—and prompted more generous donations—than any kid at the home, and I loved it. He traveled with the senior choir, sang solos with them, and then spoke before congregations who applauded not only his talent but the good work being done at Tipton Orphans Home.

Dining Room Brawls

There were frequent skirmishes in the dining room, generally between the teenage boys and their matrons. One evening, after everyone was seated, I hurried from the kitchen through the dining room, carrying a glass of juice for one of the matrons who had made a special request for it, and irked Miss Polk in the process. "Like we don't have enough to do! Here. Take it to her!"

I was about halfway down the length of the dining room when a loud yelp came from the far end, near the back door, where the older boys sat. Everyone turned toward the disturbance. The yelling accelerated and David Reed, seventeen, jumped up. His matron came out of her chair and slammed her fist against David's right shoulder. He yelled again and flung his arm around, catching her in the face. She stumbled and several matrons jumped up and rushed to the table.

That's when I saw the fork stuck in David's shoulder. His matron hadn't just hit him, she had stabbed him in the shoulder with a fork. Another boy yanked it out.

Yelling, shouting, and pushing filled the end of the dining room. Chairs scrapped the floor and banged the walls, tables jostled and moved. Dishes fell and matrons ran toward the commotion. For a few minutes, the older boys and the matrons—including the four or five men who worked for the home and ate with us—went at it so fiercely, the rest of us backed away.

I stood on a chair and saw David and two other boys fight their way through the crowd and run out the back door. It took several minutes to re-establish order and clean up the mess.

Later I learned that David and his friends had run away that evening. I knew we would never see them again because the home rarely brought back runaways over the age of twelve.

Chapter 19

The Reality Train

At times, loneliness became so all-consuming I felt as though I were dying, breath by breath. Joline had graduated and left and I knew I would never hear from her again. Kids who left rarely returned and I couldn't blame them. Even those who had sisters and brothers seldom come back to visit them, and I sometimes wondered if that was because they had been kept apart so long, they forgot each other. Or . . . maybe they just hated the home that much.

I never stopped longing to see Jenny, Amy, and Gordon, to talk with them, to hug them and find out how they *really* were. Months would pass with nothing more than a glimpse across the dining room or in church, and it sometimes seemed that everything I once believed was untrue, and I would begin to doubt reality and question my own memories.

Did I ever really have a mother, or did I dream that? Was there ever a little shack that exploded into a fireball, or was it some terrifying nightmare? Were my brothers and sisters really my brothers and sisters, or fantasies I had dreamed up? Perhaps my memories weren't really mine, but just things I had heard, and I somehow "made them mine."

Did anything exist outside of Tipton? The newspaper that I sometimes saw in the lobby might be just a prop to convince us that another world existed, when in fact, it didn't. Perhaps the illusion was maintained to give us hope and make us easier to manage. Even the town of Tipton became suspect in my mind as I considered the possibility that it existed only as an extension of the home.

When my thinking became lodged in this restricted orbit of doubt, one depressing supposition linked to the next, I moved in a daze, unable to focus on the task at hand. I observed the other girls in the dorm, or the kitchen, as if they were robots or mannequins and we were all in the middle of a stage—a flatland called Oklahoma—with parts to play, words to say, work to do.

Kitchen robots cooked for laundry, farm, and matron-robots. One hundred and eighty young-looking robots were kept in line by older-looking robots, all programmed to remain ignorant of our robotic state.

But what was the point? The robots never touched. There were no pats or hugs and so few smiles that the slightest upward turn in a matron-robot's mouth, or the tiniest nod of approval prompted feelings of undying devotion.

Maybe we were an experiment . . . a group of non-touching robots placed on earth by more intelligent creatures from outer space. Maybe we would never die, but just go on walking through day after identical day, working, going to school, and sleeping, routine broken only by violence.

Perhaps we were supposed to figure out that we were lifeless, soulless beings . . . a part of some alien project . . . to see if we were smart enough to escape.

One evening, after two days of feeling completely detached from the world around me, I overheard someone mention the train that passed through the wheat field behind our dormitory. The sound of the train had become so much a part of my life that I hadn't really heard it in years. Yet, if there was a train, then it would be proof that more world existed than Tipton.

A little before eight o'clock that evening, I sneaked out of the dormitory and walked out into the wheat field to the railroad tracks. There, I sat alone, waiting for the train. It, like the newspaper in the lobby, might only be a prop, I reminded myself. A daily prop meant to convince us that there were other places in the world.

When I first heard and felt it, I moved off the tracks and stepped back several feet. In the distance, I saw its light, heard its whistle, and waited for it to reach me. It rumbled toward me, its massive engine roaring and its clacking wheels growing louder by the second. Then, it finally thundered past me with such force, the ground trembled beneath my feet and its roar resounded through the night and filled my head. Its vibrating power quivered through my whole body, and I experienced it to the core of my being.

The train was real. There *was* more world, another town somewhere. The train roared down the track for a reason . . . taking something somewhere . . . disturbing the ground and the air as it went. Yes, the train was real. This tiny bit of truth restored my hope, diminished my doubt, and made me feel less insane.

I stood in the wheat field long after it passed, sorry it was gone, wishing I were on it, going somewhere . . . anywhere . . . and wanting it to come back and thunder past me a second time so that I could feel its power and realness again.

When the night grew quiet except for the crickets and the wind whispering through the tall grain, I turned and slowly walked back to the dormitory.

Many times after that night, when my questions returned and I began doubting my own existence and the existence of everything around me, I slipped out of the dormitory and waited in the wheat field alone . . . to be restored by the train. Sometimes I cried, other times I laughed, but both tears and laughter sprang from knowing the train was real, and therefore, so was I.

Mocked

At one of the three football games I was allowed to attend during my high school years, a letter I had written two years earlier came back to haunt me. The half-time show had just ended and the bands reclaimed their seats on opposite sides when both teams ran onto the field, ready to butt heads again.

Two of the cheerleaders from the visiting team giggled as they ran around the far end of the field and approached our side. I saw them coming, secretly envious because home girls weren't allowed to be cheerleaders. As they neared our bleachers, I lost track of them and turned my attention to the teams now on the field, being cheered by noisy spectators on both sides.

I stood at the fence with a few other home kids, hoping the night air wouldn't get any colder.

"Is there someone named Othello here?"

I turned, surprised to see the two cheerleaders.

"I'm Othello."

Instantly, their hands went to their mouths; then they giggled and walked away.

"Why?" I followed them a few feet. "Why did you ask?"

They glanced uncomfortably at each other, then covered their mouths and giggled again. I stood silently, waiting for their response. Finally, one said, "You're the one who wrote the letter saying, *May I be your daughter? I'll be good!* aren't you?"

Too humiliated to speak, I stared in disbelief.

"We just wanted to see what you looked liked." Turning quickly, they ran off, laughing.

For a moment, I couldn't move. Embarrassed into numbness, I swallowed hard against the aching lump trying to choke me. When I finally moved numbly back to the fence to stare at the game, someone asked, "What'd they want?"

"Nothing. They were just being silly."

Before they appeared, I had been shivering from the cold; now I felt so hot I thought I might suffocate. What a stupid, stupid thing I had done. How could I have been such a fool? Why didn't I know that my desperate request would be shared with kids who would laugh and ridicule me? When would I learn that adults couldn't be trusted? They would always, always, find a way to distort the truth, twist your words, and make something ugly from the most innocent request.

And yet, even as I lectured myself I grieved that the people who had received my letter could have mocked me. It was a difficult, ugly reality to accept because in my mind they had come to represent the "perfect parents"—parents I wanted to believe existed somewhere, for someone—and letting go of that idea left me feeling empty, weak, and stupid.

The Touching Sickness

The home had no counselors or therapists, just an annual visit from representatives of the State Mental Hospital in Norman, Oklahoma. The representatives came, perhaps once a year, stayed a day or two, and left with three or four children to be "committed." I had heard the home received 10 percent of its money from the state and that visits from representatives of the hospital was one of the conditions that had to be met. I never knew for sure.

However, during one of the hospital's "visits," I learned that Amy was going to be committed. Panicked, I ran to Brother Wellington's office and burst in without knocking. "Is Amy going to be sent to the mental hospital?"

Brother Wellington, who had been writing something, set his pencil aside and leaned back. "First," he began, "you're not supposed to be here."

"Has she been selected?" I stood rigidly behind a chair facing his desk.

"Where are you supposed to be right now?" He stood and moved from behind the desk. "I know you're not supposed to be here."

"I'll go as soon as you tell me! Is she being committed to the mental hospital?"

He moved behind me and closed the door, then gestured for me to sit but I didn't.

He sighed. "Well, I can tell you there's going to be a hearing tomorrow. Nothing's definite yet."

"A hearing? What do you mean?"

"An official hearing with a judge, and . . . doctors . . . and you can be there. I was going to let you know in the morning."

"But why? Amy's not crazy!"

Two men I had never seen before crossed the lobby, approached the office, and glanced at us through the large glass window. "Those men are from the hospital," Brother Wellington said. "Now, tomorrow at ten A.M., come here to my office. I'll let you speak then."

"What's the hearing supposed to do?"

"Well, you just come back in the morning . . . " He opened the door. "And you'll see. I've already notified Miss Polk. She knows you'll be leaving the kitchen to get cleaned up for the meeting at nine-thirty. Be here by ten."

The men outside the window noticed the door opening and moved toward it as I left. Knowing they wanted to take Amy away, I trembled with anger as I brushed past them.

The next morning five people sat in Brother Wellington's office—the sheriff, Brother Wellington, a hospital representative who introduced himself without using the word "doctor," Amy, and me.

"Where's the judge?" I asked, glaring at Brother Wellington. "You said there would be a judge."

"The sheriff has the authority to act in cases such as this," Brother Wellington said.

"Cases such as what?" I blurted. "There's nothing wrong with Amy! She's as normal as anybody! You can't just take her away!"

The sheriff smiled at Amy and leaned forward. "Little girl," he began in a honeyed voice, "what would you say is the worst thing you've ever done?"

She thought a moment, then said with conviction, "I ran away."

The hospital representative and the sheriff both nodded soberly. The sheriff stroked his chin. "Hmmm."

"She's run away *once*!" I said. "That doesn't make her crazy! If you think it's crazy to run away once, then almost everyone here is crazier than she is! I've run away three times!"

No one responded. Amy glared angrily at me, and I suddenly felt confused.

"That, compounded by what her matron says . . . " the sheriff said. "I think that for her own good . . . "

Brother Wellington interrupted, "One second, please." He stood and opened the door. "Othello, will you and Amy please wait in the hall?"

"No! You can't do this!"

Amy calmly stood and glared at me as she walked out. Baffled by her response and terrified that I would never see her again, a little cry escaped my throat as I hurried out, too. Brother Wellington closed the door behind me. "Why didn't you say something, Amy?" I grabbed her arms. "Why didn't you fight for yourself?"

"Because I want to go!" she whispered. "It has to be better than here!"

My head spun. I couldn't believe what I was hearing. "No! No! You don't! You don't understand! It'll be much worse! Much worse!"

"Nothing would be worse, Othello. Nothing! I hate it here!"

I grabbed her hands. "So do I! But this won't help!"

Then, while the men discussed the details in the office, Amy told me that she had been planning this for weeks.

"I heard Miss Stork talking to the sewing lady last month. They were talking about the hospital coming to take kids away." Her eyes rounded with excitement. "Then Miss Stork started talking about the touching sickness."

"The—what?"

"She said some people go to the hospital because they have the touching sickness. It makes you touch things. Everything." She touched the wall, her clothes, my arm, the door. "So I started touching things. Everything, every time any matron was around."

My fingers covered my mouth as I tried to listen and cry silently. "No . . . no!"

"And it worked!" She whispered. "Miss Stork told about me!" She nodded, a smug look on her face. "Miss Stork believed I had the touching sickness! It worked!"

"You've got to tell them that!" I searched frantically for a way to convince her but the door opened and the men stepped out into the hall. "She's not crazy!" I cried. "Please, don't take her! It was all a game! A game!"

Amy glared at me as they walked her across the lobby and out the door.

"Go back to work, Othello," Brother Wellington said. "This is the best thing for Amy and all concerned."

The pain and emptiness that swallowed me stole every ounce of energy and I cried off and on for days, afraid that Amy might get hurt or even die, and I would never know.

Jenny Expelled

When fourteen-year-old Dora Lee came to the home, it was her last hope of staying out of the Tecumseh Reform School. If she didn't adjust, she was told, she would be sent away immediately.

Miss Polk warned that anyone involved with Dora would probably end up in trouble, so when I heard Dora was placed in Jenny's dormitory—and the two had become fast friends—I worried about Jenny.

Rumors spread quickly that Dora slipped out at night and went with airmen from Altus Air Force Base, so I couldn't wait to warn Jenny to stay away from her. My chance came a few days later when Jenny came into the kitchen and went into one of the walk-in refrigerators.

I followed and closed the door.

"Hi, Othello! Miss McGregor wants an apple to take to her room." She picked one from the top of the box.

"Jenny," I began tentatively, afraid I would anger her. "You've got to listen to me. Dora Lee will get you in trouble. Please stay away from her."

Jenny looked at the apple, frowned, and dug through the box, finally selecting another one. "Dora's nice," she said. "You just don't know her."

"I know she can get you into a lot of trouble. Please don't hang around with her."

Resentment crossed her face. "I know that's what people say, but it's not true."

"It is!" I pleaded, frantic to make her believe me. "In fact, if she messes up once more, she's going to a reform school! And if you're involved with her—!"

"Oh, leave me alone!" She tried to walk around me but I took her arm. She was taller than me now, but I held my position as the "big" sister. "She's bad news, Jenny. Please stay away from her!"

She jerked her arm away. "You don't know what you're talking about! Besides, what do you want? For me to be a goody-goody like you? I would rather have Dora for a sister!"

I knew she didn't really mean it, but the sting of her words kept me from following her as she left. *She would rather have Dora for a sister?*

Stunned, I stood there thinking about how important it had seemed to be a "good example"—and for what? In the end, it didn't matter.

A few days later, Sister Wellington told me that both Jenny and Dora had been caught sneaking out with airmen and had both been sent away.

"What? You sent Jenny to the reform school, too?"

"No." A nasty smirk pulled the corners of her mouth upward before she turned her back to me and walked away.

A week or so later I saw Sister Wellington again and asked where Jenny was.

"With your brother, Mason."

Word quickly spread that Jenny had been forced to leave because she was pregnant. Embarrassed and humiliated for her, I tried to stop the rumors but knew I couldn't. When I asked Sister Wellington about it, she shrugged and said, "Well, she'd been sneaking out with airmen, so she probably was."

My sense of loss and guilt became all-consuming. Mason had been in prison . . . he played in a band, in night clubs . . . what kind of example—and how much help—would he be? And what if Daddy lived with them . . . would he try to rape her, too?

I begged God for forgiveness, for not doing enough . . . for not being smart enough to have stopped her. Now, both of my sisters were gone and I had no control over what happened to them. Only Gordon and I were left, and in all the years we'd been there, we had never been allowed to sit down and actually talk—and that wasn't going to change.

Christmas Eve Dread

I loved—and hated—Christmas. Each year, anticipation built to a frenzied pitch between Thanksgiving and Christmas Eve. It was as if I expected some miracle to suddenly change everything, and this strange expectation didn't lessen from year to year. Then, around noon on Christmas Eve, a dread would begin to seep through me, threatening to spoil everything. Regardless of the weather, Christmas Eve night was always the coldest night of the year.

I lay awake, remembering Momma's words, "I'll be home for Christmas," and secretly I waited. I had kept the ruby necklace that I made for her the first Christmas after the fire, until I was twelve, then threw it in the trash one Christmas day. But even with the necklace gone, my hope continued to build as Christmas approached.

On Christmas mornings, when everyone else excitedly opened their gifts from the churches that sponsored them, I had no interest. I felt guilty knowing that someone had shopped for me, and knew I should be thankful, but I wasn't. What I wanted couldn't be wrapped in paper or tied with a ribbon. It didn't exist. Although I knew better, in the secret-most place of my heart, I wanted Momma to return.

Best-looking Girl

Between classes, in the hall, Don Gibson nudged me and leaned down to whisper, "Guess who was voted the best looking girl in school?"

"I voted for Maggie Ward. She probably got it."

Don grinned and shook his head.

"Well, she should have." I opened my locker and exchanged my math book for my English book. "She's the prettiest."

"You did!" He stepped back, smiling, and spread his arms.

"Oh, sure I did. And you were voted most likely to succeed." I turned away and headed for my English class.

"It's true!" He stayed with me.

"Hey, Othello! Congratulations!" It was Glenda Faye. "You got prettiest girl!"

Half a dozen students who rarely noticed me, suddenly approached, all of them talking at once.

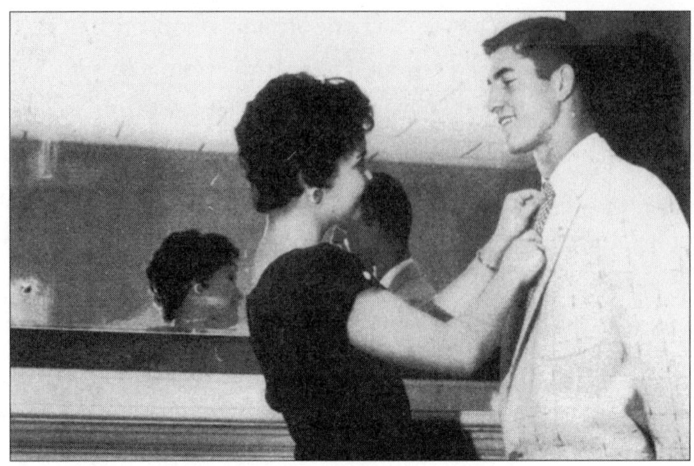

Othello James and Delbert Laing, "Best Looking," 1958

My mouth went dry. "That's impossible!"

For the next several minutes, my ears buzzed and my head felt as though it had been stuffed with cotton. *If I was voted the best-looking girl, then it was a joke. They were mocking me.*

Too humiliated to speak, I pushed through them and headed for my English class. One by one, as the rest of the class filed in, everyone had a comment. I kept my eyes on my book, embarrassed to look up.

Why would they do such a cruel, humiliating thing? I tried not to cry.

The next week when the photographer took pictures of the "best looking girl and boy" for the yearbook, I told him that I honestly didn't want my picture taken.

"You're kidding, of course."

"No, sir. Can you not take it?"

He shook his head and thought about it. Finally, he said, "Tell you what I'll do . . . " He stood. "Come with me. I have an idea." Just as we were leaving the room, Delbert, who had been voted "best looking" boy, met us at the door.

"Are you Delbert?" the photographer asked.

Delbert nodded.

"Come along."

Delbert shrugged and we followed the photographer into the Home Ec building where the photographer positioned us in front of a mirror so that only my profile was captured. As instructed, I smiled at Delbert, which wasn't hard to do because he *was* the best looking boy in school.

As we left the building, I felt grateful for the photographer's creativity. At least, he had tried to help.

Glenda's Best Friend

A few days later, as I stepped off the bus, Glenda Faye, who had lost her arm several years earlier, asked, "Do you care if I walk with you to the dorm?"

It seemed a strange request because there was nothing to keep her from doing it, and I probably wouldn't have noticed if she hadn't asked.

"I want to ask you something, but I want it to be a secret."

I wasn't crazy about Glenda because she was generally so cranky, but I decided to listen to her secret. "Okay."

After a moment, she said, "Can I be your best friend?"

Surprised by the question because I thought friendship had to grow into the "best" category, I didn't answer right away.

"I want to go where you go and do what you do."

Confused, because we were nothing alike, I asked, "Why?"

She stopped walking and stared directly into my eyes. "Because you're the best looking girl in school, and if we're best friends, everyone will look at me, too."

My first response was to laugh—and I did—but her pained expression stopped me. "I'm sorry. I wasn't laughing at you. You—you just don't understand. No one's looking at me. That 'best looking' thing was a joke. A bad joke. They did it to embarrass me because I—I don't know why. Maybe they just don't like me."

Her expression didn't change. "I still want to hang around with you. I think they meant it."

I stared at her artificial arm, which was bent to help hold her books. As usual, she wasn't wearing the hand, just the hook.

I shrugged. "Okay."

I knew Glenda was fooling herself because we had nothing in common. She liked commotion, fights, and a sense of danger. She often spread rumors to make things happen, then took sides and got into the middle of the argument. Because of her handicap, she worked in the dormitory as a "house girl" and had more time to think up mischief than the rest of us. What little free time I had, I used for drawing, playing the piano, or day-dreaming about becoming a famous singer.

For the next several days at school, Glenda followed me from class to class. We hardly knew each other and rarely spoke because we had nothing to talk about. So I wasn't surprised when after a couple of weeks, she said, "You're boring!" and disappeared. It stung a little to think of myself as boring—and I certainly hoped she wouldn't tell anyone—but I wasn't surprised she felt that way.

Camera Rage

My anger at Sister Wellington for confiscating my camera three years earlier, grew almost on a daily basis. It came to represent all the lies and broken promises of my life. Every time I saw her, I asked if she would return it, and every time, she said, "I don't think you can be trusted, yet. You'll just take dirty pictures of boys."

I couldn't imagine what kind of evil filled her mind, or what kind of dirty pictures she thought I would take. Was a picture of a boy *dirty*, just because a boy was in it? Such questions had also begun to enter my mind as I listened to the preacher and other Bible teachers. Did they constantly talk about whores and prostitutes because they thought about them all the time? And was "the truth" they taught really true, or the only "truth" they knew? What about all the other religious people who thought their "truth" was true? Since no one agreed, maybe everyone was wrong. And, if everyone was wrong, what difference did it make? Whatever was really true would keep being true, whether or not anyone ever recognized it.

The Wheat Sea

If some of our teachers hadn't discussed current events during class, I would have never known what was going on in the outside world. There were no magazines or newspapers and our television wasn't on for more than a couple of hours, except for special "approved" programs, and the news was not one of them.

Discussion in class, however, frequently left me plagued with questions. My class schedule prevented me from talking with Coach Royal as I had done during seventh and eighth grades, and my questions didn't really "fit" into our class discussions.

I tried occasionally to talk with other kids about my thoughts but more often than not, they rolled their eyes and twirled a finger around an ear, telling me I was crazy. So one Saturday afternoon, after writing a letter for Miss Polk, I risked talking with her.

"Miss Polk, Communists are just people like us, right?"

She cocked her head and frowned at me. "Of course not! They're Communists! They're bad. We're not."

"But if they'd been born here, they would be like us. Right?"

"Well, they weren't. So they aren't. It's as simple as that."

I wished it were that simple for me. "But . . . do you understand what I mean?"

She shrugged. "I'm not sure."

"Well, like Sputnik, the satellite thing that goes around the earth . . . "

"Yeah?"

"Well, what I wonder is . . . since no one on earth ever did such a thing before . . . why aren't all people, everywhere—including us—happy about it? Doesn't it kind of mean . . . well, if they could do it . . . if they're that smart . . . we can do it, too? I mean, why is it bad that the Communists did it first?"

She frowned as she walked to the other side of the stove and stirred a kettle of butter beans. "Because they might use it to spy on us. And no matter what they're up to, because they're Communist, that Sputnik is not good."

"But it's proof that people are smart. That we can think of things . . . and build things like that . . . shouldn't everyone be happy?"

"No."

"Well, what if we made friends with them. Maybe they wouldn't be so bad."

"Oh, stop this ridiculous talk and get me some bacon fat for these beans."

I cut a hunk of bacon fat and carried it to her. "Well, last assembly at school, when we were all saying the Pledge of Allegiance, I thought about the words and—"

"Get me a knife. What words?"

"The Pledge of Allegiance words," I said over my shoulder as I got her a knife.

"You mean you haven't memorized that yet?" She scoffed.

"Yeah, I have. But I was thinking about the words as I said them . . . and, well, I suddenly couldn't say some of them."

She whittled slivers of fat into the beans. "Which ones . . . and why?"

"Well, just the first part, for instance. It seems wrong to me to pledge allegiance to just Americans. Why not all people, all human beings?"

"Because you can't! You're an American. You have to be loyal to America."

"I know but . . . if God made all people, then He probably likes everybody. And if Jesus said love everybody, he probably meant everybody. Not just Americans."

"Now you're talking crazy!" She glanced angrily at me. "And I don't want to hear crazy talk. Communists are not good and God don't expect us to like them!"

"Well, don't you ever wonder about stuff like this?"

"Absolutely not! It's a waste of time. I have a kitchen to run, girls to keep busy, and I don't have time for silly talk. Now go do whatever you're supposed to be doing."

That ended our conversation, but it didn't end my confusion or my questions. As I had so many times before, I began to feel as if my world wasn't real, that my very existence was a joke. I had been born at the wrong time or in the wrong place; the people around me had answers but their answers didn't fit my questions. They rarely made sense to me.

As I walked slowly to my dorm, a vast and all-encompassing loneliness enveloped me. I felt as if I would never escape the confines of the orphanage, its dullness, its sameness, its ever-expanding deadness. My chest tightened and my breathing became labored. I had to get out of the home. Some way, somehow, I had to find another place to live or I was going to die.

The dorm was quiet and I saw no one as I plodded toward my room. Taking pencil and paper from my notebook, I began to write a letter. I wasn't sure where I would send it because I didn't know who I was writing to; I only knew I had to write for help.

> *Dear Someone,*
>
> *Come get me. I'm in Tipton, Oklahoma, at the Tipton Orphans Home. I will die if I stay here. Please, please believe me. No one here is really alive, not even me, but I will come alive if you will come and get me.*
>
> *Othello James*

I cried when I finished the letter because I had no place to send it—no special person, no secret address where it would be received and acted upon. I was crying into the wind; the situation was hopeless.

Yet, even as I thought it, one side of my mind rebelled. There had to be a way to contact someone in the outside world . . . if there was an outside world . . . and, like finding a note in a bottle that had washed up on the beach, surely someone would respond. But how would I make that happen?

Realizing how foolish it was to dream of rescue, I tore the letter into tiny pieces and stuffed them into my pocket. If anyone found it, I would be mocked forever.

Although we were not supposed to leave the dorm without permission, I slipped out and wandered around to the back of the building. There, I stared out at the great sea of wheat that disappeared into eternity. It seemed alive as it obeyed the gusting wind, bowing, rising, and bowing again in endless supplication.

Enchanted by its gentle beckoning, I wandered out into the field and let the willowy stalks blow against me in sweeping, golden waves, gently scratching and caressing my arms. The silky tips of the grain shimmered in the yellowish light of the late afternoon sun.

Almost hidden in that great wheat sea, it was easy to fantasize, to imagine that the wind, the wheat, the sun and I possessed some magical, supernatural power. Together, we could change any circumstance or situation; together, we were invincible. Together, we could rescue me.

Taking the torn, shredded letter from my pocket, I imagined tossing it into the wind to be blown in every direction and carried around the world, where magically the pieces would come together and my letter would land at the feet of the wise, benevolent soul meant to receive it.

It was a wonderful, fantastical thought! So beautiful, in fact, I could not resist it. I cried as I threw the tiny pieces of my letter into the air and watched the wind carry them away.

Take it! Take it, please! Let someone know I'm waiting! Let them come and get me!

For a moment, it seemed the wind heard me. It whipped harder and frantically swept the swirling pieces of paper higher and higher into the air. Strands of my hair beat against my face, the ends cool and wet because I couldn't stop crying. The fantasy peaked when the tiniest, highest pieces sparkled and glittered brightly in the sunlight.

As I stood there, watching the wind carry my letter to some unknown place, I knew nothing magical would happen. Still, with the wind and the wheat gently blowing against me, I reached a sort of peace. I felt certain that somewhere, in a faraway place—a large city, perhaps, with lots of bright lights and thousands of people—there was someone with answers to my questions and a million more that I had not asked. Someday I would go there. I would meet someone with answers to *my* questions—and we would talk and talk for days. It would be wonderful. Someday.

Coach's Poem

It was time for report cards when Coach Royal wrote a rhyme on the blackboard.

A-sittin' and a-wishin' makes no person great.
The good Lord sends the fishin' but you must dig the bait.

The message reverberated through me, bouncing off the walls of my brain, rearranging thoughts, reviving hopes and dreams, and restoring my weakened faith in myself. I stared at the board, recalling my mother's words: *If you want the shoes bad enough, you can have them.*

Her words and Coach's poem expressed the same idea, and as I considered them, I felt stronger and more independent. If my life was ever to amount to anything, *I* would have to make it happen—and I would.

Although I felt no real sense of direction, the poem meant more than anything I had ever learned in school. The words ignited a spark that brightened something within me.

I copied the poem in the front of my notebook.

Throughout that class, my eyes darted from Coach to his scrawling on the board. He, one of my dearest and most respected friends, would never know how these few words had inspired me, because regardless of how I would try to tell him, my gratitude swelled far beyond my ability to express it. He had liberated and empowered me, and for that hour, at least, he had made me feel invincible—a feeling far grander than my vocabulary.

Chapter 20

Junior Play

Home girls weren't allowed to play basketball or participate in track because the teams wore shorts. We also weren't allowed to be cheerleaders because of the short, indecent costumes and sinful leg-kicking routines. Even the band was "off limits" because their routines came too close to dancing.

Occasionally, however, depending on the content of the play, juniors and seniors were allowed to perform in school plays, if they auditioned for, and got the parts.

In my junior year, I tried out for three parts, hoping to land one of them. I knew I would love pretending to be someone else—someone whose words and actions could be memorized and called forth at the exact time and place. To my great delight, I was given the lead.

The added bonus—getting away from the home two evenings a week to practice—heightened the excitement. The play, a light-hearted comedy, set the tone of "fun" each evening as Miss Skagg helped us memorize our lines. I also enjoyed being with Town kids, most of whom I only knew by name, and wished this weren't the extent of our time together, but knew it was.

During the final week of practice, as I waited in the wings while others rehearsed onstage, Danny Apperson came to sit and talk with me. Danny always had a quick smile that immediately put me at ease. We talked about the play, grades, tests, and all the school gossip that I seldom heard.

"I think Billie Jo's getting married this summer. Least ways, she says she is."

Billie Jo was a Town kid and also a junior, so I knew her. "You mean she's not gonna graduate?"

He shrugged. "Not according to what I hear."

"That would be stupid. Not only that, she's the best forward on the girls' basketball team, isn't she?"

As Danny leaned down to whisper, his arm and shoulder pressed against mine. "I hear she's pregnant."

"Really?" A month or so earlier, Billie Jo had dropped her wallet in study hall. When it hit the floor, three packages of condoms fell out. At the time, the boys hooted and teased her, and I cringed, imagining her embarrassment.

I was tempted to tell Danny about it but before I could, he leaned close and whispered, "May I kiss you?"

My first impulse was to laugh. It felt like a joke that anyone would want to kiss me, but after I thought about it a moment, I decided I might never have another chance to be kissed by a boy as handsome as Danny. Unable to actually say "Yes," I just didn't say "No," and Danny accepted my silence as I meant it.

He kissed me gently, and I wasn't prepared for the rush of conflicting excitement. One kiss became two, then a dozen, not just on my mouth but my face, neck and ears, and I loved it! Had Miss Skagg not been running back and forth across the stage, shouting commands in her frantic screeching voice, Billie Jo probably wouldn't have been the only girl in our class to not graduate next year.

My body temperature rose dramatically in a matter of seconds. For a moment, I could scarcely breathe. In spite of all the wonderful desire and urgency sweeping through me, guilt rode shotgun, monitoring my responses. I pulled myself free, laughed, stood, took several deep breaths, and laughed again. Danny smiled and nodded for me to sit back down.

I shook my head, still laughing nervously. "That's so good it's not good, Danny."

"Why?" He patted the chair and grinned.

"It's just not. I *want* to graduate. It's that . . . well, it makes me feel . . . well, like maybe I could forget . . . what . . . what I really want."

"Think so?" His grin broadened. "That's not bad. That's good."

"Hello! Is anyone listening?" Miss Skagg's voice broke through the buzzing and throbbing in my head. "I need some actors out here!"

"I've got to go." I pushed past him, relieved to be saved by something other than my rapidly diminishing conscience. Rushing onstage, I tried to orient myself to the scene. Rodney Mangum, the leading man, craned his neck to look beyond me and into the wings. Seeing Danny, he raised his eyebrows and smiled knowingly.

For the rest of the evening, I stayed onstage or sat on the steps, in full view of Miss Skagg. Being around Danny was dangerous. I found his gentleness irresistible, and I knew that more time with him would only be regretted. I had to graduate. Being an example for Jenny, Amy, and Gordon was the only meaningful commitment in my life. I had made a promise and I would keep it.

I managed to stay clear of Danny for the rest of the evening, and the next morning renewed my resolve. Someone, however, had seen us kissing in the wings and by the time I got home from school the next day, word of those wonderful kisses had spread to Sister Wellington.

Sitting in her office, across the desk from her, my hands in my lap, I stared at her blue hair and fine mustache.

"You can't be trusted, can you?" Her small eyes blinked behind her glasses. "You simply can't be trusted!"

There was no sense in arguing. She would win.

"I ought to yank you out of that play! And I would do it if there was time for someone else to learn your part!" She grunted. "Actually, I'd do it if it weren't for the money the school would lose!"

I stared at her, wondering what my punishment would be.

She sighed wearily and sat back. "Well, young lady, there will be no more outings for you this year. No ball games. Nothing. Not one. You can't be trusted around boys."

Inwardly, I mocked her. I had only been to three football games in three years. What difference would it make to miss the rest?

"Go on, now. Get back to the kitchen."

On the night of the play, I managed to so completely wrap myself in the part of a dominant wife, raging against her untalented, songwriter husband, that I received rave reviews from kids, parents, and teachers. My only moment of sadness came when I realized I had to wait a year to audition for the senior play . . . and knew that Sister Wellington probably wouldn't let me participate.

My "high" lasted over a week, though, as I relived every scene and line and knew I had done a great job. Being someone else, confident of every movement, gave me endless satisfaction. Like controlling a small universe, knowing the plot and how each scene would evolve—so unlike my life!—I reveled in every minute of it.

Colonel Lykus and the Little Girls

Laundry girls delivered tubs of folded towels and cleaning rags to the kitchen but because the nursery was closer to the kitchen, kitchen girls delivered them to the nursery. One Saturday morning, after the breakfast mess was cleaned up and we were starting to prepare for other weekend meals, Miss Polk sent me to deliver clean towels and rags to the nursery.

The only dorm with its own kitchen and dining room, I entered through the front door and walked down the hall where I set the box on the kitchen counter. Through the window, I saw Miss Nelson, the matron, wiping the nose of a little girl about four years old, while a dozen other kids squealed and played in the fenced yard.

As I often did, I looked around for Maggie, the teenage girl who assisted in the nursery. I found her in the back of the dormitory, sitting on the edge of one of the small beds, comforting a whimpering little girl. I also saw two other beds with children in them.

"Hi, Maggie. Are these kids sick?"

Maggie glanced behind me, then toward the hall before she whispered, "Colonel Lykus came over here last night!"

"Colonel Lykus? What for?" Colonel Lykus and his wife were the new house parents for Gordon's dormitory, the ten- and twelve-year-old boys. They had been at the home about three months. "What did he want?"

Maggie's face soured with disgust. "What did he want? He wanted—and got—these three!" She waved her arm angrily at the girls in their beds.

I couldn't believe she meant what I thought she meant.

"I heard someone crying about eleven o'clock and . . . and came back here to check. And he, Colonel Lykus, was in the bed with Sheila!" Her eyes flashed with hatred. "Apparently, he had already raped Sue Ann and Ginny!"

I tried to take it all in. "He . . . he . . . *really*?"

Tears slipped down her face and she angrily brushed them away. "Yes, really!"

"Well . . . what . . . what did you do?"

"At first, I didn't know what to do. I mean, I flipped on the light to see who was crying and he jumped up, startled, half naked and gaping at me like a fish out of water!" She gestured wildly toward Sheila's bed. "When I realized what I was seeing, and that it was him, I turned off the light and ran to get Miss Nelson!"

I tried to imagine what I would have done. In my mind, I could see her pounding on Miss Nelson's door.

"It took her forever to answer! And when she did, I told her what I saw and she looked terrified and confused and grabbed her robe . . . but by the time we got back to the beds, he was gone!" Her face reddened and tears continued to spill. "Sue Ann, Sheila, and Ginny were all crying and holding themselves! I wanted to go after him and kill him!"

"What did Miss Nelson do?"

Maggie took a tissue from her pocket, blew her nose, and took a deep breath. "She said she would handle it. She said I might have been mistaken, that it wasn't Colonel Lykus—but it was! I saw him. I know what he looks like! It was Lykus!"

I walked to the other beds and stared down at Sue Ann and Ginny, now asleep, while Sheila continued to whimper. "We've got to make sure Miss Nelson reports it," I said.

"No!" Maggie jumped up and hurried toward me. "You can't tell. At least not yet. Let Miss Nelson take care of it. She told me not to mention it to anyone, and if she knew I told you, I'd be in trouble."

I looked at the little girls, none older than four or five. "Are you sure?"

"You can't tell!" Maggie whispered again. "Promise me you won't." She grabbed my hands. "If they move me out of the nursery and I can't be with my little brother, Ricky, I don't know what I will do! I want to work here!"

When we heard the kids running in from the play yard, I quickly vowed my silence, and left. As I walked back toward the kitchen, I remembered the chapel service when Colonel Lykus was first introduced to us.

"Now, this is an earnest man of God," Brother Wellington announced. "The very day he heard we had an opening for house parents, he called and asked for an interview. He drove six hundred miles to get here! Now, that's Christian dedication!"

Colonel Lykus stood at attention beside Brother Wellington, staring just above our heads.

"After serving his country for more than twenty-five years, he has now chosen to serve God full-time." Brother Wellington's glowing admiration prompted Colonel Lykus to smile and nod.

I believed that Brother Wellington was a good man and would never have knowingly hired anyone who would purposely hurt any of us, but I also knew he saw what he wanted to see. He wanted to see a man of God, to believe that Colonel Lykus was such a man—and that's what he saw. Lykus, however, wasn't even a man—he was less than a dog.

My stomach knotted. Some way, I had to let someone know.

Sunday, after we finished in the kitchen, I sneaked over to the nursery, shocked to see that in just one night, Maggie looked years older.

"He came back!" she whispered. "Last night he raped Emily! And I didn't even know until this morning! The poor little thing cried without making a sound!"

She ran shaking fingers through her hair and turned away, crying.

"Maggie, we've got to do something! I'll—I'll go to the Elders of the Church. They're in charge of the home. They'll do something."

Her face still turned away from me, she nodded. "Okay. Okay."

Reporting the Rapes

Finding an opportunity to talk with the Elders wouldn't be easy. It had to happen at church, so I would need several other kids to help, to be lookouts or "jiggers." I couldn't do it alone.

One at a time, I approached other girls, whispered the situation, and asked, "Will you jigger for me?"

"Yeah."

The next church service was on Wednesday evening, and I would have only a few minutes after church, while everyone stood around talking, waiting for busses. Then I would have to slip out of the crowd and find some Elders to listen to me. I knew I had to find two of them because I couldn't depend on just one. A single Elder might be like Miss Nelson . . . afraid to do anything . . . but with two, they would probably do something.

When the last song ended and the congregation began to move from the pews, my jiggers took their positions between the bus, the church, and the matrons—all of them alert and ready to "psst!" when the bus driver headed for the bus . . . or a matron wandered in my direction . . . or any other problem arose.

Darting around the side of the church, I saw Brother Jackson and Brother Eldrich, near the front of the church, talking. I glanced back to see if my jigger saw me. She did.

"Brother Jackson! Brother Eldrich! I've got to talk to you!" I kept my voice low but urgent. They frowned, and glanced behind me, questioning my unexpected presence.

"Somebody's got to do something!" I whispered. "About Colonel Lykus."

"Colonel Lykus?" They repeated in unison.

I nodded and glanced at my jigger. Everything was still okay. "He's going into the nursery and . . . and getting in bed with the little girls!"

Both men drew back, looked at each other, then at me again.

"Psst!"

The jigger waved frantically for me to come back.

"We'll take care of it," Brother Jackson said. "Tonight."

I turned and ran back into the safety of the shadows beside the church, aware that my jigger had already left.

The last one on the bus, I breathlessly found a seat and avoided the matron's eyes.

"And where were you?"

"The bathroom. I couldn't wait."

Late that night, a stern shake woke me. Brother and Sister Wellington stood next to my bed. "Get up. Get dressed and come to the Administration building."

A few minutes later, my mouth so dry I could hardly swallow, I stood in Brother Wellington's office. Both he and Sister Wellington had tired, grim expressions as their eyes met mine.

I started to sit in one of the brown leather chairs.

"Don't sit," Brother Wellington said. "There's not much to say. We just want you to know that you can't . . . you can't . . . tell lies on good . . . Christian men and get away with it." Sadness slackened his face.

"Wha—?" I thought I had misunderstood.

"Colonel Lykus is a fine, Christian man and what you did tonight—"

"But he—!"

"We can't allow you to tell this lie to anyone else. So we're taking care of it. Tonight."

They both stood. "You're going to spend some time in the punishment room, upstairs," Sister Wellington said. "You've done a terrible thing! And you need to pray for forgiveness and think about the damage you've done!"

My heart raced as they walked me across the dark lobby. I looked from one to the other, still not believing their response. "But . . . what about Emily? Sue Ann? And the other little girls? Aren't you even going to check them?"

"And while you're upstairs," Sister Wellington opened the door that led to the staircase, "you'll be thinking about how important it is not to tell such horrible lies. You can't even imagine the harm you've done!"

They urged me up the stairs, but Brother Wellington didn't follow us up. "Rumors like this hurt everyone. The church! The home! And the children!"

"But I saw the girls! I saw them in bed, crying!" I wanted to add what Maggie had told me but didn't want to get her in trouble.

At the top of the stairs, Sister Wellington turned on a light and nudged me to turn left down a hallway. "You saw children in bed. Maybe they were crying. That's all you know." She sorted through her key ring, pulled one key separate, and unlocked a door. "You will be let out in a few days when you come to your senses and apologize for lying."

The room's warm breath belched into the hall as we entered then closed around me like a suffocating veil. She switched on the light. "There are pajamas and a Bible in the drawer. There's a toothbrush and towel in the bathroom. You have nothing to do but read. Read the Bible. And pray." Her grim voice and face created a greater dread than the room. "Pray for forgiveness."

She stepped into the hallway, started to close the door and then hesitated. "You'll get biscuits and water. Nothing else until you apologize."

She closed and locked the door. I didn't move until I heard her footsteps descend the stairs and heard the door below close. Knowing I was the only one in the building prompted fears I hadn't felt in years. What was in the other rooms?

I slowly moved to the window beside the bed and opened the curtain. The outside darkness pressed against the glass, trying to get in. In the distance, I could see the light pole at the end of the sidewalk, across the campus, near my dorm.

Easing to the edge of the bed, I became conscious of the absolute silence. The sounds of crickets and locust couldn't penetrate the walls and closed window.

Knowing that the window overlooked the roof of the porch, I jumped up and tried to open it. Every movement and sound were exaggerated in the silence as I grunted and strained to raise it, even an inch. When it wouldn't budge, I tried to turn the lock but couldn't. I stood on the nightstand to grasp the lock from a better angle, but when I saw it, I realized the futility of trying. Nails had been driven in place to keep the lock from moving.

Too depressed to cry, I lay across the bed and thought about the past couple of days. What a fool I had been to think the Elders would help . . . and yet, even as I thought about it, I was still shocked that nothing was being done to stop Colonel Lykus. How many more kids would he hurt before someone did something?

Did they even bother to check the nursery and see for themselves? And why wouldn't the Elders do anything? They had charge of the home *and* the Wellingtons. They hired them!

They weren't concerned about the kids; otherwise, the Elders would have sent Colonel Lykus away—not punish me. Then it hit me. They were afraid the various congregations that supported the home would hear about it and withdraw their support . . . and there would be no Tipton Home—no money for kids, no money for matrons, no money for administrators. No orphanage.

I prayed that night but not for forgiveness. I prayed for Ginny, Sue Ann, Sheila, and Emily, and that Colonel Lykus wouldn't go to the nursery again.

I awoke to the deep resonance of the bell calling everyone to breakfast. Jumping up, I moved to the window and watched Laverne pulling the rope and letting herself be lifted by the weight of the bell. As I watched her, I recalled the time, years before, when Amy had been locked in this very room and later told me that angels came to talk to her. She was only six or seven at the time. I cried, remembering she had seen me ringing the dinner bell, and called my name, repeatedly, but I couldn't hear her.

Now, as then, life went on as if nothing had happened. I waited behind the same locked door for someone to bring me biscuits and water. In all those years, all that had changed was my age. Only one more year and I could leave.

For three days, I sat on the bed or stared out the window. No one came to the room except to open the door and put a tray inside, three times a day. Usually, it was Sister Wellington. At the end of the second day, she had asked, "Are you ready to apologize?" When I only stared at her, she closed the door and left.

I ate the biscuits, glad that I liked them, and began to wonder if I should apologize just so I could get out of the room. School would be out in a couple of weeks. Didn't it matter if I took tests for final grades?

All of the third day, I talked to myself, trying to convince myself to apologize. At first, my anger flared and I defended my actions, but I continued to argue.

Maybe she's right . . . all I saw were little girls in bed crying . . . all I knew was what Maggie said.

But Maggie was so upset . . . she had to be telling the truth!

What good did telling the truth do? Look what it gets you. If you had minded your own business, you'd be going to school, getting things done, and be a lot happier than this!

But what about Colonel Lykus? He should be punished . . . or at least sent away. He shouldn't be here, and if I apologize, he'll probably just keep doing it!

If you don't apologize, he'll probably keep doing it, too. But if you apologize, at least you'll get out of this room.

The argument lasted for hours. Finally, the door opened and Sister Wellington stood in the doorway, holding a tray. "If you'll apologize, now, I'll let you spend the night in your own bed."

Reluctantly, hating her with a fierce intensity, I nodded. "I apologize."

"For what?"

"For . . . what I . . . said."

"For telling lies on Colonel Lykus!" She snapped. "Say you told lies on Colonel Lykus!" Her hands gripped the tray.

"I . . . ah, apologize for . . . lying . . . about Colonel . . . Lykus." I couldn't look at her as I choked the words out. I wanted to push her out of the room and run forever . . . to get away from everything in the home.

She sighed. "You'll not speak of the lie ever again. Do you understand?"

I nodded.

"You'll not mention it to anyone!"

I nodded.

She shoved the tray at me. "Here. That's your supper. Take the biscuits, leave the tray on my desk, and go to your dormitory."

I took the tray and stepped into the hall where the fresher, cooler air rushed up to greet me. Without looking back, I ran down the stairs, put the tray on her desk, and grabbed the biscuits. In the darkened lobby, I paused at the water cooler and took a long, cold drink.

A warm hand touched my back and I spun around. Brother Wellington stood beside me, rubbing my back between my shoulders, a sad smile touching his lips. "I see you apologized. Good."

His eyes shown wet and I knew he was sincerely grateful that I had apologized—*to save the home*—but I couldn't stand there looking at him. I turned and bolted for the door.

Brother Wellington was a good man! Somewhere in my heart, I knew it; but I also knew he was wrong to let it go this way and punish me while letting Colonel Lykus stay.

I ate the biscuits as I walked to my dorm, wondering if maybe Brother Wellington had to do what the Elders told him. Whatever made him ignore the truth, hurt him. I could see that. Brother Wellington had a good and gentle side and tonight I saw how vulnerable he was. Sister Wellington, on the other hand, loved her job and all that went with it. I couldn't believe she even had feelings, much less experienced sorrow, guilt, or pain.

The next morning, I was stunned to see Maggie in the hallway. Drawn and pale, dark circles blackened both of her eyes.

I grabbed her arm. "They moved you!"

She nodded and pulled away.

"You said they would."

Her head bobbed again. "Don't talk about it."

Less than a week later, I was surprised to see Gordon helping with the milk delivery to the kitchen, and the instant we made eye contact, he motioned for me to follow him outside.

I glanced around to make sure Miss Polk wasn't in sight and then ran out to meet him. "When did you start working on the farm?"

"Last week." He took my hand. "I heard you were locked up."

"Yeah. You know what for?"

"You snitched to the Elders about Colonel Lykus. Everybody knows about it." He walked to the truck and said to Jerry Don, the driver, "Hey, give us a minute. Okay?"

Jerry Don shrugged. "Sure."

Gordon pulled me away from the truck. "What you don't know," he whispered, "is what the Lykuses did last night. In our dorm."

"Oh, that's right! They're your matrons!"

"Yeah. Well, not anymore. They're both gone."

"Really?" I was thrilled to hear it. "Did the Elders make them leave?"

Gordon laughed. "No. Colonel Lykus got all jealous because Mrs. Lykus was measuring us for new clothes. You know, running the tape measure up our legs and such. Anyway, he started yelling and screaming and . . . " Gordon's eyes danced as he recalled the scene, "accusing her of touching us . . . you know . . . and—and she got a pair of scissors and stabbed him! Threw them right across the room and stabbed him with them!"

"Wha—?" I couldn't close my mouth.

He laughed. "He didn't die but they made so much noise other matrons came, and well, anyway . . . they're gone! Gone when we got up this morning!" He laughed again, squeezed my hand, and turned to leave. "Hey, I gotta get, but I just wanted you to know . . . Lykus won't be humping little girls anymore!"

Jerry Don took off the minute Gordon slammed the door. We waved one last time and I suddenly felt like dancing. Not just because Colonel Lykus was gone, but because I had seen Gordon and he was the one who told me the good news. That was our first conversation in years.

Thank you, God, for getting rid of Colonel Lykus. And thank you for Gordon. I peeked around the corner to make sure Miss Polk didn't see me sneaking back inside.

Chapter 21

From Fear to Rage

Home girls rarely dated because few town boys were willing to undergo the Wellingtons' close scrutiny. My senior year, Arty Clifford bravely submitted to the examination in hopes of dating me but I knew nothing about it until he had been rejected. When through the ever-faithful grapevine, I heard, I marveled that Arty or anyone would be interested in dating me.

Then a new boy, Bud Collins, enrolled late in the year and every girl, including myself, swooned. Bud had everything. Besides being so handsome we could hardly stand it, he was an outstanding athlete, sparkled with personality, and made every guy in school rude with envy.

I admired him from afar as he flirted with all the girls around me, aware that even if I could get his attention, Sister Wellington would never let me date him. That didn't stop me, however, from "accidentally" bumping into him and spilling my books all over the hall so that he would help me pick them up (which he did) while apologizing profusely for being so clumsy. I accepted his apology with a nod and smile because, up close, Bud's gorgeous smile turned my brain to mush.

Consequently, I was completely unprepared when I was called to Sister Wellington's office one Sunday afternoon, after church.

Wearing her perpetual frown, she studied me across her desk. "I know I'm going to regret this," she grumbled, "but Bud Collins has asked to date you . . . and we've decided to let you go."

I couldn't swallow or close my mouth.

"He and his parents are members of the church, so even if *you* can't control yourself, hopefully, he can."

Fearing that the slightest movement or simplest word would be misinterpreted, I scarcely breathed.

She was going to let me date Bud Collins!

While my ears rang and my heart hammered until I feared she would hear it, she laid out the conditions of our date. We would be allowed to sit together in church (away from the home kids) and could go to the drugstore for a soda afterwards. I was to be home by nine o'clock.

The conditions didn't bother me. The idea that I would be alone with Bud for even a few minutes thrilled *and* terrified me. I had no idea what to expect or what was expected of me. Back at the dorm, however, every girl suddenly considered herself an expert, although none of them had actually been on a date.

They huddled in my room, giggling and talking excitedly.

"You've got to make sure, when you sit down, that your skirt is up just enough to let him see your knee. Carla Matthews, a Town girl, told me and she has lots of dates."

I had heard that Carla was a whore, so I dismissed that advice.

"Have you got some chewing gum? You've got to have gum so your breath won't stink."

"When he tries to kiss you, turn your head a little this way so your noses won't bump."

"You wanna wear my new stretch belt? It'll make your waist look smaller."

"Wear lipstick but not too much or it'll smear."

That evening Bud picked me up in his father's car and drove me to church. Neither of us uttered a word until he parked at the church and came around to open my door. "You look real pretty tonight."

My heart jumped. "Thank you." I could hardly make my legs move to get out of the car.

Our entrance turned every head in the church. We sat a few pews from the back door—as far away as we could get from the home kids—but every head turned a dozen times during the next hour. Some glanced back and giggled, others sneaked little waves, which I pretended not to see.

During church, Bud held my hand, interlocking our fingers. After a while my fingers ached from the pressure of his beefy hands but I was afraid to move or say anything. I stared straight ahead, too self-conscious to even glance at him when peripherally, I could see him looking at me.

After the soda at the drugstore, Mr. Everything drove out to a lonely road, parked, and immediately turned to kiss me. Having only one very unpleasant memory of being parked on a lonely road, I tensed.

Between my memory and my naivete, Bud didn't have a chance. With his first kiss, he thrust his tongue into my mouth so far I thought I would gag. I wondered if he was having some kind of seizure. The only time I had seen someone lose control of their tongue was when Jo Ann had her epileptic fit.

Ignoring my startled reaction, Bud groped at my breast and tried to choke me again with his tongue.

I pulled back again, wiped spit off my chin, and said, "I'm supposed to be back by nine."

"Relax. We have twenty minutes."

Already exhausted, I took a deep breath, wondering what to do. "If you don't mind," I said, "I'd like to leave now."

"Come on. Give me a chance."

"I want to go."

On the short drive back, I felt embarrassed, knowing that I had been a huge disappointment, but when I replayed the scene in my mind, there was nothing I would have done differently. There just wasn't enough room in my mouth for two whole tongues. A little bit might have been nice, but not the whole thing.

I knew he wouldn't ask me out again and would probably tell everyone in school that I was a dud, so I dreaded school the next day. Much to my surprise, I was suddenly the most popular girl in school—a shocking turn of events. Every guy flirted with me, whistled at me, and winked when our eyes met.

By the end of the day, however, Danny Apperson told me the sad truth about Mr. Wonderful. He smiled apologetically and said, "I know he was lying, but he told everyone he scored."

"What?" I couldn't have been more stunned.

"He said you really put out."

"I put out?"

He nodded.

Mortified, I burst into tears. "You know I didn't!"

Danny put his arm around me. "I know. If you were gonna put out, I think you'd have done it with me."

I neither denied nor confirmed the truth. All I could do was regret having been with Bud and secretly mock Sister Wellington's decision to let me date him.

Finally, in an effort to salvage some shred of ego, I stopped crying, wiped my tears away and said, "Danny, Bud is not only a liar . . . he's a rotten kisser. Make sure everyone knows I said that."

He laughed. "Be glad to."

Strip Show

It was a school night and I was already in pajamas when I needed to borrow a pencil sharpener and carried my broken pencil down the hall to Rachel's room.

"Rachel, can I use—?" I stopped and stared at Rachel who was dancing seductively in the center of the room to *no* music. Several other girls, piled on the two twin beds shoved against opposite walls, snickered and giggled, their pajama tops tied up under their breasts and the legs of their pajamas rolled to the tops of their thighs.

She glanced up, saw me and kept on dancing, unbuttoning her clothes. I watched for a minute, wondering why she would be stripping for the other girls, when I realized that everyone kept glancing toward the window.

I looked out but saw only darkness. "Who's out there?" I asked.

Rachel laughed. "Who's not?"

The other girls laughed.

It took me a second to realize that some sort of audience lurked in the night, and when I did, I turned immediately and left, embarrassed by my ignorance and naivete. It humiliated me to think that I, one of the oldest girls in the dormitory, didn't even *suspect* that such things went on.

The Other Sex

Over the next few weeks, I became increasingly aware of the sexual activity taking place around me. I overheard other girls talking and realized that some of them were having affairs with men who worked for the home. Rachel talked freely about the men she allowed to crawl through her window at night but even as I listened, I found it hard to believe. More than anything else, I wondered why they would risk pregnancy.

One evening Rachel talked at length about some of the men who were hired to make repairs in the warehouse. As I listened, I wondered what was wrong with me. I saw the men, too, but it never occurred to me to flirt or let them into my room.

I was both amazed and embarrassed by what I saw and heard, and at my own responses. Wasn't I normal? Why didn't I "see opportunities everywhere," as Rachel put it? Every time I left her room, I felt more foolish.

Then one night I was awakened by footsteps running down the hall. I heard giggling, then a muffled crash and more giggling. The matron's light came on and she hurried out to investigate. I peeked down the hall and caught a glimpse of our matron, Mrs. Jullian, disappearing into Frieda's room.

I heard Mrs. Jullian scolding someone, then she stepped back out into the hall and I dived for my bed. The next day Glenda Faye told me that Connie Jean and Frieda had let their boyfriends in, and they had made it out only seconds before Mrs. Jullian entered their room.

"They almost got caught!" she whispered excitedly.

Again, the next night, when the giggling started, the hall light came on instantly. Loud, angry voices carried from one end of the hall to the other.

"Good Lord! Look at you! Look at you!" Mrs. Jullian's voice deepened with disgust.

"Get out! Get out!" Sister Wellington's anger pierced the cinder block walls.

I, and a dozen others ran to our doors to see. Mrs. Jullian and Sister Wellington stood outside Frieda and Connie Jean's room. "Get your clothes and get out of here!"

We heard boys laughing nervously and crashing about, apparently leaving through the window.

The chaos lasted only a few minutes. Connie Jean and Frieda were dressed and out of the building with Sister Wellington a few minutes later. The next morning, they were gone.

For days the gossip continued. We never knew where Connie Jean and Frieda went but their leaving didn't deter Rachel or the others for long. The late night "dances" continued and Rachel continued to talk about the construction workers who frequented her bed.

Maybe something was wrong with me. Maybe I should spend more time thinking about boys and sex. But the truth was, I didn't. Accepting that I might be abnormal didn't change the fact that I still preferred to play the piano or draw.

With Jenny and Amy gone, and Gordon seldom seen, the only time the loneliness eased was when I lost myself drawing or making up a new song.

Saving Sister Wellington

Restlessness frequently prompted squabbles as we gathered on Saturday evening to watch TV. One Saturday evening in November, however, Sister Wellington became the object of our immediate discontent.

She had been in Mrs. Jullian's room for several minutes when she came into the living room, turned the TV off, and scowled at us. "This dormitory has become an evil place. Sinful, shameful things are going on in these rooms! And some of you are going to pay for it with your very souls!"

"I don't have a soul!" Glenda Faye shouted. "I lost it already when I lost my arm!" Then she and her twin, Linda Mae, both sitting on the couch, laughed uproariously.

Sister Wellington stepped back as if she'd been slapped. "That's not funny, Missy! Just because you lost your arm doesn't mean you're above God's laws, you know!"

Glenda stopped laughing and glowered at Sister Wellington. "Shut your ugly mouth!"

Surprised she would say such a thing, I laughed nervously with the others. Sister Wellington rushed to the couch and slapped Glenda, hard, on the face.

Linda Mae came up fighting and suddenly the whole room went crazy. She grabbed Sister Wellington's hair and yanked her head to the side. Betty Davidson, a large and generally quiet girl, rushed across the room and shoved Sister Wellington down against the arm of the couch. Simultaneously, Laverne—unquestionably the strongest girl in the home—hit Sister Wellington, knocking her to the floor. Her glasses flew off and cracked against the wall.

In a matter of seconds, they kicked, hit, shoved, and pounded on Sister Wellington while some of us cowered and others screamed or shouted for blood.

Like a pack of wild animals, they pummeled her all over the floor.

Mrs. Jullian, obviously terrified, cringed against the wall, whimpering, "Girls! Girls! Please!"

Then Laverne kicked Sister Wellington in the head and without thinking, I jumped up. I hated the old woman, too, but I couldn't watch them kill her. "Stop it! That's enough!" I grabbed Linda Mae and pulled her back. That, alone, was enough to stop them. They stepped back, trembling and panting, still twitching to fight, but staying at arms length. Within seconds, before anyone spoke, their angry expressions dissolved into shock, realizing what they had done.

Mrs. Jullian helped Sister Wellington to her feet and retrieved her glasses. The side of Sister Wellington's face bled and bright red marks covered her pale neck and arms. Still panting, she tried to straighten the bent frames on her glasses, but couldn't, and put them on anyway. Trembling, her voice weak and somewhat hesitant, she said, "Go to your rooms. All of you."

A hush fell over the dormitory for the next half hour. Silently, we relived the scene again and again, too frightened to talk about it. Then Mrs. Jullian came into the bathroom where I was brushing my teeth, and said, "Come with me."

In her room, she closed the door. Sister Wellington perched uncomfortably on the edge of the bed, her face splotchy with red marks, a Band-Aid on her cheek. She took a long, shaky breath, and said, "Thank you. I'll remember this when it comes time for football games and other special events."

I hadn't seen a game in so long I'd almost forgotten about them.

"I—I realize . . . I could have been killed," she whispered, pulling herself up as if wanting to deny it.

The silence in the dormitory for the last half hour indicated that everyone thought that, too, and they had scared themselves half to death.

Sister Wellington stood and tried to appear unshaken. "So we'll see about getting you to some football games."

I nodded. Having rescued her meant less to me than she probably imagined. I felt no sense of glory because my response hadn't been out of love or any sort of caring for her personally. It had been instinctive, the same reaction I had when Mr. Bunt beat Kenny Holister in grade school, Joe Bard beat Sue Ann in Bible class, and Colonel Lykus raped the little girls. Except, those things I couldn't stop. I also knew that no one meant to kill Sister Wellington. The girls had just gone crazy with anger and frustration, the same anger and insanity I felt.

I was, however, glad to hear I would get to go to football games and the more I thought about it, the better I felt. I hadn't been out at night since the play, almost a year ago, so the next Friday, I floated through the day, anticipating the game. I rushed home from the kitchen to change my clothes and was halfway down the hall when Sister Wellington stepped out of the matron's room and called my name. Since I had just "saved her life" a few days before, I felt no fear, only inconvenience because I wanted to clean up for the game.

This time she didn't close the door. For a moment, she looked rather nervous, her eyes shifting and darting between Mrs. Jullian and me. "Ah, I want to thank you again," she began, "for . . . for what you did . . . " As her voice weakened and she hesitated I felt the sick, sinking feeling of knowing I had been fooled again.

" . . . but I've changed my mind. I'm not letting you go to the game."

Instant rage blocked all rational thought. Only a strange sputtering sound came from my throat.

"Instead," Mrs. Jullian added, almost apologetically, "she's letting Betty, Laverne, and the twins go."

I tried to make sense of it. "*What?* They were the ones—! Why *them* and not me?"

"Because . . . " Sister Wellington smiled weakly, "they need to . . . release some of their anger. And you, well, I don't think you know why you stopped them. So . . . so I want you to stay home . . . and think about it."

White-hot fury pumped through every cell. My mouth worked. My arms twitched. "I—I *don't* know why I stopped them! I should have let them kill you! You don't deserve to live!" I ran to my room where I fumed, paced, and sulked all evening. My hatred for Sister Wellington perfected itself over the next few hours and I gloated at its shameless ugliness, resplendent in its purity.

Ticket to Hell

Several months passed before Sister Wellington came back to our dorm. Then in early March, just prior to my eighteenth birthday, she returned and called us into the living room for another meeting. Her squatty body thrust forward from tightly girdled hips; her sullen gaze moved from one face to another.

"Girls, some of you are going to hell. We know that." She glanced around for a reaction but got none. We had heard our gloomy after-life prediction for years and accepted it without regret or self-pity.

"But there's one of you going to hell for a dollar and five cents!"

I wanted to laugh but didn't. Had someone bought a ticket?

"Shameless, *shameless* things are going on in this dormitory! And all of them will send you to hell! But someone stole a dollar and five cents from Mrs. Jullian's room—and that person is going to hell, too! *That* person sold her soul for a dollar and a nickel!"

Mrs. Jullian stood to one side, watching us suspiciously, as if wondering who would confess. "It was on my dresser," she said. "I laid it there this morning and someone took it."

Personally, I couldn't imagine why anyone would take it because there was no place to spend it. I hadn't been in a store for years. What good was money to us?

"Whoever took it needs to repent, tonight!" Sister Wellington warned. "God just might snatch you out of bed before morning, and there you'd be!—going straight to hell for a dollar and five cents!"

"I think I know who it was," Mrs. Jullian began, "but rather than accuse someone, I'd prefer she step forward and confess. That's what God wants her to do."

We all glanced around to see if we could spot the "condemned" person. For the next fifteen minutes, Sister Wellington talked about the tragedy of selling one's soul for $1.05. Frankly, I agreed with her and hoped whoever took the money would step forward, repent, and let the rest of us go to bed. No one volunteered so the shaming continued. "This is a sad, sad night. Let's hope the thief doesn't die in her sleep and spend eternity burning in the hot, hot flames of hell!"

Finally, we were dismissed, the crime still unsolved.

The next morning, everything went wrong in the kitchen. None of us could get our part of the Sunday dinner ready without making mistakes and creating extra messes to clean up. When we finally got out of the kitchen, I rushed back to the dorm to dress for church. I showered quickly and made a futile search for a pair of stockings that didn't have runs. Disappointed that I didn't have a single stocking without a run, I began to despair over my appearance.

I agonized over my too-curly hair, which frizzed in every direction, and eventually gave up that cause, too, and went to sulk on the living room couch. I brooded over everything that had ever bothered me, until I finally cried. Only three more months and I could leave . . . start over . . . and maybe find a job so that I could buy a new pair of stockings.

At one point, I glanced toward Mrs. Jullian's room and caught her watching me. Irritated, I turned my back to her and continued brooding until I boarded the bus for church.

Later that afternoon, after the kitchen was cleaned, I went back to my room and sprawled across my bed to wallow in my misery. An hour or so later, startled awake by a loud crash, I jumped up to find Sister Wellington and Mrs. Jullian rummaging through my locker. A shoe box, which had been on top of my locker was now on the floor, its contents of junk scattered everywhere.

"Where is it?" Sister Wellington asked. "Where's the money?"

"What?" Still groggy with sleep, I gaped at her. "What money?"

"The dollar and five cents! We know you took it!" Sister Wellington leaned close to my face. "Mrs. Jullian told me how guilty you looked this morning! You were trying to find the courage to confess!"

Remembering my earlier depression, and realizing how it had been interpreted, my heart began to pound with anger.

"Get up and come here!" Mrs. Jullian demanded as she stomped down the hall toward her room. Indignation prompted me to follow quickly, eager for a confrontation.

"I know you're the thief!" Mrs. Jullian yelled. "Now, where's my money?" She picked up a large paddle and raised it to hit me. Sister Wellington stepped back to watch.

I raised my hands to protect myself but wasn't quick enough. The blow landed hard against my shoulder and knocked me sideways. I came up filled with a hate-driven surge of strength and grabbed the paddle as she brought it down again.

I yanked it from her hands. "You're not going to hit me again!" Swinging the paddle wildly over my head, I threatened them both. They backed away quickly. "Now, now, Othello . . . Othello . . . Just calm down. Calm down!"

"I'm not gonna calm down! And I'm not gonna take a beating for something I didn't do!"

Mouths open, faces ashen, they stumbled around the bed.

I waved the board at them. "And I'm not staying here another minute! I'm leaving today! Today! Don't try to stop me!"

They nodded, dodging and crouching. I threw the paddle down and it whacked the floor with a sharp cracking sound. They flinched.

"I'm calling someone to come get me! Don't try to stop me!"

Then I remembered my camera taken years ago and I glared at Sister Wellington. "I want my camera. Wherever it is, get it. I want it today!"

Propelled by anger and adrenaline, I marched across the campus toward the Administration building. Twice, before I reached it, I passed matrons who glanced up, frowning because I was "out of place," but in both instances, when our eyes met, their frowns dissolved into something akin to fear.

The Administration building was empty. I strode into Brother Wellington's office and picked up the phone, realizing as I did, that I had not touched a telephone since I was nine years old, the night that Daddy had me call the Baptist Home to see if they would take us back.

An operator came on the line and I suddenly realized I didn't know what to say. "Ah . . . ah, I want my Aunt Lola Mae."

"What's her last name?"

I struggled to recall. "Doyle?"

"D-O-Y-L-E?"

"Ah, I think so."

"Where does she live, hon?"

"Altus. She lives in Altus, Oklahoma."

"Just a minute, please."

For several breathless seconds, I listened to a phone ringing in my ear, then a voice from my childhood rushed back to greet me, "Nnnello. This is Lola Mae."

Anger dampened the rush of excitement that wanted to come at the sound of her voice. "Aunt Lola Mae! This is Othello. Tell Daddy to come get me!"

"Why, good land! Othello? Well . . . honey, I'm not sure I know where he is."

"Find him, Aunt Lola Mae! Tell him to pick me up in front of the home today! I'm leaving today! Make sure he's here!"

"Well, honey . . . I'll see. I'll do my best."

"Tell him to get here right away!" I knew that Altus was only twenty-five miles from Tipton and that he could be in the driveway within the hour if she found him.

"Like I said . . . I'll do my best."

When I hung up the phone, I felt the greatest surge of power and control I'd ever felt.

During the next two hours, I moved in an unfamiliar reality, a place filled with grace, power, and certainty. No matrons approached me as I packed my things into a small suitcase and said goodbye to some of the kids. I then walked over to the boys' side of the campus, to Gordon's dorm, where he sat outside, waiting for me.

"I heard you were leaving!" He laughed.

I laughed, too, amazed at how fast the grapevine traveled. He beamed and hugged me. "Good. Get out and keep going."

"I plan to."

"You going to Daddy?"

I nodded.

"You going to finish school?"

"Of course!"

He hugged me and I promised I would write. There was no sense in promising him more because I knew I couldn't take him with me.

"It's okay," he said. "Don't worry about me. I'm doing pretty good."

I knew he really was. Gordon had a charm, and so much talent to go with it, he was the perfect "show kid" for the orphanage. Besides his good looks and personality, he was smart enough to work the system—a system which worked better and easier for the boys. Their sins were never as bad as ours.

"I'll write."

Everywhere I went, matrons stayed out of my way and kids smiled and gave me good luck signs. As I approached the Administration building where I intended to wait for Daddy, Mrs. Butcher, the fourth grade teacher, stopped me at the back door. She handed me my camera, and said, "You would have graduated in three months."

I took the camera, aware that Sister Wellington didn't have the nerve to give it to me, herself. "I'll graduate somewhere else."

She shook her head slowly. "No, you probably won't. Most kids who leave without graduating, never finish school. Even those who graduate have a hard time." Her cold expression staggered me. "Leaving before you finish," she went on, "almost guarantees you'll end up a whore, or a prostitute . . . like all the others."

I recoiled, hardly able to contain myself. I wanted to hit her. "No, Miss Butcher, I won't!"

"If you were a boy," she continued, "I would predict that you'd be in jail within a month. Most of them . . . especially those who don't graduate . . . do something stupid like rob a gas station, and get caught, of course." Her smug expression implied she liked it that way.

Revolted and shaken, I pushed past her, walked through the building, and stood out front to wait for Daddy. As the minutes passed, her words rang in my ears and drummed through my head, convincing me that my decision to leave was not a mistake.

Amazingly, Daddy showed up about an hour later.

Chapter 22

The World Outside

I had no fear of Daddy. We both knew that he wouldn't get away with anything now, so he never even looked at me in a way that raised a question. Perhaps my demeanor conveyed some new sense of authority because I certainly felt it. Whatever the reason, he treated me as if I were just another person in his life—nothing special, interesting or different—at least, not sexually.

Each time he took a drag off his cigarette, with his *left* hand, I noticed an edge of dirt or paint encrusted around his cuticles and under his fingernails. A tiny man with no teeth and a concave mouth, and wrinkles bunching at the back of his skinny neck as he lifted his chin to peer over the hood of the car, he looked years older than his age, fifty-five.

As we headed for Konowa, Oklahoma, he seemed quiet and resentful, as if picking me up had created an unreasonable hardship for him. He made no direct accusations, just innuendoes.

Finally, I asked, "What's the matter?"

His eyes darted in my direction then back to the road. "I would have appreciated a little more notice."

Even though I had already accepted a lot of unhappy "truths" about him, it still hurt to realize I was only an inconvenient obligation. "I couldn't wait."

"What's a day or two difference make?"

"It makes a lot of difference when you're about to get a beating for something you didn't do."

"Hmmm." He nodded, reluctantly conceding. "You finished with school?"

"Not for three more months. In June."

Clouds of red dust driven by powerful gusts of wind buffeted the car. Budding trees fought to hang onto the new green leaves lining their branches.

"You can get a job and help out," he said. "I can't feed you forever."

"I'll get a job as soon as I finish school. I want to graduate."

He scoffed, glanced at me, and looked away again. "What good's that piece of paper gonna do? You need to go to work now, and I know two or three places that'll hire you to waitress. Tomorrow."

I sighed from the weight of his attitude. "Let me finish school first. Please. That piece of paper might not be important to you, but it's important to me."

He lit another cigarette and blew smoke toward the windshield. "No one else in the family has one or ever needed one! And we got along just fine."

"That's one of the reasons I want it," I said. "If I graduate, maybe Jenny, Amy, and Gordon will, too. It's gotta start somewhere. Why not with me?"

He didn't respond and I didn't care if he agreed. I intended to graduate and let him house and feed me until I did. For the first time in my life, I felt no sense of obligation to him and even felt that he owed me something—at least three months of room and board so I could finish high school.

"Have you heard from Jenny?" I asked.

"Heard from her? Hell, she lives with me!"

Dumbfounded, I gaped at him. "I—I thought she was living with Mason."

"Well, that lasted about six months. Since then, she's been with Rosa and me."

"Rosa? Who's that?"

He reflected a bit before he spoke. "Rosa's my wife. Sort of. We've been together several years. She's a nurse and runs a little nursing home."

"In Konowa?"

"Yeah. Just a little place. Takes care of five old people." He stubbed out the cigarette. "There's a little town up ahead. I'm gonna stop so we can go to the bathroom and get something to eat."

Just the act of walking into that gritty little diner as a "free" person, not bound to return to the orphanage for the first time in eleven years, renewed my energy. A dull gray linoleum-covered counter about ten feet long stretched almost to the far side of the room. Three men in overalls and dirty baseball caps sat at the counter, their necks and faces weathered and tanned. In unison, they turned to look at us.

Four booths sat along the outside wall, beneath a long window that ran the length of the room, their tables dirtied with plates, cups, and remnants from previous customers.

A waitress, about my age, hurried to one of the tables with a dishpan and began clearing the dishes. "Ya'll can sit here, if you want."

"I'll be back," Daddy said over his shoulder as he disappeared into a hallway marked "Rest rooms."

I sat at the freshly wiped table and took in my first "free" surroundings. It didn't matter to me that the potted plants on the shelf across the room had died of thirst months ago; that yellow, gummy grease splattered the wall behind the counter and the cook stove; nor that the floor had a "walk pattern" down the center of the linoleum. A layer of reddish dust lay thick beneath the counter stools and the booths, but the center had been scuffed clean by footsteps.

The waitress came to the table, her soft blonde hair curled only on the ends. "Ya'll want some coffee?"

Panic flitted through me. I didn't know how much coffee cost, or whether Daddy intended to have it. "Ah, can you wait until he gets back?" I nodded toward the hall.

"Sure."

I relaxed a little when she left. I had never ordered food in a restaurant, read a menu, or paid for anything with money. Hoping to keep my ignorance hidden for the moment, I preoccupied myself with my new surroundings again.

Outside, the wind continued to hammer everything in its path. Across the road, beside a little house badly in need of paint, a clothesline full of shirts, overalls, and dresses flapped in the wind, looking like ghosts trying to flee.

I'm free! Free! I wanted the truth to sink into the deepest part of my soul and make me feel the joy I knew it would, once I really accepted it.

Daddy ordered us both a hamburger, himself coffee, and me a Coke.

I had heard of Coke but never tasted one. The fizzing surface tickled my nose and I laughed, embarrassed because I hadn't expected it. I also had a hundred more questions about Rosa and Jenny but every time I asked, Daddy said, "Eat. We'll talk in the car."

The nursing home was just one of many dilapidated houses on the old tree-lined block. Sparse, dead grass, struggling to green itself, did its best to cover the yards, its winter-yellow tendrils running out to the dirt and gravel street. People on porches sat in chairs and watched as we drove by. Dogs occasionally darted into the street, barking protectively and chasing the car.

"Well, here it is." Daddy pulled into the driveway of yet another house that needed paint. Its long porch ran the length of the house and a fat woman with orange hair frizzing six inches from her head, stood and walked to the steps. Her cotton print dress hung like a limp sack from her small sloping shoulders, widening as it fell over her stomach, then dropped to her knees where thin bowed legs extended downward like wide parentheses. A pair of men's brown cloth slippers covered her feet.

"That's Rosa." Daddy turned off the ignition and opened his door.

Rosa greeted us with a wide smile that wrinkled her face like a crumpled paper sack. "Hello, young lady. My name's Rosa." She grabbed my hand and shook it firmly. "And I'm happy to meet 'cha. Your sister's not here right now, but she'll be back in a couple of hours."

Taking my elbow, she guided me toward the door. "Come on inside and get a glass of iced tea. Then I'll show you around."

Daddy had already disappeared inside, so I followed Rosa. In contrast to the bright sunshine, the little house was dark, all the shades drawn, forcing me to strain to see. I had the sense of beds all around but couldn't really see more than shadows. The smell, however, couldn't be overlooked. A sharp, acrid odor mingled with a strange unfamiliar—and foul—smell permeated the house.

Holding my breath, I followed Rosa through two rooms and into a small kitchen where Daddy sat at a table pushed against the wall. He opened a bottle of beer, let the lid lay where it fell, and lifted the bottle for a long drink.

The kitchen smelled better because a large pot of chicken bubbled on the stove. Rosa poured two large glasses of iced tea and handed me one. "Come on," she said. "I'll show you around. Have your eyes adjusted yet?"

"I think so." There were three entrances into the kitchen, the one we had just entered, one leading into another part of the house, and a back door. She waddled toward the one that opened into a small room with an empty half bed, a television, and some storage cupboards. From there, we passed through another room hardly large enough for the hospital bed, chair, and dresser that had been crammed into it.

"This is Mrs. Whittaker," she said softly. "She ain't far from heaven, I expect."

I peered down at the thin, frail woman, hardly more than a skeleton, her thin skin revealing every vein in her closed eyes, her shrunken, toothless mouth agape. Dark purple veins showed in her pale white hands as they rested flat against her chest.

"Mrs. Whittaker's been here almost a year. At first, she got around a little, but not for six months now. I have to turn her all the time. She just don't move on her own." Rosa shook her head, made a little shaming, clicking sound then waddled through a door leading into a bathroom that opened into yet another room. "This is where Russell and I sleep," she said. "It ain't much, but all we need."

The bed had been carefully made and the dresser top with its freshly starched and ironed white runner displayed her best perfume bottles, a lamp, and several books. Other than the bed and dresser, two chairs crouched in the corners of the room, one draped with Daddy's pants and shirt.

"Go out this door and you're back in the front room." She led the way. "Millie White and Gladys Trindle live here."

Seeing the front door, I realized we had just made a full circle and began to feel a little better oriented. I glanced at the beds on either side of the room. Rosa moved to one and said, "Millie? You awake?"

The husky, sleeping figure didn't move.

"I guess she ain't." She turned to look at the other bed.

"I'm awake!" a strong voice barked.

"You're always awake," Rosa laughed and turned to me. "This is Gladys and she's more trouble than ten others."

Gladys laughed and reached for my hand. "My, my! Now who do you belong to?"

"Ah, I'm Russell's daughter."

"Russell's?" She made a sputtering sound. "Who'd of thought, ugly as he is, that he'd of had a looker?"

"Come on," Rosa nudged my elbow. "She'll talk your leg off."

Gladys laughed. "I will, at that!"

The dining room, like the front room, had been converted into a hospital room. Beds stood against both walls, with rocking chairs, tables, and walkers here and there.

"Now, in here is Indian Annie and Crazy Jane. Hey! You girls ready to get up for awhile?"

A slight woman with long gray hair hanging over her shoulders smiled and sat up.

"That's Crazy Jane. You'll like her."

"She'll like me, too!" Gladys barked from the front room.

"No, she won't!" Rosa yelled back. "Nobody likes you!"

Gladys' laugh carried through the house.

Crazy Jane scooted off her bed. Once on her feet, the nightgown covering her slight body appeared to be empty. With an impish smile, she shuffled over to me and squinted as she peered at my face. "Did I hear someone say you're Russell's daughter?"

"Yes, ma'am."

"Nice to meetcha, hon." Her bony hand felt cool.

"Indian Annie?" Rosa leaned over the other bed and shook the woman's shoulder. "Wake up! You can't sleep all day or you'll be up all night."

Annie turned reluctantly. "The Indians coming?" she asked. "Do we need to hide?"

"No." Rosa yelled. "You just need to get up and sit in your rocker awhile." Then she turned to me. "She can't hardly hear."

"She's crazy!" Crazy Jane said. "When she was a little girl, the Indians attacked their place. Yeah, they did. They burned it clean down and kilt everyone but Annie. They thought they kilt her too but they only put her eye out."

A second glance at Indian Annie confirmed that she had an empty eye socket. In the dimly lit room, it hadn't been obvious at first.

"Since then, she always wakes up thinking the Indians are coming!" Crazy Jane laughed and moved to her own rocking chair where she adjusted the pillow and sat down.

Rosa helped Annie to her chair then turned to the kitchen. "I'll get you girls a little snack."

"I want apple pie!" Gladys yelled from the front room.

"So do I," Rosa shouted, "but I don't have any. Come on, Othello." She wagged her head toward the kitchen. "You can help me serve 'em some applesauce and juice."

As we prepared dishes of applesauce and small glasses of orange juice, I glanced in the little room with the half bed and TV. Daddy was stretched out, on his back, his hands above his head.

"Where does Jenny sleep?" I asked, realizing that the half bed was the only empty bed I'd seen.

"Well, she's been sleeping in there where your daddy is, but when I heard this morning that you were coming, I rented a little house down the street. It's been vacant for months. You and Jenny can live there." She hesitated and looked at me. "Is that okay by you?"

"Sure!" I laughed. "I'm so glad to be out of the home, I don't care where I sleep."

She placed the glasses and bowls on a large brown tray. "Well, it's really against regulations for Jenny to sleep here, so it's best that I get her out."

She lumbered toward the dining room. "I'll show you the place after I give my girls a snack."

We retraced out steps, beginning in the dining room, placing a bowl of applesauce and cup of juice on every table except Mrs. Whittaker's. After everyone had eaten, and Rosa had emptied a couple of bedpans, she woke Daddy. "Get up and sit in the kitchen," she said. "I'm going to show Othello the house."

Daddy pushed himself off the bed, ran his fingers through his hair, and went into the kitchen where he poured himself a cup of coffee and sat down at the table.

"You girls be good for Russell," Rosa yelled as we left. "He's in the kitchen if you need him."

We walked only half a block, two doors down from the nursing home.

The little house, unlike the other older homes, had no porch or character. A sidewalk ran straight to the door. More than anything else, the house looked like a long wooden box with a door and two windows facing the street. The dirt yard was dotted with dark oil spots as if it had been used for parking cars.

"It's not much," Rosa said as she turned the key. "But it's clean—and all I can afford."

I had instantly liked Rosa and grown fonder by the minute as she walked me through the nursing home, so if I had hated it, I would have lied. But I didn't hate it. Although small, it was new enough that the cream-colored linoleum still shown in the afternoon light.

"I rented it this morning, after your Aunt Lola Mae called and said your daddy was supposed to pick you up."

"I really appreciate it, Rosa. You don't know how much."

"We'll get some furniture over here, after Jenny gets home. She can help."

"I can't wait to see her." I admitted. "I haven't seen her in two years."

"Well, she's taller than you. I can tell you that much."

The house had two small bedrooms, a tiny living room, and a miniature kitchen and bathroom. I wondered if a bed would actually fit in the smallest bedroom, but I didn't care. It was *not* Tipton Home. It was a real house where I could live like a free person, make my own decisions, and not have a matron watching my every move.

"When's Amy get out?" Rosa asked. "Russell said she's younger than Jenny."

I was somehow surprised that she didn't know where Amy was. "Ah . . . Amy's not in the home. She's—she's in the mental hospital in Norman."

"*What?*" She stepped back, outrage twisting her face.

For the next several minutes, I told her about the "trial" and the day Amy was taken away.

"Well, I'll just check into that!" She spat the words out. "I happen to know how that system works because I was a nurse there for fifteen years, and if something can be done, I'll do it!"

"Really?" It amazed me that this strange looking old woman might have influence enough to get Amy released.

"You're damn-tootin'! I know the doctors, the administrators, the nurses, counselors, and therapists. I know exactly whose arm to twist and how hard to twist it." She moved to the door to leave. "No, no. That's not right, hauling off little kids to a mental hospital." She hesitated and then dropped her gaze for a minute, as if considering her thoughts carefully. "You know what they do with those orphan kids, don't you?"

I frowned, no idea what she meant.

"They do experiments on them. Yep." She nodded. "Fertility experiments among other things. The government allows it because they're orphans, so we've gotta get her out of there fast."

I was blinking stupidly, trying to comprehend such a hideous thought, when Jenny peeked around Rosa. "Othello!"

All thoughts vanished, and I ran to her.

"Here," Rosa thrust the key at us. "Show Jenny the house and you girls can move some furniture when you get through catching up."

Catching Up

"This is the place?" Jenny asked. "I went by the nursing home and Daddy said you were here and we were moving into our own place."

I stepped back. "Whatta you think?"

She stepped inside and scrutinized every room as if she were going to buy it. "Well . . . it's little. And it's ugly."

"You think so? I think it looks great! There's not a matron anywhere!"

She laughed. "Yeah. That's true. Well . . . maybe with some curtains and some furniture." She raised an eyebrow. "Who gets this bedroom?" She nodded toward the larger of the two.

"Well, until we get two beds, we probably both get it."

She smiled. "We'll giggle and laugh all night!"

"I know. Oh, it's so good to see you. I can't wait to hear everything . . . about Mason . . . school . . . everything!"

"Me, too. How's Gordon?"

"Just before I left, I saw him and he's okay. He didn't seem upset I was leaving."

"Hey, you two!" Daddy stuck his head inside the door. "You gonna help me move furniture?"

We followed him to the back of the nursing home and into a garage where he pulled a bed frame and mattresses away from the wall. Jenny and I took one end and he the other and we walked the mattresses down to the little house. Rosa set out sheets, pillowcases, and pillows for us and once the bed was made, we moved an assortment of tables, lamps, chairs, and a small chest.

Within the hour, the little house began to take shape and Jenny and I made the bed then sat on it to talk. Her soft brown hair hung just above her shoulders, the ends curled upward into a perfect "flip" that bounced slightly as she moved and talked. Her make-up, flawlessly applied, made her look closer to twenty than sixteen.

Since this was our first conversation since she had left the home, I asked her about the night she sneaked out with Dora Lee and got caught.

"It never happened!" She laughed.

I frowned. "Sister Wellington said you and Dora were caught slipping out with airmen from the Altus Base. Was she lying?"

"She didn't know she was lying," Jenny laughed. "The truth is I never slipped out with Dora. But I *did* tell Dora to say that I was with her if she ever got caught."

"Why? Why would you do that?"

"So I'd be sent away. I'd heard that anyone caught slipping out with boys would be sent to a reform school, and I preferred that to the home."

"You were willing to—?"

She nodded.

"Well, how did you end up with Mason? Why didn't they send you to the reform school?"

She laughed. "I had written Mason the week before. Slipped the letter out through a Town kid. I told him I was in big trouble and to come visit me." She shrugged. "The timing just worked out. When Sister Wellington locked me up in one of the punishment rooms, she said I was going to be sent to the reform school on Monday. Then Mason came the next day—Sunday. So instead of sending me to the reform school, she sent me to live with him."

"So . . . what everyone thought . . . that you were having sex with a bunch of airmen . . . that wasn't true?"

She shook her head. "No. No. In fact," she added indignantly, "Sister Wellington told Mason I might be pregnant! So, even before he took me to his house, he stopped by a doctor's office . . . for an examination to find out."

"And?"

"Well, the doctor didn't say anything to me, but I guess he talked to Mason because as we drove away from the clinic, Mason said, 'The old lady at the home told me you might be pregnant . . . but the doctor said you're a virgin.'" She rolled her eyes, remembering. "Can you imagine that old bitch telling Mason that!"

We talked until it was almost dark then walked back to the nursing home where we ate a sandwich in the kitchen and Jenny filled me in on what to expect at school. "With only three months until you graduate, you've got nothing to worry about. You're the new girl. Everyone will be nice to you."

"Have you got a boyfriend?"

"David, I guess. We've been out a few times." She shrugged and giggled. "Actually, there's this guy named Kevin I want you to meet. He's tall, good-looking. You'll like him."

From that moment until midnight, we laughed and giggled, trying to make up for all the years we'd been kept apart. Then, as I began to drift off, I remembered Miss Butcher's face and words as she stood in the doorway that morning. "You'll either be a prostitute or a whore within a month."

I wouldn't. I would never be a prostitute or whore. "Jenny? You awake?"

"Mm-hum."

I told her what Miss Butcher had said.

"What's the difference?"

"What do you mean, what's the difference? It's insulting!"

"No, I mean, what's the difference between a prostitute and a whore?"

"Oh." I thought about it. "I don't know."

She turned over. "A prostitute gets paid, I think. But they're both whores."

"Oh." A few seconds later, I remember what Rosa said about the hospital experiments. "Jenny? You still awake?"

"Yeah."

I told her what Rosa had said. She sprang up and sat staring at me. "We've gotta do something."

"Rosa said she would. She said she knows people . . . and things, and she can do it."

"She can? Good. That's good."

New School, New Boys

The next morning, Jenny and I ate a bowl of oatmeal in Rosa's kitchen and Daddy handed us each two dollars for a week's worth of lunches.

"Daddy!" Jenny protested. "We can't eat all week on two dollars."

"Then come home and eat."

Jenny argued that there wasn't time, but Daddy didn't budge.

Konowa High School was about the same size as Tipton High. Maybe 200 kids. After enrolling, I sat through the classes, looking and listening but learning little. With everything being new, and being the newest kid at school, I had more attention than I could handle. Every time I looked up, one of the boys winked or smiled.

Before lunch, Jenny had spread the word that I played the piano, so when we entered the little snack shack called "Bertha's" most of the girls politely asked about my piano playing, and most of the boys asked repeatedly, "What's your name again?"

At the end of the day, just as I was about to open the door to leave, a large, hairy arm reached around me. I thought the hand was going for my breast and I reacted so quickly and strongly, grabbing the arm and twisting it down and back, that a six-foot-tall boy landed on his back, at my feet.

Kids behind us halted and gasped. I glanced back, then at the embarrassed boy scrambling to his feet.

"Why'd you do that?" he asked.

"I . . . I thought . . . "

"Thought what? I was about to open the door for you!" he said indignantly. "I was just reaching over your shoulder to open the door."

"Oh. I thought…"

"You thought what?" Still humiliated, he glanced from me to those behind me.

"Nothing." I couldn't leave fast enough. Jenny caught up with me and laughed until tears came to her eyes.

"Well, all I could think about were Miss Butcher's words, and I thought he was, you know…"

"What was his name?"

"I don't know."

"What did he look like?"

I could still see him staring, dumbfounded, from the floor.

"Cute. Really cute. Blond hair. Tall. Big."

She frowned. "How tall? Six feet?"

I nodded.

"Oh, geez! That had to be Kevin. He's the only blonde in school that tall."

"Kevin?" I knew I had heard the name.

"The guy I wanted you to go out with!" She laughed again. "I haven't had the courage to speak to him, and you throw him to the floor the first time he tries to open the door for you!"

Over the next few days, I quickly learned that Jenny had a better understanding of relationships and how to manage them (to get what she wanted) than I did. On Friday, as soon as school let out, she told me that she had set up a double date with David, herself, Kevin, and me.

"Why? Why would you do that, after . . . after . . . ?"

"Because he likes you. He wants to go out with you. The day you threw him to the floor, he was hoping to walk out with you and ask you out himself. She grinned and cocked her head. "I have ways of learning these things. Anyway," she added, "after you did what you did, he sort of lost his nerve."

The thought of dating terrified me so I grilled Jenny on every detail—what to say . . . what to do . . . how "far" was far enough . . . what guys expected, and even how I should dress.

"Relax," she said. "You'll do fine. Besides, I'll be there to cover up any blunders."

David and Kevin arrived in David's car, both as neatly dressed as models, every hair shiny with oil and combed into submission, and smelling like a bottle of Old Spice. Jenny slid onto the front seat with David and I sat in the back with Kevin, nervously twisting the strap on my purse until at one point I thought I broke it. We ate burgers and fries at the drugstore soda fountain, made a lot of self-conscious conversation and when we finished, the boys had just ordered a second round of Cherry Cokes, when Jenny said to me, "Let's go freshen up."

For the next five minutes, backed up against a sink, I listened, dumbstruck, at what she said.

"Just for the fun of it . . . let's trade dates!"

"You're kidding."

"No! "

"Won't we hurt their feelings?"

"No. They'll love it."

"How do you know?"

"Trust me. They'll love it."

Embarrassed and ashamed to go along with the plan, I wasn't strong enough or thinking fast enough to argue confidently. So after we combed our hair and applied a fresh layer of lipstick, we walked back to the table. Doing as instructed, I sat down beside David. He inclined his head questioningly, then shrugged and smiled.

Jenny slid in beside Kevin, and the two boys glanced at each other and laughed. Nothing more was said. We acted as though the "switch" hadn't happened and when we finished our drinks, David drove out of town to park.

He turned out the lights and darkness enveloped the car. For several seconds, only the sound of the crickets assured me that we hadn't evaporated. After a moment, my eyes adjusted to the moonlight and I could see David behind the steering wheel.

Another few seconds passed and sounds of movement came from the backseat. David tentatively reached across the seat to touch my hand. "You're not gonna throw me, are you?"

From the backseat, Kevin and Jenny burst out laughing, and David and I laughed, too.

"It depends." I said.

Eternal minutes dragged by as Jenny and Kevin petted and panted in the backseat, and David and I slowly but surely gathered enough nerve for him to try to kiss me, and for me to let him.

Chapter 23

All I Didn't Know

Daddy was around most of the time, in the kitchen with a cup of coffee or bottle of beer. He grudgingly gave us two dollars a week for lunches at Bertha's and said very little to either Jenny or me. Having never held money in my hand, learning to count change was a humiliating experience. I didn't know if I should count it to be sure I hadn't been cheated, or if doing so was rude.

My socialization took constant vigilance because I had never read a newspaper or seen a televised newscast. In eleven years, I had seen only two movies, *Quo Vaduz* and *The Blue Veil*, and read as many books: *The Mystery of the Little Green Turtle* and *Rebecca*. Current events, world affairs, and politics meant nothing. All I knew about the President of the United States, I learned from an *I Like Ike* button worn by a farmer at the Tipton church. The farmer liked him.

I could, however, recite the names of every book in the Bible; quote scriptures for hours on end; name every missionary journey taken by the apostles; locate any city in the Holy Land at the time of Jesus; make up a new song every time I sat down at the piano; draw almost anything I saw; and feel stupid and guilty about everything I said, thought, or did. Unfortunately, none of these helped much as I stumbled through my last three months of high school.

Rosa was my greatest source of non-judgmental information. She waddled around like a great, wrinkled-faced duck, her false teeth moving and clicking as she patiently advised me about each new situation. I even risked confiding my most precious secret . . . that somewhere inside of me was a special, wonderful place where music existed . . . where my mind, fingers, eyes, and ears all connected . . . and where there was no trouble, only a feeling of acceptance and an awareness that "the place" would always be there for me.

"Have you ever heard of such a thing?" I asked, searching her expression for signs of rejection.

She took a swallow of coffee before answering. "Some people might call it your soul."

The idea horrified me. My soul was in constant jeopardy . . . constantly at risk of going to hell . . . that wonderful place should never be condemned to hell.

"The good Lord gave it to you." She nodded confidently. "It's the good Lord's gift."

"Then, it can't be my soul!" I argued. "Why would He give me a wonderful soul like that and then send it to hell if I did something bad? That would destroy it!"

She placed her hands on the table and slowly pushed herself up to a standing position. "Now, I don't know everything you've heard about God . . . and I don't pretend to know more than anyone else . . . but I do know..." She paused and looked at me intensely. "I do know that everybody has a kind of special place . . . a beautiful place . . . inside them. And you mostly have to get real still to recognize it. And when you do, you don't doubt it. You don't question it. You just enjoy it."

"You've felt it then?"

She picked up her empty coffee cup and waddled across the kitchen. "Everybody has, at one time or another, I expect. Some more than others. I don't know why."

I waited for her to sit again. "When do you feel it?"

"Oh, I don't know. I used to feel it when I worked in the hospital, sometimes. Certain people kind of help you feel it, I think."

"And what about the feeling that I told you about when I left the home. That feeling of power. Like nothing can stop you."

"What about it? Long as you use it for good, I reckon it's good." She gestured toward the counter. "Hand me that sack of cookies, honey. I'm hungry."

We opened the cookies and shared them, not saying much else.

After awhile, it started to rain and we sat quietly just listening to it. "I called the hospital today and made an appointment to talk with Dr. Farnsworthy about Amy."

"You did?" I loved this ugly old lady with fuzzy orange hair. "What did he say?"

"Well," she washed a bite of cookie down with coffee. "I just made an appointment. Oh, he'll help me, I'm sure of it." An evil little chuckle escaped her throat. "He doesn't have much choice. I know a lot more about him than he's comfortable with! Things he'd prefer I kept to myself."

I laughed. "Like what?"

"Well, let's just say I know he'll help me . . . and leave it at that."

Deeply satisfied that Rosa would use any and all means at her disposal, I smiled, thought of Amy, and listened to the rain again.

"It'll take awhile," she added, "because certain strings have to be pulled and bells have to be rung in order, but I'll get Amy out of there before summer. I promise."

Relief and gratitude flooded through me. "Thank you, Rosa. You have no idea how good this makes me feel."

She smiled, stood, then waddled to my side of the table and patted my shoulder. "I think I do."

My Piano

My second week in Konowa, Jenny put a dress on layaway, agreeing to pay four dollars a week—my lunch money and hers. Consequently, the last few hours at school each day became increasingly uncomfortable as my stomach growled and complained. So as soon as the last bell rang, we ran home together and finished off what the patients hadn't eaten.

Toward the end of the third week, I came home to find Rosa and Daddy standing in the middle of the street, directing two men who were delivering a tall, black, upright piano to the little house.

"A piano! I can't believe you did this, Daddy!"

He nodded, smiled a little, and glanced away. Rosa patted my arm. "It's just an old thing, but you'll enjoy it, I'm sure."

Never expecting such a treasure, I loved its scratched surface and yellowed keys. Rosa stood back and beamed and Daddy nodded, the little smile still on his face.

I hugged and kissed them. "Thank you! Thank you."

"Well!" Rosa said, dropping into the nearest chair. "You just going to dance around or play us something?"

Immediately, I slid onto the seat and began to play.

"What's the name of that?" Rosa asked when I finished. "I don't think I've heard it before."

"It doesn't have a name. It's one I made up."

Daddy, looking restless and bored, stood and moved to the door. "I'll go watch the girls."

Rosa stayed for half an hour, closing her eyes and listening as if she really enjoyed it. "You keep playing," she said when she left. "That's what it's for."

The piano, tall, black, scarred and yellow-toothed, grinned at me and dominated most of my afternoons for the next three months.

Getting Serious

David and I saw each other every evening, but no matter how heated our kisses became, Miss Butcher's words rang loudly in my ears, monitoring all my responses. In spite of this, David maintained a constant interest in me, and within a month of meeting him, he was saying things, such as "when we get married . . . " –words that created instant panic.

"I'm going to own my own auto repair shop someday," he told me with a wide, proud grin. "Like my dad's, only better." Then he added with an equal sense of satisfaction, "My mom keeps the books for the shop. Maybe you'll keep books for my shop, too, huh?" He winked and I tried to smile but the idea sounded a lot like returning to Tipton Home.

His parents were wonderful to me, but I knew I could never be like them. They had everything they wanted—a little business, a house, some kids—and each other. But I wanted more. I wasn't sure what *more* I wanted, and maybe it was only something *different*, but whatever it was, their life would never satisfy me.

His mother commented on every person in town, making statements that both amused and startled me. One evening, after supper, she stood on her tiptoes to look out the kitchen window, then laughed and said, "Millie's got another pair of boots parked under her bed tonight. That's the third pair this week."

I cringed at the thought of living in a town so small that every move was known. It was all too much like Tipton Home. I knew these were good people but Konowa was the wrong place for me and I could feel it to the marrow of my bones. I longed for lights and city streets that I had never seen, for stores filled with people, where everyone went about their business, not caring what anyone else did. Every thought and action of my life had been restricted, and I ached to change that, to explore, learn, and see what was out "there," and what I could do with it.

I talked to David about my trepidation.

"What do you mean, *go where the lights are?*"

"I mean . . . a bigger place. A place with thousands of people and things happening all the time."

"Oh." His shoulders slumped. "Well, maybe after awhile that feeling will go away . . . and you'll decide you can live here."

I shook my head. "I don't think so."

He smiled and took my hand. "Well, it might!"

Two weeks before graduation, David gave me an engagement ring. His kindness and sweetness melted my heart, and I wanted to take the ring but knew I would be lying to him. I couldn't stay in Konowa. "I can't take it, David. If I do, I'll just disappoint you."

"Take it anyway," he urged. "Just wear it awhile. You never know, you just might decide you love me enough to stay."

"It isn't you! It's me. I just can't stay here! There's someplace else . . . I don't know where . . . but someplace where I'm supposed to be. And wherever it is, it's not here."

He sighed. "Well, will you wear it until you go?"

"No, because you'll build your hopes up that I'll keep it, and I won't."

"No! No!" He held up his hands to protest. "I believe you. You're not going to stay here. I just want to be engaged to you until then . . . to know that we came close . . . very close to getting married. Because I'll always love you."

I let him slip the ring on my finger.

Graduation Plans

I ordered the minimum number of graduation announcements, and mailed only four. Other than my brothers, Don and Mason, and my Aunt Lola Mae, the only other people I thought *might* be interested in my graduation were Lewis and Lou Ellen Foster, the couple who had given me the camera that Sister Wellington confiscated years ago. I wanted to believe they really liked me and would be glad to know I was graduating.

I sent Don's announcement to his last military address and hoped it would be forwarded. As I sealed Mason's announcement, I doubted he would be able to leave work to come, and knew Aunt Lola Mae wouldn't come, so I hoped with all my heart that Lewis and Lou Ellen would.

I assumed Daddy would attend, so a couple of weeks prior to graduation, I walked over to the nursing home to mark the time on the kitchen calendar.

Daddy watched me circle the date and pencil in the hour, and said, "I ain't goin'." He cupped both hands around his beer bottle as Rosa stepped away from the stove and stared defiantly at him.

"I ain't!" He repeated. "I ain't goin'!"

My chest tightened. "Why?"

"I don't have a jacket."

"I'll get you a jacket!" Rosa scolded, "Or you can borrow one!"

He shook his head, lifted his beer, and drank.

Discouraged, I went back to the little house and sat down at the piano. Minutes later, Daddy threw the door open and stepped inside. "You're just like your mother!" he yelled. "Just like her! She was never satisfied. Never satisfied! She always wanted two dresses! Was never satisfied with one!"

The ludicrous remark almost strangled me as I tried not to laugh.

"Now, me!" he ranted, "I'm not like that! I'm happy with the shirt on my back! One shirt!" He spat the words at me. "But you and your momma—you always gotta have more!"

Trying to imagine being happy with one shirt or one dress, I finally laughed.

He stormed at me, his arms raised threateningly. "Now, listen here, Sister! I'll tell you one thing, and you can count on it!" He wagged a finger in my face. "I've never let one of my kids interfere with my happiness, and Sister, I don't intend to start now! If you want to graduate, then graduate! But don't expect me to be there because I don't care!"

He left in the same furious huff as he had entered, slamming the door behind him. I took a deep breath and tried to separate my thoughts. That he had never let his kids interfere with his happiness was one of the saddest things I'd ever heard . . . but that he proudly admitted it, hit me as one of the funniest ideas ever expressed. *Boasting* about it was incomprehensible. I laughed until my face hurt. How could anyone admit to that?

After awhile, however, his saying he didn't care that I was graduating created a sickening heaviness that made me doubt *I* should care.

The Interview

A pressing truth began to dominate my awareness. I needed a job. Daddy had mentioned several times that a coffee shop in town needed a waitress, and I might have considered it but I couldn't count change accurately enough, and I knew it. I had, on the other hand, three years of typing and two years of shorthand completed, so I decided to look for work as a secretary.

I found three secretarial positions listed in the paper, all of them in other towns. The one in Muskogee sounded best so I called, made an appointment for the next afternoon, and skipped school to take the bus to Muskogee. I found the address with the help of a map, and walked four blocks in my high heels only to discover the door to the business locked. Frustrated, I stepped back to double-check the address against the ad in the paper.

Just then, a car pulled to the curb and a sandy-haired man about thirty-five, yelled out the window, "Are you here for the interview?"

I nodded. "Are you Mr. Steward? The man I talked to yesterday?"

"Yes, something's come up and I can't do it right now."

I sighed. "You want me to wait?"

He seemed to think about it. "Well, if you'd like, you can ride along with me and I'll interview you on the way. I need to pick up some packages."

Without a second's hesitation, I thanked him and got in the car. He pulled away from the curb and asked, "You out of high school yet?"

"I will be next week."

He smiled. "I'll bet you're happy about that."

"Yes, sir."

"You a good student?"

I shrugged. "In some classes. I typed sixty-five words a minute. And take dictation ninety words a minute."

"Oh, yeah?" He laughed and nodded as though he were impressed as he stopped at a stop sign, then turned right and headed down another street. "I'd say that's pretty darn good!"

His sandy-colored hair, caught in the air from the window, whipped across his forehead. "You said on the phone that you live in Konowa, didn't you?"

I nodded "That's right."

"Did you grow up in Konowa?"

"No, sir. I grew up in Tipton. There's an orphanage there. That's where I lived."

"Oh." He nodded slowly as if considering what I'd said. "No family?"

Hesitant to tell him about Daddy, I shrugged. "Not much."

"I see. Hmmm. Must be hard."

Wanting to assure him I would be a good employee, I quickly added, "And I'm a hard worker. I know how to work. And I'm honest and . . . and you can depend on me."

"Now, that part, I would have guessed. I'll bet you're as good and honest as they come."

My confidence grew as he drove to an old building that looked like an abandoned warehouse then parked in a lot behind it. There were no other cars in sight and when he got out of the car, he said, "You mentioned you were taking a bus . . . what time do you need to leave to catch the bus back to Konowa?"

"Three-forty five."

"Good. There's plenty of time." He got out, then before closing the door, he leaned down and smiled at me. "Why don't you come in with me? I'll give you a couple of boxes to carry."

We walked up a concrete loading ramp littered with assorted trash and covered with a layer of red grit. "Mr. Steward, does it sound like I can do the job?"

He took keys from his pocket, unlocked the door, and smiled. "You sound just fine." He held the door for me and turned on the light as I stepped inside a large, empty room. A great relief swept through me. One obstacle down. *I had the job!* Life was getting better by the minute.

We stepped around a pile of boards and empty cardboard boxes, as I followed him into a second, smaller room. Several small boxes were stacked in the corner, and the faded light filtering through a single dirty window cast a dim yellow glow over everything.

I didn't see him step behind me but when his hand touched my neck, I spun around, my heart racing, every muscle tensed.

"Whoa!" He laughed, pulling his hand back. "I . . . I was just admiring your pretty neck."

As his eyes nervously studied my face, he reached again to touch my neck.

"It's just a neck." I swatted his hand back, not sure what to do. My heart hammered so fast, I could hardly breathe.

"Come on," he whispered. "I won't hurt you."

Was it expected? Did I have to do this to get the job? Did he lock the door with a key from the inside, too? Frozen, I stood like a block of ice as he touched my face. I smelled garlic on his breath, felt the wetness of his mouth on my neck, too horrified to move.

He started to unbutton my blouse and my hands came up. "No! Please, no!"

He pushed my hands aside and I erupted into a frenzy of flailing arms and scrambling feet, but he blocked my every move and we suddenly fell to the floor.

"No, no, no!" The words echoed through the empty warehouse. I lost my shoes, felt him pulling my bra up over my breasts and pushing himself against me. The dirty tile floor pushed hard and cold against my back.

"Shhh! Shhh!" He whispered in my ear, as if trying to comfort me. "Don't resist. Don't resist."

I didn't resist much longer. A deepening sense of futility extinguished whatever spark had prompted me to fight at all. I felt his hand move inside my panties before my mind focused on the exposed and broken light bulb in the dirty ceiling outlet. A gaping hole exposed the fragile burned-out filament. It wouldn't matter how many times the switch was flipped, the light wouldn't shine again.

I was still staring at the light bulb when he said, "You don't have to worry about getting pregnant. I've been fixed." Then he stepped into what I guessed was a bathroom and came out carrying a dirty blue towel. "Here."

I grasped the towel, but oddly, couldn't feel it. My hands moved awkwardly, numb and dead. I sat up slowly, wondering if he would watch while I cleaned myself, and was relieved when he picked up one of the small boxes and left the room. As I heard his footsteps move across the floor, I worked as quickly as I could to pull myself together, thankful that my clothes were only dusty, not torn. I had just put on my shoes when he came back.

"You'll make your bus in plenty of time." He smiled, his mouth tight, his eyes only sweeping in my direction. "I'll take you to the bus stop."

"Do you really need a secretary?" I finally asked, once we were in the car.

He didn't look at me when he answered, "No. Sorry."

He didn't sound sorry.

Feeling came back into my hands as I sat at the bus stop but my feet went numb, and when I stood to get on the bus, I stumbled. The driver moved quickly to help me.

"I guess my foot went to sleep."

It was a short trip back to Konowa because my mind ran faster than the bus. Lies seemed to be the biggest problem in the world. *Lies and my stupidity*. I knew I wouldn't die from an unwanted penis being stuck into my vagina, because I'd experienced that before. But it *was* possible to die from lies that hurt so much they made you want to kill yourself. And when the lie meant you wouldn't get a job . . . a job you needed . . . if you ran into enough of those lies, you could probably starve to death.

Another liar. God, how I hated liars! People promising one thing but giving you another, building up your hopes, making you think everything was okay, then leaving you feeling like a stupid fool again.

Fear and despair brought a rush of tears. Prior to this moment, I hadn't considered that life outside the orphanage might be as bad as life inside. If that was true, as it now appeared to be, I had wasted my whole life fooling myself.

Go, Spider, Go!

David drove me to the graduation ceremony. I had no intention of telling him about the "interview" because it hadn't affected my decision to leave Konowa as soon as I could.

I sat in the front row and as the speeches droned on and on, I watched a small gray spider slowly creeping across the floor, along the base of the stage. It was just a little garden spider, careful to stay near the relative safety of the stage wall, seeming to have some place it wanted to go. Occasionally it stopped and rested before continuing its slow, uncertain trek.

About halfway through the speeches, David tapped me on the shoulder and gestured behind us. I looked back and saw Daddy entering the room.

He looked uncomfortable as he took a seat, wearing a light colored casual jacket I'd never seen before. I smiled at him, glad he had come, but I wasn't sure he saw me.

The spider neared the steps just as the speeches ended and the principal started to call our names. Nervously, I watched, hoping the spider wouldn't be stepped on, after working so hard to get that far. When my name was called, I walked slowly and carefully, keeping my eye on the spider. Somehow, within that hour, it had come to symbolize all I felt. If he could make it across the room without being squashed, everything would be okay for me. Just as I reached the steps, the spider was directly beneath me. I stepped over him, letting him pass safely.

Go, Spider, Go!

I walked up to accept my diploma. We had both made it.

Assuming that Daddy's appearance at the ceremony meant he had regretted his words and had a change of heart, I asked David to take me by the house. I wanted to thank Daddy for coming, and hoped the ceremony had prompted a little pride. David waited for me in the car.

The "girls" were all asleep for the night and Daddy was in the kitchen with Rosa, his borrowed jacket hanging on the back of his chair. He lifted his beer and drank as I approached.

"Thank you for being there tonight," I said to him. "It meant a lot to me."

He threw a nasty glance in my direction and set the beer down. "Well, I damn sure didn't want to go! I went because she wouldn't shut up about it!" He poked the air toward Rosa.

"Well, a kid only graduates once, Russell."

Silenced by the exchange, I looked from one to the other.

"Well, that's good!" he said, "'Cause I damn sure wouldn't go again! Ever!"

I felt myself inching backward, unable to respond.

"Furthermore!" he yelled, "if you weren't my own flesh and blood, you wouldn't be living here right now! And now that you've got this almighty education, get your ass out and go to work! I'm not supporting you!"

Defeated, stumbling and crying, I rushed out of the house and ran across the yard to David's car. I slumped against the door and blubbered every word that had been said.

Fury crossed David's face for a moment then melted into compassion.

"Let's get out of here."

Chapter 24

Trying to End It

That evening, sitting in his car, David tried to console me, promising me a life that would be much better once we were married. But all the confusion I had ever felt seemed to rise and engulf me at once and as he held me and kissed me, apologizing for my father, I wasn't really there. I was in some strange void where nothing made sense and no matter where I looked, I saw only blurry lines, shadows, and distorted angles.

Then suddenly, I was lying on the seat and he was on top of me. I saw the moon, through the windshield, bright and round overhead—and one horrible thought filled my mind: *pregnancy!*

"No!" I pushed at him. "Stop! I'll get pregnant!"

He jerked back and came all over my thigh. "You won't," he said when he caught his breath. "You won't."

"Take me home."

"I'm sorry." He reached for my hand. "I'm sorry. I just—just—"

"It doesn't matter! Just take me home!"

Jenny had left immediately following the graduation ceremony to spend the weekend with a girlfriend so I had the house to myself—to wonder why I had been born. What was the point? When would anything really be better? Daddy didn't want me to stay and I didn't want to stay, but I had no where to go. If I stayed and married David, we would both regret it. And now I could see that Miss Butcher was right . . . I was probably nothing but a common whore.

I thought about the supply of pills that Rosa kept in the nursing home. I knew she had just bought a new prescription of Dexedrine to help her lose weight. Tomorrow, I would take them all. Why spend the rest of my life stumbling around, unable to tell a rapist from an employer? Better to end it all now.

Then David came by early the next morning and sat on the couch opposite me. "Are you feeling any better?"

"No. I want to die."

"Good god! Don't talk like that! How do you think it makes me feel?"

Realizing that I didn't care how it made him feel, I said nothing.

"Why don't you just marry me and let everything work out naturally."

"Because it won't work out. Getting married isn't going to make me happy. I have to do something—*something!*—for myself and I don't know how . . . or what!"

I asked him to leave but he didn't move.

"Let me stay with you awhile. I can help you through this."

"No. I want to be alone."

When he finally left, I walked directly to the nursing home, took the Dexedrine from Rosa's cabinet and went back to the little house, where I locked the door and counted the pills. Twenty-one. Without another thought about it, I washed them down, several at a time, with water then I sat in the living room staring at the old piano. At that moment, I realized that Rosa, not Daddy, had bought it for me.

I wanted it to be Daddy, and because he was there when it was delivered, I decided it was Daddy . . . but now with two more months of experience behind me . . . I knew that Rosa had bought it.

My Bible lay on the table beside me but I didn't pick it up. Every scripture I had so carefully underlined in the home, condemned me in some way. It seemed almost laughable now. What difference did it make?

I didn't move or try to move for almost an hour. Then, I heard David come to the door. He called my name, and for the first time I knew the pills had taken effect; his voice sounded warped and echoed in my ears. When I didn't answer the door, he pounded fiercely. "Othello! Open the door! Open the door!" He beat it again and again. Finally, I decided to get up and let him in. What harm could it do? The pills were down.

I stood and took one step on legs that wouldn't hold me. I fell, face down, but the fall didn't hurt. When I tried to move, I had no strength and, strangely, I felt no alarm. The floor was cool against my face and nothing disturbed me enough to want to move. The house grew quiet again so I assumed David had left. Then suddenly, the door crashed open, flooding the room with light and chilly air.

David had gotten Daddy and together they shouldered through the door. The empty Dexedrine bottle was still on the table and David saw it immediately. "How many did you take?" he shouted. "How many did you take?" My mouth didn't want to move so I didn't answer.

"We've got to get her to a hospital," David said, yanking me up to a sitting position.

"Hell, no, we don't!" Daddy growled. "Rosa will take care of her. I'm not paying for no hospital bills!"

"But . . . you've got to!"

"Let's get her over to the nursing home."

One on either side of me, they pulled me to my feet and I stumbled between them as they walked me to the nursing home. All the while, Daddy spewed his anger, but his words had little effect. "What will the neighbors think? How can you embarrass me this way? Everybody will think you're a drunk or a drug addict!"

When I felt Rosa checking my pulse, I opened my eyes. David sat at the foot of the bed, his lower face shadowed with dark whiskers, his eyes riveted on my face. He blinked, looked again, and smiled. "She's awake!"

Rosa's fingers tightened around my wrist. "Good Lord! You gave me a scare! Two or three times I thought for sure you were a goner!"

Later I learned that I had been unconscious for two days, and David had never left my side. He placed all his hope in Rosa's skills because Daddy refused to take me to a hospital.

Daddy was so angry with me he wouldn't look at me.

My Saviors

When I regained some strength and went back to the house, Jenny talked to me for a few minutes and then remembered I'd received a letter. I opened it and found a "Congratulations Graduate!" card from Lewis and Lou Ellen Foster. In all the commotion and emotion of the past week, I had forgotten I had even mailed them an announcement.

Now it seemed unimportant. I opened it, removed the letter and a $20 bill.

> *Dear Othello,*
>
> *Lewis and I were in South America when your announcement arrived, otherwise we would have been proud to attend your graduation. We are very proud you stuck to it. We've thought for a long time that we'd like to have you come and live with us, and perhaps go to college, if you want—which we'll pay for as long as your grades indicate you're interested.*
>
> *The $20 is to help you decide what you want to do. If you want a new dress, buy one—or anything else you want. But if you want to come and live with us, use the $20 for a bus ticket.*

After her signature, she included their phone number.

I read the letter several times, each time growing more excited. Even in my groggy, thick-headed state, I knew I held the ticket to my freedom. This was the answer . . . my chance to start over.

I called immediately. "Mrs. Foster?"

"Yes?"

"This is Othello."

She made a little squealing sound. "Yes, dear!"

"May I come tomorrow?"

She laughed, heartily, and the sound of her enthusiasm lifted my spirits instantly. "Of course, you may! Do you know what time?"

"Not yet. But I'll find out and let you know."

"Wonderful!"

Thank you, God. This was the opportunity I needed and longed for. It would get me to the city, to choices, ideas and possibilities—where I could start again.

Jenny and I cried together that night, saying our goodbyes.

"I don't blame you. You've got to go. I'd do the same."

"Would you? Would you leave me here with Daddy and go away to start a new life somewhere else?"

She nodded. "Yeah. And you'd do exactly what I'm doing . . . you'd insist that I go."

I knew she was right but my instinct to protect her forced me to ask, "Do you think you'll be safe with Daddy?"

The question startled her. "Safe? What do you mean?"

"I mean . . . sexually."

"Sexually?" Incredulity raised her voice and widened her eyes. "He's never tried anything with *me*! It's always been *you*."

Her quick, unequivocal response eased my fear. "Then, I have one last request . . . will you help Rosa follow-up to get Amy?"

She gave me the answer I expected. "Of course, I will. If she'll let me, I'll go to the hospital with her."

I sighed, at last able to release some of the tension. I copied the Fosters' phone number and gave it to her. "Let me know if there's anything I can do to help."

She smiled. "You know I will."

Don't Look Back!

David drove me to the bus stop in front of the drug store at five-thirty the next morning. In the shadowy grayness of the empty predawn street, we stared at each other and I cried as I gave him back his ring.

"It's okay," he said, "you told me it would happen. I knew I couldn't keep you."

"I'm sorry."

"You would never be happy with me, but I wanted you to be . . . Wanted to make you love me so much you wouldn't leave. But . . . I knew. You need to be somewhere else. Maybe it's like you say . . . where the lights are."

In the distance, the rumble of the approaching bus grew louder. Never had I felt so torn and twisted up inside. How could I leave the first person who had ever really loved me? How could anyone do that? I had to be the worst person on earth to walk away from him, and yet, I knew I had to.

When the bus pulled to a stop, David grabbed me in a strong embrace and whispered frantically, "I love you! Please remember that! Remember I'll always be here for you."

I nodded and tried to talk through my tears, but couldn't.

"No matter what!" he insisted, "You can always come back. Any time."

Stepping onto the bus was the hardest thing I had ever done. The fear of leaving behind my only hope, the only love I might ever know, held my feet like magnets. Then, finally, the door closed behind me and I saw David shrinking in the distance, staring after the bus. Slowly, I made my way toward the back, aware of the few sleeping passengers on either side. I sat on the backseat and tried to stop crying.

As the miles slipped behind me, my mind turned more and more toward Lewis, Lou Ellen, and the possibilities that lay ahead. It felt wonderful to know that, at last, I had someone to help me think and make decisions, to help me find a sense of direction—and get where I wanted to go.

Slowly, I began to consider the possible opportunities. Maybe I could go to an art school and become an artist . . . or a composer. Yes, a composer. Were there schools for that? Of course, I would have to learn to read music and that sounded hard—and *boring*.

Maybe I could become a nurse. Lots of girls did that. But even as I considered it, I shook my head. I couldn't take care of sick people—I'd be depressed all the time, myself.

A few miles further down the road, we stopped at another small town drugstore and picked up a single passenger. When the door closed again, a young woman about my age, wearing a long-sleeved shirt and carrying a small suitcase almost like mine, walked awkwardly toward the back.

"You care if I sit with you?" She nodded toward the long bench seat, her limp brown hair hanging in oily strands.

Secretly, I minded because my own thoughts were more exciting than anything she would say, but deciding to be polite, I said, "Go ahead."

We bumped along in silence for awhile and I returned to considering the options of my new life. Going to college had never been a serious consideration because only one or two of the home girls had done that. Only the boys were encouraged to go to college. So now, I wondered what colleges Lewis and Lou Ellen might suggest. The only ones I knew about were those supported by the Churches of Christ, and I wasn't sure I wanted more churchy stuff.

"Where you going?"

The question jolted me back to reality. "Ah, Wichita Falls, Texas."

"Oh. You got family there?"

"Sort of."

"Oh."

I looked at her closely for the first time and noticed the dark circles under her eyes. A thin, olive-skinned girl, she wore no makeup and seemed unconcerned that a strand of hair had fallen over her right eye. "Where are you going?" I pretended interest I didn't feel.

"To my grandma's. In Lawton."

I nodded, hoping she wouldn't respond.

"See these?" she held out her arms, palms up, in front of me.

I glanced at her empty hands and shrugged. "What?"

"These!" She pushed back the cuffs of her sleeves, exposing gauze- bandaged wrists. "I tried to kill myself."

The fear that ripped through me stiffened my whole body. I knew she was going to tell me something horribly sad and I couldn't bear to hear it. I wasn't strong enough. It took every ounce of resolve I had just to sit there, and I knew that if I listened to her, my tiny reserve would vanish. My newfound hopes and dreams would disappear.

"I slit my wrists." The note of pride in her voice repulsed me. The revulsion made my stomach queasy, as if I had just brushed against something so evil, it threatened my very existence. There was no time to think, only to run.

Jumping up, I quickly moved toward the front of the bus. Panting, as if I'd been running, I dropped to the seat behind the driver and didn't look back. I felt ashamed for not listening to her, for not trying to make her feel better, but I couldn't. There was nothing in me that could help, but there was something in her that terrified me . . . that threatened to steal my newly promised freedom—*if* I let her sad thoughts enter my head.

I had to get away, completely away, and start over. I had to imagine that everything was going to be okay. It was mean and thoughtless to ignore her, and I knew it, but my guilt did not alleviate the greater fear that I had to separate myself from her immediately *because I wanted to tell her everything! About the fire that killed my mother . . . about Sister Wellington . . . about Daddy . . . everything! And if I even mentioned it, all of my resolve would vanish instantly, and I knew it.*

Keeping my eyes fixed on the passing flat landscape, now bathed in the early morning sun, I dared not look back. Not even a glance. Not at the girl, not at my memories of David, or anything else. The invisible, fragile thread that held my thoughts together would snap if I even turned my head or thoughts to glance back.

I had to find a way to build something from the rubble that had so far been my life, to use the sharp edge of fear, now slicing through me, to cut a new path and carve a new existence. There had to be a way to do that, to create something of substance from the pile of rubble and prove I wasn't worthless. I didn't know how I would do it; I only knew I couldn't look back.

I took a deep breath and exhaled slowly.

I have a place to go. That's more than I had last week. Whatever lies ahead can't be worse than what I'm leaving behind.

The sun warmed my face and arm and as I settled back to feel it, I slipped off my shoes. The floor felt warm beneath my bare feet and vibrations tingled up through my legs, just as they had before Momma died and we rumbled from town to town in the truck.

I glanced at my feet and saw the high heels Rosa had bought me for graduation. Shiny, black patent leather, just what I had always wanted—*pretty shoes*.

I remembered the day when I was seven and lifted the heavy Sears & Roebuck catalog to the table, demanding, "Momma! I want them shoes." Her unwavering gaze had met mine, and with a voice cradled in patience and gentleness, she replied, "And *I* said . . . if you want 'em bad enough you can have 'em."

If you want 'em bad enough, you can have 'em.

At last, I had pretty shoes. *Thank you, Rosa. Thank you, Momma.*

The steady roar of the engine and the rhythmic drone of the tires on the highway began to repeat the words: *If you want it bad enough, you can have it. If you want it bad enough . . . .*

The tightness in my throat began to ease. I noticed thick, green trees and flowers along the road. Had they been there all along?

If you want it bad enough . . .

The words comforted me and I recalled the night I first learned to read and how I realized then that words running through my mind influenced my emotions.

When did I forget that? I knew it once. How did I forget something so important?

. . . you can have it.

I would start again. Do things right, and prove that my life wasn't some stupid accident, beyond my control.

If you want it bad enough . . .

I wanted to do something valuable, to make something of myself. I could do more now than cut out paper dolls. I could type. Take shorthand. I could get a real job. If I remembered what Momma said, it would be easier. Much easier. Like now . . . just remembering had made me feel better. If I kept remembering . . . never forgot . . . *if you want it bad enough . . .*

I glanced back at the girl on the rear seat. Her hollow, blank expression, fixed in my direction, pushed an enormous wave of guilt through me. Immediately, I averted my eyes and turned to the front again, but her haunting, dead gaze lingered in my mind.

Maybe I should just sit with her . . . not let her talk about cutting her wrists . . . stop her if she tried . . . could I do that? Could I keep her from dragging me down?

Apparently, something within me thought so because even before I finished the thought, I was on my feet and moving toward her. Her relieved expression encouraged me to keep walking.

"I'm sorry I moved away," I admitted, deliberately avoiding her eyes. "But . . . but I can't . . . can't listen to you talk about sad things."

"Why?"

"I just can't." Sitting stiffly erect, I stared at the back of the bus driver's head. The top of his navy blue cap was darkened by hair oil. "I'm . . . I'm going to . . . to start over myself, and I'm afraid that—well, if I listen to . . . or talk about really bad things—well, I might not make it . . . myself."

She didn't respond for several seconds then said, "Then I can't talk. Because it's all bad."

"Don't tell me about it!" I scolded through gritted teeth. "Or . . . or I'll have to leave again!"

The seat vibrated and bounced as the bus traveled a rough patch of road and only the tires and engine broke the silence.

I glanced at her. "Can't you tell me something good?"

She sighed and stared out the window before answering. "No."

My mind scrambled madly for a suggestion. "No? Nothing's good? What about your grandma? Isn't she good?"

"She's sick."

My resolve began to slip. "Well . . . are you going to help her? *That's* good."

"She's supposed to help *me*!" She scoffed. "My parents say she's my only hope. They're tired of trying."

I clutched the edge of the seat, not sure if I was trying to hang on or jump up. "Well . . . why can't you help her? I mean, help her do things . . . clean the house . . . or cook for her. If she's sick, she needs help."

She raised a skeptical eyebrow and shook her head. "You don't understand. Even if—"

"Do you *want* things to get better?" I interrupted. "Things like *your life?*"

She drew back, offended. "Of course, I do!"

"Then . . . *do* something—something that makes you feel better. Like helping your grandma."

I couldn't believe the words spewing out of my mouth, and even felt guilty for saying them. I had no right. I hadn't begun to turn things around. So far, all I had were shaky hopes and vague dreams, and I'd only just begun to try and define them. But, again, my guilt didn't stop me. "We've both gotta *do* something!" I remembered Coach's poem about sitting and wishing but didn't recite it for her.

She raised her eyebrows, folded her arms and sat back, staring at me as if she were considering my words. After a moment, she took a long, shaky breath and said, "Well . . . Gram's in a wheelchair . . . so I could probably do a lot. Not just cooking and cleaning and stuff . . . but . . . maybe take her for walks. You know, push her around outside . . . into town . . . get her out of the house."

Still feeling like a fraud, I rested my head against the back of the seat and closed my eyes, reluctant to say anymore.

"She was a school teacher. Real smart. I—I dropped out of school. She probably hates me."

Without opening my eyes, I asked, "Whose idea was it for you to go live with her?"

"Hers."

I turned to look at her. "Then she doesn't hate you."

The bus slowed as it rumbled into the outskirts of a small town.

"We're going to make a ten-minute stop here, folks!" The driver yelled over his shoulder. "You can get off and stretch a few minutes, if you want."

"What's your name?" the girl asked.

"Othello."

She frowned. "O—what?"

I repeated it, slowly.

She rolled her eyes and we both laughed. "Why would anyone name a kid that?"

"I don't know."

"You going to change it?"

"Probably not. What's yours?"

"Retha Mae."

I rolled my eyes. "That's better, huh?" We both laughed again.

When the bus stopped at Higgins Drug & Soda Fountain, Retha Mae and I bought orange soda pops and Baby Ruth candy bars. The driver took two suitcases from the luggage compartment and handed them to a balding man in a rumpled gray suit. He had slept the whole time I was on the bus and now squinted against the sun as he stumbled down the street between his luggage.

Another passenger boarded and the driver pulled away from the curb.

"What are you going to do in Wichita Falls?" There was a note of interest in Retha Mae's question.

"Go to school. And work, maybe."

"High school or college?" She nibbled unconsciously at the candy as she talked.

A rush of pride swelled through me. "I just graduated."

"Oh." Sitting sideways on the seat, now, she studied me closely. "Have you got a boyfriend?"

I felt an invisible guard rise between us. "I can't talk about that."

She nodded. "Okay."

Through the window, we both watched a flock of small birds swirl through the air and try to find landing spots on a telephone line.

"I heard," she said in a somber voice, "that it tickles their feet when someone talks on the phone." We both laughed uproariously.

When the last of our pop and candy was gone, she twisted the empty wrapper around a finger. "If I help her, Grams might help me finish high school, huh?"

"Probably. Is that what you want to do?"

She almost smiled and nodded.

"How bad do you want it?"

"Pretty bad. But it's hard, you know. I dropped out two years ago."

I thought of my own situation and realized that in just the past hour I had grown stronger. Saying things I didn't quite believe—but wanted to—gave me strength. "My Momma used to say, if you want something bad enough, you can have it."

She squinted at me through narrowed eyes. "You think it's true?"

I shrugged. "Yeah, probably. If you don't look back till you get what you want, then I think it could be true."

After a moment, Retha Mae took a brush from her purse and with long sweeping strokes, began to brush her hair. "How do you do that—not look back?"

The feeling of being a fraud returned. "I don't know. I just know I'm not going to."

Retha Mae put the brush in her lap and stared straight ahead. Maybe she was looking at the bus driver's dirty hat. Maybe she was watching the road. It didn't matter because her eyes weren't dead anymore, and when I saw that, I felt a kind of happiness for both of us. The new life in her eyes was all the evidence I needed to know that I would make it, too, and every mile that slipped beneath the wheels of the bus deepened my conviction.

I wanted a new life—and I wanted it *bad*.

Epilogue

Amy, Virgiinia and Othello

About the Family

My oldest brother, Don, continued his military career, retiring after twenty-five years. He has three children, five grandchildren, and resides with his wife, Juanita, in Belleville, Illinois. A self-described "gadget inventor," he spent several years designing and improving simple household items. Don is, and always will be, my hero.

Mason worked as a paint-and-body man most of his life, satisfying his creative urges with inventions that he researched and developed in his home laboratory, dubbed his "electric room." He died of cancer in 1993. He had two children, a son and daughter.

Thurmond struggled with alcoholism most of his life and committed suicide in 1975, at the age of thirty-five. He left two children, a son and daughter, who came to live with me.

Jenny is an artist, writer and poet, and real estate broker in Southern California. She has two children, a son and daughter, and two grandchildren.

Amy became an elementary school teacher and resides with her husband in California. They have two sons and three grandsons.

Gordon's creative and entrepreneurial spirit led him first into Madison Avenue advertising where he was Creative Supervisor for Saatchi and Saatchi for fifteen years. Also an inventor (who sometimes collaborated with Mason before his death), Gordon is now CEO of his own company, Trinity Motors. He invented a highly efficient generator/motor that generates "free" electricity while operating as a regular, electric motor. His Web site is: www.trinitymotersinc.com.

My father died in 1989, at age eighty-four, in a nursing home in Oklahoma.

David, my first boyfriend, opened his own shop, married a wonderful woman, and together they raised several children in Weatherford, Oklahoma.

Me? The year-and-a-half I spent in the loving home of Lewis and Lou Ellen Foster gave me an opportunity to more or less adjust to the outside world. Aware that I wasn't ready for college, I enrolled in a business college, with the lofty ambition of becoming a secretary.

One evening at the Fosters', Jenny called and needed help. Daddy had left Rosa and taken Jenny with him to California, where he abandoned her. She was stranded in a fourth-rate motel, with no money. While still on the phone, I told the Fosters the situation and they immediately called friends who lived in the area. These friends, Maury and Aileen Lewis, gave Jenny a home until she finished high school.

A few months later, when Rosa succeeded in getting Amy out of the hospital, Maury and Aileen Lewis generously opened their home to her, too.

At this point, I must interrupt myself and say that to cover both my personal "at home" life and my professional life would require writing another

300 pages. Suffice it to say that I married, divorced, and raised two sons, Mark and Bryan, and a niece and nephew, Joanne and Sonny. My brother Thurmond committed suicide when Sonny was nine and Joanne was five. Both had been sorely neglected and abused, so you can imagine that it would take another 300 pages to adequately tell the whole story.

I began writing in 1963, four years after leaving the orphanage. It was my intent to let the world know what was happening to children placed in homes. I also thought the world would rush to their rescue, and was stunned to learn otherwise.

I sent my first article to a magazine whose editor promptly wrote back and asked, "Who are you trying to kid? Things like this haven't happened since Dickens wrote about them." On the same rejection slip, he also scribbled, "You need to choose a less pretentious pseudonym."

I was stymied. My vocabulary didn't include the words *pretentious* and *pseudonym*, so I reached for my dictionary, looked up the words, and felt truly insulted. Not only did he not believe what I had written, he didn't believe my name!

Depressed, I typed up 150 pages of notes about my first eighteen years, determined that one day I would write about it and they would believe it. In the meantime, I would write fiction. My first novel, *House of Secrets*, written at age twenty-five, was published by Avon Books and sold 57,000 copies.

It never once occurred to me that I didn't have enough information, training, or skill to write a novel. I wanted to do it . . . I *loved* doing it . . . and it never entered my mind that it wouldn't sell.

Zebra Books bought my next two novels, *Satan's Daughters* and *Whispers from the Dark*, and both did well, selling between 55–60,000 copies. Between these publications, I wrote columns for a local newspaper, sold mystery stories to Alfred Hitchcock and Ellery Queen magazines, and any horror magazine I could find.

Eventually, I turned my attention to children's books. First, I wrote *Whoever Heard of a Fird?* A fird is part fish, part bird, and throughout the story, he is looking for a herd of fird, but nobody has heard of a fird. All the characters were two-feature creatures: bertles (part bear, part turtles) dickens (part dog, part chickens), etcetera. I loved this story passionately, so when every children's publisher in New York had rejected it, I decided to have even more fun with it, and wrote twelve songs—one for each two-feature creature. Then, of course, it was rejected twice as fast.

From 1975 to 1988, I taught two creative writing classes—one through the University of California, Irvine, extension program, and one at Cypress College in Cypress, California. Royalty checks were few, far between, and small, so when I learned about a hypnosis training center in Los Angeles, I immediately enrolled and attended evening and weekend classes. I became a hypnotist, then a master hypnotist, and eventually a certified hypnotherapist—and finally had a way to earn a living doing something else I loved. I opened an office and began working the week after I graduated. However, I never quit writing or marketing my work, and constantly had manuscripts to work on between hypnosis clients.

One evening I pulled *Fird* out and began drawing pictures of the characters. I listened to the music and excited myself all over again.

Determined to find someone "in the know" to listen to it, I stormed Hanna-Barbera. I literally bluffed my way into the parking lot and ran from a parking lot attendant who was chasing me and screaming: "Lady! Lady! Stop! You can't go in there!"

But I did. Inside, I bluffed my way up to the music director's office and stormed him, too. He was enraged that I had walked in without an appointment and was asking him to listen to my work. "You can't just barge in here!" he shouted. "You have to go through the proper channels!"

I explained to him that I had tried but all the channels seemed to be clogged, so I wasn't leaving until he listened to my work.

His eyes bulged, his face turned purple, and through clenched teeth he snarled, "Lady, I'll call security and have you thrown out!"

I sat down. "Go ahead. That's probably all the publicity I need. I'll call every paper in town, and tomorrow morning there will be a headline somewhere that says, 'Writer tossed out of Hanna-Barbera!' Then, maybe someone will call and listen to me."

He groaned. "Lady, things like this only happen in B movies."

I said, "Your life is now a B movie."

He finally sat down, dropped his head into his hands and took a deep breath. After a long silence, he said, "Okay."

I knew I only had one chance.

I spread the manuscript and pictures over his desk, then sat down at his piano. *You have one chance!* I reminded myself. Then I began to narrate the story (which I had practically memorized), played the piano, and sang the songs. I was about a third of the way into it, when he said, "What did you say your name is?"

"Othello."

"Othello." He smiled and shook his head. "Well, Othello, this is the greatest thing that's ever come across my desk."

I thought I would pass out. Three months later, I received a phone call from Hanna-Barbera saying they were interested in buying the *Fird* if they could buy all rights. My heart sank. I knew I would make more money if I could hang onto even a small percentage. I asked how much they were offering for "all rights," and he said there was no sense discussing that unless I was willing to sell all rights. I said, "A good offer might change my mind." He hemmed and hawed and finally said, "Probably around a hundred thousand."

That sounded like a million dollars to me, but I knew that even a tiny percentage in the long run would be better, so I turned them down.

I have never regretted that decision, because with the validation I received on my work, I was energized to keep trying. However, I stopped looking for publishers and started researching companies that produce recordings for children. I fell in love with Caedmon Records' recording of *Peter and the Wolf* and rushed my material off to them.

They loved it! It was still another four years before it was published, but the wait was worth it. Stage and film star, Joel Gray, recorded the book and the songs, and Michelle Dorman, a brilliant young artist, won awards for her beautiful illustrations of my characters.

One moment during this period stands out above all the others. I was invited to New York to hear Joel Gray record my songs. That alone, was enough to thrill me, but before it was over something even more wonderful happened. At one point, Joel stopped the music and called to the director in the booth where I was standing, "Have Othello come down and sing this part with me. I'm not sure how it goes."

As I stepped down to the studio floor, absolute joy swept over me. I had never felt such a rush of pride, and for the first time in my life I thought, *Momma, can you see me? Can you see me now?*

Nothing ever needed to top that moment; I had been validated for life.

Hanna-Barbera wanted to use some of the *Fird* characters for Saturday morning TV cartoons. They produced a fabulous five-minute animated video to promote the book and a line of plush toys based on *Fird* characters. Remco Toys licensed the toys and marketed them under the name *Firffles*. *Fird* licensing went to dozens of companies for over 100 products, which included everything from lunch boxes to underwear.

I also had three other books (with music) published by Caedmon: *Lilly, Willy and the Mail-Order Witch*, and *Hector McSnector and the Mail-Order Witch*. Two of the books were illustrated by the highly acclaimed artist, Timothy Hildebrandt, and were recorded by Broadway star, Tammy Grimes. *Snyder Spider's Surprise*, the second in a planned series of *Fird* books, was illustrated by Michelle Dorman.

Four of my children's books, also published by Caedmon, were marketed as *The funny Bone Poems*. They were illustrated by award-winning artist, Sandy Huffaker, and recorded by Sandy Duncan.

Hanna-Barbera expressed interest in also adapting the *Mail-Order Witch* series to Saturday morning cartoons. Life was beautiful and I felt sure I was "on my way."

Then the bottom fell out.

Hanna-Barbera and Caedmon were finalizing the contract details for Saturday morning cartoons when Disney ripped off the whole project. Within a week, everyone's giddiness turned to stunned silence. Disney took my two-feature creature idea and produced a rip-off version. Weeks later, I watched *Wuzzles—a* watered-down version of my characters, *Firffles*—on Saturday morning TV.

Fortunately, and unfortunately, the *Wuzzles* bombed. Obviously, I wasn't sorry to see them go, but when I called Hanna-Barbera to ask what it meant as far as the *Fird* was concerned, I was told: "Well, they bombed so terribly, we'll just have to wait a few years and let the bad taste get out of everyone's mouth. No one is going to take a chance on your stuff now."

I asked how many "a few" years were, and he said, "At least ten."

Caedmon and everyone involved assured me that there was nothing anyone could do. The advice was unanimous: *forget it and move on.*

During 1988–89, Caedmon Books was bought by Harper-Collins and all of my children's books were suddenly lost. They couldn't be found on a Harper-Collins computer screen or a bookstore shelf anywhere. I did my best to trace their disappearance, but was never able to learn anything.

"We have no indication that we ever had them," one honest and talkative Harper assistant told me. "I guess they just fell through the cracks." This was the answer despite the fact that I had letters and royalty statements from them that dated back to the acquisition of Caedmon. It wasn't until late in 2004—almost twenty years later—that I received a reversion letter, and the rights to my books are again mine.

The good news, if there is any good news in this, is that every one of my children's books has survived, despite the acquisition disaster. They are listed on Amazon.com as "collectables," and a copy of *Whoever Heard of a Fird* sells for $150–$250, depending on the day, the condition, and whether they have more than one available.

In 1987, when sexual abuse made headlines every few days, I wrote and self-published a little book called *Life after Trauma and Abuse*. I had spent more than ten years counseling clients and using hypnotherapy, and I felt sure I could help.

I scheduled seminars up and down the West Coast, appeared on several local television shows, and sold about 5,000 copies of the book. However, while speaking to a large audience in Los Angeles, I realized that most abuse victims weren't interested in help; they wanted *revenge*. The few who were really interested in help, wrote wonderful letters thanking me for writing the book.

As I worked with more and more abuse survivors, I became acutely aware of my own spiritual awakenings. This stirring began in the early '80s and by 1988, I was enrolled in Science of Mind classes, headed in the direction of becoming a Religious Science minister.

All the while, I maintained an active hypnotherapy office. Many of my clients had abuse issues and most of them were overweight. This prompted me to put together a weight loss program called "Body Designing." It included private hypnosis sessions, a book, and four hypnosis tapes. The program was a huge success for the clients and for me. Even after I closed my office, I continued to market the program and receive "success" letters.

In 1993, I began my ministry serving as pastor for The Church of Life, an independent Church of Religious Science in Tustin, California. Today, I am a licensed minister for The Christian Church (Disciples of Christ) in Indiana. I write meditation music for our services and have just finished a new book called *The Father Within*. I also write a weekly opinion column (social and political commentary) for the *Kokomo Tribune*.

After spending most of my adult life divorced, I finally met and married a wonderful man. Don and I reside in Kokomo, Indiana. He is a blessing in every aspect of my life—a true helpmate.

I am still as fascinated with the mind/body/spirit connection as I was the first day I discovered it while teaching myself to read. I see the thought/emotion connection as one of God's most precious gift to us. It is a way to save ourselves from unnecessary suffering. Once we know how to use this wonderful gift, we are no longer doomed to remain victims. We can learn to use "the connection" to create a better world for ourselves and everyone around us. I know, because of the changes I've witnessed in others and the changes I have experienced.

I began this book forty years ago, wanting to awaken the world to what too often happens to children in orphanages. There are still many orphanages in the U.S., primarily owned and operated by churches. However, my desire to help has broadened as my understanding has grown. Pain is pain, regardless of the memory that prompts it.

Millions of people are smarting from abusive experiences. Few of them grew up in orphanages but they all have one thing in common: They hide their guilt and shame like soiled undergarments. They have no respectable, guilt-free "under-self" to put on, and they do not know where to find one. Consequently, every moment of their life is inhibited and limited to some extent.

I wrote the following and final chapter of this book hoping to ease someone else's pain.

Is the Next Chapter for You?

I don't know. Did some past experience leave you feeling as if you had lost the best part of yourself—your innocence and ability to love? Are you haunted by specific memories? Do you find yourself so confused and frightened that you silently scream, "Someone, help me!" when there is no one around but you? Do you occasionally feel as if you are stuck in an absurd play and you don't know your part—and worse, you don't deserve to know? Are you terrified to make decisions because you might make the wrong one . . . so you make the same decision you always make in that particular situation? Then, do you hate yourself afterwards because you didn't have the nerve to do what you really wanted to do?

If you have never experienced any of these doubts and fears, then the final chapter is probably not for you.

On the other hand, if you have experienced all of these responses—and you know the final chapter is for you—it does not mean you are crazy or that you are damaged beyond repair. You are, however, severely limiting your responses to life.

It is possible to ease beyond guilt, grief, anger, and pain and create a completely new image of yourself. No one can do it but you, so your success will depend entirely on "how bad" you want to live a more rewarding life. If you truly want to free yourself emotionally so that you can fulfill your own desires, there are tools that can help. It all depends on whether you really want to change the ending of the story of your life.

Regaining Self Respect

For over twenty years, abuse issues have been addressed in every conceivable manner, and while there are some fine programs, there are others that only validate the pain and help the victim blame the abuser. Validating the pain may be temporarily soothing but it is rarely productive; the victim already knows who to blame—and no one will ever find self-respect by blaming "the past" for conditions *in the present*.

Dealing with "The Effects" of Abuse

Victims of abuse feel as if they have been robbed of innocence and no longer have control over their lives. This is *not* true; it only *seems* that way. When others hurt us, regardless of the reason, they do not actually take innocence or power away from us. However, when we are young and do not know how or why we suddenly feel such a loss, we also do not know where or how to find and reclaim those wonderful feelings.

Almost without exception, when we are victimized as children we reach erroneous conclusions about ourselves, our relationship to others, and the world. The mere fact that our parents or caregivers treated us with disregard made it easy to reach flawed conclusions, such as: *I am not loved; therefore, I am unlovable. I must be a horrible person, but I don't know how to be different. I don't know how to make others love me. I have no control over my life!*

Such conclusions quickly became beliefs that sank deeply into the subconscious and have continued to operate as "truths," negatively influencing every decision we have made. If we take no steps to undo these beliefs and remain "a victim," we choose a life that offers no genuine rewards and only meager short-lived satisfactions—most of which are derived from punishing our abusers and blaming others for our unhappiness and failures. Unfortunately, these small "victories" never prompt feelings of real pride and always impede our success.

Moving beyond abuse is difficult but not nearly as difficult as continuing to live as "a victim."

Those of us who experienced childhood abuse generally need help from every available source, but we should never forget that *no one can help us more than we can help ourselves*. Counselors can educate and inform and act as catalysts for change, but they cannot make us change our minds about ourselves, nor can they reclaim our innocence and sense of power. This is a task that must be performed by every individual sufferer.

Only those who want to move ahead and leave victimization behind will put forth the effort required to succeed, because it takes real effort to replace one belief system with another. It also requires constant vigilance—paying attention to emotions *and the thoughts that create them*—as well as replacing hurtful memories with ideas that create a sense of value and self-worth.

Moving from a belief that you are a victim to a belief that you are in control of your life means constantly correcting your thoughts and words, and bringing them into alignment with what you want—a belief that you can accomplish anything you set out to do. Old thoughts and words will slip back dozens of times a day when you first begin but, as with anything else, the more you practice, the easier the task becomes.

Are You Willing?

You cannot be a victim and also be in control of your life. Moving from "victim" to "being in control of your life" means you must be willing to give up the idea that you are a victim. Generally, the very idea of giving up your victim status is confusing and insulting. It's as if you are being asked to do the impossible: to give up yourself—your true identity.

Yet, you were not born with the mindset of a victim. That is a learned response, which has become a firm belief. You are much more than a victim, and to allow yourself to continue believing that you are defined by your experiences will only limit the rest of your life.

You are capable of enjoying all the beauty and grandeur that life has to offer and to partake in all of life's sweetest experiences. Yes, it hurt your feelings to be treated abusively. It grieved you to be neglected, beaten, or mistreated. Yes, you experienced terrible pain at the time these things happened, *but your mind was not permanently damaged. It works as perfectly now as it did when these things happened—and your mind is the only tool you need to change the direction of your life*.

Building "Mental Muscles"

It all begins with mental exercises.

Imagine that a "couch potato"—an out-of-shape observer of life—decides he or she wants to become an Olympic champion. Obviously, it will take greater determination and effort for the couch potato than it would for a normally healthy, "in shape" person. The same is true for those who have been beaten down emotionally but who *truly* want to live happy, fulfilling, and productive lives. They can do it, but not without developing the "mental muscles" necessary to succeed.

Mental exercises build "mental muscles" that enable you to get up when you fall, and keep you on track as you develop and implement plans to reach your various goals. Mental exercises are the first important step, because you will need them to "muscle out" the doubts and fears that, otherwise, will destroy your confidence and undermine your resolve.

Mental exercises are specific words and ideas that you repeat on a regular and sustained basis. They are affirmations that restore your belief in yourself and bolster your confidence so you can succeed. A list of exercises will be included later.

Why Mental Exercises Work

Mental exercises work because:

- Every thought creates a corresponding emotion.
- Emotions create conviction—belief.

- Belief prompts action.
- Action produces results.

Example: As a child, you are repeatedly beaten, and think: *I am not lovable*. (1) This thought creates painful emotions. The pain convinces you that your thought is true, and you cry. (2) Believing you are unlovable, you shut down your emotions, thinking this will "protect" you, and (3) you modify your behavior to coincide with your belief. Perhaps you withdraw and risk less, or become hostile and more aggressive, but regardless of how you manifest your belief that you are not lovable, you will (4) produce a specific result.

If you choose to shut down your emotions, you will probably be known as "cold" and "uncaring"; if you become hostile and aggressive, you will probably end up in jail.

Through this example, we can clearly see that our thoughts and emotions create the outcomes of our lives. This invisible cause-and-effect principle is constantly at work determining everything we say and do. Only by changing the initial *cause* (belief) can we change the *effect* (outcome) of our lives, and the only way to change an unhappy and unhealthy belief is to constantly feed ourselves new, happy, healthy thoughts.

Planning Success

Before you can succeed at anything, you must *decide* what you want to do, and *create a plan* of action to make it happen. This is true whether you are a victim of abuse or came from a solid, loving background. No one stumbles into success.

Children, whose ideas have been ignored or belittled, grow into adults who have (1) no respect for their own ideas and (2) no confidence they can create a plan for their own success.

The biggest stumbling block is that abuse victims feel *entitled* to their pain and anger—and they are! What they frequently fail to realize is that they are also entitled to happiness, and it is not possible to be both a victim *and* happy. The issue, then, is not one of entitlement but of choice between opposite realities—that of being a victim . . . or a happy and successful person.

Overcoming the effects of tragic events is not easy but it *is* possible, and definitely worth the effort. There is no sweeter feeling than proving your value to yourself—and one way to do this is to *ignore the past* and keep working toward your goal. Pursuing a goal is exciting and rewarding in its own right, and accomplishing it is indescribably delicious! And, the moment you achieve your goal, you will realize you haven't been permanently damaged. You will see that you have taken control of your life and achieved your dream—something that couldn't have been done if you were *permanently* damaged.

Some call this *denial*, and it *is*! It is a form of denial that allows you to be happy and accomplish your goals. The alternative *is also* denial—of happiness and success—and leaves you convinced that you are a helpless victim.

Which would you rather deny? The choice is yours.

Taking Control

To take control of your life, you must take control of your mind. The good news is: *You already have the only tool you need to create a new reality!*

You have the power and ability to *stop* thinking of yourself as you did as a child. *I'm alone . . . I'm no good . . . nobody cares about me . . . I'm not like everyone else*. There are a thousand such demoralizing thoughts and all of them can be recognized quickly because without exception, they leave you feeling depressed, lonely, and victimized. When you tolerate these thoughts and feelings, you *are* victimized, but you are victimizing yourself! You are repeating ideas that you learned as a child, and continuing to use them against yourself.

Encouraging Affirmations

To end the barrage of insults and depressing ideas, you will need to make a list of at least ten statements that make you feel strong. These are ideas that encourage, strengthen and support you so that you can continue moving ahead.

Examples of encouraging affirmations

- I can control my life because I can control my thoughts, my emotions, and my responses.
- I am intelligent. I can stop abusing myself.
- My life is important. I will make it important.
- I am calm and confident in all situations.
- Everyone deserves love, including me.
- I can devise an intelligent plan for my life.
- I will make a plan to do something I love, and follow my plan.
- Every day I grow more accepting and acceptable, and feel more accepted.
- Every day I grow more loving and lovable, and feel more loved.

Initially, such statements will make you feel as if you are lying to yourself. The tendency is to think, "Who am I kidding? I can't change what I am." *Say the affirmations anyway.* Make your own list of positive statements. The more you say them, the "truer" they seem to be *because repetition of positive ideas breaks down the old belief that you are a failure, and you will begin to see yourself as someone who can be happy and successful.*

Looking for a Rescuer

Most abused children secretly wish to be rescued by some benevolent soul who will suddenly whisk them away and make their life worth living. The thought of this fictitious person is so pleasant that it becomes a wonderful dream, a fantasy relived daily. These children silently and constantly pray: *Please, God, send someone to take me away. Send someone who will be kind and make me happy.* This burning desire for rescue eventually becomes a "secret belief"—hidden even from the believer—but it is there, influencing every decision: *Someday, somehow, someone will come and take me out of this miserable situation, and I will be happy.*

Tragically, this desire for a rescuer is carried into adulthood—from relationship to relationship—and always ends in disappointment, tears, and anger. Although the rescuer is always blamed for the failure of the relationship, victims do not escape unscathed. *The failed relationship reinforces their belief that they are stupid or unlovable.*

Don't be fooled into believing someone else can rescue you!

The idea that someone else will suddenly change the way you feel about yourself, *is a lie.* Your feelings about yourself and your life are based on your beliefs, and no one can change your beliefs about you—*except you.* And until you do, life is one, long, futile search for acceptance and happiness. Every relationship is strained and eventually falls apart as you turn to lovers, friends, and spouses, expecting them to do the impossible: make *you* happy.

You must become your own rescuer or you will never feel worthy of success.

There is no magic pill, no "perfect" person, and no ideal situation that will erase the negative ideas you have accepted about yourself. Some people will support you more and longer than others, but no one can replace what only you can do. Some situations are more satisfying than others but even a "dream" situation will not erase the negative beliefs you hold about yourself. You must make the corrections.

This may sound like more responsibility than you want, but the alternative is even less desirable: a lifetime of horrible memories and constant defeats.

You have a Power within you that always responds to love—and nothing else. You can pray for love and acceptance and for God to take away your sense of loss, but unless you are willing to cooperate with the Rules of Love, you pray in vain.

If, however, you are willing to cooperate with the Rules of Love—for even thirty days—you will begin to convince yourself that you have complete control of your life. And . . . *if you want it bad enough, you can have it.*

When we feel unloved, we feel depressed or *dis*pirited because love is an attribute of Spirit. We also lose self-respect and harbor feelings of anger and resentment, guilt and shame. Consequently, it is only when we restore love to our own minds that we begin to feel loved and respectable again.

Almost everyone is familiar with the idea that "God is love" (1 John 4:8) but few know how to use this information to their benefit. They pray for help and love but do not know how to actually *use* love to help themselves.

The Happiness Program (below) is designed to use *love to restore love* in those who feel it is lacking. This program is not only for those who have been raped, beaten, or neglected in the traditional sense of "abuse." Anyone who senses there is more to life than they are presently experiencing can benefit from *The Happiness Program*.

Within thirty days, it is possible to experience tremendous relief in areas where pain and resentment have had crippling effects for years. A deep sense of satisfaction, purpose, and well-being can be reestablished in that short time. After the initial thirty days, those who work the program can decide whether they want to continue following it until it becomes a "habit"—just as their feelings of loss and victimization have become a "habit"—or not.

The Happiness Program

The Happiness Program is a thirty-day program of mental exercises that I developed in 1986 and used as the basis for seminars entitled "Life After Trauma and Abuse." It is based on spiritual principles aimed at restoring love and eliminating fear from your life. It dramatically demonstrates the positive effects of accepting full responsibility for your thoughts and emotions and focusing your full attention on love.

Anyone wishing to bring more happiness and love into his or her life will find the program extremely helpful. It is laid out in "steps" that, if followed as directed, will clearly demonstrate your ability to take control of your life.

The Happiness Program can be worked alone or in groups. There are certain advantages to working with a group, such as sharing experiences and finding inspiration in each other's successes, but anyone who is serious about changing his or her life can do so by working the program alone.

Hundreds of people have worked the program alone and experienced wonderful effects on their life. I have used it in groups at church and at my office, and seen the same benefits there, as well. So whether you choose to work the program alone or start a group and share it with others is entirely up to you. Ultimately, of course, it is up to *you* to do the exercises and stick to the program.

Read through the entire program before beginning the first step. The first day of the program will require two or three hours, so it is best to set aside a morning or afternoon to begin. After that, only a few minutes a day are needed to work the various steps.

Step 1

(To be done the first day of the program, and repeated every day for thirty days.)

When you are ready to begin the program, mark thirty consecutive days off a calendar. These can be the most important thirty days of your life. Each day, put a checkmark on that day to remind yourself of your progress. As you check off the day, think to yourself, "Today, I choose to be happy." As you think this pleasant thought, allow the expectation of a pleasant day to create a sense of happiness within you.

As the day progresses, stop several times to "sense" how you are feeling. If you are experiencing anything other than happiness, try to identify what you are feeling, and say to yourself, "I am feeling ____________________ (anxious, afraid, worried, angry, etc.) and I prefer to feel happy." Then, once again, remind yourself, "Today, I choose to be happy." Allow the pleasant thought to again create a sense of happiness within you, as if you *expect* a pleasant experience.

Step 2

(To be done the first day only.)

Take one hour or less to list on paper every past, painful experience that makes you unhappy when you remember it. No priority need be noted. Make no judgments as to whether this experience should make you unhappy. If it makes you unhappy, it makes you unhappy, and therefore should be listed.

Examples of past pain might be:

- When my mother/father died.
- When my mother/father abandoned me.
- When my husband/wife left me.
- When my brother/sister was killed.
- When I lost my job.
- When I declared bankruptcy.
- When my best friend lied to me.
- When I lost my diamond bracelet.

Next, write across an envelope the words "Past Pain." Put the list in the envelope. Do not seal. You may take five minutes from each day to add to the list any experiences, which come to mind later. Do not dwell on the memories when they occur to you; simply make a mental note to add them to the list and then dismiss them. Commit yourself to the idea of leaving these thoughts on this list, refusing to consider them for thirty days.

Step 3

(To be done the first day only.)

Take one hour or less to list on paper every future concern and fear which you can do nothing about. No priority need be noted. A fearful thought creates fear. Make no judgments as to whether these thoughts should frighten you. Fear is fear. It cannot be judged to be good or bad, right or wrong.

Examples of future fears, which you can do nothing about:

- Dying in an automobile accident.
- A spouse or lover leaving.
- Earthquakes, tornados, terrorist attacks.
- A child's sexual preference or orientation.
- A family member's alcoholism.
- What other people think.
- What other people do.

Next, write the words "Future Fears" on an envelope, put the list inside the envelope but do not seal it. Each day you may take five minutes to add to this list if new fears come to mind. Do not take more than five minutes. Commit yourself to the idea of leaving these thoughts on this list, refusing to consider them for thirty days.

Step 4

(To be done the first day only.)

Take one hour or less to list all the fears, concerns, and worries which you *can* do something about. This is a list of *your* worries and concerns and therefore *you* are responsible for getting them done and relieving your own anxieties.

Examples of fears I can do something about:

- The car will break down.
- I will lose my job.
- I may not get a certain job.
- I'll never finish school.
- I don't make enough money.
- I'm not a good parent.
- I'll always be alone.
- I may be an alcoholic.
- No one loves me.

Next, beside each fear, make a note as to *what* you can do to relieve this fear, and *when* you can do it. Leave this list out so that you can refer to it each day. *Do* what you can do, and forget what you cannot do that day. (Also be aware of the difference between "cannot do" and "will not" do. Honesty is essential to your success.)

Your list and responses might look something like this:

- That the car will break down.—*I can't afford to take it to the shop, so I'll ask my brother (neighbor, friend), who works on his car, to take a look at it. I'll do that this weekend.*
- That I may lose my job.—*I'll be more punctual and more careful. I'll volunteer to work late if the boss needs me. I'll do this tomorrow.*
- That I'll always be alone.—*I'll make myself more available. I'll attend office parties and accept invitations from friends who go out in groups to socialize. I'll accept the next invitation.*

Step 5

(To be done the first day and added to frequently.)

Make one last list. Take as long as you like. Write across the top of the page: "Thoughts that make me happy." No priority need be noted. Make no judgments as to whether these thoughts should make you happy. If a thought makes you happy, put it on the list.

Make several copies of this list. Put a copy in every room of your house or apartment. Put a copy in your wallet, briefcase, or purse. Put a copy in your car, office, or any other place you are likely to be. Literally, paper your life with this list. Leave yourself no room for deception, to say, "I couldn't think of anything happy."

Example of thoughts that make me happy.

- Holding my grandbaby.
- Being thin and sexy.
- Kissing my boyfriend/girlfriend.
- Having perfect health.

- Having $100,000.
- Winning an award.
- Lying in the sun in Florida.
- Buying a house.
- Having my husband/wife love me.
- Having my parents' respect.
- Hugging my children.
- Getting a promotion.
- Owning your own business.
- Being promoted and getting a raise.
- Losing forty pounds.

Read your "Thoughts that make me happy" list several times a day, and as you read it, take a few seconds to imagine that what you are reading *is happening*. Feel your grandchild's arms around your neck . . . imagine looking at yourself in a mirror and admiring your thin, sexy body . . . or being called in for a promotion at work. In other words, allow the thoughts to bring you a sense of happiness *on the spot*.

Step 6

For the next thirty days, read "My Thirty-Day Commitment to Happiness" at least twice a day, preferably in the morning and evening. To "forget" to read these statements actually makes a statement: *I do not really want to be happy*. (This is fine, of course, and should bring a certain degree of satisfaction because what you do not want, you do not have.)

My Thirty-Day Commitment to Happiness

- For thirty days, I will take a vacation from the pain of my past and let it take care of itself.
- For thirty days, I will accept responsibility for all my feelings. I will blame no one, no circumstance, and no condition for the way I feel and behave.

- For thirty days, I will accept no responsibility for another adult's feelings, circumstances, or conditions.
- For thirty days, I will not judge nor criticize anyone or anything, including myself.
- For thirty days, I will be unconcerned about what others think of me. They may think what they choose. I can't stop them anyway.
- For thirty days, I will refrain from mentioning my troubles or unhappiness to anyone. I will talk about only what makes me happy.
- For thirty days, I will make no sacrifices. Others (with the exception of small children) must look after their own well-being. I have spent a lifetime attempting to help, and everyone is just as unhappy as they ever were. I deserve a break, and for thirty days, I am taking one.
- For thirty days, if I cannot watch TV or read the paper or visit with others without making judgments and feeling depressed, angry, or unhappy, I will not do these things.
- For thirty days, when I am tempted to feel selfish and guilty for being happy when others are not, I will remind myself that my unhappiness will not make them happy. Then, I will do something that makes me happy.
- For thirty days, I will look for love everywhere. I will search for it in every person, situation, and circumstance. Where I cannot identify it, I will say, "I know love must be here. That I do not see it does not mean it is not here."
- For thirty days, I will allow myself to feel good about the idea that within every situation love can be found.

Step 7

(Do be done every day for thirty days.)

Set aside fifteen minutes in which to grow quiet and let your mind dwell on the idea that love is power, and love is within you. It is within your mind, it is helping to keep your body functioning, it is given to others every time you smile or speak kindly, and it is now changing your life for the better.

If feelings of sadness or regret come to you, that is because you have unknowingly made some judgment, such as: love *is gone . . . love is not possible for you . . . or you don't deserve love,* etc. In other words, you have actually connected the idea of love with the idea of loss or pain, and not kept the true meaning of love in mind. Do not grow impatient with yourself. Simply dismiss the judgments, the ideas of loss, and for fifteen minutes dwell on the idea that love is everywhere, within everyone—including you—and it is the most powerful force in the universe.

Let your mind consider all the ways love is powerful. Consider the bonds it creates and how it overflows into everything you do—from the care of your home, children, and pets, to the joy you feel when you are doing work you love. You want to be extremely familiar with all that love does, and know how to recognize it in every situation, because love is the power that will assist you in getting where you want to go.

Step 8

With every unpleasant encounter, think to yourself: "People are doing the best they can—including me." And let go of the unpleasant feelings that came with the encounter. If you can't let go of the unpleasant feelings immediately, repeat the thought again and add one other: "I have a choice in my response."

Step 9

(Begin the fourth week of the program.)

This exercise should be started the fourth week of the program because for many people, it would seem unreasonably difficult if begun sooner. However, after three weeks of mental preparation, it becomes acceptable to even the hard-core "miserable." This step allows you to "practice loving" on a daily basis.

Exercise for practicing love:

With every person you encounter during the day, regardless of how casual or fleeting, think to yourself the words: "I love you." Think them without judgment or criticism as to what type of love you are referring to. Do not allow yourself to be dissuaded by self-criticism, such as: "I don't even know that person." Of course, you do. That person is like you. That person wants to love and be loved. That person may be experiencing all the anxieties that thinking of fear produces—but then, not wanting to even think the words "I love you" is a thought prompted by fear.

What fear could stop you from *thinking* a loving thought, if love is the feeling you desire? And what fear could keep you from wanting to share love, except a thought that you—or the other person—is unworthy of love?

As you *think*, you experience. This, of course, is the benefit of this exercise. By thinking "I love you" to everyone you meet, you immediately experience the beneficial effects of the thought. You begin to feel lovable and loved.

Especially when involved in an unpleasant or angry situation, think, "I love you—and somewhere beneath our fears, I know you love me, too." This is the way to maintain a loving perspective in even the most difficult circumstance. The rewards realized from a more loving perspective cannot be overstated. Begin the exercise as soon as it seems reasonable to do so, and certainly no later than the fourth week.

Step 10

(To be done between the first and fourth weeks.)

Decide *what* you want to change about your life. Write it down, create a realistic plan to accomplish it, and set a realistic date for having it accomplished. Then, list five things you can do to begin, and *do* those things. When one item is completed, scratch it off and add another. Write a positive statement—an affirmation—declaring that you will succeed. Such a statement encourages you, and helps you stay focused.

Again, the steps are:

- Decide what you want.
- Write an affirmative statement describing it.
- Decide what you must do to accomplish it.
- List what you must do.
- Set a date for its accomplishment.
- Write an affirmation.
- Each day, scratch off the things you have done and add another, until your goal has been met.

Let's assume that your goal is to finish your education, and you know that if you apply yourself, you can do it within eighteen months. Your goal-setting plan might look like this:

My Goal
I will finish my education within the next eighteen months. I will accomplish this by doing the following things.

1. Talk to a school counselor.
2. Apply for a school loan.
3. Set up a schedule of night classes.
4. Get up early to study before going to work.
5. Give my family quality time on non-class evenings and weekends.

Daily Affirmation: *I will do this because it will make me happy, and to prove that I have control of my life.*

If your goal is to lose thirty pounds, your goal-setting plan might look like this:

My Goal
I will lose thirty pounds. I will do this sensibly by losing two or three pounds a week. By ___(date)___ I will weigh _____ pounds. I will accomplish this by doing the following things:

1. Follow a sensible diet.
2. Exercise at least thirty minutes a day.
3. Prepare and take my lunch to work.
4. Encourage myself with positive affirmations.
5. Listen to relaxation tapes and stay relaxed.

Daily Affirmation: *I will do this because it will make me happy, and to prove I am in control of my life.*

The goal-setting format is simple, *and* it works. It is effective, even in cases where you must keep doing more and more things to accomplish your goal—such as trying to find employment in a depressed area. In such a case, the daily affirmations will be far more helpful than you can imagine. They will keep your attitude positive when you would otherwise be tempted to quit.

You are always free to write your own affirmations. *You are the only person who knows exactly where you need encouragement.* For instance, in trying to locate a job when unemployment is high, you will need to think creatively. A good affirmation in this circumstance would be: *I am keenly alert to all possibilities and see creative solutions in all situations.*

No one has more influence in your life than you. Never pass up an opportunity to encourage yourself.

Once you have succeeded in meeting your various goals, you can look back at all the abusive memories that you thought were holding you back—and see that they weren't. Memories have power only when you are willing to give them power—which means, *when you think about them.* Thinking about *anything* gives that idea power.

As You Work the Program

Do not be discouraged if, at first, you find old thought patterns inundating you at every turn. This is to be expected. This is subconscious resistance generated by old beliefs that (1) you do not deserve to be happy, and (2) that your suffering is "proof" that you have nothing to do with the pain you're experiencing. Be willing to challenge these erroneous ideas for at least thirty days.

As old and painful thoughts come to mind, stop them as soon as you become aware of them, and choose a happy thought. The only reason you hesitate to do this is because you have accepted a belief that you are not "good enough" to deserve happiness. Do it anyway. If you wait until you feel "good enough," you will never be happy. It is not possible to start loving yourself until you begin doing loving things for yourself—and thinking loving thoughts *is doing* something loving.

Keep in mind that reprimanding yourself for having made mistakes is to *continue* making a mistake.

In only thirty days, it is possible to experience the true power of love and to recognize that you are in control of your life—your happiness, love, success, and prosperity. If, after thirty days, you want to change your mind and feel guilty or unhappy again, you are certainly free to do so.

The power of love that helps you overcome the effects of painful experiences is eternal. It cannot be taken from you, but you can forget you have it. Love cannot be felt until it is given away—and with every thought you think, you are "giving" either love or fear to yourself and everyone around you.

Love will always rescue you if remember to use it, but it cannot rescue you if you choose to remember pain and fear, instead.

God is love. Love is always with us and willing to help if we remember to use it.

Tips to Remember:

- The past cannot hurt you unless you choose to remember it.
- Memories have no power over you; they cannot alter your decision.
- Every thought creates a corresponding emotion—so think encouraging thoughts!
- There are two thought categories: love and fear. Thoughts that make you happy and create a sense of well-being are *loving*; thoughts that hurt and create doubt are fear-based and will undermine your success.
- You have a choice between thoughts. Choose wisely.

- You cannot control others, situations, circumstances, the past, or the future—nor do you need to. You only need to control *your* responses to them.
- Pain is an effect created by something that has already happened. What has happened is in the past. All pain is in the past unless we bring it into our present thoughts. Present thoughts of past pain create present pain.
- Fear is created by thinking of something that might happen in the future. Fear cannot exist in the present unless we are presently thinking fearful thoughts.
- Fearful thoughts will immobilize you. Replace them immediately with encouraging thoughts.
- What you believe creates the reality you experience.
- Denying yourself happiness does not make you "good," it makes you and everyone around you miserable.
- There is a Power within you that is sufficient to overcome all obstacles. It doesn't care what you call It, but It is there and It responds to love—your loving thoughts, your loving your life, your loving others, your loving your dreams and pursuing them. If you will remember to love your life, family, friends, the day, your work—love will empower you, and soon you will love all that you have accomplished. You will also love the truth that you—and only you—control your life.

God gave you that control because God *is* love.